The Politics of War

WITHDRAWN

The Politics of War
A study of the rationality of violence in inter-state relations

Charles Reynolds
Senior Lecturer in International Politics
University of Durham

HARVESTER WHEATSHEAF
ST. MARTIN'S PRESS, NEW YORK

First published 1989 by
Harvester Wheatsheaf
66 Wood Lane End, Hemel Hempstead
Hertfordshire HP2 4RG
A division of
Simon & Schuster International Group

and in the USA by
St. Martin's Press, Inc.
175 Fifth Avenue, New York, NY 10010

© 1989 Charles Reynolds

Printed and bound in Great Britain by
A. Wheaton & Co. Ltd, Exeter

British Library Cataloguing in Publication Data

Reynolds, Charles, 1937–
The Politics of war.
I. War. Political aspects
355'.02
ISBN 0-7450-0201-3

1 2 3 4 5   93 92 91 90 89

Library of Congress Cataloging-in-Publication Data

Reynolds. Charles.
The politics of war / Charles Reynolds.
p.   cm.
ISBN 0-312-02022-8 : $39.95 (St. Martin's : est.)
1. War. 2 Violence. 3. International relations. 4. Military
policy. 5. Limited war. 6. War and politics. I. Title.
U21.2.R49 1989
355'.02—dc19   88-23621
                                      CIP

To Pauline

Contents

Preface   vi

1 Politics and Strategy   1

2 Rationality and Action   32

3 Classical Strategy   59

4 Scientific Strategy   86

5 Weapons and Strategy—Conventional Practice   120

6 Weapons and Strategy—Nuclear Theory   155

7 Reasons and Violence   186

8 Reasoning and Violence   224

9 Conclusion   263

Select Bibliography   271
Index   280

Preface

Man, so we are told, is a rational animal. It is this capacity to reason that, apparently, distinguishes him from other animals. The human species is also virtually the only species to engage in intra-specific violence. The other major exceptions are rats and ants. Very few social groups within the human species abstain from this form of violence and it may be supposed that where they do so, as in the case of the Esquimaux before their discovery by civilisation, the violence of nature precludes that of man. This book seeks to link these two basic human characteristics by asking the question in what sense is violence between states rational?

I am not, however, concerned with the phenomenon of human violence as something to be explained, an aspect of the human condition as it were, but with the notion of its instrumentality. In particular it is war as an organised and directed violence between states and factions, and its threat, that is the focus of this study. This is violence with a purpose, devised by men and not by nature. Ethologists and socio-biologists have an explanation of human violence in terms of its alleged function in promoting the survival of the species by the promotion of fitness. Natural selection however, cannot be the purpose of human violence, destroying as it does the best of the gene-pool—the healthy and the young—leaving the unfit, impotent, and the old, inviolate. Even this is no longer the case. Moloch in this century chooses not the young fighting male but devours all alike; men, women, and children. Casualties in the First World War were mostly soldiers, in the Second World War they were mostly civilians, and a Third World War using nuclear weapons would make no such discrimination.

For the first time in human history a precise calculation of the consequences of the use of weapons in war can be made. Paradoxically, this advances the prospect of using and threatening violence between states, rationally. Both the necessity for, and the possibility of, controlling violence are conducive to this end. A distinction between the use and threat of violence for security and non-security objectives can be made with the advent of strategic nuclear weapons and the rationale of mutual defensive deterrence. My central concern in this book is with the Clausewitzian notion of war as a political instrument. What conditions must be satisfied for war to be policy by other means? The importance of control and of a commensurate relation between war—the means—and politics—the ends—are crucial in this respect. Rationality consists of making this relationship and maintaining it. This leads on to further questions. How can violence be used as a means to an end without either the means changing the ends sought, or, in the effort to secure them, destroying any balance between means and ends? If war is to be rational, that is effective as a means of securing political objectives, it must be controlled and the conditions for effectiveness both known and satisfied.

Both the world wars of this century escaped control and became security or total wars. Yet the end of security was never attained. Allies became enemies and enemies allies. There was little rationality in this. All other political objectives sought through violence became subordinate to a concern for security, resulting in the goal of unconditional surrender and the negation of compromise and negotiation, or a political solution. This is the reversal of the notion of war as policy by other means. And a third and nuclear world war would produce neither victors nor vanquished: all involved would perish. If this argument is accepted total wars are inherently irrational since they cannot be a means of achieving any political objective; rather they become ends in themselves. Preventing limited forms of violence from developing into Armageddon must be a pressing concern for those engaged both in war and preparations for war. Given that this can be done, and this will be a subject for examination in this book, limited wars can be rational, in that they can achieve their object effectively. Again for this to be the case they must satisfy certain conditions and be subject to control. The implications of this position will be considered.

There is a progression in this book from theory to practice. I have thought it necessary to examine some of the theoretical aspects of strategic theories and their attempts to prescribe for political practice, at a fairly basic and abstract level. In particular two concepts—reason and action—have been analysed as central to any thesis of the instrumental use of violence in inter-state relations. Strategic thought is heavily dependent upon the notion of rational action. Attempts to systematise reasoning in order to relate conditions and their satisfaction to results, presuppose a theory of human behaviour or, at least, a theory of rationality. Thus before looking at such attempts in detail, a number of first order questions seem relevant, if only to clarify the central issues involved. Is strategic argument more than practical reasoning? On what grounds can strategic prescriptions be assessed as relevant and effective? What grounds are valid for choosing between alternative and contradictory strategic options? These questions cannot be answered without some account of the relationship between reason and action and of the nature and implications of these concepts in the context of human choice.

From this somewhat abstract level of analysis the enquiry moves on to the argument that strategic prescriptions entail an explanatory basis if they are to be authoritative and effective. What sort of explanation is entailed? Does it correspond to the kind of subsumption theory or deductive-nomothetic model found in the natural sciences? Is it purely normative, so closely bound up with values and beliefs as to defy empirical generalisation? Is it historical in character and useless for any practical purposes other than serving as an educative device for practitioners? After dealing with these questions, practice is placed in sharper focus with an emphasis on specific uses of violence and the context of decision-making and action. The elements of threat and preparation for war in the form of defence policy and weapons procurement programmes, are also considered as aspects of practice in the instrumental use of violence. The concern here is for the level of perception and consciousness and the postulate of a common rationality, in what is essentially a set of adversarial relationships between states.

A book of this kind owes a great deal to the commitment and scholarship of many people both dead and alive. I am very conscious of this debt, as I am for what I owe to the milieu of free enquiry and disinterested research in which I am privileged to work. It has a fragile existence. It is said that the first casualty of war is truth. It is also at risk in times of peace, especially where national security is invoked by governments to curtail freedom of speech and to curb free enquiry. I hope to have made a modest contribution to redressing the balance, within the limited means and sources at my disposal.

I am extremely grateful to Dorothy Anson and Jean Richardson for their efficiency and hard work in preparing this book for publication. I owe more than I can say to my wife for her encouragement and support.

1 Politics and Strategy

War, conceived of as organised violence between and within states, designed to achieve a political object, is the central concern of this book. I am not however, concerned with war as a phenomenon to be explained. The causes of war, or of wars, are beyond its scope. War is taken to be a complex of actions explicable only in terms of human reasoning. Human actions, with their unforeseen consequences, are the product of intentions and purposes articulated by individual human agents, anxious to protect and secure their interests, acting for the most part as agents of the state, or of political factions. Elucidating this tangle of motive and purpose, of action and reason, is the province of the historian, armed with rules governing the nature and status of evidence, and concerned to establish what was actually the case. No general principles about war can be derived from this activity or its reconstruction. Yet as we shall see, those engaged in the practice, as opposed to the study, of war, seek guidance as to its proper and effective conduct. They find inspiration in past cases and in lessons, positive and negative, learnt from them. Practitioners of violence also engage in closely reasoned analysis based on possible and probable contingencies or 'scenarios'. This compound of fact and fiction tends to be abstract and schematised. It is concerned not so much with the past as a guide but with the immediate future in terms of the capabilities of extant and developing weapons.

This nexus of precept, conjecture, understanding, hypothesis, and practice, is generally called *strategy*. It takes two broad forms, depending on its emphasis. The first derives its prescriptions from the study of past practice supported by a level of a-temporal generalisation. This is what I have termed the *classical* approach, and it will be considered in detail in a later chapter. History informs it, and the rules it seeks to inculcate are extrapolated from a close study of the conduct of wars. It is not explicitly concerned with formulating a theory of war or of the practice of war. The other approach, which I have termed *scientific*, is more strictly theoretical. A theory is sought, or at least is implicit, which seeks to explain conduct on the grounds of a generalised rationality. The practical injunctions it urges

1

upon practitioners are the derivations not of an understanding based on past practice, but of an analytic framework which leans heavily upon ordering and conceptual categories.

Both these approaches have this in common; they seek to offer advice as to the proper use of violence, or its threat, to achieve a given end, perhaps with economy, or some limiting condition. They are concerned with the instrumental use of violence either by states or by political movements. How may violence be used effectively and what sort of capacity for violence is most effective in a given situation, are their central questions. They take as a starting point organised violence as both legitimate and normal as a means of achieving political ends. Although, as we shall see later, reservations are sometimes made as to the legitimacy of the ends. Defence is deemed to be respectable in this respect but imperialism is no longer fashionable.[1] There are also formal reservations about means, expressed in conventions limiting or banning the use of certain weapons and regulating, or seeking to regulate, the conduct of war. In general, however, strategists are content to leave questions of this kind to politicians and confine themselves to the question of the effectiveness of violence. This of course begs the major question what are wars for? a question which is not answered by winning them. If war is to be considered to be instrumental we are as much concerned with the result, that is with the ends, as with the means. This involves a concern with politics as much as with the more narrow aspects of the mechanics of violence.

Politics is often taken to be a conciliatory rather than a coercive practice. The activity of resolving conflict and, following Aristotle,[2] the model has been that of government by consent, exercising a restraining influence on sectional interest and promoting consensus. Conciliation rather than repression has been the favoured method. However, *vide* Machiavelli,[3] there is a parallel tradition which conceives of conciliating opposed interests as but one aspect of politics. The framework for this consists of a means of enforcement or maintaining a necessary form of law and order. Governments have the primary responsibility for maintaining this framework. Conflicts between citizens are thus controlled both by rules and by their enforcement. Violence in a controlled and regulated form is as much part of politics as conciliation.

Advocates of revolution or of radical political programmes, with the possible exception of anarchists, do not quarrel with this view of the role of government as enforcer. It is not the enforcement of rules which they question, but the authority and legitimacy of the government and perhaps of the rules themselves. The right of the state to use violence, through its agent the government, against its citizens is not disputed. Civil war and revolutionary war are thus means of changing governments and their associated political systems. I shall be concerned with this aspect of instrumental violence in a later chapter. There are strategies of radical political change through the use of violence as well as those more familiarly associated with international conflict.

Politics *between* states in this respect are of a different category, since no general consensus exists on any form of international order. While violence is always an element in national politics it is subject to constraints and rules that are more or less observed. There is a framework for the resolution of disputes, with the government acting as an arbiter, monopolising the use of violence and delegating it where necessary. Overt physical violence is comparatively rare within the state. This of course is open to qualification if we take a long historical view. Nevertheless, physical violence and its threat is much more in evidence in international politics. It appears to be the most commonly accepted means of resolving disputes and is subject to little or no constraint or political control. It is a commonplace to regard the world of states as anarchic with violence as its *ultima ratio*. Without subscribing to this view it is true to say that inter-state relations are more governed by the threat of violence than are relations between the government and citizen. The view that international politics is inherently violent is both prevalent and taken as a justification for the arming of the state. War is something to be feared as well as used.

Thus international politics, while not qualitatively different from domestic politics in that violence is an integral part of both forms of politics, present a permanent threat of war. A Marxist[4] would of course claim that this was the case for the state in the form of class war stemming from the contradictions of capitalism. This aspect will be examined later. The point here is that this omnipresent threat is, partly at least, a consequence of the various capacities for violence developed by the state as a response. Without going into this argument in detail at this stage, expectations of proper or appropriate action within the state are based on a view of violence different in kind from those concerning the behaviour of states. Apparently arbitrary behaviour can be expected from the latter and insecurity is the consequence of this belief. This is not generally the case within the state although we should be careful in taking both contemporary practice and a particular type of state as our points of reference. In the main the use of violence by the state against the citizen is made palatable by the emphasis upon individual conduct, and the consequences for the individual within the rule of law and civil order in the event of any breach of the law.

It becomes a matter for rational calculation whether the chances of detection and punishment are sufficient to deter most breaches of the law, both for the individual and for the enforcers. The rationale of deterrence is sought by the latter; the costs are calculated by the former. Although not in any way a precisely calculated ratio it is one that permits a degree of rationality on both sides, for both the crime and its penalty. It concerns the individual and his conception of a relationship with the state. It is possible to act rationally in terms of this relationship. Violence, in the sense of punishment, and even perhaps in terms of criminal behaviour, is mediated by custom and consent, as it is not between states. Rational conduct is possible where a specific social context of rules, conventions and penalties, overt and covert, exists. It has a social basis. The normative principle is one of order; an order maintained and enforced by the government that permits individuals to have a social existence. The world of states is deemed to be rather different. The notion of civil order which is presumed to exist within the state is absent outside it.

A synonym for order is often termed peace. Although the concept is rarely closely defined, the central assumption is that its antonym, war, is undesirable. All nation-states are in principle, peace-loving, and war is either a product of forces over which individual states exercise no control, or is the consequence of militarist and aggressive policies pursued by certain states. There is an inherent incompatibility between these two attributions. An irrational foreign or defence policy is thus one that enhances or creates those conditions which promote war between states. A rational external policy seeks to achieve the opposite. Avoiding war or seeking to mitigate its consequences is the only reasonable course of action for the nation-state. Such thinking is manifest in the peace-creating universalist institutions established after the two World Wars of this century—the League of Nations and the United Nations. It is also manifest in the rhetoric of disarmament and arms control negotiations, and in the statements of politicians justifying their arms procurement programmes to their people.

The paradox implicit in the maxim that he who wishes peace must first prepare for war[5] will be examined later; the point here is that on the one hand there is an almost universal ethic which condemns war as inherently immoral, and for our purposes, irrational, and on the other, an almost universal practice of war-making and preparation for war. Ethical, and other constraining influences on the practice of war, will be considered in a later chapter. My concern here is with the rational use of war. War may be an evil but it is generally considered to be a necessary evil, pending some Utopian time when it will disappear. It is necessary both for the protection and defence of states as political entities, and for the preservation and promotion of their interests in the face of predatory competition. The question of the legitimacy of such violence is secondary to the question of its necessity. Property and human rights are protected within the state by the rule of law backed by the monopoly of violence possessed by the state and its agents. At least this is a model of the modern state perhaps more often aspired to, than realised, in the modern world. However, beyond the state there is no ambiguity. There is neither a rule of law nor a coherent and institutionalised form of violence to support it. The state is forced upon its own resources and efforts to maintain itself and its political system. The extent to which the threat of violence or its use can provide for this, is one aspect of its rationality considered in this book.

The notion that the world of states is void of rules or of any means of regulating competitive relations between states is extreme. Certainly no form of world government has actually existed apart from forms of regional imperialism where a kind of *pax romana* has prevailed. And it is equally true that attempts at creating a system of international law with regulatory institutions have not produced any real restraint over national willingness to break conventions where this appears expedient. But while enforcement of rules is weak and ultimately depends upon a balance of advantage as perceived by the contending states, there are rules in inter-state relations. Nation states in fact accept a system of constraints and inducements to negotiated agreements rather than violent methods of promoting their interests, as the norm. The point is not that there are rules, but that these rules and their observance are the product of a rationale in which the extremes of the pursuit of national self-interest are moderated by the multiplicity of interests that require some minimal cooperation between states. Slavery for example, was difficult to eradicate because some nations benefited from it. This was not true of piracy—the private as opposed to the official form of privateering. With the expansion and growing importance of trade, piracy was a menace to all states engaged in what was a multilateral and not bilateral set of transactions. They cooperated in its suppression. This depends upon the perception of interest held by the politicians. They must be willing to forego immediate advantage in order not to sacrifice longer-term interests. The calculus of relative advantage is neither permanent nor binding on the state, but it presupposes some minimal form of world order. Even when violence is pursued or threatened, the successful state, like the successful criminal, wishes to enjoy his spoils in peace and this requires a measure of consent, not only from his victims, but from the world community in general. Moderation in demands and in the degree of violence would thus appear to be rational in this respect.

War and peace, in this view, are not poles apart but complementary. Most modern wars, however total they appear to have been, have taken place within a context of reasoning that assumes some minimal form of order, either to be restored, or modified, after the violence is over. They are essentially political contests. It is true that the more total they become, the more their political rationale becomes subordinate to the level of violence. In this sense they can be said to have lost rationality in proportion to the loss of control exercised by the contenders over the scale of violence. Equally, a moralist would find it difficult to detect constraint and political sense in the extension of destruction to civilians or in violations of neutrality extending the war to declared non-belligerents. In comparative terms inter-state violence has become more widespread in its effects, as weapons have become both more deadly and more indiscriminate. Nevertheless, it could be argued, until the advent of nuclear weapons at least, that the civilian population and the socio-economic structure of the state, its means of productions, and its economic relations with other states, are legitimate targets since they provide the means by which the war may be prosecuted. The babe in arms and the potential mother provide recruits. There are few civilians who are irrelevant to total war and so innocent victims.

The main point however, is that the extreme conditions of war and the means with which it is prosecuted are not the focus for an explanation of inter-state relations and the role of violence. The states involved in such conflicts sought to attain ends through the use or threat of force and while the scale of devastation, and indeed, the outcome of the struggle, have been unforeseen and counter-productive, the ends could only be realised by treating violence as instrumental and not as an end in itself. This notion of purpose and its associated rationale was never lost, even in the midst of the greatest such conflict of this century—the Second World War. As we shall see, this may not be the case for nuclear war. In non-nuclear war violence was rational because it was a means to an end: where this was not the case, then irrationality prevailed. Perpetual war was not part of this vision. Even Hitler, who with his Social-Darwinism,[6] came near to a theory of war for war's sake, believed that fighting was necessary to the survival of the state. In improving the quality of the *herrenvolk* and protecting the racial-state, war was instrumental and not an end in itself.

It is perhaps because of the need to restore 'normalcy' as a condition of success in using violence, that resort to war and war itself have always been condemned or justified in moral terms. War guilt and the question of responsibility are connected to the legitimisation of conquest and the promotion of interests. It is not so much as to the victor the spoils, as showing that war booty—the acquisitive side of victory—is really reparation. Such arguments are not merely lip-service to morality, as an attempt to return to normality through a peace which allows the retention of the gains won through successful violence. Hence the representation of war as an evil and the responsibility for it placed upon the defeated. Success and its material consequences are thus legitimised. Clearly this requires the acquiescence of the defeated, in some measure at least. This can be achieved through a repudiation of the political system that had engaged in the war.

Whether we regard the international condition as violence punctuated by relatively brief periods of peace, or as peace punctuated by relatively short outbursts of violence, the notion of anarchy has little empirical evidence to support it. States engage in actions which presuppose attainable goals, whether through violent or non-violent means, within a context of expectations of proper action on the part of other states. No statesman, however powerful in material terms he conceives his state to be, has ever believed in a complete freedom of action on the international stage. If indeed this condition ever existed for a state, the consequences would be not anarchy but world hegemony with its own form of order and law enforcement. Violence, in short, is but one of a number of forms of human action that are rule-guided, even when the rules constitute a vestigial framework, subject more to breaches than observance. It is analogous to crime. The criminal seeks to profit from his actions and in his conflict with the law acts out a rationale shared by the policing authorities. He is no anarchist and his breaches of the rules amounts to an acceptance of them in that *his* title to life, freedom, and property, are as important to him, as to his victims. The problems of revolutionary war and of the just war will be left to later chapters. The point here is that while the justification of the use of violence may be made in moral terms—in terms of rule-breaking—the practice presupposes a rationality in terms of its effectiveness in promoting the interests of the state. It is this rationality that is the central concern of this book. It may be that the elimination of violence from human relations is a good thing but this would, in international politics, eliminate the nation-state as well. The disappearance of the state would merely shift the problem to a different sphere.

Those, for example, who advocate the promotion of world peace through universalist organisations[7] have either based it on the dominant group of states—'a world of mice ruled over by lions' or have conceived of a global police force operating through the aegis of a world political authority with supranational powers. These represent organised or institutionalised forms of violence. Peace has to be policed and this implies the same monopoly of violence at the global level, with its political implications, as that enjoyed by a relatively few nation-states in the modern world. The problem is really political in that it implies a surrender of political autonomy by states to a new political entity. It is hard to envisage a voluntary relinquishment of sovereignty in this respect. And to talk of imposition is to talk of using violence, or its threat. Essentially the maintenance of peace depends upon a means of enforcement in the same way as law and order is enforced within the state.

More commonly the notion of an armed peace has prevailed, especially with the advent of nuclear weapons. Peace is seen in terms of a tangible guarantee of the territorial and political integrity of the state. This is achieved, or maintained through what are somewhat euphemistically called defence policies. Ideally local superiority in the means of violence is a basic requirement. Such superiority is restricted, in that it depends, on firstly, a political system based on alliances that modifies the environment of the defending state in its favour, and secondly, on the production of weapons and their deployment as an effective deterrent to a potential aggressor.

The relevance of weapons technology will be considered in later chapters. Arms races and radical innovations in weapons are clearly important as influences upon both peace and security. The idea of security is central to the notion of international peace. It depends, in the absence of a supranational authority exercising some of the functions of a state, upon individual national perceptions and responses, to what is conceived of as a threat. Self-preservation in a world of potentially inimical states is the end sought. It does not preclude cooperation and joint defensive measures with other states, but these are negotiated and maintained only in terms of the prevailing concept of national security and where this changes as circumstances and the relevant factors vary, so are these relationships re-interpreted. Security as an end is simply the preservation of the political entity—the state. In practice it is a complex of empirical conditions and values. The point here is that it is state-centric. The state itself is sole judge and executor.

International peace is thus a product of the satisfaction of national security needs. And the same could be said of war. Notions such as the balance of power, or of the rule of law, in regulating changes in inter-state relationships, or in resolving contentious issues, reflect the view of those anxious to preserve for them what is an advantageous political situation that more or less guarantees their security. Challenges to this and advocates of a countering violence reflect the view of states whose security needs, as they are interpreted, are not satisfied. This can be crudely represented into a contest between the 'haves and the have-nots', but the point here, as we shall see developed later, is that security for one state can affect that of another, depending on a combination of circumstances and conditions that escapes direction and control. For example, the upsurge of imperialism in the inter-war years, with Japan, Germany, and Italy seeking territorial expansion was, in part at least, caused by the economic damage of the recession.[8] Economic autarky was seen as a means of insulting their economies from such cataclysms. This meant emulating those imperial powers which had acquired their empires under more favourable conditions and were able to use their resources as a means of relief from the collapse of the world economic system. This was exacerbated for Germany in particular, by the fact that the victor powers stripped Germany of her imperial possessions after the First World War. Autarky was seen in security terms, and war was a necessary means to obtain it. The German challenge was necessary for survival. Yet if the world economic system had proved immune to recession and if national politicians had observed a higher priority in maintaining it than relapsing into short-term nationalist solutions, imperialist policies would not have been seen as a means of national salvation. These are of course counter-factual conditions. The point here is that security can come to mean control over an inimical environment and where this environment largely consists of other states the consequence is international violence. This is not axiomatic, for cooperation can also be a solution, although as we shall see, maintaining this presents serious difficulties too.

Peace is thus conditional upon satisfying conditions for state security. While these are predominantly assessed in military terms they also include political and ideological considerations. The stability of a government, or a political system, for example, depends not simply on its powers of coercion and successful use of force, but also on its freedom from external and internal subversion. The degree of vulnerability to this form of pressure is an important factor. The threat to the state posed by its coexistence with other states and the absence of any superior regulating authority, is not purely a matter of the relative balance of forces. External support for political factions, economic leverage, terrorism, the exploitation of sources of disunity, propaganda, and the dissemination of dissent etc., are all means of weakening political rule and reducing the will and military capability of a state. The condition of France in the 1930s is a case in point, when Germany embarked on such a programme designed to weaken French opposition and will to fight. Some have argued that this proved effective in helping towards the French military and political collapse in 1940 but this is perhaps open to question.

If the problems posed by security competition on the military level were resolved by some miracle, the problems of covert means of threat and persuasion would yet remain as a danger to the political system. Peace and security thus take on a broader aspect than merely the absence of overt violence and its threat, emanating from other states. Ideological and economic competition between states are relevant to the problem of security. Thus the issue at stake moves from the preservation of the territorial integrity of the nation-state to the protection of a political system or a 'way of life'. Or rather the two become indivisible. Peace is never an end in itself but is defined by, and related to, an empirical state of affairs with specific conditions requiring satisfaction. Even if these conditions were accepted and recognised by all states belonging to the world system, maintaining them could not be disassociated from violence. Enforcement, that is the effective use of violence to preserve this state of affairs is a prime or sufficient condition; a violence controlled and administered as a means of maintaining peace. It is thus essentially political. The central question, if peace is desired, is not the eradication of violence as a means of resolving the security problem, but controlling it, and using it to provide security. This would require a political locus other than the nation-state.

Whatever view of the world of states is taken to be its true representation, whether of ordered anarchy or uncontrolled violence, and whatever the aspirations of those of idealistic temper, it is the views of those who act in it that are our central concern. As we shall see when we consider the question of approaches to strategy later in this chapter, the emphasis is on the perceptions of those engaged in political practice and not those imposed on them. The problem of the rationality of violence, which is the central concern of this book, depends upon an examination of reasoning in practice not in the abstract. This last will certainly be considered in various chapters but the main thesis of this work is that an explanation of the use of violence in international politics and its rationale lies in the reasoning of those who employ it. Although we shall be considering strategic thought in terms of the prescriptions of the strategists, the views of the politicians and their conception of the world in which they operate, (which may indeed incorporate the theoretical level), are central to our understanding of war. Strategic prescriptions are related to a limited instrumentality directed to the successful use of violence under combat conditions. What some writers have called 'higher strategy' is too often ignored or treated as the province of the politicians. The central question of this study is *what is war for?*—and this cannot be answered without an examination of the political rationale.

Few politicians have believed in a wholly anarchic world and the very nature and character of inter-state relations indicate that this is so. Diplomacy implies rules; negotiation implies the possibility of agreement; and agreement implies in turn the principle *pacta sunt servanda*,[9] that is, it has a contractual basis and is binding on the parties. One of the more foolish of Hitler's actions was his violation of the Munich agreement in 1939 by completing the dismemberment of Czechoslovakia.[10] In occupying

Bohemia and Moravia he revealed to his opponents that negotiation was nugatory and that war was the only alternative. Nevertheless, most politicians have accepted that national interests, either the basic interest of security, however this is defined, or lesser concerns, can be pursued through the aegis of violence. In believing this, and indeed the belief is central to the idea of national security where the principal threat lies in the omnipresent possibility of violence, they have not necessarily preferred violent to non-violent means in achieving their object. They have however, accepted it as one of a number of efficacious methods of fulfilling the national will. It has been argued by some commentators that the acceptance of violence as part of the diplomatic repertoire has been a major contribution to the prevalence of violence in inter-state relations. They point to what I have termed the power-security hypothesis as a form of self-fulfilling prophecy.[11]

This deserves some examination. The argument is at the basis of *real politik* and may constitute in practice an element in the belief system of international actors and so form part of, or be related to, their reasoning. In addition I said earlier that strategic thought is largely preoccupied with the sub-political level, that is, concerned with means rather than ends. Nevertheless, as we shall see later, there is often a submerged thesis or set of assumptions about the nature of the milieu in which states exist. This thesis generally corresponds to the notion of security competition and its rationale. In any case the argument itself purports to be explanatory in a general sense, and this claim should be examined. From our point of view, if it is true, the development and use of forms of violence as a means of achieving security and promoting national interests is inherently irrational if the consequence is total war. Politicians who sought to provide security or negotiate through strength would be acting irrationally.

Is this the case? The power-security hypothesis asserts the inevitability of competition between nation-states since the only ultimate guarantee of security is a national ability to defend itself against likely aggression. Since the threat is seen in terms of capability for violence and not in actual intentions, because of the fact that weapons apparently can be evaluated more easily due to their material nature, while good will is less tangible, then all nations with this capability are potentially at least inimical. It is true that some of these for various reasons can accommodate their respective fears, although not necessarily their rivalries, in the form of associations or alliances designed to restrict chance and uncertainty. Within them the essentially national preoccupation with security is only masked by the fiction of a collective response to the threat of aggression. Such relationships are inherently precarious as the relative balance of capabilities changes through technological innovation in weapons or the fluctuations of governments. Allies become enemies and enemies friends. There is no common security denominator and each member state interprets its own security problem in the light of its own circumstances. The force of an alliance lies not in providing an overwhelming military response to aggression, or its threat, but in precluding diplomatic manoeuvring between politically uncommitted states designed to isolate and pressurise individual states.

The central thesis of the power-security hypothesis is that security fears are based on the relative military capacities of states that potentially enable them to violate each other's territorial integrity. The consequence is a drive to counter this by developing a superior countervailing military capacity and by seeking to control the external environment through power politics. Arms races and wars combined with imperialist policies are the result.

Such competition is alleged to be both permanent and inevitable, since so long as one state with the requisite resources holds this view, all the others are compelled to follow suit. The world of states is inherently competitive in terms of armaments and military capacity. One state's security is thus always another state's insecurity. The only solutions to this condition of permanent security competition are if one state succeeds in achieving the world hegemony that alone can provide it with a guarantee of its own security, or by the abandonment of the nation-state as the primary political entity in world politics. Neither of these options has proved realisable in the past, either through world or regional conquest, or by substitution for the nation-state through the creation of universalist organisations.

According to this argument, diplomacy and 'normal' inter state relations are permeated by security fears at all levels, including trade and economic exchange. The apparently sensible advice that 'he who wishes peace must first prepare for war', has the paradoxical effect of making war more likely. National war preparation induces a similar effect on other nations and exacerbates the basic security problem. The whole situation is seen in terms of relative capabilities for violence and not in terms of the intentions of governments. International politics is thus power politics, since no nation-state can afford to isolate itself from the struggle. Small relatively weak states become involved as pawns in the overall power struggle between the major rivals. They have the difficult choice of seeking protection, at a price, from one of the major contenders, or of trying to maintain a precarious independence through neutrality. Either policy has its risks and must ultimately depend on the volition of the major powers. Associations have proved dangerous and one-sided, and neutrality has been violated.

Parallel with this drive to extend national authority over a dangerously unstable environment, has been the development and sophistication of the basic instrument—the means of violence. Innovation in weapons technology has not only been the tangible form of the contest, it has also exercised a directing influence on it. From sea-power to air-power, from air-power to the ballistic missile, the changes have altered the relative importance of space and territory and of the political significance of states. In an age of steam a state seeking security through its navy required a global network of coaling stations and ports in order to deploy its force effectively. The creation of this network, in tandem with an Empire, gave temporary superiority to the British Isles. The strains of maintaining this position against the rivalry of other would-be naval powers, principally, Japan, the United States, and, locally, France, Germany, and Italy, proved too much for its resources. Oil, and the development of aircraft produced the aircraft carrier, which given the relatively limited range of extant aircraft also required advance bases to be effective. Similarly, the innovation of the atomic bomb was less radical in its effects because of the limitations of its carrier—the long range bomber. Thus space and territory were important to national security, partly because of the geographical distribution of the great powers, who found in each other's existence the primary threat to security, and, reflecting this, partly because of logistical and technological requirements of the weapons system they had devised to meet this threat. Similarly, the advent of the ballistic missile imposed its own demands on the security system while reducing the importance of space and territory.

The implications of this argument will be considered in later chapters. The point here is that it reflects a dynamic which is beyond the control of any one state, however powerful. And such a dynamic is the product of an apparently rational response to the perception of threat by states. Responding to the capacities for violence possessed, or being created, by other states, the nation-state seeks security by matching them, either alone or in association with other states. The consequence is an intensification of the security competition as other states in turn respond to this development. They are all caught up in a network of such responses which they do not control, and which, according to the power-security hypothesis, not merely perpetuates chronic insecurity but leads to war. Such wars are never conclusive however, and re-combinations of states in new security associations occur at their end. The security dilemma is never resolved.

Now the power-security hypothesis appears plausible at this general level. States, or rather statesmen, are concerned mainly with security in terms of the relative capacities for violence possessed by other states. All nations, whatever their political systems, whether neutral or allied, economically and militarily strong or weak, democratic or totalitarian in government, ideologically closed or pragmatically open, have defence policies and create capacities for violence. And a good deal of their concern for security stems from fear[12] not of intentions but of each other's arms and this in turn produces competition.

If we take one example, in the last world war and the events leading up to it, there seems an almost exclusive concern for security. Hitler believed that Germany, disarmed by *diktat* after the First World War, was especially vulnerable, given its geographical position in Europe. The political creations of the peace treaties had produced a situation in which Germany was surrounded by a *cordon sanitaire* dominated and controlled by France. The French themselves had refrained from making the peace settlement even more draconian towards Germany only by being placated with a security guarantee from the United States and Britain. This combined with the League of Nations, reparations, and disarmament, gave France some assurance against future possible aggression from Germany. The refusal of the United States to ratify these treaties, and of Britain to guarantee France unilaterally, left the French without a major ally against German resurgence. The consequence was a series of post-war actions, such as the combination with the smaller nations surrounding Germany, and with the Soviet Union, and the occupation of the Ruhr in 1923, designed to provide security but having the effect of underlining German weakness.

Hitler's solution was to dismantle through unilateral action the Versailles and Locarno agreements and break up the *cordon sanitaire* through diplomacy. His policies of territorial expansion, autarky, and racial purity, were designed to free Germany of economic and political entanglements to achieve a genuine independence.[13] Only by pursuing these policies did he believe that Germany could be secure both from foreign invasion and from the economic disruptions of a world market economy driven into recession by financial manipulators. The point here is that, shorn of its racism and of Social-Darwinism, it was a rationally conceived policy. Security for France, or for Britain, was achieved at the expense of Germany. The pursuit of German security entailed the satisfaction of certain conditions, the most basic of which was rearmament redressing the balance.

The fatal flaw in this argument lies in the nature of the opposition. Not only was his rationality not shared by his opponents; his objectives, and his ability to achieve them by force, constituted a danger to other states. It was not that the political settlements made after the First World War were deemed sacrosanct to the victors. They were in any case something of a compromise between their competing interests. It was not in British interests to aggrandise France at the expense of other European powers since this would compromise its traditional interest in preserving a European balance as a basis for British security. The legitimacy of Poland, Austria, and Czechoslovakia, was challenged by Hitler on the grounds that the principle of self-determination had not been observed; that they had been imposed on, and not negotiated with, Germany; and that they were in effect instruments designed by the victor powers, especially France, to contain a weakened Germany. This case was largely accepted by France and Britain, by default in the case of Austria, and by negotiation in the case of Czechoslovakia.

The difficulty came with Hitler's relatively modest demands on Poland. The difference was however, that German rearmament had proceeded to the point when this was a major threat to the rearming, but relatively weak, France and Britain. Moreover, Hitler had broken the Munich Agreement and so made the prospect of a genuine negotiated settlement of outstanding territorial problems very doubtful. Attention thus moved from diplomacy and negotiation to security and confrontation. It was not so much what Hitler formally demanded, as his capacity to realise it by the successful use of force, that produced the war. The irrational content of his programme—the racism and persecution of minorities—while deplored by British and French liberals—were not reasons for war or its threat. The war was not inevitable because of the nature of the political systems involved, but because of the security threat implicit in Hitler's war preparations and the duplicitous nature of his diplomacy.

Hitler, for his part, believed that while he was strengthening his position in Europe at the expense of France, he was not seriously threatening Britain and only marginally threatening France. His intentions were certainly designed to create a situation which divided the opposition and which destroyed the Versailles system. But his route lay to the East.[14] He conceived his policy as Clausewitzian[15] in character, that is, not as a general threat to the existence of other major powers, but as a rational use of violence and its threat, to secure political changes that were limited in nature. The level of violence implicit in this programme was not in his view a challenge to security but limited as in the Eighteenth Century. He did not conceive, that, smaller countries apart, he was, in effect, through the development of a war capacity, directly challenging the integrity of his opponents. This threat and the French and British response to it produced a war in which the central issue was not the political quarrel over Poland that occasioned it, but the continued existence of the combatants as major powers.

Such a war could only be rational if it produced a situation in which one or other of the warring states achieved a lasting security. This as we know did not happen. The nations that 'won' the war did not win the peace they desired. But the point here is not that failure is somehow inherently irrational, but that rationality constitutes a relationship between means and ends so that there is a high probability that the former will realise the latter. This will be examined in the next chapters. In this case security fears were aroused to such an extent by, what on the face of it, appeared to be a rational policy employing violence, that a security as opposed to a political war was the consequence. The existence of states became the central issue, together with their political systems, and not the limited political objectives the initial contest appeared to be about.

The point is that this is not inevitable as a consequence of the power/security hypothesis. It is not a dynamic that forces politicians to dance to its tune. The explanation of why this war turned out as it did lies in the perceptions of those who fought it. They were all forced in a sense to make unpalatable choices, but they were choices. What concerns us is not the alleged irrationality of a security policy based on the notion of countervailing capacities for violence, and its counter-productive effects producing chronic insecurity in the world of states. The relationship between means and ends is the central concern. Thus while the beliefs of politicians are important, in that *their* view of the world is relevant to their formulation of objectives and their choice of action designed to realise them, we cannot impose a superior view without justifying it.

Politicians, it is true, have to face the consequences, often unforeseen, of their actions. As we shall see, the vacillations of the French and British governments, firstly over challenging Hitler about the occupation of

Prague in 1939, and secondly, during the *drôle de guerre* period, stemmed directly from the desire not to fight the kind of total war which was implicit in their threat of force. They did not want to provoke all-out war by taking irreversible military actions against Germany. Hence the hesitations over violating the territory of the Low Countries and of the Scandinavian states. Limits on bombing were imposed.[16] It was essentially a defensive strategy that was being pursued, designed to persuade the Germans, if not Hitler, that the war was impossible to win. The point here is that politicians, even in facing total war, do not readily lose sight of its political consequences. The concern for security is not related in practice to an absolute condition of military superiority but to a calculated balance of forces and the assumption of relative advantage as well as of mutual benefit. As such the notion of security is inherently subjective and conditional, depending on the perceptions of the agents concerned and of their awareness of the relevant conditions that require satisfaction. In the event they may miscalculate and misinterpret each other's actions. Hitler and his opponents certainly did; he clearly believed in limited war in the form of a blitzkrieg, a rationally controlled war designed to secure political objectives. The opposition, fighting under local disadvantages, wanted to frustrate him without extending the war into its total form. Both found themselves in fact fighting a security war they did not want. This was always a possibility given the nature of the challenge. Paradoxically it was Hitler's initial successes and Britain's refusal to accept the political consequences, that pushed the war into its total phase.

The emphasis placed upon the mechanics of security competition and upon military capability is an error if an explanation of violence between states is sought. The reasoning which provides the explanation is that of those engaged in the contest. It is their conception of security which matters and not that derived from an analytic framework imposed upon a political situation. I will return to this point in later chapters and consider at this stage the relation of strategic thought to political practice. As will be clear from the preceding discussion, strategy is conceived of as a programme of action which relates means to ends in a rational manner under conditions of opposition or bargaining. The means are not necessarily those of violence or of its threat, but contain some element inimical to an adversary or negotiating partner, even where this is minimal such as a refusal to cooperate or participate in some desired programme or action. Diplomacy and negotiation are closely related to such 'strategies' where concessions are bargained for and positions of strength are related to positions of weakness. Accommodation as well as violent confrontation can be the consequence of such strategies. The possibility of violence is, however, always present, given the existence of military capabilities.

It was argued earlier that an emphasis on means alone ignores the means/end relationship and produces prescriptions that are empirically and theoretically vacuous or limited to the operational or technical level. The objectives sought, and the relationship between them and the means, thus become secondary. Strategic prescriptions that lack a theoretically adequate basis or some authoritative ground are invalid however plausible they may appear. It is thus necessary when seeking to establish an effective programme of action, or strategy, to provide a ground for its acceptance. Or to put it another way, what is *effective* action is derived from an adequate *explanation*. It depends on a theory. This is because the theory provides an explanation as to why the proposed course of action will lead, with a high degree of probability, or with certainty, to the desired result. The end state of affairs is explained as the consequences of specific necessary and sufficient conditions. If the relationship between these conditions—the means—and the result is not explained, then prescribed actions not merely lack authority, they fail to be instrumental. Any success in their application is entirely arbitrary. The implications of this argument will be examined in later chapters.

Strategy, in my view, consists of the level of reasoning and action, in which both means and ends are mediated in action so that the latter are formulated and attainable through the creation and exercise of the former. The nature of this reasoning will be examined later on. The point here is that to be rational both means and ends must be commensurable. In deciding on objectives the politician draws upon resources, organises and deploys them, and so on, but should not allow his course of action to be determined by his selection of the means. To illustrate this point, none of the belligerents of 1939, France, Britain and Germany, had prepared for a war which fully mobilised and deployed all their resources. The war they contemplated at that point was a war of existing military capabilities, although Britain and France were engaged in frantic attempts to supplement their deficiencies, particularly in their Air Forces.[17] But the ostensible object of the war was to force Germany to withdraw its troops from Poland. The level of hostilities between Sept. 1939 and May 1940 failed to achieve this. The threat then became one of total war in which the existence of the combatant states became the main issue. Yet none of these states had actually prepared for such a struggle. The defeat of France did not produce the political accommodation that Germany sought and the war drifted into its total phase. Neither the means—the war capacities which were being created or which existed at the time—nor the ends—the political objectives sought—were defined or made commensurate. The consequence was a directionless war lacking rationality. It became a war of resources and it was these that determined its intensity and scale, linked solely to the objective of unconditional surrender. There was no clear link between strategy and politics.

One of the virtues of the power-security hypothesis is its emphasis on the distinctive character of security as a national interest. It focusses attention on the security problem for the state and on its importance as an influence in inter-state relations. Without accepting it as a determinant of international politics, the distinction it makes between security and other national interests pursued in the world of states, is crucial for strategic thought. If control is to be exercised over violence so that it can act as an effective means to secure a political object, this distinction must be maintained. As we saw earlier a political war became a total or security war because of the failure to do this. Security is not an absolute state of condition, although it is often referred to by politicians in these terms. It is in practice a belief concerning a set of political and military relationships and capabilities generally acceptable to most states and compatible with attempts at securing relative advantage in international politics. Violence, although disreputable, is confined to two main objects that when kept separate permit its control. National security is one; and is conceived of as maintaining the territorial and political integrity of the state. The other may be any objective that does not jeopardise this and threaten the existence of other states. It follows that to confuse these is to initiate a war in which there is no commensurate relation between means and ends unless the end of achieving world hegemony is sought. Rational violence is thus the effective use of force to achieve a limited political end, without this end and the means chosen to fulfil it changing their character or relation. The question of what constitutes effective action will be examined later; the point here is that security and non-security ends must be clearly distinguished, and what is deemed to be an appropriate strategy limited by this distinction. As we shall see later, the problem is not defining rationality in war and strategy, but in actually fulfilling its conditions. However, making this distinction is an important first step. Strategic thought, if it is not to be positively dangerous to those who accept its prescriptions, must distinguish between what is appropriate as a basis for defence in terms of action, and what is appropriate for the promotion and protection of non-defence interests.

Let us now turn more directly to strategic thought. It is common in strategic commentary to refer to mistakes and missed opportunities as well as to success and effective leadership and planning.[18] The commentary is critical, not perhaps in a negative sense, but designed to be helpful to practitioners. Without necessarily drawing general conclusions about the nature of war and applying them to its proper conduct in the present and future, they nevertheless present an account which assesses action on critical grounds relating action to achievements or results, usually in terms of battlefield victory. The theoretical implications of this will be examined in the next chapter, but some preliminary remarks are appropriate here. The assertion of judgements of this kind depend for their validity upon two distinct grounds. Firstly, they may be related to the application of a theory that postulates a causal relationship between pre-conditions, which include the level of action, and a result, a state of affairs which is inevitably produced by the fulfilment of these conditions under a covering law. This is at least implicit in such assessments and more will be said about its implications later.

Secondly, the assessment may be limited in nature and confined to the circumstances surrounding specific military action. A mistake may be taken to be a failure in fulfilling an intention or action which for one reason or another did not succeed in its object. In this case the reasoning of the agent is directly relevant. In this particular context we can only talk about non-fulfilment of *his* intentions, that is, he failed in what he set out to do. There is no associated explanation as such, merely an identification of reasoning and related action. The agent himself may have his 'explanation' in the form of an *ex post facto* rationalisation. For example, Hitler 'explained' his failure to achieve his stated objectives in operation *Barbarossa*[19] by blaming the early onset of winter, the delay in beginning the offensive caused by his need to intervene in Yugoslavia and Greece, and the incapacity of his generals. His generals[20] blamed his interference in operational planning and changes in the direction of the main thrust. We need not accept these reasons as explanatory; the point here is that failure is identified in terms of the agent's intentions.

But the second case, that of the attribution of error by strategic commentators, carries a clear implication that alternative actions (or inaction) and decisions would have averted disaster or produced success. Mistakes were made. And the notion of mistake implies the possession of a superior form of reasoning which offers a ground of truth against which errors can be identified and condemned for what they are. What is this reasoning, and in what sense is it superior as a ground for judging the reasoning of agents whose actions are under scrutiny? Hitler's generals criticised his obstinacy in holding ground rather than making strategic withdrawals. He was condemned for giving priority to economic objectives rather than concentrating on the defeat of the enemy forces in the field. His defence, so far as it was articulated, was that he was primarily concerned with achieving his political objectives. Defeating the enemy was a necessary step to their fulfilment but the point of such defeat was to achieve a real and not an apparent advantage for Germany. Possession of the grain, minerals and oil, of key economic areas in the East, was essential not merely to the prosecution of the war but to the very point of the war. In the event he was able to do neither and his defeat was total. The point here is that a critical assessment of the strategy he adopted can only be made by having grounds that are themselves unassailable. In other words it presupposes a superior knowledge. This knowledge is not simply *ex post facto*, referring to facts the participants could not have known at the time, but is theoretical in character. It is based on an explanatory form that permits prescription.

The logical and empirical implications of this argument will be considered in the next chapter. The point here is that if critical strategic assessments are made, we are entitled to ask for some justification of the grounds on which they are based. Moreover, since more than mere criticism is involved in the examination of past wars and campaigns, the need for a validated theoretical explanation is particularly important if this is used as a basis for advice to practitioners. Essentially strategic thought is prescriptive; it seeks to establish a rational ground for doing something on the basis that the prescribed action will produce a given result. It is thus intimately related to practice and is not merely a commentary on it. Let us look at the less rigorous argument that this ground is based on an understanding of past experience. The implicit assumption is that the level of violence and its employment in the past can be used as a means of assessing appropriate action in the present and the future. This is rather more than historical investigation, for the historian has no lessons to offer. His enquiry stops at the point where by the skilful use of surviving evidence he is able to reconstruct a past situation and so make it intelligible to his readers. There are many problems in the establishment of historical knowledge and some of them are relevant to the strategist who concerns himself with making parallels with the past.

The problem of anachronism for example, where extrapolations from the record of the past are deemed relevant to the present causes certain difficulties. Both the analyst and the practitioner assess action in a temporal context which links past and future in a highly ambiguous way. Essentially, they are concerned with appraising how a given course of action will produce a given result in terms of a set of variable conditions and factors. The strategic analyst looks at the past in order to appraise actors in terms of their relative success or failure in attaining their object. He also extrapolates from the historical record quasi generalisations which permit him to make judgements about effective action in the future. To take one example, Liddell Hart's study of the Battle of Cambrai in 1916;[21] he concluded that the true role of the tank was not appreciated and the initial tactical success was therefore not exploited. This lack of appreciation led directly to the French collapse in 1940. If the French Army, possessing as it did superior tanks, both in performance and numbers, had only learned the lessons of Cambrai and organised its armour as did the German Army, the outcome would have been very different. This is of course tautologically true. The counter-factuals in this type of argument presuppose a level of causality that is not validated by any explicit theoretical explanation.

The point here is that both the analyst and the practitioner are concerned with examining past situations of decision and action in warfare in terms of their relevance to the future course of action. The type of reasoning involved is projective and seeks to extend apparent lessons learn from the past to guide practice. In the case of this example, Liddell Hart's argument fell on deaf ears because neither the British nor the French governments sought the offensive. The British Army was extremely small and there was no place for highly mobile concentrations of armour in it. The strategy to be adopted was defensive and in keeping with a small army and the exploitation of the navy and air force. The French, for their part were not thinking of invading Germany or of a quick campaign with decisive battles. Holding the German forces and applying pressure through economic blockade and peripheral operations would suffice in bringing about Hitler's defeat by demonstrating that he could not win. Both governments were afraid of aerial bombing, relying on the experience of the Spanish Civil War and the German and Italian use of aircraft against unprotected Spanish cities such as Guernica as a precedent. As it turned out it was the blitzkrieg and not the blitz that proved the greatest danger. As experience changes so do the appreciations.

Given the great difficulty relevant to this case as to the present nuclear age, of evaluating new military technology and the necessity, given the volatility of the element of arms competition, to plan and develop over a period of time, it is not surprising that contradiction and ambiguities abound in strategic thinking and defence planning. The panzer division was an admirable formation for the blitzkrieg and so was the tactical airforce designed to support it, but when the war became a prolonged total war what were the appropriate weapons then? Hitler's forces became obsolescent and a major effort was required to innovate during the course of the war. But by the time his new types of tanks, jet aircraft, snorkel equipped submarines, and ballistic missiles appeared, it was too late. His opponents had been caught at a disadvantage but not decisively defeated. They were able to catch up.

Of course the practioner, if he survives, learns by what he conceives of as his mistakes, and so policy and strategy are essentially pragmatic. It is at the planning stage in time of peace that the reflective and theoretical aspects of strategy assume importance. The simple aim of total war—the unconditional surrender of the enemy—gives a direction to strategy lacking in conflicts that are more limited where a complex of interests and relevant factors complicate judgement. An armed peace is one based on hypothesis and scenario. It is conjectural. A distinction should thus be made between the type of reasoning which is concerned with a time continuum from past experience, as it is interpreted, into a future, in order to make rational choices in terms of weapons procurement, alliances, and defence in general, and the reasoning of those engaged in actual conflict. This is a distinction between the hypothetical basis of defence-policy with its relatively long-term perspectives and the short-term strategy of action. The former is concerned with the problem of security and its conditions; the latter with the immediate problems of victory and defeat.

There are two main points that emerge from this; firstly the temptation to argue from hindsight and to interpret *ex post facto* the continuum of reasoning of political and military leaders should be avoided. Of course we know in a sense what happened and it is tempting to explain in terms of success and failure, forgetting that these are relative to the intentions and reasoning of the agents concerned. If, for example, Hitler had not had to support the Italians in the Balkans and counter the coup in Belgrade, he would have invaded the Soviet Union earlier and this would, perhaps, have nullified the effects of the early onset of winter. The British success in promoting opposition in Yugoslavia and in supporting the Greeks against the Italians and Germans, in a sense caused this delay.[22] Only with hindsight could it be deemed to be instrumental in foiling Hitler's campaign in Russia. And this of course is only apparent instrumentality. Who could have foreseen an early winter?

This leads on to the second point; any attempt to extrapolate lessons from history involves theory construction. If we wish to designate a given manoeuvre or decision as a mistake we are in effect stating that we know what would be a correct or effective course of action. Being wise after the event is relatively easy. The grounds on which we criticise action also prescribe it. It does so not because of some lesson learnt from the past but because an a-temporal level of generalisation is implied, that links conditions and action for a given class of situations so that the result invariably follows. There is an implicit claim to knowledge of the relevant factors based not on historical precedent but on a causal relation between events, actions, and conditions, in terms of inducing a particular state of affairs. Rational judgement in strategic matters is the choice of an effective course of action, one that brings about the desired result. Strategic advice presumes that there is this knowledge. Whatever its form it cannot be derived from unique situations in the past. It is a universal knowledge based on timeless principles. This argument will be considered at length when classical strategic thought is examined in a later chapter.

It is sometimes argued that rigorous theory or genuine laws relating to the proper conduct of war are either impossible or else irrelevant to strategic thought. Its purpose is not to engage in what can only be empirically vacuous conceptual schemes, a kind of military metaphysics, but to provide a form of understanding that aids practice. This constitutes a kind of hermeneutics as a basis for utility. It asserts an understanding of the actions of others through a common consciousness and rationality. The basic assumption is one of an underlying psychological awareness that applies to all human actions regardless of time and place. From Zenophon to Montgomery military (and political) leaders have been inspired by the same kind of reasoning in action.

What I have called 'expectations of proper action' form the basis of practical reasoning. Action is undertaken in the belief that it occurs within a framework of assumptions about appropriate responses from those on whom it impinges. Instrumental action is intended to elicit a specific response. This is an expectation that in practice may be disappointed but it provides a basis for action derived from learning and experience within a social context. It is *socially* derived. Taking it out of this context and applying it to past societies or societies with very different mores would produce some alarming results. Action within this novel context, to be effective, would have to be based on learning a new language and a knowledge of new social roles. Minimally some common ground would have to be established. This is largely taken for granted in social life, and vastly improved communications have provided opportunities for developing this common ground. In some cases, most notably that of Japan in the Nineteenth Century, contact with other cultures has been a traumatic experience.

Thus while it may be rational to operate on this assumption in a known social milieu, it cannot be rational to extend this assumption into a radically different social context. It is an assumption that is tested in practice and through practice. It is relevant to the practitioner rather than to the theoretician. It becomes relevant to the latter when it is used as the basis of a universal rationality alleged to apply to all cases in which violence is instrumental. Where this rationality is assumed to exist in the formulation of an appropriate strategy—either in terms of means or in the definition of ends—the consequence of action will not be as expected. The assumption is one that must be empirically derived, as in the case of practical reasoning, through a process of trial and error. The alternative is a theory of rationality or of rational behaviour, that assumes some of the characteristics of grounded theory in science and is open to test. Without such a theory we have no means of deriving knowledge from self-knowledge and escaping its innate subjectivity. As we shall see, many strategic models or scenarios make the assumption of a common rationality in devising means of attaining political objectives through violence or its threat. This turns out to be an extension of practical reasoning into a context that is in fact imponderable, as where radically novel weapons come into existence, or differing in important respects from the social milieu of the strategist. The example of nuclear ballistic missiles and the theory of deterrence illustrate this. So does the case of the Vietnam War and the problem of forcing an appropriate response from the North Vietnamese government within the context of a limited war.

The direct consequences of an emphasis on understanding as the goal of historical enquiry and using this as a basis for strategic prescription is a form of rationalisation that is non-explanatory. This is conceived of by some strategic thinkers as a means of establishing what is an appropriate reason governing choice in a specific situation. The question of appropriateness can be argued in two different ways. Firstly, it can entail a reference to a grounded theory that establishes which preconditions need to be satisfied for an event to take place, whether the event in question is a state of mind or a state of affairs. In other words it permits both an explanation of reasoning as a process and an explanation of its consequences, i.e. where it operates, in terms of stipulated actions. Or, secondly, the reference could be to a socially derived criterion of reasonableness, rather on the legal principle of beyond reasonable doubt or what a reasonable person would do or deem to be rational in given circumstances where direct evidence is scant. The implications of these two positions will be considered in detail in the next chapters.

It is clear, however, that where a grounded theory is lacking, the second of these two references is innately subjective. What counts as an appropriate action in a given situation is a matter of assessment, wholly dependent upon a social context and socially derived rules of conduct. In no way of course does this permit any predictive derivation of a result. The language is that of justification and not explanation, in that no necessary and sufficient conditions for a result—i.e. the terms of the action—are stipulated. Rather the action is deemed to be justified in terms of an associated reasoning and not in terms of a guaranteed result. And so far as the historian is concerned it is a dubious ground on which to infer the reasoning of agents, acting in very different social contexts, from that which provides the language of justification, *vide* criticism of the Whig school of history.

Similarly, the strategist, if he relies on this kind of rationalisation as a basis for his advice to practitioners, is engaged in a vicious circularity. Deriving his rules of rational conduct from his own society, and using them to appraise past uses of organised violence and then extrapolating lessons from this appraisal, asserting their relevance for the present and future conduct of war, adds nothing to our knowledge. The prescriptive level of his argument is not made more authoritative by such an appeal given the circular nature of its interpretative base. This aspect of strategic thought and its relation to history will be considered in detail in the next chapter. The point here is that the assertion of a common rationality, such that in any age or society the actor is motivated by the same reasoning as that which prevails in our own, is extremely suspect. It is not an assumption but a theory that requires proof.

There is an additional problem in using historical reconstruction as a basis for strategic prescription. In explaining action, that is seeking as an historian to establish what actually happened, it is important to establish what was contemplated at the time as options or alternative courses of action. This is particularly true for acts of violence intended to produce a specific result. Acts of this kind are undertaken within a framework of reasoning in which various balances of profit and loss—of optimally effective action—are made. What is actually done, is done as a consequence of an analysis, more or less elaborate and sophisticated, from which emerges the chosen course of action. In short, fully to understand and explain an act of violence or its threat, it is necessary to place it in such a context. Such a context is of course that deemed to be relevant or pertinent by the actor and not imposed on the situation by the historian or strategist. Here it is the reasoning of the actor that provides us with an explanation of what happened.

Thus, in explaining a war, or at least, the initiation of violence between states or political factions, it is important to examine the specific level of action in terms of the purposes it was intended to serve and of the alternatives considered, by the actors. Such considerations as economy, the problem of control, the effects prejudicial or otherwise on other objectives sought or positions maintained, the relevance of ideological or ethical aspects, the perception of rules, or legal constraints, and the likely effects upon popular support or popular opposition, are all aspects of the specific decision to act, and require elucidation before the act itself can be explained. And this, of course, is equally true where inaction is the preferred choice. Such a context of decision is innately political and is also unique in its particular combination of factors.

For example, much of the attack on what is termed 'appeasement'[23] in the 1930s rests upon the anachronistic argument that if Hitler's programme of action could have been checked at an early stage the consequent war could have been avoided. Chamberlain's policies are criticised for encouraging Hitler to believe that Britain would not seriously oppose him. Acting on this belief he seized what he thought was an opportunity for German expansion at the expense of its neighbours. But this argument presumes omniscience on the part of Chamberlain and ignores the difficulties of preventive diplomacy and pre-emptive war. A knowledge of Hitler's intentions is presumed and his opportunism ignored, not to speak of the attitudes of other states such as Italy, the Soviet Union, and France. The temporising policy which Chamberlain adopted, seeking a definitive negotiated settlement acceptable to Hitler and which effectively tied him, was related to an appreciation of Britain's military strength, or lack of it, domestic political difficulties, and the absence of any direct challenge to British interests.

In short, the reasoning which underlay his policy is ignored and argument by hindsight substituted for it. The avoidance of a direct challenge to Germany was a reasonable choice given what was known at the time, and it left it open to Britain, rearming where it was weakest, to take what options were available, depending on Hitler's subsequent moves. The rationality of the challenge when it was eventually made in 1939 over Poland is perhaps open to discussion, but it came when Hitler had clearly broken an agreement he had freely entered into, and so closed the possibility of further negotiation. This was compounded when the Soviet Union was removed from the diplomatic scene through the Molotov-Ribbentrop Pact. Appeasement in any case begs the question as to what crucial interest is at stake. If it was presumed that Hitler wanted total war, a presumption entirely lacking in evidence, then indeed an earlier war or confrontation would have been rational. But this is dubious. In any case such a confrontation would have to meet with success and given the military state of Britain, and its geographical position, this was to say the least highly unlikely. Equally, it is difficult to argue that Hitler directly threatened any specific British interest in his territorial demands on Czechoslovakia, Austria, and Poland. And rearmament in the air on the part of Britain closed the one major gap in its security that could be exploited by a German threat.

The point here is that it is crucial to evaluate what alternative courses of action exist in an adversarial situation in terms of the perceptions of the agent. The imposition of a range of options known only to the latter-day, or contemporary 'observer', is not only a-historical and rationalising, but incapable of sustaining an explanation of action that can be used to support strategic prescription. Looting history for parallels and precedents is a doubtful exercise when history itself as a source of genuine knowledge is perverted in this way. The problem can be stated thus: when we offer an explanation of strategies it must be in terms of the reasoning of those engaged in action. Reconstructing their perceptions and rationale may entail the examination of its theoretical structure, elucidating the assumptions and hypotheses of the practitioners. So far as this goes it is history that is being done. Its focus only takes on an abstract and theoretical form where political reasoning contains a high theoretical content. The nearest analogy is with the relation between an ideology such as Marxism or liberal-democracy and socialist and democratic politics. If the examination moves away from the link between theories of this kind and political practice, to a concern with the former, that is with theory proper, it changes its character.

In this context, no one, for example, can demonstrate on empirical and theoretical grounds that defensive deterrence is actually instrumental in preventing war between the major nuclear powers. Deterrence theory and its derivations is relevant to politics only in terms of its status as a set of assumptions and as an influence upon strategic decision and weapons procurement. It is essentially a belief. It constitutes a basis for decision and choice where it is relevant and is reflected in the various weapons systems adopted, in negotiations over defence, arms control and disarmament, and in a nation's general strategic posture. A whole world of intangibles is involved here, especially since the question of values and the political system cannot be separated from questions of defence. Action and inaction thus have a political context that is complex and inter-related whatever its particular focus. Strategic argument that ignore this ignores the overall problem of ends pursued by the state. For example, the willingness to accept deprivation in material terms and to accept limitations on freedoms and political expression, not to speak of the sacrifice of life, is based on the paramount importance of the preservation of the state. Nationalism becomes dominant in belligerent countries and total commitment to the struggle is the consequence. This commitment may be placed in jeopardy however, and the consequences for the state and its political system radical. War is the father of revolution. Adopting a particular strategy and using violence in a particular way may destroy the state itself.

It is interesting to note that all major revolutions including that of the French, developed out of war,[24] with the intervention of foreign powers and its consequences. In the case of the Vietnam War, with all its limitations and the cajoleries and manipulations of the administration, dissent was a major factor in bringing about an American defeat in terms of achieving the limited objective of maintaining a friendly government in power in South Vietnam. The political system was able, barely, to contain the opposition without radical constitutional and political changes, but it left its mark on American politics. The historian with his concern for reconstructing political reasoning is generally aware of this contextual relationship between areas and foci of decision and action. Particular developments may be singled out as important, giving them the importance attributed to them by the actors involved, but again this is a matter of context.

It is when the assumptions underlying this reasoning are subject to critical analysis that the enquiry becomes ambiguous. More than reconstruction is involved here. The strategist however modest in his claims, wishes to inform practice, to guide it in the right direction and to proffer authoritative advice. There is the implicit claim of expertise in the instrumental use of violence in politics. For this claim and its associated debate to be both valid and effective, there must be some means of referring theoretical strategic argument to some criteria of evaluation that stand above it. Without this it remains largely a matter for the politician, and the choice of advice becomes entirely subjective and dependent on political expediency. As I said before, politicians tend to accept the advice they wish to hear. What would constitute such criteria will be examined in later chapters. The strategist unlike the historian enters into the actual reasoning of politicians by accepting the stated ends, or at least taking them as axiomatic, and is mainly concerned with devising an instrumental means for their achievement. Yet in doing this the question of a proper relationship between ends and means is avoided. This is at the root of strategy. The effectiveness of the chosen means is a function of whether the ends are attainable within prestated conditions and limits. But the strategist has no say over what these ends are; this is the province of the practitioner. Only when the two are combined does this problem disappear. This still leaves the problem of determining a proper relation between means and ends, in terms of commensurability and effectiveness, open.

If we take the example of the Vietnam War[25] to illustrate this, it is clear that President Johnson would take no strategic advice that brought into question the ends he sought to achieve. Yet it is and was far from clear that maintaining a client government in South Vietnam was important to the United States in any tangible sense. Its significance in terms of prestige and commitment to the global containment of communism is perhaps a different matter, although the stakes here could only be heightened by an exaggerated importance being attributed to the issue. The terms of failure were in a sense established by the rhetoric of commitment. It was impolitic at the time to question the overall commitment to global containment even though it was becoming increasingly clear after the Cuban missile crisis that a nuclear balance between the Soviet Union and the United States was emerging. This had the two effects of making security dependent on the principle of defensive deterrence and of making some form of strategic accommodation with the Soviet Union a necessity. War became something to be avoided rather than used as a means to achieve security. The second effect was, given the constraint on general war, political situations could be exploited by both sides and success and failure postulated depending on local or regional circumstances. Given the proximity of Vietnam to China and to the Soviet Union, and the self-imposed limits set by the United States, it was not obvious that the latter state enjoyed the advantage. Thus the Vietnam War was commenced at a time when security needs precluded both the threat of general war and the global containment of communism. The premises in short were obsolete as the war began. This became increasingly obvious to the administration as the level of cost (material and human) mounted, and opposition strengthened in the United States. The question was asked, what was the war for? There was no obvious or convincing answer.

The role of the strategist in all this was to concentrate on means. Given the limits set on the war, principally that banning an extension of ground combat into North Vietnam, the chief instrument of victory was seen as aerial bombing while maintaining a holding operation in South Vietnam. The problem was seen as breaking the will of the North Vietnamese government by making the cost of supporting the insurrection in the South too high. The successive bombing campaigns had the principal effect of increasing the level of North Vietnamese involvement in the South and forcing a corresponding increase in American ground forces to match them. This they never succeeded in doing although they inflicted numerous military reverses on North Vietnamese troops and checked the Tet offensive. The air war was, however, totally ineffective, and one can surmise that the air force was used after this ineffectiveness was apparent solely because it was the only military instrument entirely at the command of the President. The Army was withdrawn by Congress, and both its size and its effort were limited in any case by the need to keep the war itself limited and to preserve a measure of political support at home. In the end aerial bombing was used to obtain an ignominious peace and even here its role is dubious. Although the limits were preserved in spite of the extension of operations into Laos and Cambodia it is hard to escape the conclusion that the war escaped control. What was expected to be an effective demonstration of force designed to maintain the political status quo in South Vietnam became a minor war of attrition in which, paradoxically, the cost in political and military terms was seen as too high for the United States to sustain. The ends and means were not commensurate, or at least showed signs of becoming badly out of proportion. Once this was understood the war was ended, leaving the difficulty of extrication as a separate problem. If strategy and politics had been coordinated from the beginning and ends and means related properly, although success could by no means be guaranteed, the actual policy and its implementation would have been more rational.

The point being made here is that strategic prescriptions presume courses of action that are concrete and tangibly directed to a definable purpose. The political milieu in which these prescriptions are applied is not so simple. It is complex, and those acting within it are rarely able to take one course of action without it impinging on a whole range of interests and commitments. The elements of value, of relative and shifting priorities between preferred outcomes, militates against the adoption of simple strategies. This is true even in the context of total war where the main aim of violence is the complete defeat of the enemy. A range of complicating factors and interests operate even here, precluding the adoption of single-minded strategy of victory. As we shall see in a later chapter, Churchill was more anxious to remove the Hitler regime than to destroy Germany as a state capable of acting as a barrier to Soviet expansion. It was a painful choice to him to accept the necessity to do so, and he sought to adopt a strategy that at the very least would pre-empt the Soviet Union from influence in the Balkans and Eastern Europe even though it was the Soviet Union that sustained the major effort in fighting Germany. Thus if it is not winning *per se* that matters, it is winning under certain conditions, and achieving the kind of peace that best suits the victor's interests, that is politically important. The purely military level is subordinate to this and strategy must combine the two levels—the military and the political—if it is to be genuinely instrumental.

The case is even more complicated in times of peace when defence and security are central to policy or where limited wars within a framework of mutual defensive relations are fought. Whatever the outcome of the Vietnam War, no American President, or Russian or Chinese leader for that matter, wanted to provoke a general nuclear war. It was fought under the compelling need to keep a general peace and arms control negotiations continued between the major powers during it. The strategist cannot thus conceive of military instrumentality as in a sense a-political. His prescriptions depend for their persuasiveness and force upon the relevance they have for the politician in terms of the satisfaction of his objectives. These may not coincide with what the strategist assumes to be paramount. Equally, the politician needs to know what are the implications in military terms of the prescriptions urged upon him by the strategist. In either case it is clear that the basis of strategic prescription must be the prevailing political rationality, not that of the past. An appeal to precedent in order to be valid must not simply be simply an appeal to alleged instrumentality; it must show the two cases to be the same in all respects including the reasoning of those engaged in them. If we regard such reasoning as unique to time, place, and the individuals concerned, it is hard to see how this can be the case.

The alternative in terms of strategic method is to stand outside the actual context of reasoning and apply a different rationality; one derived from a genuine a-temporal theory of action. A strategic theory of this sort would inform action by showing a causal relationship between conditions, a governing principle, and a result. The actor then has the choice, should he so wish, to procure the result, by fulfilling the conditions. In short he obeys the rationality dictated by the theory. This is a genuine instrumentality in the same way as an applied science is the basis of technical performance. To be relevant, it would have to embrace human reasoning since this is the basis of action. But reasoning itself would be explained within the theory of action, as mental states induced by the operation of certain conditions within the framework of laws. This would provide a genuine scientific basis for strategic theory.

At the moment we have technology but not science. Or at least science has a very limited application to strategy related to the technical performance of weapons systems. Their apparent precision and the ability to specify masks their ambiguity in political terms. If we take the Strategic Defence Initiative[26] for example, current strategic debate focusses on two areas of contention. The first is whether a defensive shield, either complete, or partial, can be achieved through current technological knowledge and at a reasonable cost. It must be said that this is an imponderable. Translating theory into practice in the form of a completed programme that performs according to specification must always be subject to doubt. But while this is mainly the province of the scientists, it is the second focus that is most relevant to strategy. What would such a defence shield do? If its purpose is to provide security what does this entail and would it in fact achieve this object? The implications of these questions will be examined in later chapters. The point which can be made here is that unless they can be answered satisfactorily the question of technical competence is of secondary importance. The rationale is political not technical. If the consequence of a perfect defensive shield against ballistic missiles is an enhancement of other threats to national integrity for which no defence is provided, or if the result is an arms race in which both competitors achieve another stalemate, then developing it is hardly a rational course of action. It cannot be said from the outset that a unilateral decision to embark on such a programme will not produce such consequences. Rationality in international politics is not a matter for one state or for one strategy; it is shared.

To conclude this introductory discussion of the use of violence as a political instrument and its associated strategic prescriptions, let me return to the theme of this book. It is that any strategic argument which seeks to direct and inform practice needs to satisfy certain conditions so that the desired end is, in fact, achieved by the means recommended and employed. The rationality of such arguments does not depend upon making out a plausible or acceptable case for the recommended action, but in showing that the result is either highly probable or certain. What this entails will be examined in the next chapters. As I hope to show they entail the formulation of a grounded theory which acts both as a framework of reference and a means of validation for recommended courses of action. In the absence of such a theory strategic prescriptions are empirically vacuous, and in the context of the rational use of violence in a nuclear age, highly dangerous. The problem, as I have tried to argue, is not that violence is either evil or irrational as a means of achieving political ends, as that it is both when it escapes control and becomes indiscriminate. Except for those who believe that violence is an evil in all contexts, violence is a necessary adjunct to politics. It is a means of maintaining basic political conditions for all other human activities to be conducted rationally. The problem lies in controlling and regulating it, and this is essentially the primary concern of strategic thought whatever its secondary concerns. If it is to be instrumental in fulfilling human purposes then the use of violence must be commensurate with the ends sought. It must be limited. What this entails and how such control is to be achieved are the central questions of this book.

NOTES AND REFERENCES

1. It is astonishing with the retreat of the European states from their Empires, how the set of assumptions and beliefs about the 'white man's burden' that was used to justify the imperial presence so rapidly disappeared into a kind of ideological oubliette.
2. Aristotle, *The Politics* trans. T. A. Sinclair, Penguin, Harmondsworth, 1964.
3. N. Machievelli, *The Prince*, Everyman, London, 1938.
4. See K. Marx, *Das Kapital* and V. I. Lenin, *Imperialism: the Highest Stage of Capitalism.*

5. Qui desideret pacem praeperet bellum. Vegetius. De Re Mil.
6. See C. Reynolds, *Modes of Imperialism*, Martin Robertson, Oxford, 1981 and A. Hitler, *Mein Kampf*, trans. Ralph Mannheim, Radius Books, Hutchinson, London, 1969, pp. 121 and 137. Also pp. 124–6.
7. See F. P. Walters, *A History of the League of Nations*, OUP, London, 1967, and Inis L. Claude Jr. *Swords into Plowshares*, rev. ed. University of London Press, London, 1964. The functionalist argument asserts the development of interdependence between states as part of a process that will produce supranational institutions. This process is generated by the inability of the modern nation-state to fulfil important economic and technical functions unilaterally, or through *ad hoc* arrangements with other states. This belief in the supremacy of economic forces found its most naive expression in Norman Angell, *The Great Illusion*, Heinemann, London, 1933, published in the year Hitler came to power.
8. See *Modes of Imperialism, op. cit.* for an account of economic imperialism in its modern guise.
9. *Pacta sunt servanda.* This is the principle of international law that asserts freely negotiated contracts between states as binding since consent implies obligation.
10. In March 1939 Hitler took advantage of the Tiso coup in Slovenia by occupying Prague, declaring Bohemia and Moravia as German Protectorates and recognising the state of Slovakia. In so doing, he not only broke the Munich agreement and destroyed Czechoslovakia but acquired non-German territory and population, thus abrogating the principle of self-determination he had invoked to support his demands for the Sudetenland.
11. See Hans Morgenthau, *Politics among Nations*, Alfred Knopf, New York, 1951; see also F. H. Hinsley *Power and the Pursuit of Peace*, CUP, Cambridge, 1967, and K. Waltz, *Man, the State and War*, Columbia University Press, New York, 1965.
12. On the importance of fear see Barry Buzan, *People, States and Fear,* Wheatsheaf Books, Brighton, 1983.
13. *Mein Kampf, op. cit.* p. 128.
14. See Hossbach Memo. Doc 386–PS in *IMTC The Trial of German Major War Criminals*, London, HMSO, Vol. III p. 297, also Obersalzburg Speech. Doc 798–PS *ibid.* p. 585 and Boehm Memo. Doc 789–PS *ibid.* p. 4572.
15. Carl von Clausewitz was one of the very few writers Hitler cited as an influence upon his ideas. See *The Testament of Adolph Hitler*, Hitler-Bormann Documents, Feb-April, 1945, ed. Francois Genoud, trans. R. H. Stevens, intro. by H. Trevor-Roper, Cassell, London, 1960.
16. On the '*drôle de guerre*' period see Dudley Saward '*Bomber' Harris,* Cassell, London, 1984, p. 76, apropos of March 1940 "At this period of the war there was little real bombing as the government was not at all anxious to commence a Blitz and thereby encourage swift retaliation from the Germans", see also *British Policy in the Second World War: Documents,* ed. Llewellyn Woodward, HMSO, London, 1970, Vol. 1.
17. See Lord Vansittart, *The Mist Procession*, Hutchinson, London, 1954, p. 443 and also Viscount Templewood, *Nine Troubled Years,* Collins, London, 1954, p. 131.
18. A good example of this is the official enquiry set up by the French after the defeat of 1940. Commission d'Enquete Parlementaire sur les evenements survenus en France de 1933 a 1945, Paris, 1951-1954; see also Eleanor M.

Gates, *End of the Affair. The Collapse of the Anglo-French Alliance 1939–40*, Allen & Unwin, London, 1981.

19. For an account of Hitler's decision to invade the Soviet Union see C. Reynolds, *Modes of Imperialism, op. cit.*

20. See H. Guderian, *Panzer Leader*, trans. Constantine Fitzgibbon, 1952, Faber edition, London, 1974, pp. 265–8 and 432–43. See also Erich von Manstein, *Lost Victories*, ed. and trans. Anthony G. Powell, Methuen, London, 1958.

21. See Basil Liddell Hart, *A History of the First World War*, Cassell, London, 1970.

22. For an account of British policy in the Balkans see Elizabeth Barker, *British Policy in S.E. Europe in the Second World War*, Macmillan Press, London and Basingstoke, 1976, Chap. 9, pp. 78–95.

23. For the argument against appeasement see Martin Gilbert and Richard Gott, *The Appeasers,* Weidenfeld and Nicolson, London, 1963. For a defence of Baldwin see Keith Middlemas and John Barnes, *Baldwin*, Weidenfeld and Nicolson, London, 1969. For a more balanced view see Maurice Cowling, *The Impact of Hitler: British politics and British policy 1933–1940.* CUP, Cambridge, 1975.

24. Vide the French involvement in the American War of Independence; Austrian and Prussian intervention in the French Revolution; British, American and Japanese intervention in the Russian Revolution and Japanese, Soviet and American involvement in the various stages of the Chinese Revolution.

25. See L. B. Johnson, *The Vantage Point,* Popular Library, NY, 1971.

26. This was a proposal made by President Reagan in an speech in March 1983 that the United States should develop a programme designed to destroy incoming missiles.

2 Rationality and Action

A major implicit claim in strategic theory is that it provides an authoritative basis for military and political practice. It is essentially prescriptive. This is true even where 'theory' is overtly historical in character or a piece of strategic reasoning. An explanation of a battle, a campaign or a war, carries with it the assumption that events, actions and decision are so related as to produce certain results. These may be evaluated and criticised in terms of relative success or failure. The ends sought may similarly be scrutinised and held up to criticism. At one level this is military history and at another strategic theory, but the common element is a presumption of knowledge on the part of the observer as to the relation between means and ends so that success and not failure is the consequence of action.

The military historian may not be concerned with extrapolating 'lessons from the past', but in formulating an evaluation of the relationship between reasoning and practice in the context of war or preparation for war, he is in fact theorising. As we shall see, his conclusions are very often used as data by the strategic theorist, although they are the product of an implicit theorising and so not neutral or objective. The strategic theorist, of course, is directly concerned with prescription. His expertise lies in his ability to state with authority 'how to do it'. Although this authority may in practice stem from fortuitous coincidence with events, or from the parallelism of his advice with what politicians want to do, in principle it must derive from the adequacy of his theory.

The questions asked in this chapter are: what kind of theory is entailed in stipulating violence as a means to the achievement of political ends, and what are the conditions that need to be satisfied before it is deemed adequate? Answering these questions involves placing them within the framework of the general problem of the theoretical explanation of human conduct. Violence is only one aspect of social interaction and an explanation of this phenomenon would be incorporated within a theory of social behaviour. I am not concerned, however, with *explaining* violence in human affairs, but rather with the problem of its *utility* as stipulated by strategic theory. It may be the case that this more restricted view of theory is itself inadequate since it constitutes a sub-class of a much larger theory. The implications of this possibility will be considered.

Nevertheless, the focus of this study lies in the attempt to relate general propositions about human action in terms of capability and performance, to rationality. On what grounds can we postulate that a specified course of action will lead to a desired result? Under what theoretical conditions is violence or its threat rational in the sense that it constitutes a means? What are the grounds for making prescriptive statements concerning the effective threat or use of violence? Clearly, these questions extend beyond the fields of military history and strategic theory. They involve some basic questions about theory and its application to human action and rationality before turning to the strategic arguments themselves in later chapters.

Theory is a very loose expression and conceals a multitude of arguments and positions. It has been an exhaustively contested question whether the form of theory characteristic of the natural sciences is appropriate to the general explanation of human conduct. It is clear that in practice some level of generalisation exists in almost any attempt to account for human conduct, whether the focus is restricted in time and place and explicitly historical, or whether it lies in practical reasoning. If such accounts are to be the subject of evaluation, or where they contain some claim to authority or knowledge as a basis for practice, then their theoretical claims, implicit or explicit, need examination. What can be made of the proposition, for example, made by Colin Gray, with its apparent contradictions, 'strategy ultimately is about policies that work or do not work, in practice in one place, in one period; it is not about strategic "truth".' If the strategic theorist denies the universality of his 'theories' what is the force of the particular 'truth',[1] he urges upon the politicians? Why should we accept *his* prescriptions? In the nuclear age these questions are of more than passing interest.

Let us begin then by looking at the logical and empirical attributes of scientific theory. Our question is, can this mode of explanation be applied to human action and rationality so that we can derive an applied science of human conduct from a general theoretical level for, in this case, the effective use of violence?

First of all what is meant by scientific theory? It should be stressed that the major theoretical element relevant to strategic theory and the explanation of human action is causality.[2] Statements made by strategists that relate to, for example, capability, (itself causal in nature) and consequences in terms of action, are implicitly or explicitly invoking a theory of causation.

To ascribe a cause in simple terms is to say that certain occurrences (events) are related to other occurrences so that where one is found, so is the other. A causal theory asserts firstly, a set of statements describing the occurrences in terms of time and place; secondly, a set of universal hypotheses, and thirdly, the logical deduction of the event from these two sets. It must be capable of empirical test through observation and experiment so that the conclusion, that is the deduced state of affairs, occurs without exception. The event is then said to be explained and since the theory is universal, constitutes merely one instance of a class of such events. Thus wherever and whenever the combination of preconditions, necessary and sufficient, occurs, then the event in question will occur. The explanation of why this should be so involves the stipulation of such conditions within the framework of deductive argument. The theory thus explains the occurrence of classes of events by subsuming them within a covering law. It is important to note that this description of theoretical explanation turns on its logical structure. It says nothing about what is claimed as knowledge—the content as opposed to the form of the argument.

What makes this argument explanatory and not merely a closed analytic conceptual scheme is a form of testing that is logically independent of the theory itself. The conclusions of the theory are a logically necessary consequence of the initial premises and conditions, governed by the law. The theory is deductive. However, the process of testing through experiment and observation is inductive in character. The theoretical conclusions are tested by reference to experience. This enables the selection and rejection of competing hypotheses in conjunction with other criteria. It also enables a distinction to be made between hypotheses which in principle are testable and hypotheses which are not. Only the former can constitute an explanation.

There are however, some difficult problems associated with this model of causal theory and its testing. Firstly, if a covering law model is tested against finite experience and is treated as an empirical explanation, on what grounds can we consider its laws as universal? We have to support the logic of a law with assumptions about the uniformity of nature: assumptions that are metaphysical in character and which postulate that nature is constant and unchanging. Such an assumption cannot of course be tested. Secondly, if we assert that such explanations are confirmed by experience, although we may have evidence from observation and experiment that the confirmation of the law occurred at the time of test, we cannot know on grounds of experience that this will hold good in any future test. Thirdly, if an inductive principle is postulated what inductive principle justifies this? We are forced into infinite regress if we seek to establish one. Fourthly, it can be argued that the method by which a covering law is tested leads to circularity, for the evidence of observation and experiment is itself stipulated by the theory. Fifthly, if less then universality is claimed for such laws, i.e. it is argued that they are merely probable, then any law could be confirmed on a frequency principle of probability since any proportion of instances could be regarded as confirmatory. Sixthly, accepting that successful prediction occurs, i.e. establishing a confirmation between theoretical conclusions and experimental results, why should we change from one theory to another where they both meet this condition? On what grounds should we choose between rival or incommensurate explanations, both of which have been successful in terms of this test?

There are many other problems but my point here is that the *logical* structure of a covering law model is not a sufficient criterion for the identification and evaluation of an explanatory mode. The notion of an empirical test which validates universal generalisations is not itself a *logical* criterion for the acceptance or rejection of theories. Thus while a causal explanation entails a particular logical structure there are other criteria, of a non-logical nature, which require satisfaction before the putative explanation is deemed adequate and genuinely explanatory. This is recognised by Hempel, who argues that one of the conditions for adequacy is that the law-like statements must have empirical content. 'They must be capable of test by experiment and observation'.[3] He also asserts empirical conditions; namely that the factual references must be true and that the explanation as a whole be confirmed through evidence. Thus although the logically necessary relationship between premises, general laws and conditions typifies this form of theoretical explanation, it must be qualified by an insistence on the satisfaction of criteria, empirical and conventional in character; such conditions are not logical conditions but derived from practice itself.

The relationship between scientific theory and practice is for some philosophers of science crucial. They point to the 'predictive control' of science and the practical application of theories, as a demarcation principle for science itself. Without entering into this debate or accepting that instrumentalism is indeed the hallmark of science, it is certainly the case that successful prediction is a consequence of both the logic and the satisfaction of empirical conditions for scientific hypotheses. And from this we can see that there are important consequences for practice. Leaving aside the contentions concerning the nature and status of theory as a basis for scientific knowledge' if we are in possession of a theory which, albeit, in abstract terms, tells us that a conjunction of conditions governed by a law-like proposition will produce consequences wherever and whenever they occur, then we have a powerful instrument for directing activities so that this state of affairs is either induced by creating the conditions, or utilised in some form of practical activity.

But a genuine applied science is only possible where there is a genuine body of theory; genuine in the sense that it has been adequately tested. The implications of this argument for this enquiry are obvious. If we possess such a body of theory relevant to 'situations of social choice', then we will be able to induce desired states of affairs. In the case of strategic theory this would mean that the instrumental use of violence would have an effective basis so that specified ends could be properly formulated and realised through its means.

The question as to whether this model of theory is appropriate to explanation of human reasoning and action is left open at this stage. However, it is clear that such a model is essentially deterministic; where causal conditions and their governing principle are satisfied then the effect inevitably follows. This must be qualified; as Mary Hesse points out. 'Determinism is the characteristic of a theory according to which from a complete description of the present and perhaps some past states of a system, all future states can be precisely and rigorously calculated'.[4] And, as she argues, no natural science can claim this since it can never be known. The complete information required to test the theory is not, nor can be, in our possession. But this qualification is true of all forms of test and, as was argued earlier, tests against experience are inductively based. No theory can be said to be complete and no test final. Nevertheless, causal theory enables prediction, and exceptions in terms of test disqualify the tested hypothesis. Stating the result that should be observed or obtained by experiment is a pre-conditon of the theory's adequacy. Finding this result confirmed or fulfilled constitutes its adequacy. As such, a prediction, i.e. that *this* result should obtain, is an essential part of the theory.

The application of covering law, or subsumption theory, to human conduct is open to question. Human action, as will be argued later, is closely related to reasoning. In principle, this last could be explicable by a general theory although this would make intentions, purposes etc, epiphenomenal and not the central focus of explanation. In this case we would talk in terms of causes of reasons. Such a theory is implicit in any attempt to relate preconditions to consequences as an explanation of human action. If this is done either in strategic enquiry or in broader fields of the social sciences—economics, politics, sociology, psychology or in history, then such theorising entails the satisfaction of logical and empirical conditions appropriate to covering law explanation. Strategic theory is in this sense a sub-branch of general behavioural theory. It implies or is derived from such a general theoretical construct.

In practice these entailments are only implicit in extant strategic reasoning. As we shall see strategic theorists have not in general sought to establish a *general* theoretical basis for their strategic prescriptions. This is not to say that such a theory is unnecessary. As was argued earlier, applied science is a derivative of 'pure' or theoretical, science. Without the latter a kind of vulgar empiricism or practical reasoning serves as a substitute. If the emphasis is placed upon instrumentality without an adequate theoretical basis, then not only do prescriptions lack authority they also lack effectiveness. Trial and error might serve to produce a desired result in the end, but in the area of warfare the consequent waste and human suffering seem a high price to pay.

However, saying that general theoretical conditions are neither satisfied or central to extant strategic reasoning is not to say that other forms of theory are not present. Indeed a later chapter will be concerned with a form of theory—rational action theory—that is central to strategic thought, and is applicable only to situations of social choice within terms of limited generality. One form of theorising, probability theory, has been urged as more appropriate to explanation of human action. In formal structure it differs little from covering-law theory except that it is inductively rather than deductively based. Instead of an absolute conformity between conclusions and empirical instances it depends upon establishing a specified number of confirming instances. Prediction becomes probability, or projection.[5] Clearly fallibility does not apply here and the adequacy of this theoretical construct depends upon a prior statement of expectation in proportional terms being confirmed by the incidence of that degree of instances.

Forms of this approach to explanation such as frequency theory and statistical generalisation depend upon the isolation of a finite number of equal possibilities and then relating this to the probability of the event according to the proportion of possibilities favourable to its occurrence. The process is inductive; as Hempel puts it, 'We find a certain relative frequency for a series of observed events and assume that the same frequency will hold approximately for further confirmation of the series ....'[6] Clearly the series is finite and some criterion of selection and limit must obtain. Probability statements of this kind are ratings of propositions about the future, those which are probably true as opposed to others, and so provide a guide to choice.

However, statistical generalisations and frequencies based on them or from which they are derived, are, so far as human affairs are concerned, relatively short term in character. They are projections of associated restricted classes of events in terms of the distribution of instances of such associations over a finite period. The probability of the occurrence of the association is a function of the frequency of distribution. While this may be relevant, and perhaps useful, for demographic or meteorological projections (or forecasts) it is not relevant to strategic theory with its complex of variables related to human action and reasoning. And even in these two examples the finite time scale allows only a limited application to practice. Long range forecasts and projections are notoriously fallible.

It is also important to note the frequency principle applies to events and not actions. The significance of this distinction will be discussed later, but the point here is that the notion of an event in the sense of a reasoned action is irrelevant to this form of generalisation. It is materialist in concept. Only things susceptible to quantitative treatment can be the subject of this kind of probability statement. Questions of motive and choice do not enter into this form of statement, although of course, it may be used to supply data informing choice. Whether human actions or their consequences can be treated as material phenomena in this way will be considered later but the relevance and utility of this sort of theorising depends on being able to treat them so.

To take an example; the arms race phenomenon has been explained in terms of a process of *schismogenesis* or *symmetrical reciprocity leading directly to war*.[7] This is a function of the rate of armament expenditure in a competitive situation. Where 't = time; x = defence; y = menaces;' and 'k = 1 = a positive constant' termed a *defence coefficient*, then for Nation A, $dx/dt=ky$ and for Nation B, $dy/dt=kx$. If x and y increase without limit or control then war is the inevitable result. Richardson, the author of this theory, adds to this simple equation the factors g and h (grievances and ambitions) and a and b (economic limitations) and refines it thus; Nation A $dx/dt=ky-ax$ and for Nation B $dx/dt=lx-by$ representing the economic limitations factor; and to $dx/dt=ky-ax+g$ and to $dy/dt=lx-by+h$

respectively to include the grievance factor.

On the basis of these equations Richardson examines the statistics of armaments expenditures and trade figures preceding the two major wars of this century in terms of *warfinpersal* that is the *money value of arms expenditures divided by average wage*. This kind of correlative reasoning is intended to indicate the probability of war. From similar associations in the past extrapolations can be made to determine the likelihood of war stemming from uncontrolled arms races.

There are obvious flaws in this approach. The major one consists of the importation of qualitative concepts such as grievances and ambitions into statistical argument. Such concepts cannot be quantified and relate to reasoning and choice. The argument becomes a kind of hybrid, confusing what can be treated statistically with what cannot. The confusion arises out of the treatment of what is essentially human action as a series of finite statistical events—arms purchases, exports and imports etc. which are the consequences of reasoned action. Similarly the reduction of arms races to a bilateral competition in expenditure on arms is a gross oversimplification of reality. Both the kinds of arms purchases and the multilateral character of security competition and its geopolitics are ignored. Statistical generalisations of this order are really only summary statements of limited consequences of reasoning. It also ignores the fact that mere expenditure calculated over periods of time is not reflected in actual capability at any one time. Weapons systems take a relatively long time to develop and expenditure figures give no indication of this. It is true also that large amounts of money are allocated to projects which are ultimately aborted or to projects which become obsolete on completion.

The kind of probability theory most relevant to strategy is related to expectations of proper action, on what it is reasonable to expect, and this depends upon evidence. Tendencies and regulations in human conduct rather than statistical frequencies are the focus for this kind of theorising. Again it should be stressed that a level of generality applies so that human action is seen in terms of classes rather than individual action. The object of such an approach is to confer some predictive quality on statements concerning human action on the basis of probability.

This form of probability rests on the extrapolation of common features in decisional situations in the past. Situational logic as Popper terms it,[8] consists of an idealised reconstruction of the problem 'in which the agent finds himself'. The problem-solving action he takes is then deemed 'appropriate' or adequate to the situation. According to Popper this 'method of situational analysis may be described as an application of the rationality principle'. We thus have a model situation and a general rule of conduct appropriate to it. This enables both an appraisal of past situations and a guide to future conduct—something of interest both to military historians and to strategists. It offers a basis for prescription and for explanation.

The identification of the situation as a situation of a particular kind also allows the specification of appropriate reasons or rational action. The emphasis placed on the situation itself by Popper as a *problem* indicates that the rational solution is derived from it and its conditions rather than vice-versa. In a sense the problem-situation dictates its own solution. Such situations are deemed to recur and so we have the principle of regularity in human conduct with associated rules of behaviour. The practical consequences of this are clear—so long as it is possible to identify situations, actual or potential, then we are in possession of a means of directing action successfully—i.e. solving the problem.

As it stands this argument seems more easy to state than to fulfil. Its implications will be discussed later but some points can be made here. A principle of rationality is asserted; is this relative to the agent, to the observer, or to both? Since it seeks to generalise it would seem that a normative principle is invoked common to all such situations of rational choice. Is this principle a rule derived from observation of practice, that is conventional in character, or is it external to practice, a means of assessing and justifying it? If the former the question of *appropriateness* does not arise since the mere identification of the rule being followed allows us to explain without any prescriptive or practical implications. If the latter than rationality or *appropriate* action involves a relation between means and ends that is stipulative. If this action is taken in this situation then this result will follow. The implied generalisation is not a law but a statement of probability.

These points will be discussed in detail when rationalisation and reason-giving explanation are considered later in this chapter. Their implications for strategic theory are however obvious. If a principle of rationality can direct effective action and is derivable from the analysis of past situations of choice, then we have a means of basing strategic prescriptions on solid ground. A variation of this argument also supports this possibility. This places the emphasis not so much on the situation itself but upon the agent. Again in the mode of *expectations of proper action* the agent is disposed to act in a particular way when faced with a particular problem situation or exposed to a set of stimuli provided by certain empirical conditions. This theory of dispositions has been developed into a socio-biological or ethological theory of animal behaviour.[9] Without going into the argument that cultural practices are determined in some way by a mixture of genetic and environmental conditions, the point is that phenomena such as wars are explained in terms of a maladaptive survival mechanism. This, formerly functional in man's early history, has become dysfunctional, and the contribution that aggression, the product of this mechanism, makes to survival now militates against it. However, such a general theory of atavistic impulses while offering a general *explanation* of war, the drive to power, and imperialism in modern times, is inherently non-rational. The biological theory, as it might be termed, treats human action as unmotivated and unreasoned. Man is an animal and is controlled by biological forces that he does not control. Although some ethologists are prescriptive in that they offer remedies for controlling violence, the theory itself is determinist; it is hard to see how on the terms of the theory man can escape being an animal.

However, if we treat dispositions in the sense of *rational* responses to specified situations—the other side of Popper's equation, then probability statements can be made in terms of propensities to act in a particular way. Singular instances can be referred to a class of dispositions and similarly, situations that elicit this response can also be classified. The generalising bais for strategic theory can thus be established. The disposition to act in a rational or appropriate way is derived by extrapolation and then projected where similar situational conditions are detected. In strategic analysis a common rationale is postulated. The implications of this approach will be considered later.

The search for probabilities in human conduct is directly linked to notions of utility. It is an attempt to derive knowledge about the future from what is known about the past. In the case of strategic reasoning, as we shall see, the probability of actions is related to notions of rationality within a given situation termed a scenario or contingency. Controlling the situation in the sense of maintaining or creating conditions is as important as taking action. Environmental control with its dimension of threat has been dominant during the nuclear period for reasons which will be discussed later. The emphasis has been placed on weapons procurement and *defence posture* rather than on action. In the absence of past experience of nuclear war there has been a heavy dependency on hypothetical reasoning void of empirical reference or factual base. This should not minimise the other mode of strategy, the actual use of violence as a means of attaining political objectives. This was the dominant mode in the pre-nuclear period and is still relevant even within the restrictions of the nuclear balance. As we shall see it has taken new forms, such as proxy warfare, terrorism, revolution and counter-revolution. In such cases probability statements can be based on experience and thus become directly relevant to strategy.

Probability statements derived from past regularities in terms of situational logic turn on some notion of rationality. Before looking more closely at the relation between reason and action let us look at what is sometimes called teleological explanation. This seeks to relate processes and change to an overall end or purpose. Connections between events or more loosely, behaviour, are purposive in that they lead directly to a state of affairs realised only by the preceding sequence. An explanation is thus based upon a knowledge of the end and the means by which it was achieved. The means were thus purposive, i.e. directed to that end.

This is perhaps most easily seen in the functional properties of organisms where these operate to promote the continued existence of some biological entity.[10] However, the notion of function has been used in social and political analysis to indicate the relation between certain institutional practices and the maintenance of a structure or system.

Structural-functionalism has been a dominant theoretical mode in anthropology for example.[11] It has also been applied to international relations in the form of systems analysis. A balance of power system constitutes a characteristic behavioural pattern, the members of which by changing their affiliations with one another prevent any one of their number from dominating the rest. The system overall is maintained through a complex of diplomacy and military preparation which is understood only through the overall rationale of balance. It is functional in terms of preserving the end of balance.

More transcendental views have been taken of particular social forces. Here the notion of immanent purpose dominates. Marx for example, thought that social organisation emerged from the necessities of war forcing family and tribal groups to coalesce and adopt practices, including those related to material production, that in turn created cohesive societies. Kant too, saw war as a progressive force. The 'unsocial sociability' of men *constituted* 'the means employed by nature to bring about the development of all the capacities of men. . . .'[12]

The problem with this view of purpose is that it is not explanatory but descriptive. We need to know the ends in terms of a completed series of changes before we can talk of purpose. This form of teleology offers only definitions that relate to past practices. The notion of system is tautological since we are unable to identify a system and its functional relationship other than in terms of its characterisation. A system is as a system does. While it may make sense to relate function to organisms, using it in the context of human conduct seems to be a misplaced analogy. In any case it is useless from the point of view of strategic theory, since it only serves as a basis for describing relationships in static terms i.e. retrospectively: it cannot serve as a basis for practice and prescription.

Colligations are another form of teleological argument.[13] Human action is seen not in terms of unique circumstances and individual reasoning but as a continuing process or trend. According to one proponent of this argument, 'the historian is often at least, in a position to say what was happening with full awareness of the situation, for the processes with which he is concerned are in typical cases, completed processes, and he can trace the stages of their history with a sure consciousness of where they were leading.'[14] Such processes are not causal, it is argued, and thus no general law is adduced in order to explain the connections between events or why the alleged pattern occurs. As such this approach does not fall in the explanatory rubric of the national sciences and the level of generalisation is descriptive rather than explanatory.

Concepts that *order* events are central to colligations and they include process, trend, development, movement, rise, decline, system, progress, cycle, revolution, evolution and so on. They operate 'quite independently of choice'[15] so that the individual, whatever his intentions, is caught up in a set of operating circumstances that produce eventually a final state of affairs, probably not in his own lifetime. Only the historical observer looking retrospectively at the past can discern such processes and of these only those that can be shown to have a result. Of those that operate on him he is of course quite unconscious, although if intellectual constructs are subject to the colligatory process then the argument would apply to his 'history' too. In this context it is pertinent to note that Marx and Engels's own notions of the historic process and its determinism would apply to Marxism too.

There is some ambiguity in this approach as to the part reasoning plays in formulating a colligatory account. While independent of *individual* reasoning there are cases of prolonged purposive action as with long-term policies, or a unity of purpose as in political or ideological movements, that lend themselves to colligation. 'Britain', for example, (rather than individual British statesmen) is alleged to have pursued balance of power politics in Europe for some three centuries. Purpose here is seen as a collective property. It belongs not to the individual but to social groups. A collective consciousness is asserted, finding its identity in the pursuit of long term programmes.

There are a number of problems with this approach which will be considered in detail at the end of this chapter. For our immediate purposes colligations, since they deal with completed processes and trends, do not seem to be directly relevant to strategic theory. Since they do not provide an explanation of why the process operated as it did, we cannot extrapolate from a knowledge of past processes any generalisation to support strategic prescription or theory. In this sense the past, conceived of as a colligatory process, cannot provide a guide to the present. As agents we are unaware of the consequences in terms of colligation of our actions.

However, this approach is conceived of as 'historical' and as we shall see the historical past provides a source for strategic prescription and a support for related generalisations. Military history and strategy are closely related. The view that the past at least affords parallels or analogies for present practice and that situations of strategic choice present similar rationales regardless of their temporal character, has been generally accepted in strategic thinking. Clausewitz himself well understood the methodological problems of the scientific approach with its law-like statements on the one hand and the historical approach, with its emphasis on the reconstruction of situation and reason on the other. Neither, he thought appropriate to strategic theory, and the approach he advocated has more than a passing resemblance to the colligatory exercise.

Another reason for relating this approach to strategic theory is that very often such theorising implicitly supports or is derived from a view of historical development that is colligatory. The power-security hypotheses, for example, the basis of *realism*, is often imported as a set of basic assumptions about the world of states by strategists. Such assumptions and the model of action-reaction-interaction on the level of state violence and preparation for violence between states, are innately colligatory. Thus patterns imposed on the present are often derivations of those assumed to have existed in the past. The continuum of security fears,[16] with its seemingly permanent insoluble problems, and their temporary solutions producing unforeseen consequences, appears to have substance and to lend support to strategic prescription.

The teleological approach is perhaps a mistake when applied to human conduct. The end pursued by non-reasoning processes governed by some immanent purpose is not the same as an end pursued by reasoning individuals. It is this last that is central to strategic theory. Purpose within the rationale of human action postulates a different kind of end. As one commentator argues, teleology should be applied solely to 'the description and comprehension of organic behaviour'[17] because of this ambiguity.

It was said earlier that this sort of theorising approach is concerned with the relationship between events rather than between human actions and reason. In other words individual reasoning is classified as epiphenomenal. Let us now look at the two concepts—reason and action[18] in more detail to see what the implications of this distinction amount to.

Action in this context is conceived of as a decision or irreducible physical movement related to intention. Involuntary acts produced by physiological processes, or which happen spontaneously as reactions to stimuli, are not so related and are irrelevant to this inquiry. Strategic theory is concerned with the instrumentality of violence. It is therefore occupied with the problem of *effective* action and with stipulating its terms and conditions. The focus of our inquiry is thus instrumental action; action related to the fulfilment of a purpose. It constitutes that class of decisions and acts stemming from human agency and intelligible in terms of violition (purpose, intention, motive and reason etc.)

It is important to stress that action does not constitute an event. It is not an observable phenomenon although aspects of it may be observed. Consequently, it is not susceptible to the same explanatory treatment as repeatable physical events in nature. In a sense a battle, for example, can be treated as a finite event or series of events located in time and place. It can be given an identity and an associated description. It would be a mistake, however, to seek to explain it on this basis. Treating it as a natural phenomenon entails satisfying the criteria properly belonging to the covering-law mode of explanation discussed earlier. Yet although a battle consists of a series of physical happenings they are unintelligible except in terms of reasoning. The description would be incomplete without this nor would we be able to explain what was happening.

To depict an action as the product of human agency it is necessary to identify and describe it and this in turn requires a description of the intentions of the agent. Such a description must encompass further descriptions, notably of what the agent takes to be the milieu in which he acts, of what he conceives of as instrumental, that is, the link between means and ends, and of what he conceives of as desirable in terms of relative preference—that is his contemplated ends. The action is only understood where these descriptions are considered to be complete. And the reference is always to the agent and not to some preconception of relevance adopted by the observer. The latter can only know or apprehend the action in question in terms of this reference and on the basis of evidence of it.

Another reason against treating action as if it were an event or natural occurrence is that when we are dealing with instrumental action we are concerned as much with inaction as with action itself. The point here is that if action is taken as premeditated and a matter of choice then amongst the rejected choices are a number of contemplated courses of action that provide the context for the choice actually made. In order to explain this last the context of choice, especially where this constitutes a process of optimalisation, needs to be examined. Furthermore, deciding to take no action is itself a form of action, where the agent is content to let circumstances or the situation develop either in the sense of 'the ripeness of time', or because it is likely to produce the desired state of affairs. Clearly inaction and non-action are rational choices but hardly events in the sense of material phenomena. They are not therefore susceptible to causal explanation. Yet it must be part of strategic theory to be able to prescribe when not as well as when to act.

In short, if we wish to treat action in the same sense as physical events are treated in the natural sciences then the entailments of covering-law explanation become relevant.[19] If however, action is understood to be intentional or instrumental then other explanatory forms becomes relevant. The principal one directly relevant to strategy is rational action theory and this will be discussed at length in a later chapter. The point here is that there are genuine alternatives depending on how the concept action is treated; what should not be done is to conflate them and so make a category mistake.

The notion of action in this context is related to instrumentality—to the means—end relationship. We are thus concerned with the idea of power or capacity for action, and this has been treated theoretically.[20] The importance of this concept for strategic theory lies in the notion of potentiality, that is power as a latent capacity. A good deal of strategic prescription is concerned with creating such a potential in the form of weapons systems designed to operate under certain future contingencies as well as being relevant to more immediate uses of violence.

Arguments that turn on the notion of capability carry the implication that there are certain attributes of states, or certain factors in a political situation which constitute necessary preconditions either for the successful achievement of an objective or for a particular action. If we can stipulate these for a specific situation then we have a means of stating what the outcome will be, depending on their presence or absence. Power in this sense is an unrealised potential that permits on the simplest level statements of possibility, and when directly related to evidence, can be given more precision as statements of probability. The relevant evidence relates to past action. Generally, power is treated in terms of an inventory, that is, as a material capacity to perform physical acts such as violence.

Having attributes, however, does not entail any particular action unless we can establish a general explanatory link between these and action itself. For power to be actualised in human relations something is required inseparable from the notion of capability. This is the disposition to act in terms of a purpose. The postulated capability is therefore a means related to a will to act in pursuit of an end. This is another way of saying that capability to act and action itself are constitutive parts of the same process. We cannot know one without the other and it is tautologically true to say that in order to act we must be capable of action.

The question of *effective* action is another matter. By this is meant a capability to perform successfully, and this entails stipulating and satisfying theoretical conditions. In terms of human action we can act and fail to achieve our purpose. In this sense we have the capacity to act but not the capacity to succeed in our object. If we wish to make prescriptions about necessary capability in terms of successful action, then a causal theory is involved that specifies necessary and sufficient conditions, together with the relevant covering-law. The derived hypothesis must be capable of empirical test. But, as we have seen earlier, human action cannot be treated in terms of covering law explanation. The element of reason is intimately bound up with action but does not entail it. Action with this dimension cannot be treated as an event.

Statements about capacity are really statements about performance. The asserted capacity can only be known through its actualisation. Power is, therefore, as power does. Statements about potential power are empirically vacuous where they are not theoretically justified. We can only know of what we are capable *ex post facto*. In practice assessments of past performance provide an inductive basis for prescription. Extrapolations from the past support probability statements about performance as a guide to practice. They constitute evidence in support of the postulated relationship between capability and effective action.

This sort of extrapolation, however, treats performance as independent of the intentions and purposes of the performer. Only the material aspects of the performance are selected. If capability and its relation to action is treated in this way, then either a continuum of rationality is assumed or deemed to be irrelevant. As we shall see later the assumption of continuity of reasoning leads to anachronism and circularity. And treating reasons as irrelevant means treating potential for action as material phenomena requiring theoretical explanation. The 'evidence' adduced from past performance to support prescriptions for action is thus prejudiced from the beginning if these assumptions are made.

In the field of strategy reliance on this sort of extrapolation can be a dangerous policy. Novel tactics such as the blitzkrieg, using panzer divisions with close tactical air support, can confound expectation and produce defeat. In the case of novel weapons systems such as the nuclear missile, it is even more dangerous, given the absence of any experience of nuclear wary. If the dimension of reasoning is ignored the emphasis in strategic theory is placed upon material capability without any reference to the ends for which it is a means. This is linked both to the physical performance of weapons systems and to relative balances in these in the world of states. In defensive terms this capability is seen as a counter to any postulated attack by an adversary. Similarly, offensive use is related to the defensive capability of the opposition. Crude assessments of capability of this kind are unrelated to the political context.

The problem is that capability cannot be assessed in terms of its relevance or effectiveness prior to its realisation in action. Effectiveness must be seen as the fulfilment of a specified end, in this case either national security, however this is defined, or the promotion or protection of national interests. The assertion of a capability unrelated to these is inherently open-ended. We are entitled to ask capability for what? In the pre-nuclear era there was an inherent ambiguity in the relationship between capacity for security and capacity for the pursuit of non-security ends, in military terms. No weapon could be treated as serving one purpose or the other. This ambiguity presented serious problems especially to those who sought negotiated rather than enforced 'agreements'. For example, the appearance of aircraft as a major weapon aroused fears of vulnerability to attack which were generalised rather than specifically related to political contingencies. The security dimension with its inherent leanings towards worst case analysis tended to dominate the more pragmatic political and diplomatic dimensions. Thus the debate in Britain on the question of whether to adopt a bomber force as a deterrent, or whether to develop fighters instead as a defence, did not consider the specific circumstances in which these aircraft might be used. A generalised capability based on material performance is no capability in terms of political performance. Or to put it another way it is the latter that should dictate the former.

In the event numbers were paramount and the *size* rather than the postulated function of the Luftwaffe was the major issue in strategic debate. Hitler and Goering encouraged this emphasis since it appeared to weaken the British will in negotiation. But in fact the Luftwaffe was designed to fulfil a tactical support role rather than to act as a strategic bomber force. Hence the emphasis was placed on coordinated land warfare rather than on direct assults against civilian targets. In this context the Battle of Britain for both sides was more improvised than planned, as was the blitz itself. The point here is that planning an effective capability depends upon responding to the *reasoning* of an adversary rather than to calculations of relativities in armaments. British military planning was derived from previous experience in the First World War. Economic blockade was preferable to massive battles of attrition. Hence a long war was postulated, prosecuted by the Navy with the Air Force providing defence. Germany, however, thought in terms of a short war, utilising the advantages of a head start in rearmament and avoiding a war of attrition in which the superior resources of the opposing states could be brought to bear. The Battle of France, a considerable gamble, was the consequence.

In the nuclear age this ambiguity over capability seems to be avoided through the common rationale of deterrence. Ambiguity mainly exists at the sub-strategic level where non-nuclear allies and their security are involved. However this negative capability is also open to question, although at least its relevance to the fulfilment of a purpose is very much clearer than the postulated defensive capabilities of the pre-nuclear period.

Outside practice, the point remains that statements of capability require the element of intention or purpose before they can be given empirical reference and meaning. In other words to talk of capability is to talk of the potential for action in terms not merely of its effectiveness but in terms of what this effectiveness is directed towards. Machines have capability. They can be used in various ways and this use is written into their design and specifications. The destructive capabilities of nuclear weapons can, unlike weapons in the past, be precisely measured, but although this has consequences for the conduct of war and the provision of defence, it is the purpose for which this destructive capacity is used that is important. And we cannot state in advance of use whether or not capability in this sense exists or not. Nor can we cite precedents in support, not merely because of the lack of experience of nuclear war, but because of the inability to separate capability from its context of reasoning.

So far this discussion has concentrated on the dimension of action. The point has been made that actions, unlike physical events, can only be understood in terms of intentions and purposes or reasoning. Let us therefore look at reasons more closely. The implications of this connection for strategic theory is that some general principle of rationality is involved in any attempt to prescribe for effective action. This is central to rational action theory, to be discussed later on.

First of all let us look at attempts to explain past human action in terms of a construct of reasoning. The postulate of rationality is conceived of as a means of determining what is an appropriate reason governing choice in a given situation. It contains a generalising element in that rules or law-like principles which guide or determine decision in one such situation can be extended to cases of the same kind. Similarly, their application or relevance can be inferred by identifying individual cases as belonging to that class. Hence at one and the same time an act can be adjudged as being rational and as producing a given result.

A distinction should be made between explaining an action by inferring the reasons from the action itself on the basis of an assumption of common rationality, and judging either the inferred reason or an actual one as being rational. This is to say finding out what the reasons were by inferring them from what a reasonable man would do in the circumstances, is one exercise, and judging them as reasonable according to specific criteria of rationality, another. The former is concerned with explanation but the latter is evaluative. Both are exercises undertaken by the observer and not the agent. If we take the first distinction, reasons here can be conceived of either as causes or as reasons which are linked to some normative principle of rationality. An explanation proceeds by showing that actions of that kind are caused by a disposition to act in that way and specifying its conditions, necessary and sufficient together with a covering-law.

The objections to treating reasons as causes in explaining past actions are broadly the same as raised earlier. More specifically, if we conceive of acts as intentional or purposive, are we constrained to treat the latter as necessary and sufficient conditions for the former? In what way can we show that a reason entails an action, where the reason is an intention, in such a way as to be able to infer or predict the reason from the action? Can reasons be treated as sufficient or necessary conditions for a class of actions? An agent's reasons may be anything which he conceives to be good or appropriate as a justification for his action. He is concerned with justification not with the assertion of any general truth. This is to make a distinction between holding a reason to be relevant or good, and conceiving it as a cause or a necessary condition for doing something. Of course, an agent is not precluded from conceiving his reasons as necessary preconditions for the ends he seeks, or as a determinant of either the means or the ends in terms of following a theory. But there is a distinction between this type of reason and the former. To conceive of having a reason as a disposition for doing something is to make intelligible the action through eludicating the reason. But if we want to treat the disposition as a cause we have to hold wanting to do something as logically distinct from doing it and then formulating a causal relation between the two, so that the latter invariably follows from the former. Now whether the agent believes this or not, having a reason, whatever its nature and whatever the belief system to which it is related, is sufficient to make his related action intelligible.

The point here is that a causal explanation which treats intentions or reasons as causes does not supersede or preclude an explanation which simply proffers the agent's reasons in order to make the associated act explicable. They are two quite different explanatory forms, and so we are not constrained to adopt a causal mode if we wish to explain an act by citing the agent's reasons. We are however constrained to adopt the causal model if the reference is not to the agent's reasons but to a governing principle of rationality and so if one is cited then a covering-law is necessary. The illegitimacy is not one of confusing two types of explanation but in implicitly adopting the general mode without fulfilling its logical conditions. This kind of argument is independent of the agent whose reasoning, as apart from his reasons, is irrelevant to the putative explanation. It belongs to the generalising or theorising form of explanation discussed earlier.

The normative notion of rationality however can be attributed to the agent's own conception of rational behaviour. It can be either imposed upon a class of actions in terms of appropriateness, according to notions commonly accepted by agents in that situation as being rational, or it can be referrable to the conceptions of the individual agent. The importance of making this distinction lies in the truth conditions of the reference. If we 'explain' an action by asserting a normative principle which permits a statement of what is appropriate action in a given state of affairs, then the reference of such an account is to the principle itself. But on what grounds is this justified? Why should an agent accept it as a basis for his actions? Did he in fact accept it as such? This latter question is of course begged. But it is this question which is important in explanation for, if we wish to refer to an account of an action to something which validates it, it is insufficient to cite a normative principle of rationality in the absence of evidence that it was to that which the agent himself appealed. As in the case of a causal argument which is accepted by the agent as a basis for his actions, the point is not the substance of such arguments, but whether they were actually cited as reasons. If, in short, he has reasons then these, and these only, can constitute an adequate reference for an explanatory account of his action. The question as to whether the observer thinks these reasonable is irrelevant, as is the question of their nature and status as reasons. And the question whether the agent considers them reasonable is nonsensical for they *are* his reasons.

Thus the imposition of an observer's criterion of rationality on an agent's action is non-explanatory, given the absence either of a theory containing such a principle as a covering-law and susceptible to an empirical test, or of an alternative means of validation. In effect what is being done here is not explanation but judgement. The judgement consists of stating a criterion for an appropriate relation between reasons and actions, either in terms of means and ends or in terms of the belief system of the agents. Here again the distinction between a reference to the observer's reasons and those of the agent becomes blurred. In the case of the former the judgement takes the form of asserting on various grounds appropriate conditions and actions for the fulfilment of a stated purpose. Selecting these and acting on them will in effect not only succeed in the achievement of the end for which they are a means, but be the only rational way of proceeding. The degree to which the agent conforms to this model is a measure of his rationality. But we may ask again what justifies this argument? In the absence of an adequate explanatory basis which would permit prediction, and a testable statement of necessary and sufficient conditions, we have to take it on trust. The point here is that the argument as it stands is non-explanatory. Judgements of rationality are not explanations of acts.

If however, we examine the agent's own reasoning and discover that he in fact adopts this procedure, while we are not in a position to establish whether his reasoning was good on any authoritative explanatory grounds, we can distinguish between forms of reasoning or establish whether it was reasoning. Julius Caesar was a successful general by any standards, but he appeared to rely on the aspect of the entrails of chickens in order to make up his mind to act on a number of occasions. The question was Caesar rational to do so is totally irrelevant if we wish to explain why he did what he did in terms of his reasons. What is being argued here is that where we have evidence of reasoning which somehow connects means to ends on the basis of the agent's own conceptions, then we are in a position to refer an account to such evidence in a way we are not when we make a reference to notions of rationality which are alleged to govern actions. Either these last are normative, or imply a general theory; if the former, no explanation is forthcoming, and if the latter, specific truth conditions are entailed which need to be satisfied if we are to explain.

No judgement as to the reasonableness of an agent's reasons is necessary in formulating a reason-giving explanation. We can know what his reasons are on the basis of evidence, but we cannot presume that knowledge which allows us to say that they will produce specified consequences. The question as to what constitutes a correct or a good reason is decided by the agent, and the historian or strategist, if he wishes to explain rather than to judge, is constrained by that decision. To understand an action, or to make it intelligible, is to understand the intention or purpose which coexisted with it. The meaning of the action lies in this; and it is the meaning it had for the agent. But to *explain* the action all we need to do is to relate the evidence of intentions to it. It is at this point that the observer or historian begins to construct an account. This is to argue that explanation lies in making such a reference, and that meaning and understanding are products of it. There are a number of difficulties in doing this, but the point here is that no judgement as to the rationality of the belief system of the agent, his conceptions of the relation of means to ends, or the ends themselves, is entailed by this notion of explanation. Nor are we constrained to formulate any general law or causal hypothesis in adopting it.

 One last objection to the substitution of the rationalisations of the observer for the reasons of the agent, is that it is innately anachronistic. What is deemed reasonable or rational, as we have seen, can be referred to causal explanation or normative judgement. In the former case the theory is a-temporal and treats an action as one of a class; and in the latter case the principle is either inseparable from the society which considers it relevant or appropriate or is metaphysical and outside time. But even if the rationalisation consists of no more than making an inference from the evidence of action of what would be reasonable as an intention or purpose, and citing this as a reason which makes the action intelligible, it is still anachronistic. The historian or strategist who does this is treating himself as a homologue for rational man and is referring past actions for which he has no direct evidence or intention, to what he conceives of as reasonable. And this like the 'experience' of the idealist will vary from historian to historian, and strategist to strategist. Such an account will be one of the personal or social predelictions of an age, not of the age which it purports to explain, through the actions of its people.

It is sometimes argued that actions can be made intelligible by means of a reference to rules. This argument places the agent in a context in which both he and his associates act according to a set of pre-conceived conventions. These consist of expectations of proper action which allows the identification of the meaning or the significance of acts. Acts are thus 'social' in the sense that the agent conceives of what is appropriate, i.e. the rule 'governing' his action, relative to his contemporaries' conceptions of appropriateness. Such expectations are represented or expressed in language used to indicate or describe external forms. The language thus reflects the agent's understanding of the context of usage and the conventions which govern it. The observer elicits an 'understanding' of the meaning of the agent's actions by referring them to the particular conventions or rules which are appropriate to their contexts. He can not only make them intelligible in this way, he can also evaluate them in terms of whether the rule was followed or not. It acts as a standard of reference. Hence mistakes or incorrect rule following are possible and are subject to assessment. The observer can make a judgement.

This notion of 'understanding' is related to a theory of meaning rather than to explanation. If we identify an act or an expression in terms of a rule then this is to make it intelligible. We can make sense of an action or know what it means in terms of the socio-linguistic context in which it occurs. Each such context has its own criterion of intelligiblity—its own language. But learning the language, or knowing the rules, i.e. the common context of expectations and conventions, allows us to describe but not to explain. And the description performance has to be in the linguistic form common to the describer and the described. However, knowing what something—an act or an expression—means, while an essential pre-requisite for any explanation, does not entail any truth-condition. It is a matter of identification. Understanding, therefore, is a product of knowing in any given case what a particular agent meant, in terms of a relationship between his reasons, intentions, purposes, etc., and their context. On my earlier argument, to explain an action is to go further than to elucidate its meaningfulness for the agent, it is to show what his reasons were on the basis of the evidence we have of them. And this entails no reference to rules which he may or may not follow or of which he has no cognition.

There seems to be a tautological element in the argument that all social action is rule-governed on the grounds that this is the only way of establishing its intelligibility. It would seem to be a condition of communication—a condition of language itself—that the meaning of expressions is referrable to some criteria accessible to those who seek to communicate. And this is found in actual usage, in language itself. This seems to be a definition of intelligibility. We may accept that knowing a language is essential to an understanding of actions expressed in it and that actions *per se* need to be interpreted in the light of linguistic expressions which represent social relations. But this takes us no further than description in terms of that language. If we wish to explain why an agent performed a particular action we need to refer it not merely to his linguistic forms, that is to make sense of it through a socio-linguistic reference, but to what the individual agent actually held to be a reason. And while this may be rule-governed, equally, except in a loose linguistic sense, it may not. The relevant rule cannot be inferred from action, not can it stand outside it, without indulging in rationalisation. Conventional and unconventional behaviour are related not to conventions which are independent of the agent but depend upon *his* conception of the appropriate, not that of the observer. To discover this is not to study linguistic usage or social custom but to enquire of the agent his reasons. Casting these into the category of rule-following (or breaking) does not add to the force of the explanation.

A further point is that talking of action in terms of the meaning it has for the agent, appears to deny the notion of an explanatory mode. Or rather any notion of rules and linguistic forms specialist in nature, on this argument, is supernumerary to lay language which expresses action. We cannot, other than through an act of translation, explain the latter by means of the former. And it is difficult to see the point of such a translation if all we are concerned to do in understanding social action is to learn the language in which the rules and contextual awareness are expressed. The historian, sociologist, anthropologist, etc., in pursuing such an understanding abandons any claim to distinction and becomes, like the agent, actors in society. They 'explain' or 'understand' as he does. Even if it is argued that these various discourses have their own rules and linguistic forms, it is difficult to see their relevance for the explanation of actions which are explicable only in terms of the rules and language of the agent. Whatever it is that they explain it cannot be these. And, conversely, if they do make a claim to explain human actions in terms of their own conventions then they are, on this argument, mistaken.

But as was argued earlier this would exclude any notion of truth or of communicable knowledge. Explanations derive their force from the ability to refer to some grounds for believing them to be true or adequate. Such a reference is indeed conventional, but conventional in the sense of belonging to a specific set of criteria peculiar to the discourse and consciously adopted by its practitioners. To resolve a puzzle of meaning we refer to the context of usage and either we then understand the expression, or we do not. A claim to know in the sense of 'true' knowledge entails more than this kind of meaning—clarification, and while the criteria of reference and of validation also are referrable to linguistic usage in order to understand their meaning, their provenance and use are not simply functions of language. They are consistently adopted as a means of establishing a discourse as relevant and as a means of permitting a choice between alternative and competing putative explanations. In this sense they are rules, not mere rules of meaning, but constitutive and regulative rules of an explanatory mode. They allow both the definition of knowledge and the possibility of a growing or perhaps a changing knowledge. A meaning criterion does not. Either we understand in the last sense or we do not. The only puzzle is incomprehension or misunderstanding.

It is important to distinguish between making sense of a belief by establishing its meaning in terms of a specific socio-linguistic context of usage, and justifying it. The theory of meaning discussed above asserts a form of cultural relativity in which the different contexts of usage are in effect incommensurate. There is no common standard of meaning invariance which allows us to compare or to judge actual usage. But justifying beliefs, that is holding some ground on which a belief can be deemed true or false, or indeed talking of truth or falsity, does imply standards of sorts. The question of their nature and reference is distinct from questions of meaning, although clearly the two are related. The military historian in seeking to give an account of a past to which he has no direct access faces problems of meaning. He cannot enter the world of usage other than indirectly through philology and literary survivals. He is intimately concerned with the problems of translation and interpretation even when he is dealing with earlier forms of his own language. And this activity itself is governed by rules and techniques peculiar to it. But the point here is that these are contingent problems which apply to all translation, and the historian does not have to accept the cultural relativism of a theory of meaning of this kind.

Nor does he have to be a participant in social practices in order to understand them. Clearly, *qua* historian, he cannot do this in any case for past societies. What he is required to do is to understand what these practices meant to those engaged in them. And this no more requires participation than a spectator needs to be able to play a game in order to follow it. It entails learning the language and knowing the rules. And this is certainly a necessary condition for any explanation of human action. But while the historian, as with anyone else engaged in explanatory discourse, is concerned with meaning, the autonomy of his activity depends not on the understanding or possession of a special language, but on its reference to evaluatory criteria which determine the adequacy of the preferred explanation. On this argument such conventions constitute the main criterion of the demarcation of an explanatory mode.

The relevance of this analysis of reason-giving explanation to strategic theory lies in the assertion of a rationale for action in a world of states. Strategic argument, and indeed practice itself, conceives of the use or threat of violence as a means of persuasion rather than as a blunt instrument. Even where there is overwhelming military superiority the political object is to be secured with economy or without prejudicing other objectives by excessive use of force. Threats are more important than their actual and often problematic implementation. A successful threat however, depends on persuading the opposition as to its credibility. A strategy therefore must have as its basis an appeal to a common rationality in which rewards and punishments, cost and benefit, values and ends, are commensurate between the contenders. Threats must not only seem to be credible in material terms; they must both threaten and convey some tolerable alternative.

The point is that the element of reasoning that underlies actions related to strategy, must be both communicable to an opponent and to some extent shared by him, if it is to produce success. Without such a common rationale actions will be misinterpreted and the consequential reactions may be far from what was expected or desired. The reaction of the British and French governments to the Molotov-Ribbentrop Pact is a good example of such a miscalculation on the part of Hitler.

Moreover, if this rationale is deemed irrelevant or ignored, and the emphasis placed on relative capabilities in purely military terms, then an uncontrolled arms race is the likely result. As we have seen earlier, the notion of capability begs a number of questions not the least of which is the problem of relative value. If we ask the question capacity for ... what? it cannot realistically be a quantitative estimate of damage inflicted on an opponent as an index of success. Damage itself is a subjective concept. If the object sought is political and not merely the infliction of destruction for its own sake, some estimate has to be made of the opponent's own scale of values and related reasoning. At the level of threat this is particularly important since it may be assumed that the achievement of the object by threat is preferable to incurring the costs of uncertainties of its implementation. But to be effective the threat must not merely be capable

of physical implementation, it must generate the appropriate response
from the adversary and this is dependent upon his values.

If then a common rationale is a postulate of an effective strategy, from
whence is it derived? On the arguments above it would clearly be a mistake
to make it a simple projection of one's own value system. In a world of
states such a postulate would lead to ineffectiveness or alternatively the
degeneration of strategy into brute force. The former can be said to have
been the case in the prosecution of the Vietnam War by the United States.
A war fought within limits and in this sense 'rational', nevertheless was
fought between contenders adhering to quite different value systems. The
United States, placing a higher value on American lives, reflected in
domestic pressures on the political system, and believing in the rationality
of the gradual application of force, tried aerial bombing as a means of
bringing the North Vietnamese to abandon their intervention in the South.
The latter, not sharing this value nor under pressure from democratic
processes, were willing to accept everything short of invasion the United
States could do to them, and this last was precluded by the limits set by the
American government. Even in the case of the latter where brute force
predominates over strategy, as in the Second World War, especially in the
war against Japan, the relevance of alien values became apparent in the
attempt to persuade the Japanese to surrender. This was achieved only by
Allied recognition of the peculiar status the Emperor held in Japanese
society. It is true that this surrender might have been achieved through
further brute force in the form of continued atomic bombing, but the
consequences would have been an atomic waste-land that perhaps would
only have benefited the Soviet Union.

In short, strategic reasoning is as much concerned with the consequences
of action as with action itself. Such consequences are seen in terms of
adversarial response. If this is to be favourable to the object sought or
merely to be anticipated, then the reasoning of the adversary must be taken
into account in formulating the appropriate strategy. To this extent a
common rationale emerges, based not upon projections of rationality that
are essentially either rationalisations or normative in character but upon
mutual recognition of interests, constraints, values, preferences and
commitments and so on. This rationale is, as we shall see, more closely
related to reason-giving explanation than to any generalising theory.
Central to it is the postulate of an intelligible world, intelligible to those
states that constitute it. Rational action is thus in a sense a rule-following
activity with an assumption that the actor acts in a manner parallel to that
of others and related to a common understanding. Successful action
postulates a receptivity on the part of other states, passive or active, forced
or voluntary; a receptivity only possible given common ground.

The central point is that the projection of a rationale based on the
rationalisation of the strategic observer derived from his experience, or
from extrapolations from the past, can lead neither to effective
prescription or effective explanation. Where a common value system

existed as perhaps could be argued for Eighteenth Century Europe, then strategic reasoning could be pursued within a common framework, with prospects of relative success. Certainly the cabinet wars of that century were pursued within limits. It is perhaps no coincidence that the first total war in modern history—the Napoleonic Wars—was accompanied by serious ideological divisions between states.[21]

It is perhaps appropriate to summarise the arguments at this stage bearing in mind that later chapters will be concerned with specific strategic theories. It was argued that a general explanatory framework such as the deductive-nomological theoretical mode of the natural sciences was not relevant to explanations of human action where this last involves considerations of purpose. Such a mode is implied however, where notions of cause or of necessary relationship between events, or indeed any form of generalisation about human behaviour, are employed in the argument. The empirical and logical conditions relevant to this mode of explanation then become relevant and we are entitled to ask for their satisfaction before accepting the 'explanation'.

Such implications exist in all of the various theoretical approaches examined. Probability theory, situational logic, colligation, and rationalisation, all seek to sustain a level of generalisation about human conduct that is explanatory. It could be argued that the implicit theory be made explicit and its theoretical conditions be satisfied. This is especially the case where purposive human actions are externalised and treated as events or material phenomena. Such treatment is a-temporal and the dimension of human reasoning is essentially epiphenomenal or irrelevant. Viewing 'events' such as major wars as material phenomena to be explained in causal terms, is question-begging if the explanatory theory is not made explicit and its adequacy established through empirical testing.

The dimension of reasoning itself may be said to be susceptible to covering-law explanation. This moves the argument one stage back to a consideration of the causes of specific reasoning. Rationality is thus conceived of as a response to environmental stimuli; given a knowledge of the biological mechanism involved and of the appropriate stimuli, then human behaviour can not merely be predicted but actually induced and directed according to the degree of control over the relevant conditions. The notion of agency, that is of purposive, intentional, reasoned human action, is thus superseded by a theory of human behaviour. If this sort of argument is asserted, and indeed it is implicit in rationalising theories that appeal to a generalised consciousness or the primacy of the milieu, then testable empirical hypotheses should be produced. Where these are not forthcoming we are entitled to dismiss any claims to explanation.

An appeal to probability as the basis of theorising about human action is also open to objection. The same problems associated with the treatment of reasoned action as a class of repeatable events, explicable through covering law theory, also exist for probability. A frequency principle is open to manipulation by setting temporal limits to the incidence of instances. Similarly, the class of instances is finite and dependent upon a criterion of selection subject to the problem of infinite regress. What justifies this?

'Expectations of proper action', or probability can be expressed, as we have seen, by what is termed situational logic. This is dependent upon an idealised reconstruction of a problem situation. The appropriate action is one that is 'rationally understandable' or adequate to the solution of the problem. But on what grounds can rationality and the situation be assessed? Is it the assessment of the actor or the grounds for his assessment which is in question? In spite of some ambiguity it seems that Popper inclines to the view that human action can be assessed and explained in terms of objectivised situations and responses. The observer, he argues, is in a position to determine both what the reality of a situation is, and what counts as an adequate response to it. As he puts it, '... the explanatory theory of action will, in the main, consist of a conjectural reconstruction of the problem and its background'.[22] But clearly he means the conjectures of the observer, not of the agent. As such these are a 're-enactment of experience'; an assertion of the parallel nature of the experiences of the observer and of the actor. Although Popper dissents from this aspect of Collingwood's position,[23] he asserts that the observer is postulating what he calls a 'meta-theory' about the agent's problem situation and his associated reasoning. At once and the same time a reconstruction of the 'problem situation' and of the *adequacy* of the agent's response to it are made.

So far as the reconstruction goes, if we are concerned with explaining action, then reference must be made to what evidence we have of the actor's own visualisation of his situation. It is not what appears to be relevant to the 'observer' that matters but what appears as relevant to him. It is *his* problem. Strategic decisions in the past must be related to the decision-maker's appreciation of his predicament, and it is a recon- struction of this awareness that is the province of the military historian. But it must be based on evidence. Inferences and non-grounded conjectures are relevant only in directing the search for evidence and are not substitutes for it. And it is always possible that new evidence might come to light and so change the reconstruction and with it, our knowledge.

If it is made clear that such a reconstruction depends upon evidence of the actor's consciousness and intentions then there is no problem. It is with the second part of Popper's notion of situational analysis that serious problems arise. On what grounds can we determine the adequacy of the actor's responses to the problem situation as he sees it? This involves strategic theory rather than military history. Here Popper seems to be advocating a kind of common rationality so that good and bad reasons can be evaluated by an objective observer. But in what sense is this evaluation objective?

This brings us to colligations and rationalisations that import normative criteria of rationality into the argument. These approaches, including the teleological approach considered earlier, are open to charges of historical anachronism and cultural relativism. They are essentially views of the past from social and temporal vantage-points not shared by those whose actions are the subject of interpretation. Where the reasoning of the agent is ignored, the emphasis shifts to what is deemed instrumental in human action. This constitutes two elements; what directs human action and what human action is directed to. Both imply the general theoretical construct relevant to the natural sciences. It is the latter that most concerns strategic theory.

Yet as we have seen, the dimension of reasoning cannot be ignored in conceiving action as instrumental. Ends are as important as means. The choice of means, however these are conceived, is as much dictated by value-related ends as by strictly limited notions of capability. Rationality thus becomes normative in character and is related to justifiable action in terms of some ethical code or set of rules, as much as to standards of effectiveness. If strategy is treated, as it has been throughout this work, as action directed to the fulfilment of political purposes, then instrumentality has to be related to the nature of these purposes. It is not a mechanical or teleological relationship between means and ends. Theory in this context becomes more than an explanation of physical phenomena, their causes and relationships linked to the manipulation of nature. What level of generalisation is obtained by it and what relationship it has to practice will be examined in the next chapter.

NOTES AND REFERENCES

1. Colin Gray, *Strategic Studies,* Greenwood Press, Westport, Conn., 1982, p. 98.
2. By causality is meant reference to a principle of association so that –P is a sufficient condition of q; where p is q will be too. This corresponds to Mill's Canons of Agreement. See J. S. Mill, *A System of Logic*, Longmans, London, 1965. If two or more instances of x. Its temporal case determines whether it is a cause or an effect. The criterion of differences is where x or non–x occurs and A is found in x but not in non–x. A is the effect of cause, or necessary condition when x and non–x have every other circumstance in common save A. It must be said that these canons involve infinite regress and are non-explanatory as they stand. We cannot answer the question why x occurs. They are merely associative in principle.
3. See Carl Hempel, 'Reasons and Covering Laws in Historical Explanation' in S. Hook, *Philosophy of History*, New York University Press, NY, 1963, pp. 143 (ff.) and *Aspects of Scientific Explanation*, Free Press, Glencoe, 1965, p. 102.
4. See Mary Hesse, *the Structure of Scientific Inference*, Macmillan, London, 1974
5. See M. R. Ayers, *The Refutation of Determinism*, Methuen, London, 1968, p. 43.
6. See Carl Hempel, 'Explanation in Science and History' in *Frontiers of Science and Philosophy*, ed. R. G. Colodny, Allen & Unwin, 1962, pp. 7–33.
7. See Lewis Richardson, *Arms and Insecurity,* ed. N. Rachevsky and Ernesto Tucco, Boxwood Press, Pittsburgh, 1960.
8. See Karl R. Popper, *Objective Knowledge,* Clarendon Press, Oxford, 1972, pp. 186–90.

9. See for example R. A. Hinde, *Animal Behavior - a synthesis of ethology and comparative phychology*, McGraw Hill, NY, 1966 and Konrad Lorenz, *On Aggression*, Methuen, London, 1966.
10. See Michael Ruse, *The Philosophy of Biology*, Hutchinson, London, 1973, and Mary Midgley, *Beast and Man*, Harvester Press, Hassocks, Sussex, 1979. For a critical discussion see *Modes of Imperialism, op. cit.*, Chap. 5, *Socio-biology and Imperialism*, pp. 172 (ff).
11. See Robert K. Merton, *On Theoretical Sociology*, Free Press, NY, 1967, Chapter iii *Manifest and Latent Functions*, pp. 73 (ff). J. D. Carthy and F. J. Ebling eds. *The Natural History of Aggression*, Academic Press, London, 1964, and M. A. Kaplan, *System and Process in International Politics*, Wiley, NY, 1964.
12. See W. B. Gallie, *Philosophers of Peace and War*, CUP, 1978.
13. The expression colligation was first used by the philosopher Whewell but see W. H. Walsh, Colligatory Concepts in History, in *Theories of History* ed. Patrick Gardiner, Free Press, NY, 1959.
14. *Ibid*, p. 129.
15. *Ibid*, p. 130.
16. See for example Barry Buzan, *People, States and Fear, op. cit.*
17. John MacMurray, *The Self as Agent*, Faber and Faber, London, p. 149. See also Michael Oakeshott, *On History*, Basil Blackwell, Oxford, 1983, p. 102 and Carl G. Hempel, *Aspects of Scientific Explanation, op. cit.*, p. 257.
18. On this subject see A. R. Louch, *Explanation and Human Action*, Basil Oxford, 1966, Binkley, Bronough and Marras eds *Agent, Action and Reason*, Univerity of Toronto Press and Blackwell, Oxford, 1971; G. W. Mortimore and S. Benn eds, *Rationality and the Social Sciences*, Routledge & Kegan Paul, London, 1976; S. Hood ed., *Philosophy and History*, New York University Press, NY, 1963; Donald Davidson, 'Actions Reasons and Causes', in *Journal of Phil.*, LX, No. 23, Nov 7, 1963, pp. 685–700 and Carl Hempel, The Concept of Rationality and the Logic of Explanation of Reasons, in *Aspects of Scientific Explanation, op. cit.*
19. Or deductive-nomological explanation as it is sometimes called. These conditions, according to Hempel, are
    1) an explanandum (consisting of sentences describing the phenomenon to be explained) must be deducible from the explanans through a statement of necessary and sufficient conditions.
    2) the explanans must contain general laws.
    3) the explanans must have empirical content, i.e. be capable of a test by experiment or observation.
    4) 'the sentences constituting the explanans must be true'. The whole constitutes a covering-law explanation of classes of instances of events.
20. See for example James G. March, 'The Power of Power' in David Easton ed. *Varieties of Political Theory*, Prentice Hall, Englewood Cliffs, 1966, pp. 40 (ff).
21. In this sense it had similarities with the Thirty Years War and its ideological basis. The apocalyptic nature of this struggle was only abandoned after the adoption of the principle *cuius regio; eius religio*, in effect accepting a political basis to religious heterodoxy.
23. See R. G. Collingwood, *The Idea of History*, New York, Gallaxy Books: Oxford University Press, Oxford, 1956.

3 Classical Strategy

From the beginning of civilisation man has sought to establish general principles for the proper conduct of war. Sun Tsu, perhaps the earliest recorded strategic theorist,[1] asserted that five elements governed all war as constant factors. These were the moral law, heaven, earth, the commander, and method and discipline. Some of these are familiar to us, but by the moral law he meant the cohesive, unifying and legitimising aspects of political authority, exacting obedience and stimulating morale. Heaven was the natural environment in the form of the seasons and the weather, a kind of climatology. Earth constituted spatial relations, terrain, and topography in general. The other elements relate to qualities of leadership, training and logistics.[2]

On the basis of these permanent factors Sun Tsu derived from his actual experience of war a number of precepts that, in his view, determined success or failure in war. Surprise is important, both in terms of the intentions of the commander and in the operational plan.[3] Delay is dangerous and so protracted wars or campaigns should be avoided.[4] Decision, when it is sought, should be quick. Similarly, instead of expending one's own resources, those of the enemy should be used whenever possible. Incentives for troops were important; these should be material in character.[5] The principle of concentration is noted; large forces—*ceteribus paribus* will always conquer small forces. Good intelligence is essential, since knowledge of an opponent's disposition and intentions 'cannot be obtained from experience nor by any deductive calculation'.[6] Equally, good communication between one's own troops is crucial, especially where large armies are concerned. It is in the principle that fighting is not the point of war, that perhaps Sun Tsu was most innovative. Fighting should be avoided; as he puts it, 'to fight and conquer in all your battles is not supreme excellence, supreme excellence consists in breaking the enemy's resistance without fighting.'[7] A good general is one who not only wins but wins with ease'.[8]

If we disregard the idiom in which these precepts are expressed, and the differences between his age and ours, there is little here that would surprise contemporary strategic theorists. The same elements in war appear to persist across the ages and to derive from a common experience. One or other of them may be more or less relevant and receive emphasis or neglect, but in general there is a common-sense basis that seems almost universal. They make sense. It is true that the choice of emphasis characterises a particular strategic approach. We can contrast, for example, Sun Tsu, who prefers strategem to confrontation, with Vegetius,[9] writing in the reign of Constantine, who insists on the decisive battle. This points to one major distinction that will be developed in later chapters, that is, it is the political context that determines the preferred strategy and not vice versa.

Sun Tsu was an active general at a time when the contenders in war were political states fighting what was the equivalent of limited war. No ruler was then concerned with conquest on a large scale, or sought to fight ruinous wars of attrition. Cost, as in the eighteenth century, was all important, given limitations on man-power, an agricultural economic base, and the adverse effects in political and economic terms of excessive taxation. Vegetius, writing in a completely different political milieu, was concerned with maintaining imperial policies and the power of the Emperor where these were challenged by barbarian hordes. These last were confronted by small but professioal armies. Far from approving of masterly inaction or strategem, he argued that 'The maxim of Scipio that a golden bridge should be made for a flying enemy has been much commended;'[10] but he went on to argue, this ploy should be used to make the slaughter greater. Such slaughter was necessary to inculcate the myth of imperial invincibility and the high cost of seeking to challenge imperial rule. Quick and bloody decisions were thus central to the imperial strategy.

The appropriate strategic lesson is thus one derived from a specific political context and not one imposed on it. It is not one that obtains its force and authority from the abstractions of strategic theory and is then imposed on political practice. Rulers invariably listen to the advice they wish to hear. And this advice, whatever its technicality and quality of reasoning, depends for its persuasiveness on the purposes the ruler wishes to fulfil. It is this connection between political purposes and their context, and strategic principles and their logic, that is the hallmark of what I have called classical strategy. The two kinds of reasoning are intimately linked.

As we have seen from Sun Tsu, the classical strategist is one who derives from experience, or the study of past experience, transmitted through the historical record and the accounts of practitioners, general principles about the proper conduct of war. Their relevance depends on the bearing they have for the political ends sought. He is not however, an historian. Yet he relies heavily upon a form of historical reconstruction that is not interested in the past for its own sake, but for the sake of lessons that can be derived from it. The past is interrogated in order to discover why success or failure was the consequence of the organised violence employed; what circumstances are appropriate to the use of violence; what kind of violence is most effective; and what methodological principles can be extrapolated from this exercise to guide future practice and future strategic reasoning.

Thus the classical strategist is not interested in historical truth if this is considered to be as Ranke put it, 'what really happened'.[11] Mere reconstruction is not the point. He is interested in why decisions and the course of events produced a certain result, either in accordance, or discordance, with the intentions of the actor. It is true that this interest is often limited to success in battle rather than to any wider purpose of the use of organised violence. This is often because of the difficulty in finding sufficient evidence and of establishing through the historical record the shifts and changes of policy as circumstances and objectives alter, and so affect the context of reasoning. Battle appears to be more finite and concrete. It is easier to assume that the purpose of war is victory, interpreted as success on the battle-field. Very often this is indeed the case. But as the more subtle of strategic thinkers remind us, equally, this is very often illusory. As we shall see, it was Clausewitz's great contribution to strategic thought to urge that war is merely an instrument of policy and not an end in itself.

Battle-field victory, if it is to be genuinely instrumental, must fulfil the original political purpose and so achieve the aims of the war. It may be that battle-field victory is not necessary in order to do this. The strategem too is a method that may be equally effective. The strategist who stresses the mechanics of victory as paramount, ignores the political context and the political purposes of the contest. Equally the political leader who ignores the conditions for military success where military success is politically necessary, is unlikely to succeed in his object.

The dispute between Hitler and his generals over the campaigning in the Soviet Union well illustrates this. In taking the decision in August 1941 to divert operations from Moscow to Kiev and the Crimea, Hitler justified himself to his critics by saying, 'My Generals know nothing about the economic aspects of war.'[12] This decision was regarded as profoundly mistaken by the generals, although some elements of special pleading cannot be ignored in their representations. Similarly, at the end of the war when the position of Germany was desperate, Hitler decided to make Hungary the centre of his operations, transferring troops from the Western Front to do so. Guderian attacked this decision on the grounds that slowing the Russian offensive, that is acting defensively, was the best prospect. As Guderian recorded, 'After I had disposed of the military reasons that he [Hitler] advanced he produced economic ones: since the bombing of the German synthetic oil plants, our retention of the Hungarian oil fields and refineries became essential to us and assumed a decisive importance for the outcome of the war. "If you don't get any more fuel your tanks won't be able to move and the aeroplanes won't be able to fly. You must see that. But my generals know nothing about the economic aspects of the war".'[13] From Hitler's point of view, in any case, the whole purpose of the war was to secure economic autarky for Germany. The prospects of achieving this had become remote by this time!

The problem for the classical strategist is that he wishes to derive from the past use of organised violence prescriptions relevant to his time that can lead to success in war or in making a threat of war. Such prescriptions are not of their nature rigorous formulae with an a-temporal or universal theoretical basis. They are not scientific; the entailments of scientific strategy will be considered in the next chapter. They are not the product of deductive reasoning susceptible to empirical test. This is the main distinction between classical and scientific strategic thought, and it is one of logical form rather than of empirical substance. They are both closely related to practice and so prescriptive in character.

Classical strategy derives its general principles from experience; an experience mediated through common sense. It thus appeals to a form of rationality that is innately social; normative rather than abstract in character. The problem with this is that it is linked to societies and to social practices that have something in common.[14] Their scale of values and order of preferences, together with their definitions of appropriate and legitimate means and valid ends and their relationship, must, in essence, be the same. Deriving strategic prescriptions that are universal or a-temporal in some aspect, assumes a common rationality for mankind in terms of the use of violence. If strategic thinkers in the past are deemed relevant to present practice, or if contemporary strategists assert their utility, the basis of their relevance must lie in establishing this common rationality. This issue is largely avoided by classical strategists who are unconcerned with methodological argument and the problem of justifying their prescriptions. Nevertheless, if scientific strategists are conscious theorists, classical strategists who seek to generalise about the proper conduct of war are implicit or unconscious theorists. The true distinction between them thus lies not in the character of their prescriptions or their derivation, but in their respective claims to authority. Classical strategists stress the essentially human aspects of war. As Marshal Saxe put it, 'All sciences have principles and rules: war has none ... success depends upon an infinite number of circumstances which human providence cannot foresee'.[15] Expressions such as 'the fog of war' and concepts such as 'friction',[16] morale and even luck, abound in the literature to remind us that war is a chancy business and that guidance as to its proper conduct that does not recognise this, will lead to disaster. They also constitute like Delphic prophecy, a means of qualifying strategic advice without excessive commitment to a course of action. This may have been of more use in a more despotic age than now, although given the earlier comment about rulers listening only to what they want to hear, it is not altogether irrelevant even today.[17] Inaction, or caution, is less dangerous than action and elan. Classical strategists tend not to be dogmatic or prisoners of their logic.

From this it appears that classical strategists are concerned more with the art than the science of war. I turn now to a supreme exponent of this approach, Carl von Clausewitz, who above all strategic theorists understood the importance of politics in relations to war. My justification for devoting the rest of this chapter to a consideration of his contribution to classical strategy, lies in his insistence upon defining rationality in warfare as constituting a commensurate relationship between ends and means. The centrality of this to strategy can hardly be exaggerated. He was deeply concerned with the ultimate end of war in its terms of instrumentality in serving a purpose that is essentially political. Only when war is conceived of in this way can it serve as a rational instrument. Careful definition of achievable ends, calculation of the kind and degree of force required to achieve them, and a refusal to change either the ends or the means throughout the contest, are the central lessons of his teaching. Whether he was successful in establishing the necessary conditions that must be satisfied to obtain the desired result, is another matter, as we shall see. Nevertheless, he realised that the relationship between violence and politics, represented by strategy, was of supreme importance. It was this that constituted its rationality and made violence instrumental.

Another reason for treating Clausewitz as a strategic thinker above his fellows is that he was very much concerned with justifying his prescriptive arguments. He was not seeking merely to ground his strategic advice on a firm and authoritative basis, but he was further concerned to examine what such a ground could validly be. His interest in method was therefore devoted to making as clear a case for his strategic argument as possible. In this he was above the intuitive and descriptive level of many classical strategists, who proffered their assertions without revealing the framework of assumptions from which they were derived and so exposing them to criticism. One of the main contentions of this study is that if advice to practitioners is to be deemed to be authoritative there must be a means of referring it to grounds that are open to critical evaluation. There is an assumption of some form of truth in strategic prescription. It is reasonable to ask what it is and from whence it is derived before we can take strategic argument seriously, whether as practitioners or as commentators. In this respect Clausewitz set an example not often followed by his fellow strategic thinkers.

Other reasons for treating Clausewitz as a paragon amongst classical strategists are his experience and his influence upon practice. He had direct experience of war at all levels, including that of a general officer.[18] This of itself would not be of sufficient weight to treat him as an authority. To paraphrase Frederick the Great's comment when the claims of a general for promotion were pressed on him in terms of the many years of involvement in war he had spent—he said 'So has an army mule!' Combined with the quality of his thought and of the clarity with which he perceived the central problem of war, his war experiences makes Clausewitz no armchair strategist. He has influenced many practitioners, including Hitler, who claimed, to Guderian, 'There's no need for you to try to teach me. I've been commanding the German Army in the field for five years and during that time I've had more practical experience than any gentlemen of the General Staff could ever hope to have. I've studied

Clausewitz and Moltke and read all the Schlieffen papers.'[19] Clausewitz, of course is not responsible for the consequences, or for the misinterpretations and misuse, of his arguments. Hitler did not fight a rational war in the Clausewitzian mode, but there were reasons for that which Clausewitz himself did not fully comprehend.

The two major questions with which I shall be concerned in this chapter are: what is the nature of Clausewitz's theory of the conduct of war? and, what is its practical value? Can a theory emerge that is capable of being successfully translated into practice? It should be said at the outset that any attempts at exegesis of Clausewitz's work is faced with the major difficulty that it is unfinished and is largely composed of notes and projected chapters.[20] Out of the eight books he contemplated writing, only Chapter 1 of the last book is in what he deemed to be a completed state. Possibly Chapter 2 and 3 of that book are more or less finished and this may be the case for Chapter 2 of Book Two and of Book Eight. But as a whole *Vom Kriege* is an incomplete draft. Consequently, repetition, ambiguity and brevity permeate the work. Clausewitz was particularly anxious to establish a proper relationship between theory and exposition. Methodological considerations were very important to him. The result is that philosophical and analytic arguments coexist with prescriptive and practical reasoning, illustrated by historical examples. This is an open invitation to selective argument for those interested in special pleading. As part of this method he also ventures into the reconstruction of past wars and campaigns, and so historical arguments are interspersed with the analysis. As editors of *Vom Kriege* have found,[21] it is not an easy task to establish precisely what Clausewitz meant and it would be a bold student who asserts dogmatically (as Clausewitz himself never does) an unambiguous body of doctrine.

Quite apart from these difficulties the task of exegesis is itself open to criticism. For any writer, and especially so in this case, it is impossible to refer a 'correct' interpretation to some external set of criteria that renders it definitive. Clausewitz wrote his work over a long period of time with the recent past—*his* recent past—uppermost in his mind. Modern readers have very different experiences and a different context to which to refer and the general problem of cultural relativity discussed earlier is relevant here. One of the major points made by Clausewitz is that war has social origins and is intelligible as a product of human reasoning. The innate relativism in this argument, which will be discussed later, underlines the problem of interpretation, for its relevance is very much a matter of reference and this in turn depends upon what is deemed to be of practical value. In this sense *Vom Kriege* can be made to support almost any position concerning the nature and use of war. His mode of analysis was intended to be the basis of general conclusions about war and its instrumentality, and thus to act as guide to future practitioners. The necessarily discursive character of analysis and the unfinished state of the work thus permit a variety of interpretations.

Attempts to make Clausewitz relevant to the nuclear age illustrate this inherent relativity and the open-endedness of his central argument relating as it does rationality to instrumentality.[22] General arguments are refuted, but not supported, by singular instances, and, as he was himself well aware, historical examples by careful selection may be made to support almost any argument. This applies no less to his attempt at justification as to criticisms of it based on empirical examples. As we shall see the absence of common ground, either theoretical or empirical, in the form of an attested historical interpretation, is a major problem in providing an authoritative basis for this kind of prescriptive argument. It also makes Clausewitz's concern for methodology particularly pertinent.

Two levels of analysis exist in *Vom Kriege*: the first consists of conceptual analysis of the nature of war, and the second, of practical applications admixed with historical interpretation. War is examined on the basis of its essential or ideal nature and wars are interpreted partly in the light of this analysis, and partly as critical reconstructions of reasoning. These two levels are united in the method of what Clausewitz called *kritik*[23]—or criticising the means employed—as a means both of explaining and of directing the practice of war.

Two models of war emerge from this examination. The first is that of the ideal or pure form of war in which all the resources and efforts of the state are committed to the destruction of the enemy. In Clausewitz's view this was the consequence of a logical progression of hostilities stemming from the operation of some six factors. First among these is the effect of the enemy's reaction to the initiating state's acts of violence. An interaction takes place, resulting in ever increasing efforts on both sides to obtain decisive victory. As he puts it 'so long as I have not overthrown my opponent I am bound to fear he may overthrow me. Thus I am not in control; he dictates to me as much as I dictate to him.'[24] The consequent competition leads to the utilisation of all resources at the belligerents' disposal and the intensification of the will to resist. War then becomes total. In effect he is arguing that it has escaped control.

Another factor that may induce war in its most perfect form is the importance of the end sought. If the issue at stake is deemed crucial to both contenders then the maximum effort will be made to secure or defend it. The pursuit of regional hegemony for example, or the desire for an integral part of the opponent's territory, or an ideologically based threat to the opponent's political system, would act as incentives to total war.

A third factor, and one which Clausewitz particularly noted from his experience during the Napoleonic Wars, was the involvement of peoples as well as governments in waging war. The Cabinet Wars of the Eighteenth Century were fought by relatively small professional armies using government resources secured by limited taxation, and were short in duration and restrained in their destruction. Economy in operations and the avoidance of extremes were the product of the political systems engaged. With the French Revolution came a very different type of war fought by a new type of state. Imbued with revolutionary ideology, and supported by a national system of arms production, financed by an effective and national organised system of taxation, large conscript armies achieved startling successes against opponents that did not enjoy these advantages.

Clausewitz was at pains to point out that war is social in character. Its nature and conduct is derived from the societies that fight them.[25] Consequently, the direct involvement of the masses, influenced by ideology and nationalist sentiment, and conceiving of their government as an expression of their will, produced a new and less controllable form of war. It tended towards the extreme, especially where political systems *per se* were in conflict. Although Clausewitz did not envisage ideological war as such, he was aware that popular wars—that is wars of the people—were likely to produce total war. If indeed wars come to have this ideological dimension, then the outcome can only be resolved by conquest, or conversion through conquest, as in the earlier wars of religion, since the contest is not soluble in any other way.

Fourthly, the logical tendency of war to become extreme is reinforced by the element of irrationality in which the ends sought, if not total, are pre-empted by an undue emphasis on the means employed. The initial end pursued at the beginning of hostilities becomes subordinated to the attempt to conquer the enemy, given his continued resistance. Thus control over the use and deployment of resources, both human and material, is lost. For Clausewitz this is a highly irrational development since part of his central thesis, as we shall see, is that only the requisite means should be used to secure the ends sought. The ends are political and the means—the use of violence—military. If the end becomes the destruction of the enemy's forces and this last is in turn the product of maximum effort, then the original end, whatever it was, becomes subordinate to this.[26] The inherent tendency to move in this direction is clearly irrational since rationality consists of making means and ends commensurable. Only if total war was sought at the beginning would this be rational.

Fifthly, war may entail the survival of the state itself, in that the goal of the destruction of the enemy's forces may involve the occupation of the enemy state. Hence the struggle becomes one related to national security and not to any other political issue. Pursuing hostilities to that point inevitably makes the war total, since every effort may be presumed to be made in defence of national existence. Although Clausewitz did not conceive of security as an end in itself, he believed total war to be a war of life and death for the state. Such an end subsumed all others, since any end may be achieved at the expense of the defeated state. Outside the precedents set by Napoleon in his conquests, the only case in the previous century was the disappearance of Poland as a state.[27]

Finally, wars may become total where what Clausewitz called blind panic enters into the struggle. Rational calculation is abandoned for the pursuit of victory at any price. Again such a development is more likely where the people are directly involved, and where they are in a position to threaten or influence governments.

Here we have a picture of war in its most ideal form, where the political and the military aims are fused in an all-out effort to achieve the defeat of the enemy, and where defeat is defined as complete submission to the will of the victor. It is inherently irrational in all cases except where the original end was in fact transcendental, so that such a war was intended from inception. Success in such an apocalyptic contest is conditional upon possessing the requisite resources and having the will to go on to the end. The resultant peace is a diktat imposed by the victor power and not a negotiation. This is not so much a fulfilment of the intentions of the victor as the creation of a situation in which *any* intentions may be fulfilled. As such, the end of battle-field victory is paramount over any lesser political consideration. Fundamentally this is waging war for war's sake. The only rational aspect of it is where a state seeks imperial hegemony over other states. And this view of war, as we have seen earlier, is implicit in a view of international politics as a permanent struggle for power.

Clausewitz considered absolute or total war as an ideal or model, derived from his analysis of the nature of war. At the same time, he argued that it had appeared in reality with the twenty-year contest between France and the other European states in which he had himself fought.[28] Thus the Napoleonic and Revolutionary Wars approached this ideal and the possibility of its recurrence could not be excluded from the future. Yet he did not think this likely, since there were a number of factors that in practice militated against war progressing to the extreme. It is interesting to note that most of these ameliorating factors, unlike those that made war total, are associated with reasoning. Factors that force war to its extreme form consist of structural or impersonal forces that tend to direct human action.

Thus the second model of war—the war of political calculation—is a product of reasoning that focusses on a number of factors. First, restraint is observed where total victory is seen to be improbable due to inadequate resources, adverse spatial relations and associated technology, and the balance of political affiliations between states. Secondly, the cost of achieving such a result is seen as unacceptable in terms of the postulated gain. Pyrrhic victories are generally avoided. Thirdly, limited ends pursued through violence place limits on the extent and scale of the latter. The means are controlled and limited by the ends. Fourthly, the tendency of alliances to be divisive as the balance of successes or failures affects one or other of its members, thus weakening the bond of common interest inducing caution and restraint. Fifthly, the fact that all human endeavours fall short of perfection—due to what Clausewitz calls *inertia*[29]—exercises a braking effect on action. In the area of strategy this corresponds to the notion of friction at the tactical level, where success tends to peter out and effort slackens. Sixthly, the elements of luck and circumstance introduce a random and indeterminate effect in war, creating a level of uncertainty, again inducing caution and reluctance to take risks and go to extremes. Seventhly, restraint is induced by the inability of the state to mobilise all its resources due to domestic political conditions. The need for governments to maintain their power in terms of popular consent, even in times of danger to the state, or in autocratic political systems, exercises a constraining influence on progression to total war. Finally, the sheer irrationality of going to extremes for limited political ends, provides a check on military extremism.

All these factors are presented in the analysis as elements of reasoning in the calculations of governments in determining the amount of force to employ. They are constraints common to all governments. The consequence is that in practice limited war is both the most common and the most rational form of war. The justification for this view and the distinction between prescription—what ought to be the case—and practice—what actually is the case—will be examined later. I am concerned at this stage to summarise Clausewitz's substantive arguments.

On the basis of this analysis with its fundamental distinction between two kinds of war, Clausewitz goes on to outline his notion of the rational conduct of war. His first major point is that the purpose of the intended war should be clearly defined as a statement of aims.[30] Such aims are not military but political; that is, while the defeat of the enemy forces might be a necessary condition, it is not a sufficient condition, for victory. Battlefield victory should not be confused with the ensuing state of peace and the fulfilment of the political object. From defining the aim the political leaders, taking the advice of their military commanders, assess the comparative forces of all those states likely to be involved in the achievement of the objective is calculated in the light of this appraisal. The basic calculation is designed to achieve a commensurability between means and ends so that the latter are attainable by the former and the former do not dictate the latter. The means chosen—the level and degree of violence—should not be out of proportion to the ends sought, nor should the ends themselves be subject to change or open-ended in character. This means-ends relationship is at the core of the Clausewitzian thesis of the rational use of war.

Moving closer to the world of practice, he then deals with the general principles governing the effective use of force. First, he argues that the offensive must strike directly at the enemy's 'centre of gravity'.[31] Depending upon circumstances, this can be his main army, the capital, the army of his major ally, or the community of interest of the opposed alliance: Strategy may be served by attacking its weakest link, or even by fomenting a popular uprising using political faction or dissent as a main target. In general, however, the 'centre of gravity' consists of the enemy's main forces since this is his principal means of resistance. Clausewitz then goes on to argue that the maximum effort must be made in terms of men and material in order to achieve a decisive victory, thus forcing the enemy to make peace and concede the political issue at stake. Such an effort must be made quickly, keeping the enemy off balance, and denying him the time to rally or recover.[32] This drive against the centre of gravity must be made without diversion to secondary objectives or dispersing forces. Concentration of force is a central strategic principle.

The end of such a war is a negotiated peace in which the victor secures his object. Diplomacy is thus restored as the normal means of conducting international relations and resolving disagreements. War thus constitutes a normal, rather than radical, means of settling disputes. It presupposes a common rationality and a common framework of rules and observances which allows for the relatively restricted use of violence. Political reverses through military defeat are acceptable on the basis that they are not too severe, that they do not radically alter the political status quo; that they do not threaten the existence of the state; and that they are themselves reversible through a more successful use of force in the future. Such wars, to be acceptable in this way, must thus be limited in terms of damage inflicted, in duration and cost, and in the changes they enforce. Given these assumptions, it is easy to see why Clausewitz considered war to be not 'a mere act of policy; but a true political instrument, a continuation of political activity by other means.'[33]

The main purpose of *Vom Kriege* is to provide guide lines for the proper use and conduct of war as a political instrument. To this end Clausewitz outlined a number of prescriptions. Once the true nature of war is understood and the distinction between absolute, or the perfect form of war with its inherent irrationality, and limited war, governed by political calculation and reasoning, is made, then specific conditions for success in the latter can be stipulated. Success in such a war is the consequence of accepting and understanding principles derived from the structure of war.

What is entailed in doing this? As was remarked earlier, Clausewitz set himself the task both of theorising about the proper conduct of war and of theorising about theory itself. He tried to state as explicitly as he could the method of analysis and the justification for it. Few strategic theorists have been so conscious of the need to justify the 'theory within the "theory"' as Clausewitz. He recognised that the authority of his practical and prescriptive thinking depended upon the adequacy of its theoretical base, and this in turn depended not on the force of his argument, but upon a defence of his notion of theory. The whole question of the relationship between theory and practice turns on this. The problem as he saw it was to relate the conceptual analysis of war and its ideal form to war as concrete experience in such a way as to derive guides to practical success. The one level is abstract and a-temporal, and the other empirical and innately temporal. In what sense do propositions derived from the former allow us to explain and to prescribe for unique and individual situations of human choice in the field of strategy?[34]

He considered the problem of theory. In a sophisticated analysis of the formal requirements of the mode of science he came to the conclusion that a rigorous scientific theory of war was not possible.[35] This was because of the difficulty in quantifying the relevant variables, in particular, that of the factor of reciprocity in inter-state relations, and those relating to emotions and morale. The complexity and indeterminacy of these variables, the element of cognition in human relations, and what he termed 'the moral quantities',[36] militated against the strict formulation of a scientific approach to war. But if science was not possible, scientism was nugatory. He condemned theorising *per se* where this involved purely abstract, conceptual, or *a priori*, approaches. In his view such theorising led to a formal dogmatism which was neither rigorous nor practically useful. In a remark highly pertinent to contemporary jargon-ridden 'theory', he said, 'Much greater is the evil which lies in the pompous retinue of technical terms, scientific expression and metaphors which these systems carry in their train and which like a rabble—like baggage of an army broken away from its Chief—hang about in all directions.'[37] There is indeed, as we shall see in later chapters, a good deal of hanging about, especially in nuclear strategic theory.

If the entailments of science could not be met in formulating strategic theory, what of a historical approach? His view of history and of historical method is interesting since he revealed an awareness of the dangers of hindsight and of making anachronistic judgement. He thought that the historian should place himself in making his interpretation 'exactly in the position of the commander'.[38] There were, however, a number of difficulties in doing this. The chief one, familiar to all modern historians, was the incompleteness of the evidence relating to the actual reasoning of the historical agents. He could have added that where this is apparently provided, in the form of direct accounts made by commanders, confusion and controversy, rather than access to the truth, is the consequence.[39]

It was thus a counsel of perfection to insist on a complete knowledge of motivation, intentions, reasoning, etc., as the basis of an historical reconstruction. His main objection to an historical approach as a means of deriving strategic principles, rested on his conception of the purpose of the enquiry. History, he argued, is primarily an investigation into the facticity of past events, into what actually happened, and so is not concerned with either generalities or the question of instrumental effectiveness.[40] While strategic theory too must be concerned with facts and rooted in experience, its prime purpose is to transcend the particular so as to make prescriptions for present and future practice. It is not merely a commentary on past events, but a means of making judgements based on general propositions common to all occasions in which war is used as a rational instrument. Although such judgements can of course be applied to past situations of violence and political choice, their *utility* stems from their application to continuing practice. Clausewitz intended his work to be useful.

In rejecting a scientific approach as too difficult and an historical approach as not directly relevant, Clausewitz was trying to assert an autonomous and distinctive method of analysis which could be applied to the past, present and the future. This method he terms 'criticism' (*Kritik*)[41] and it consisted of evaluating the means employed, or in other words, analysing the rationality of the use of violence in terms of its component factors and the situation. *Kritik*, or critical analysis, has three aspects.[42] It entails, first, an historical approach in the form of a narrative of facts. Secondly, it involves the tracing of effects back to their causes, and thirdly, an 'investigation and evaluation of the means employed'.[43] It is thus in part a form of historical interpretation in which judgements about the efficacy of command decisions in war are made by the strategist, and, in part, a conceptual framework from which the basis of these judgements are derived. Such a framework is itself a-temporal and is based on the analysis of the logical relations between propositions about the nature and conduct of war. It is not, however, a causal hypothesis; it is a model of rationality. The prescriptions derived from it are axioms and not laws; maxims governing the rationality of choice and decision in the employment of violence. They are what the rational observer would consider, on the basis of his personal experience of war, to be guides as to what is a reasonable decision in a given situation.

Thus the central question which Clausewitz asks himself is: how can this act be explained rationally in terms of a desired outcome? He answers this not by appealing to the actual reasons preferred by a statesman or commander, but by relating these to the possible alternatives—alternatives not necessarily perceived or even considered by the historical agent.[44] Thus for Clausewitz, rationality consists of an appropriate choice of means, related to the end sought, guided by general principles common to all situations of combat or involving organised violence. He uses 'historical' examples, firstly, as sources for general propositions, secondly, as illustrations of his analytic propositions, and thirdly, as evidence to support his generalisations. The past provides him both with his materials and his proofs. A strategist, according to Clausewitz, is a judge who is involved in the practice he is assessing; as he put it 'critical analysis is not just an evaluation of the means actually employed, but of all possible means, which first have to be formulated, that is invented. One can, after all, not condemn a method without being able to suggest a better alternative.'[45] He answers the question on what grounds can the claim to this knowledge be based, by saying, 'The proof that we demand is needed whenever the advantage of the means suggested is not plain enough to rule out all doubts; it consists in taking each of the means and assessing and comparing the particular merits of each in relation to the objective.'[46] While this is relatively easy, given hindsight, for the historian, he urges its utility for the practitioner. 'Critical analysis, after all, is nothing but thinking that should precede the action.'[47]

There are serious problems with *kritik* as a method of deriving strategic prescriptions for practitioners. It is inherently ambiguous and lends itself to constant qualification, since historical examples are used, both to exemplify the concept or definition, and as exercises in the critical analysis of actual strategic and political decisions. We are never sure whether a reference to the empirical level is an illustration or a demonstration of the principles. And as Clausewitz himself points out, there are always exceptions to rules.[48] The theoretical level informs the level of experience and vice versa, and there is always room for luck, genius, and the 'moral quantities', to intervene.

However, this method is open to fundamental criticism not because of its ambiguities, but because it confuses a number of distinctive modes of explanation without providing a viable alternative. Anxious to escape from the rigorous demands of scientific theory, the abstract and empirically empty oversimplifications of systematic theory, or scientism, and the temporal limitations of history, Clausewitz chose a method which leads inescapably to subjective rationalisation. 'Criticism' (*Kritik*) is not a valid means of relating theory to practice so that practitioners may be guided to success in their use of violence. Of course a good deal depends on what is claimed for the Clausewitzian method. If we take the reduced view that it provides a level of understanding, heuristic in nature, which somehow helps the political and military practitioner to make rational and effective decisions about the use of violence, then clearly a rigorous assessment of its epistemological and methodological implications seems excessive. Clausewitz, a modest man, continually stressed the equivocal nature of his argument in order to avoid the charge of dogmatism which he levelled at the former theorists of war. As he well understood, 'Nor can the theory of war apply the concept of law to action, since no prescriptive formulation universal enough to deserve the name of law can be applied to the constant change and diversity of the phenomena of war.'[49] He was interested in opening not closing the military mind.

But is *Vom Kriege* simply an elaborate pedagogic exercise; a training manual for the intellect? If it is only an heuristic device why should it be taken seriously by those engaged in war? Only those engaged in action can decide what is of use to them or what it is they desire, and no observer, academic or otherwise, can determine these questions in advance. Anything or nothing can have heuristic value and no such claim can be justified prior to practice. What makes Clausewitz so important in my view, is not the understanding he may or may not have had of his epoch, or of any other, but the questions he raised about the relation of theory to practice. It is precisely because he raises fundamental questions about the nature of his analysis that his work assumes a universal significance. On his own account his method was more than simply an intellectual exercise. As he argued 'The influence of theoretical truths on practical life is always exerted more through critical analysis (*kritik*) than through doctrine. Critical analysis being the application of theoretical truths to actual events, it not only reduces the gap between the two, but also accustoms the mind to these truths through their repeated application.'[50] His notion of theory was neither a formal abstract conceptual system, nor a mere educative device, but a form of analysis which, in his view, bridged theory and practice.

I want to make three criticisms of his 'theory' of war as a rational instrument of policy. The first is that theory entails explanation and that if a proferred theory is not grounded upon an adequate basis, no claim for its practical utility is tenable. I want to argue that Clausewitz's theory is inadequate in this respect and that it is essentially a technique that is fundamentally flawed. Secondly, I want to argue that the postulated relationship between the conceptual level is groundless and consists of a false dichotomy. And, thirdly, I want to argue that the method of criticism is essentially a rationalisation, subjective in nature and useless for any practical purpose. As we shall see in the next chapter, these criticisms apply to all attempts at employing the concept of rationality within an analytic scheme in order to derive prescriptions for practitioners. In this respect, as was pointed out earlier, while classical appears to differ in form from scientific terms they are the same and depend equally on an unstated and unfulfilled theory.

First, why should prescription, or to be more precise, prescriptive theory, be dependent on explanation? What sort of explanation does it entail if this is the case? As we have seen, Clausewitz offers a number of precepts which stand as guides to action. To restate these, from the notion that war in its extreme form is absolute, he argued: that victories should be sought quickly, 'direct at the enemy's power';[51] decisive battles should therefore be fought; 'all forces which are available and destined for a strategic object should be simultaneously applied to it';[52] that there was an inherent contradiction in the notion of a purely defensive war,[53] and that although winning with economy was preferable, ultimately all national capacity must be utilised if necessary;[54] that technological innovation was not as important as the organisation and logistical efficiency of the state,[55] and lastly; that the inculcation of high morale was a major factor for success.[56] From the principle of reciprocal relations we have two pieces of advice; that the range of the possible responses to be taken into consideration at the planning stage of hostilities;[57] and that the threat of intensifying the conflict could act as a deterrent to the enemy.[58] And from the proposition that war is 'policy by other means' we have the precept that the means should be related to and commensurate with the ends.[59] As he put this it was, 'the principle of only applying so much force and aiming at such an object in war as just sufficient for the attainment of the political object'.[60] A statesman should, when contemplating the use of war, take into account his national resources, those of his putative enemy, the character of the governments and political systems concerned, and their external relationships. Here we have a picture of war as a political instrument, to be used with discretion by a rational statesman, who must observe certain precepts, bearing constantly in mind the governing precept that the ends sought should be commensurate with the means employed.

Now we can regard these in a variety of ways. Are they maxims? A maxim is a rational principle concerning a type or class of action which does not have specified conditions for its application. It is a-temporal. If we are faced with two apparently contradictory maxims such as, for example, *look before you leap*, and, *he who hesitates is lost*; the force of one or the other depends upon a statement of conditions equivalent to an explanation. The maxim constitutes a kind of statement of what is reasonable in a given situation. *Look before you leap*, because there is, or may be, a ditch on the other side of the obstacle. But as a general cautionary principle it loses its force if one is being pursued by a bull at the time. Whether there is a dire choice between having ones neck broken by the ditch, or by the bull, is left to fate to determine. The point here is that if maxims are to be useful or relevant, their empirical vacuity must be filled with clearly stated conditions of application. In short they become prescriptions and their force is derived from the associated explanation.

A distinction can be made between prescriptions which belong to practical reasoning and those which logically entail an explanation of a general kind. In the first case all we need to know is whether it works and not why. If an appeal is made to experience then such a reference is to actual practice—to some precedent. The prescription worked in past situation x, this is a situation similar to x, perhaps it will work in this case. We are persuaded of this only if we recognise two things: that the two situations share the same basic characteristics, and the prescriptive statement formed part of the reasoning of those engaged in the former situation. Hence we are not concerned with a rationalising or hypothetical argument provided by an external observer, but with what actually prevailed in the situation taken as a precedent. The reference involved is directly to practice. We believe or take on trust such prescriptions and the consequences that follow from their adoption.

But to step out of the realm of practical reasoning into prescriptive theory entails a very different type of reference. The force of prescriptive statements which are related to a theoretical argument does not depend upon either belief or a persuasion that individual experiences are shared or parallel, but upon a level of attestable explanation. Why is this so? The point is that without such a reference we have no grounds either for deeming them as authoritative or for judging them. Nor can we choose between competing and incommensurate prescriptions. It is this reference and this sort of ground that Clausewitz seeks to provide, although it is seen as an alternative to either science or history. It depends upon showing not that history repeats itself, but that there are demonstrable relations between factors, so that a prescribed course of action produces a given result. It may not be the case that the result invariably follows from the associated conditions, but there must be some means of showing that a high degree of probability exists. As Clausewitz clearly recognised, the reference entails general propositions: 'War, though conditioned by the particular characteristics of states and their armed forces, must contain some more general—indeed a universal—element with which every theorist ought above all to be concerned.'[61]

Prescriptive statements which are not referable to a validated mode of explanation are examples of practical reasoning. They are essentially *ex post facto* judgements about the rationality of action in a given historical context, and as such are not really prescriptive because there is no basis for their extension into truly testable propositions about rationality in a given clas of action. Such a basis would exist only if there were a reference to a general theoretical explanation. We need to know why a postulated course of action would produce a given result before we can authoritatively recommend it to practitioners. As Clausewitz himself understood, to do this would mean satisfying the logic of a covering-law explanation and stating the sufficient and necessary conditions together with an empirical generalisation, for rationality in warfare. Whether this is at all possible for human action is another matter, as we saw in the last chapter. But it is this type of explanatory mode which is implicit in strategic theorising. As

Clausewitz put it, 'It is legitimate to judge an event by its outcome for this is the soundest criterion. But a judgement based on the result alone must not be passed off as evidence of human wisdom. To discover why a campaign failed is not the same thing as to criticise it; but if we go on and show that the causes could and should have been seen and acted on, we assume the role of critic and set ourselves up above the general'.[62] Now from his contention that criticism is at a higher level than the reconstruction of the actual reasoning of the agent—i.e. history, and that it is based upon principles derived from a conceptual and analytic framework, we can see that he makes an appeal to some form of general or theoretical explanation. But if it does not correspond to the kind of theory to which I have referred, what is its nature, its appropriate test, and the status of prescriptions derived from it?

This brings me to my second point of criticism, that the postulated relationship between the conceptual framework and experience, is a false dichotomy, neither producing, nor based on, any adequate explanatory form. According to Clausewitz, his method is directed towards the formulation of a number of propositions concerning the nature and proper conduct of war. Analysis brings out some of their logical implications together with their inter-relationships. The resultant conceptual framework is then referred to a number of interpretations of the rationale of action in past wars. These general propositions are then modified or qualified in the light of actual practice, or what is interpreted to be practice, and become not logical necessities, but probabilities, or even possibilities, which are alleged to exist in war. According to the argument, these should be taken into account by those wishing to use war as a political instrument, if they are to act both rationally and effectively.

The theory—the conceptual level—is always in principle referrable to practice—the level of experience—and vice versa. But what is the nature of this reference? Now the notion of experience used by Clausewitz is very ambiguous. Sometimes it is used to mean the accumulation of knowledge through practice as direct experience. It is also used simply as a reference to past facts. Again, it is used to mean the judgements of the agent, or alternatively, those of the rational observer, and so on. But most frequently it refers to the rational interpretation of events by the theorist. 'Experience' in this sense is not self-evident factual 'evidence' but a form of argument in its own right. It is itself an interpretation. Such an argument is a selection and presentation of facts, together with a process of reasoning, which takes the form of a set of judgements about the rationality and efficacy of decisions and actions in warfare. So the crude juxtaposition of theory against reality in the form of experience, turns out to be a contrast between conceptual analysis and historical interpretation. The relationship is not explanatory in the sense that the former is used to explain the latter, as in the relation between scientific theory and the empirical testing of hypotheses. Rather the exercise is an attempt to make the two levels coherent so that one does not contradict the other, and are in some way compatible. But 'experience' is not concrete observable reality 'out there'.

Since the organising reference is to rationality in action it is conceptually formed and stands as an interpretation of sorts. It is the product of the observer not of the agent.

Similarly the conceptual framework is modified and its propositions are so formulated as to allow as much qualification as possible, so that they do not either appear impossibly dogmatic or contradict the proferred interpretation. It is therefore not purely a realm of abstraction. The two are inter-related in a way which precludes any correspondence in which the empirical level confirms or refutes the conceptual level. Putting it another way, 'experience' is conceptually formed and becomes a rationalisation referrable only to the concepts which mould it.

The problem can be stated in terms of whether empirical examples *illustrate* or *demonstrate* the principles derived from the conceptual analysis. If the former is the case then we are not presented with an empirical explanation of a general kind from which we can derive authoritative prescriptions. The conceptual world is clarified by reference to historical 'examples' which are interpreted and formulated with an illustrative function in mind. The method here is circular. We are given an intelligible and coherent world which prescribes not effective action but a way of looking at events and their alleged rationale. No reference can show this world to be true: it merely helps to make it intelligible; but of course intelligible only in terms of this particular conceptual scheme. And we have no way of showing that this scheme is better than any rival alternative. The justification of 'criticism' in Clausewitz's view, is by referring the rationalising judgements at the empirical level to his principles, but we can see that this is no justification at all if the principles themselves cannot in turn be justified.

If, however, demonstration is required, then these principles must be treated as empirical generalisations which are capable of empirical verification. Such generalisations would be a-temporal and applicable to all situations sharing the same characteristics. They correspond to the laws of the natural sciences and bear the same empirical relationship to explanation in science. In short, my point here is that the relationship postulated between theory and reality, in which the latter somehow tests or confirms the former, requires the formulation of testable hypotheses. Clausewitz clearly recognised this requirement but rejected it in favour of a subjective level of interpretation which, however intellectually stimulating, is nevertheless void of any evaluatory or explanatory criteria. He did not succeed or indeed attempt the establishment of a criterion for critical analysis. Instead he formulated a kind of hybrid which, in my view, confuses two quite distinct types of argument—conceptual analysis and historical interpretation—neither of which in any case could lead to empirically testable hypotheses applicable to the proper conduct of war. Its focus lies in a framework of rational action referrable firstly, to the rationale of the conceptual framework with its precepts and guidelines, and secondly, to the rationale of situations of actual war. The postulated link between them in the method of criticism is highly ambiguous.

My third main criticism of Clausewitz's method and of the general approach in the classical school which it represents, is that 'testing the means employed', that is examining the rationale of action, constitutes a rationalisation and not an explanation of rationality. It is useless for any practical purpose. The central assumption of this method is that the human agents whose actions and decisions it seeks to explain and assess, act rationally. By this is meant that they are concerned with the achievement of a goal or purpose, and that the means chosen to implement it are in some way, good, commensurate, or appropriate. Ostensibly this entails making a judgement but, as I have argued, such a judgement is itself dependent upon an adequate explanatory mode if the aim is prescriptive theory. On what grounds can we determine the commensurability or appropriateness of means—related ends in terms of human action? This is done, more implicitly than explicitly, by asserting a level of rationality relevant to all situations of strategic choice. Such a level of rationality constitutes an 'objective' referent, holding good for all instances of such acts or decisions. The referent is not the actual reasons which are preferred by the agent, but what is entailed in the situation itself. We thus talk of the logic of the situation, of the rationale of action, and assess reasons and action in terms of ends and means.

Clausewitz makes a distinction between an account of the reasoning of participants in action based on surviving evidence, and an account which amounts to a form of judgement concerning the rationality of the actions and of the agent's reasoning. Although he frequently refers to the former in his 'historical' analyses, he makes it clear that his method is primarily concerned with the latter. It is important because only an analysis of rational action in using violence, rather than of actual reasoning, can provide the a-temporal propositions logically necessary to a theory of the proper conduct of war. It is essential to distinguish between using a concept of rationality to *judge* or *evaluate* actions or reasons as rational, irrational, or non-rational, in terms of a means-ends relationship, and the use of a theory of rationality which *explains* action in such a way as to provide a basis for prescriptions that are effective in practice. Since Clausewitz is not primarily interested in making *ex post facto* judgements about military action, or in creating a kind of taxonomy of rational action, but in relating theory to practice, it is the latter exercise which concerns him. And it involves an *explanatory* reference to rationality.

But what justifies this reference? On what grounds can we appeal to a level of rationality which transcends that of the historical agent? In what sense is such an appeal objective? How can we relate it to practice? It seems to me that there are three possible references, only one of which properly refers to an *explanatory* mode which would validate this level of generalisation. The first possibility is a reference to a principle of rationality that generally holds for all actions of that class, under specified conditions. Examples of this are found in contemporary economic and sociological theorising—the principle of the maximisation of profits, or of satisfaction. As we shall see in the next chapter, using such principles, models of rational choice or action can be constructed which have no direct empirical application but which would show within the terms of the model what would constitute an optimal course or decision. This approach is characteristic of the scientific school of strategy. Such a model is a conceptual construct dependent on the logical relations of its definitions rather than upon any kind of empirical referent. In the absence of a higher level theory or testable hypothesis, it remains an abstract or idealised exercise. Rationality here is an analytic or definitional concept.

Secondly, a reference to a normative principle might be entailed. For example, the notion of a balance of power system, or some notion of inter-state equilibrium, might be deployed so that the political use of violence can be evaluated in terms of a functional relationship to the stability of the postulated system. The difficulty here is that while such a principle enables evaluation and judgement it cannot itself be validated. Unlike the model of rational choice where the means-ends relationship is the focus, this type of reference is more concerned with ends-means. Value-judgements and socially derived notions of what is reasonable, or desirable, under given circumstances dominate this kind of argument.

Thirdly, a rationalising argument could be referred to a principle of causation in which the action is seen as a necessary consequence of specified conditions governed by a general law. In this case the reasons of the agent, where they are relevant, are explained by the covering hypothesis in such a way that his actions are necessarily entailed by them and the reasons in turn by their causes. Such a hypothesis must be capable of an empirical test and so provide an adequate explanation from which predictive statements about the connections between reasons and actions can be made. This in principle would constitute a viable way of deriving an applied science of human action and so relate theory directly to practice. It would have very little to do with our present historical understanding of human action. The implications of these arguments will be examined in the next chapter.

Much of the ambiguity, not only of the Clausewitzian analysis, but of the classical school in general, stems from their use or abuse of history. I will turn to this later. So far as Clausewitz is concerned there are elements of all three forms of argument in his work. The ambiguity arises not because of its unfinished character but mainly from his conscious rejection of genuine theoretical explanation in favour of the form of subjective judgement he terms 'criticism'. His notion of commensurability between means and ends, however valuable as a practical injunction, is not given an explanatory basis so that judgements based on it can be properly evaluated. The assertion that the ends must be commensurate with the means, if rationality is to prevail in warfare is, as it stands, simply a definition of rationality. We are offered a rationalisation, the truth of which is not testable either in the form of empirical hypotheses, or as reason-giving explanations, referrable directly to evidence of the actual reasons of the agents whose actions we seek to explain. The latter is in any case ruled out by this explicit rejection of an historical mode of explanation in favour of prescriptive theory. So far as the former is concerned, what we need to have if we are to be guided into the right choice of action, is some testable statement of conditions, governed by a general proposition, applicable across time to situations that are replicable. What we are actually given is a mixture of conceptual analysis and rationalisation, which however subtle and intellectually stimulating, does not accomplish Clausewitz's stated aim.

The emphasis placed on war as a rational instrument brings into focus the problem of ends. This is essentially a political problem. But what constitutes an end? What rules or guides to the formulation of ends and the link with means are provided in the Clausewitzian analysis? The major omission in *Vom Kriege* and indeed in all strategic theorising that concentrates on the instrumentality of violence, is a study of politics complementary to the study of the proper conduct of war. In the absence of such a study the analysis inevitably degenerates into an examination of technique, and this is either inherently open ended and abstract, or obsessed with the tactical level. A notion of strategy which confines itself to urging an optimal course of action, without considering the policy basis of choice, or of the ends sought, leads to irrationality, since the circumstances and the reasoning may so alter as to make the desired objectives themselves change, so rendering the original course of action irrelevant or even self-defeating. Alternatively, the choice of means may in the course of events dictate the ends sought. So the study of the *use* of war requires a parallel study of politics in order that its place as an instrument of policy can be understood and explained. Clausewitz certainly understood the first part of this problem but he did not relate it as it should be related to the political context.

He imported into his argument assumptions that were derived from recent political practice, assumptions which were not as rigorously examined as those related to the actual conduct of war. He believed that peace is the end sought, a peace that of course favoured the victor power, but one that restored the former diplomatic harmony of nations with its rules and peaceful means of resolving most disputes. War was not a fundamental challenge to this international political system because it was (or should be) limited. He believed that it became a challenge only where it became unlimited, that is, when it escaped rational control. Common rationality, with its inbuilt limits on both ends and means, was a necessary assumption. In this Clausewitz assumes a balance of power between the major European states akin to that of the Eighteenth Century. This precluded any attempt made by one state to aggrandise itself at the expense of the others. As it achieves success in war, so imperilling the balance, or manifests through its diplomacy an attempt to do this, the other states ally against it. Alliances shift and change, and given this volatility, there is a reduced inducement to challenge the system because of the uncertainty of ultimate success. Thus there is an implicit acceptance of rules of war and of its scope that limits the effects of war and its political results. Such an international political framework assumes the rationality of a commensurate relation between ends and means. Clausewitz accepts this as given, as in fact a basic normative condition. He has no explanation for its alleged existence.

Yet if we adopted another view—that of the power-security hypothesis discussed at the beginning of this study, we would have a very different set of assumptions. The world of states constitutes an anarchy in which abortive attempt after abortive attempt is made to achieve the world hegemony that alone guarantees security for the successful state. Every war in this context, potentially at least, is a total war. The concern for national security is paramount over other political interests, and technological development in the means of violence reflect this. If one state's security means another state's insecurity, a permanent power struggle is the consequence. A theory of the instrumentality of war and of its rationality, given these assumptions, would be very difficult from that offered by Clausewitz. It is true that such a view requires an adequate explanatory basis as much as that of the balance-of-power model of international politics. That is to say that it is no more valid. The point is that assumptions of this kind may prejudice a strategic theory, and in any case, should be made explicit and subjected to critical examination.

Clausewitz regarded the Napoleonic wars as aberrational since, in his view, war had escaped control and was being pursued to its limits regardless of end.[63] It was always a possibility inherent in the nature of war that this might be the case. Nevertheless it was an irrational development. It was brought about by the involvement of the masses in politics after the French Revolution. Wars reflected this involvement and instead of the dispassionate calculation of forces, became wars of emotion divorced from reason. This may reflect a conservative temperament but the political systems that dominated his day were not democratic. Equally, they could not command the resources both human and material that later democracies could deploy in warfare. The involvement of people did not merely increase the potential for destruction, it also involved their commitment to war. This could only be achieved by conviction obtained through the manipulation of nationalist and revolutionary sentiment. The concomitant of this was that whatever the calculations of the rulers in engaging in violence, their instruments—the people—had to be convinced that their sacrifice was not for sordid national advantage but for some noble aspiration, at the very least, the defence of their homeland. This modern phenomenon has produced a dimension to war understood by Clausewitz, but not included in his analysis. He had little conception of the problem of security emanating from fears of rival capabilities rather than from belligerent intentions.

If the masses are involved in international violence, both as victims and as instruments, on a scale unrealised in Clausewitz's time, weapons technology since then has radically altered. This aspect will be discussed in later chapters, but the point here is that current means of destruction are very much greater than those of the past, and in the nuclear ages so much so that the political system—domestic and international—is itself placed in jeopardy should these weapons be used on any scale. This has had important consequences for the rationality of war as a political instrument, as we shall see later. Humanity may or may not survive a nuclear Armageddon, what is certain is that the political entities that fight it will not. No political end could be served by it. Paradoxically, as we shall see, the inhibition on total war imposed by the present nuclear stalemate and its associated reasoning has for the first time made limited war a rational, and controllable option. And it has been an emotion, fear, that has done this, not reason.

However, to return to the classical theory and the Clausewitzian expression of it, I said earlier that this approach abused history. It should be clear by now what I mean by this. The past is taken to provide examples to support general principles that can be used to serve as a guide for effective action using violence as a means to an end. But if every past situation is unique in the sense that the context of reasoning supporting actions, deemed relevant to the present, is unique, such an extrapolation is a distortion. Ultimately, this type of theorising turns on individual perception—the psychological element—as a component of reasoning employed in collective bargaining. If rationality is a characteristic of what statesmen think is rational, in terms of an ends-means relationship in their contests, then this is innately subjective. Any explanation of this is historical rather than theoretical in character, unless an explanation of the reasoning process in human beings is essayed. Thus, unless some form of universal rationality is argued, placing reasoning in a genuine theoretical context, historical reasoning, or its historical consquences, taken out of context, cannot be used as a basis for prescription.

A psychological dimension, or in other words, a context of practical reasoning, is dependent upon a level of perception and understanding revealed, in so far as it is accessible, through evidence of the actual reasoning of those engaged in interdependent actions. An explanation of the ensuing course of action, as we saw in the last chapter, is essentially historical in character, that it is unique, *ex post facto*, and referable to an independent criterion based on the adequacy of the available evidence. It is not possible to extrapolate from this and derive a level of rationality without anachronism.

Each such context is unique in this sense. The classical strategist is thus compelled either to treat rationality and reasoning as genuinely universal, begging the question as to the justification of such an assumption, or to treating the past as a quarry for illustrative events, ignoring the associated reasoning, and relating these to contemporary rationality. Neither of these can serve as an authoritative basis for prescriptions for effective use of violence. Clausewitz states the position succinctly: 'No one starts a war, or rather no one in his sense ought to do so, without first having clear in his mind what he intends to achieve by that war and how he intends to conduct it. The former is its political purpose, the latter its operational objective.'[64] The problem is, having defined what is rational, and making it dependent upon a commensurate relationship between means and ends, how could this be given a general empirical application and so made practical? How could war be kept in its limited form and how could it be made instrumental for the fulfilment of a national purpose? This problem is not solved by Clausewitz or by the classical strategists he represents.

To conclude, it might be instructive to imitate the classical strategists and take a brief look at the last World War in the light of Clausewitz's teaching. Hitler thought he was fighting a limited war on the lines recommended by Clausewitz. His political appraisal of the international situation of the late 1930s had a clear end—securing for Germany territory in the eastern part of Europe. This entailed *inter alia* the destruction of the political system set up by the Versailles and other treaties. His calculation of forces took into account the relative military strengths and weaknesses of his potential opponents and allies—Britain, France, the USSR, and Italy. His pact with the Soviet Union and Alliance with Italy removed fears of a multi-front war. He took a risk in concentrating his forces against Poland, but this was a calculated risk based on intelligence and the actual deployment of the allied forces. He believed that his campaign, directly against the centre of gravity of the Polish forces, would achieve a quick victory, rapidly allowing him to re-deploy his troops against the West, and so it proved.

On the political level, however, he was mistaken in thinking that the Molotov-Ribbentrop pact would stop Britain and France from honouring their guarantee to Poland. Although this caused him some hesitation he believed, and events proved him right, that he could defeat Poland before his opponents could effectively threaten him. In this he was following Clausewitz's precept that decision should be sought without delay, for time was on the side of the weaker power. After the defeat of Poland his opponents were obdurate in rejecting his peace offer. He was thus faced with a bigger war than he would have liked, but one which he was prepared to fight, in spite of the misgivings of his generals.

The plan to defeat France again followed Clausewitzian principles, although here he was prepared to accept advice and modify it. The plan he adopted, following Manstein's advice, was intended to achieve a swift victory against the only field force that mattered—the French Army. It was risky but the alternative—a prolonged war of attrition—was riskier still. Moreover it was the kind of struggle his opponents, unprepared for war as they were, wanted to force upon him. He thus concentrated his forces against the weakest part of the enemy's disposition, and, avoiding all temptations to deviate, cut through, to win in a six week campaign. France was compelled to seek terms and Britain was forced to withdraw from the continent.

This military victory, although it opened the way to European domination and confirmed the acquisition of territory in the East, was not accompanied by a negotiated peace. Britain refused to accept battle-field defeat. It was this refusal that turned what Hitler believed to be a limited war in the Eighteenth Century manner, following the Clausewitzian notion of rationality, into total war. Britain was acting irrationally. It is interesting that Hitler explained the obduracy of Britain as caused by the personal animosity of Churchill and the cloudiness of his political judgement through excessive drinking! But indeed on the standard of rationality asserted by Clausewitz, Britain's refusal to accept the arbitrament of battle and come to terms, was irrational. It was not that the chances of success in continuing the war were so remote in 1940. Indeed invasion was expected and the victory in the air was by a very slender margin. It was that success in war was defined in total terms. Victory consisted of the defeat of Germany in terms of its political system. The two were seen as synonymous. Total war was implicit in the decision to go on fighting. The end was seen as security.

The consequence was an inherently irrational war that can only be understood by reference to the reasoning of the contenders. New weapons came into existence, including the atomic bomb. The struggle became transcendental and on a scale unforeseen by those states that originated it. All this testifies to the point made by Clausewitz, that ends and means must be commensurate if war is to be a rational instrument. But it also testifies to the difficulty of actually doing this. What theoretical basis can be provided for effective control over violence? Whatever it is, and this will be discussed in the next chapter, it cannot stem from the experiences of the past, whatever these are alleged to be.

NOTES AND REFERENCES

1. Sun Tzu, see T. R. Phillips, *Roots of Strategy,* first published 1940, reprinted Greenwood Press, Conn. 1982, p. 21.
2. *Ibid*, p. 21.
3. *Ibid*, p. 23.
4. *Ibid*, p. 23.
5. Throughout the ages inducements other than glory have been offered to soldiers, ranging from loot to pensions. Hitler rewarded his generals with cash and estates. The Democracies were perhaps more subtle awarding titles and promotions to their generals.
6. *Roots of Strategy, op. cit.* p. 61.
7. *Ibid*, p. 29.
8. *Ibid*, p. 29.
9. Vegetius *De Rei Militarii* writing in the reign of Constantine.
10. Phillips, *Roots of Strategy, op. cit.* p. 146.
11. See Michael Howard, 'The Use and Abuse of Military History' in *The Causes of Wars,* Unwin, London, 1984, pp. 200–10.
12. See Guderian, *Panzer Leader, op. cit.* pp. 198–200.
13. *Ibid*, pp. 393–4.
14. The successful use of the stratagem, as opposed to brute force, for example, depends entirely upon shared assumptions and a common rationality possessed by all contenders.
15. Marshal Saxe, *My Reveries on the Art of War*, cited in Phillips *op. cit.* p. 190.
16. Von Clausewitz coined this useful expression to indicate the delays and unforeseen circumstances that interpose between human decision and action

84   *The Politics of War*

and their consequences, see Carl von Clausewitz, *On War* trans. Col. J. J. Graham first pub. 1874, revised edition Col. F. N. Maude 1909, 3 vols Routledge Kegan Paul, 1949, Chapter vii Friction in War, pp. 77 (ff), and also Carl von Clausewitz, *On War*, ed. and trans by M. Howard and P. Paret, Princeton University Press, NJ 1976, Friction in War, pp. 119 (ff), I have referred to either of these two editions where I think one or the other expresses the sense more clearly.

17. Churchill's relations with his generals in North Africa illustrates this point.
18. For an account of his life and times see, P. Paret, *Clausewitz and the State,* OUP, 1976.
19. Guderian, *op. cit.* p. 378.
20. As he told himself, 'I look upon the first six books, of which a fair copy has now been made, as only a mass which is still in a manner without form and which has yet to be revised .... Still, notwithstanding this imperfect form I believe that an impartial reader thirsting for truth and conviction will rightly appreciate in the first six books the fruits of several years' reflection and a diligent study of War, and that, perhaps, he will find in them some leading ideas which may bring about a revolution in the theory of war', Berlin 10th July 1827, Maude-Graham edition *op. cit.* Vol. 1 p xxv and xxvii.
21. See Howard-Paret edition *op. cit.* Peter Paret the Genesis of *On War*, pp. 3. (ff).
22. See A. Rapoport ed., Introduction, *Clausewitz On War*, Penguin Harmondsworth, 1968, for a highly anachronistic view of Clausewitz's thinking. For a more closely reasoned analysis see Raymond Aron Penser *la Guerre* Vol. 1, and *L'Age Européen Planetaire,* Vol. 2, NRF Editions Gallimare Paris, 1976.
23. Maude-Graham edition *op. cit.* pp. 130 (ff) and Howard Paret edition *op. cit.* pp. 156 (ff).
24. Maude-Graham, *ibid*, p. 5.
25. *Ibid*, p. 3, p. 23, p. 29.
26. See *Ibid, Ends and Means in War*, pp. 27 (ff) and Howard-Paret ed. *Purpose and Means in War*, pp. 90 (ff).
27. This was the Third Partition of Poland in 1794–1975. Poland was further partitioned under the terms of the Molotov-Ribbentrop Pact of August 1939.
28. See Maude-Graham edition *op. cit. Absolute and Real War*, Vol. III, pp. 79 (ff) and Howard-Paret edition *op. cit. Absolute War and Real War*, pp. 579 (ff).
29. Maude- Graham, *Ibid*, p. 22.
30. He said, "......the political view is the object, War is the means and the means must always include the object in our conception" *ibid*, p. 23, and again, "No war is commenced, *or at least should be commenced* [my italics] if people acted wisely without first seeking a reply to the question, What is to be attained by and in the same?" Vol. III, p. 79, or in the Howard-Paret edition "No one starts a war—or rather no one in his senses ought to do so—without first being clear in his mind what he intends to achieve by that war and how he intends to conduct it." p. 579.
31. Howard-Paret, edition, *ibid*, p. 596.
32. *Ibid*, p. 597.
33. *Ibid*, p. 605.
34. I am indebted to the Editor of the *British Journal of International Studies* for permission to reproduce part of my article on Clausewitz *(British Journal of*

International Studies, 4(1978) pp. 178–90).
35. See Graham-Maude edition for *Methodicism* Vol. 1. pp. 122 (ff) and Howard-Paret, *Method and Practice, pp. 151 (ff)*.
36. *Graham-Maude, Vol. 1, pp. 101 (ff)*.
37. *Ibid*, Vol. 1, p. 154.
38. Howard-Paret, p. 163.
39. For example see Montgomery of Alamein, *Memoirs*, Odhams, Watford, 1958. His account of the Battle of Alamein not only ignores the role of intelligence and the Ultra intercepts, but also the contribution of his predecessors in command. The former can be excused by the demands of security but the latter is inexcusable.
40. See Graham-Maude Vol. 1, pp. 157–64.
41. *Ibid*, Vol. 1, pp. 130–55.
42. *Ibid*, p. 130.
43. Howard-Paret, p. 156.
44. Graham-Maude, Vol. 1, p. 140.
45. Howard-Paret, p. 161.
46. *Ibid*, p. 163.
47. *Ibid*, p. 168.
48. Graham-Maude, Vol. 1, p. 123.
49. Howard-Paret, p. 151.
50. *Ibid*, p. 156.
51. *Ibid*, p. 596.
52. Graham-Maude Vol. III, p. 157, and Howard-Paret, p. 622.
53. Howard-Paret, pp. 600 and 616.
54. *Ibid*, p. 617.
55. *Ibid*, pp. 330–47.
56. *Ibid*, pp. 184, 186, 189.
57. *Ibid*, pp. 92, 586.
58. *Ibid*, p. 93.
59. *Ibid*, pp. 30, 177, 585.
60. Graham-Maude Vol. III, pp. 104 and 585, Howard-Paret p. 594.
61. Howard-Paret pp. 593, 594.
62. *Ibid*, p. 627.
63. *Ibid*, p. 584.
64. *Ibid*, p. 579.

4 Scientific Strategy

If lessons from the past are fraught with ambiguities and dubious as a basis for strategic prescription, what of more schematised and abstract attempts to provide a guide to the effective employment of violence in inter-state relations? This chapter is concerned with the scientific or theoretical approach to strategy. The larger implications of theorising about human conduct were discussed in an earlier chapter and this examination of rational action theory and bargaining theories should be considered in this context. They are, however, more limited attempts to provide a rational basis for decision by offering a schema for making optimal choices in situations of conflict. They are scientific in the sense that not only do they have implicit entailments corresponding to those found in the logic and empirical conditions of the natural sciences, but they make explicit claims to authority based on their alleged capacity to generalise about rational conduct. If we think this way, their proponents argue, then we are more likely to arrive at a correct decision and so achieve a desired result.

The central thesis of this work is that strategic prescriptions entail a level of explanation in the form of an attestable theory. If strategy is to be scientific or to have the authority of science then certain preconditions must be satisfied for any postulated level of action derived from a theoretical construct to be deemed relevant and effective. There should be a ground on which to determine the authority of strategic prescription. Without it there is a serious problem of justifying strategic argument. This is especially important where this concerns the use of nuclear weapons.

As we shall see, strategic theorising in this century—the century of total war—often takes the form of a debate betwen rival schools of thought. In this respect it has a good deal in common with other attempts at basing prescription on theoretical postulates in the social sciences, most notably in economics. In this context the difficulty of resolving controversies, and the persistent open-endedness of debate, stems from the absence of common ground and the lack of generally accepted criteria for assessing the claims of rival theories. Practice then becomes the arbiter and either endorses one school or relegates the debate to increasingly abstract metaphysics. It is perhaps no coincidence that many strategic theorists who profess the scientific approach began their professional lives as economists.

However, I do not propose to repeat the arguments of a previous chapter by pursuing the problems of explaining human conduct in terms of their philosophical and epistemological implications. Rather I wish to examine more closely the aspirations of the scientific school to see what coherence or agreement exists and to relate specific prescriptions to practice to see whether there is any utility or even relevance in their application. The strategic theorists with whom I shall be concerned are primarily exercised by the problem of control over the use of violence in order to make it effective in some specific way, in terms of cost or damage limitation, for example. Control is seen largely in terms of capability or power; that is a closely defined ability to engage in specified actions directed to the achievement of a desired result. Violence is instrumental, and therefore rational, only when it can be controlled and so directed. As we shall see this is more often assumed or postulated than being the subject of explanation and so stipulating its terms and conditions as an instrument.

There are three main aspects of this notion of control or directed capability. The first is central to rational action theory and consists of control over the means-ends relationship. This postulates that a relatively limited end can be achieved through knowing the relevant strategy to adopt. Each such end has an optimum course of action—or strategy—that ensures success according to an external criterion such as cost. Such a strategy is value maximising. The second aspect is political in that control over the ends sought is dominant. Limits on levels and types of action are imposed and related to rules. This is the essence of limited war where tacit or explicit rules of engagement are understood by both sides in a conflict, or where one state declares its limits in order to reduce the area of engagement by reassuring other states as to its intentions and so averting a possible intervention and extension of the conflict. As we shall see, this form of control is highly important in defensive strategies where weapons procurement and engagement in conflict is potentially dangerous under nuclear conditions. The ends sought must be made clear to potential opponents to avert misinterpretation and consequent disaster. Finally, control over means is important and this has a technological aspect. Weapons are the visible symbol of national capability to use violence. In the pre-nuclear period they were essentially ambiguous in this respect. They could not be related to any specific end. Attempts to control them by relating them to specific purposes through regulation and disarmament failed largely because of this imprecision and the consequent inability to resolve national security dilemmas. In the nuclear age, although there is some ambiguity, the role of nuclear weapons can be more tightly related to security than was the case in the pre-nuclear period, and arms control, rather than disarmament, became a means of introducing rules governing function and use recognised by the nuclear powers. Thus uncontrolled arms races and competition in weapons procurement arising out of the imprecisions of defining offensive and defensive weapons were averted in the nuclear age by negotiation and self-imposed restraints, as well as by the physical qualities of these weapons that lent themselves to more precise definition.

A good deal of strategic debate centres around the putative significance of weapons systems and their effects on the pursuit of national interests, from security provision to the achievement of lesser political objectives through the means of violence. This has been generally true of all weapons, nuclear and non-nuclear. As we shall see the bomber was seen both as a strategic weapon capable of directly threatening national security and as a policing device capable of subduing unruly tribesmen at a cost significantly less than that of a punitive expedition.[1] It is interesting therefore to relate strategic debate concerning prescriptions for the proper use of weapons to actual practice. Consequently, two such examples, one non-nuclear and the other nuclear, will be examined in the next two chapters. These are the roles of tanks and aircraft and the role of ballistic missiles in achieving political objectives other than security.

In the case of the tank and aircraft it is instructive to relate various theories concerning mechanised warfare and strategic bombing to experience in war. Both weapons were innovatory and theories evolved prior to use. They bore the same relation therefore to the problem of instrumentality as is the present case with nuclear weapons. The prescriptive level associated with these theories is thus on a par with that provided by nuclear strategic theory. Of course with hindsight certain of these theories may be vindicated and others discredited as they are matched with experience itself. This is at best a dubious procedure and the point I wish to make in the following critique is not that *ex post facto* we can point to the inadequacies of the Douhet[2] approach to strategic success as exemplified by Bomber Command's abortive attempt to defeat Germany from the air, as that there is something inherently wrong about the theoretical argument in the first place. Similarly with nuclear weapons it would be a pity to fight a nuclear war in order to prove or disprove the hypotheses currently on offer.

Where innovation in weapons technology occurs, an appeal to the past as a means of justifying strategic prescription is invalid as a method. An appeal can of course be made to general strategic principles to which the new weapon can be related as a more expedient or less costly means of fulfilment than extant arms. The proof of this cannot however be related to experience and the force of the argument rests in the force of the principles themselves. As we shall see, a retreat in the direction of theory away from practical specifics is very often a recourse employed by strategic theorists when faced with imponderables in terms of action. In the case of the tank, for example, although Liddell Hart was conscious of the novelty of the armoured fighting vehicle, nevertheless he sought to place it within the framework of his theory of the 'indirect approach',[3] itself justified by carefully chosen historical examples. The combination of circumstances that made blitzkrieg successful was beyond his ken, and the Fabian tactics of the indirect approach and the avoidance of battle—field confrontation in the style of the trench warfare of the First World War gave the tank a different role to that perceived by Manstein, Guderian, and Hitler.

If then there is no prior experience of use, on what basis does the nuclear strategic theorist proceed in formulating his prescriptions for the instrumentality of nuclear weapons? It would seem that an authoritative basis for such prescriptions lies in a foundation of a-temporal propositions about the instrumentality of weapons under precisely stated and definable conditions. Within the structure of such a theory the technological aspects of new weapons—not merely their physical capabilities but their potential for achieving the intended result—can be assigned a precise significance. They are therefore subordinate to the overall requirements of the theory and in principle can be designed to fulfil a given function. It is not therefore a case of the theory fitting the facts, as the facts, in this case the technological performance of the weapons system, fitting the theory. Such a theory is of course more than a statement of the conditions for technical performance—control of means—and subsumes all three aspects of control defined earlier. The emphasis on technical capability in some of the strategic literature is as misguided as that which stresses general principles unrelated to the actual instruments of violence the weapons themselves.

However, before examining this aspect of strategic debate in detail I want to turn back to the 'scientific' aspect and consider its general characteristics. From this the more specific area of bargaining theory will be analysed. It should perhaps be said that while many writers on strategy explicitly reject a scientific approach to strategic problems, asserting in support of their position the inappropriateness of rigorous scientific method to human behaviour that depends on such factors as chance, morale, will, and material factors such as 'friction', terrain, and the weather, nevertheless in seeking a level of generality to support their critiques and prescriptions, they are implicitly pursuing science. As was argued in previous chapters any attempt to explain singular events— battles, campaigns, wars, etc. in terms of general propositions is innately theoretical, and to be successful must satisfy the appropriate logical and empirical entailments. The rejection of 'science' is often accompanied by the adoption of some covert theory not open to critical scrutiny.

In an earlier chapter I argued that any attempt at explanation that seeks to prescribe action must include some account of intention. The reasoning of actors in the human, as opposed to the physical domain, is central to the account. How is this incorporated in the formulation of a scientifically based strategic theory? Is it in turn explained or treated as mere epiphenomena? Earlier we saw Clausewitz asserting a common rationality as a basis for his strategic prescriptions. This was partly derived from and partly applied to, actual historical cases of the use of violence. At the tactical level, he argued, it was easier to apply a level of reasoning derived from generalisation although these were expressed in terms of rules or maxims. At the strategic level, however, because of the many imponderables governing human action it was more difficult. His solution, a hybrid between science and history 'testing the means employed' was criticised for its innate subjectivity and relativism. Once outside a framework of common assumptions and values in the form of a society understood by the commentator as part of his own practice as an actor, the assumptions about rationality become anachronistic and relative in character. Hence, Clausewitz, aware of this problem, eschewed, unlike many other strategists, references to classical antiquity for his sources and illustrations and used his immediate past going back no further than the cabinet wars of the previous century to support his argument. In this sense he was a contemporary historian. Indeed, rationalise as we may, it is hard to explain the significance of Caesar's auguries before crossing the Rubicon. What have the entrails of chickens to do with successful generalship?[4]

In the case of scientific strategy we have a different claim in respect of rationality. As we saw earlier a scientific theory of action has certain requirements which require fulfilment if the expression 'scientific' is to be more than merely analogous. Strictly speaking it is a-temporal, containing a level of generalisation which is empirically testable through derived hypotheses and which after successful test, allows us to claim that we have explained certain states of affairs. The type of explanation is one which subsumes a singular instance within a class of such instances governed by a general proposition loosely called a law. It is this kind of theory that can properly be described as scientific, and it is implicit in any claim or theoretical construct which seeks to offer an authoritative means of fulfilling stated ends. An applied science is only possible where there is an authenticated pure science. Strategic theorising seeks to direct practice so as to achieve desired results and to this extent implies, and is dependent on, a genuine theoretical basis. The problem of incorporating reasoning, intentions, etc. etc., within such a theoretical framework has been approached, as we shall see, through the aegis of decisional and bargaining theories. This is essentially a sub-theoretical level, confined in the main to means-ends relationships. I intend to argue that in turn it is dependent upon postulates that amount to asserting a general social theory. In seeking to treat rationality as a *theoretical* concept, as opposed to one derived from descriptive commonsense evaluations of contemporary social life, the argument moves into the realms of science. In practice, as we shall see, the implications of this argument are not appreciated or understood by many strategic theorists, who confine themselves to the more limited levels of abstraction which deals with optimal choice. They are concerned with defining ranges of options and selecting the most economic, cost effective, valuable, simplest, unconstraining, etc., course of action in the context of conflict.

In addition to this sort of theorising there is a further more restricted level constituting a form of operational research. This involves considerations relating to the choice of means in terms narrowly conceived of as performance but also more broadly as capability. Indeed there is often a tension between these two notions and weapons procurement programmes are often remote from the political contingencies they are ultimately intended to serve. Only very limited variables can be considered in planning the research and development of weapons systems and given the time scale involved from blueprint to deployment, these rarely include the intentions of those who use them and those whom they are used against. As we have seen, capability does not constitute mere technical performance and the latter must be defined within the concept of role with its political connotations. In the context of battle the problem is simplified to some extent by the need to outmatch the opponent's weapons and the pursuit of battlefield victories. In the context of politics the problem is more complex given the relationship of military threat to successful diplomacy. The introduction of certain types of weapons systems can have a counter-productive effect, either creating crises or nullifying a national position—in the jargon having a stabilising or de-stabilising effect.

All these theoretical endeavours are characteristic of the scientific approach to strategy, and recipes and prescriptions derived from them are urged on or by political practitioners as a means of achieving desired ends. Before examining them in detail let us consider what is distinctive in this school compared with the classical approach. The first point to make is that there is a heavy emphasis on technology in the scientific approach. Weapons systems are seen more in terms of their performance than in their use. Clausewitz, and other classical strategic thinkers such as Jomini,[5] paid little attention to technological innovations in the conduct of war. Although there were some changes in weaponry in their time it is true to say that these were not radical. War for them was practised on the basis of timeless principles, and although human factors such as morale, luck, skill, talent, etc., were variables, nevertheless they were constant in terms of their relevance to success in war. Weapons as such, received little consideration; all the radical innovations had occurred in the areas or organisation and logistics. Even these were not considered of permanent significance. The organisation for total war in Revolutionary and Napoleonic France was thought by Clausewitz to be an aberration; a deviation from rational war.

The basic arms had been in existence for a considerable period—the foot-soldier, armed with short range inaccurate fire-arms; the horse-soldier, lightly armed with lance and sword; and the artilleryman, and bombardier, with their relatively imprecise means of long range devastation, had been the staples of warfare for a long time. The navy, in some ways more innovative in terms of technology, was deemed, in continental terms at least, to be peripheral to the main zone of combat—the land. Change in warfare was largely in the tactical areas with permutations in the deployment and organisation of these basics. Military genius lay in the ability to manoeuvre for success.

Even in the great military successes of Napoleon little in the way of technological change in warfare occurred, apart from improvements in existing weapons, such as the rifle and some refinements in explosives. Napoleon's successes were attributed to his talent and to the organisation of the French nation for war, based on central control over munitions production, manpower, and taxation, as well as by his ability to draw on the resources of the conquered territories. With the exception of Russia, France was the most populous European state and, following the Revolution, had a strong centralised government capable of mobilising the resources of a developed economy for the purposes of war. Napoleon was defeated by the emulation of other European countries, notably Prussia, who, too, prepared for prolonged and total war, and eventually succeeded in overwhelming him with superior forces. The role of Britain, providing subsidies for opponents of France, diversion in the Iberian Peninsula, and using the navy for blockade, was a significant one, but central to the defeat of Napoleon was the appearance of large standing armies raised by conscription and supported by national taxation, directed by governments determined on a complete and not partial military success. It was the scale of this twenty years war that so impressed Clausewitz and others, and not its innovations in weapons technology.

Another distinctive feature of contemporary scientific strategy which distinguishes it from the classical school is its concern for defence or for what is called the 'strategic level'. This is primarily a preoccupation with the provision of security for the nation-state. As we shall see later in this chapter, types of bargaining theory are directly related to the inhibiting effects of nuclear stalemate between the major nuclear powers and the problem of deterrence. The avoidance of a suicidal total war, rather than an acceptance of its risks, is a major constraint upon the formulation of defence and foreign policies and a central element in contemporary strategic doctrine, although there are some strategists who incorporate risk-taking into their strategic prescriptions. The problem of security, or the defence of the state at all levels, from the provision of immunity from invasion or destruction, to the protection of the regime and the prevailing political system from terrorism and subversion, was not so significant for the classical strategists, who either assumed limits on war as a consequence of political rationality, did so or because they were only concerned with the tactical level, or simply attaining battle-field victory. Guerilla war was recognised as a phenomenon, but relevant to strategic thought. In any case wars were limited as much by the relatively restricted technology of the day as by the thinking associated with it. The impetus to innovate in weaponry in order to achieve total victory did not exist.

As a consequence of this concern for security, and the problem of avoiding general war as an irrational method of achieving political objectives, contemporary strategic theorists have been much occupied with the notion of threat. Although classical strategists were concerned with what might be called the psychological dimension of war—victory consists of breaking the opponent's will to resist—they were not much involved either in relating this to political objectives or with formulating the necessary conditions. Battle-field victories were the objectives. The ramifications of the dimension of threat, ranging from the use of deception to the subleties of escalation, playing upon the opponent's values and susceptibilities, indeed the art of winning without actually fighting, are largely absent from the prescriptions of the classical school.[6] In scientific strategic thought, although force is an important element in achieving political objectives, where these last are limited and present no direct challenge to the integrity of the adversary state, it is generally considered better to operate at the level of threat rather than its implementation. Not only is this more cost-effective, it also lessens the risk of an active conflict breaking its limits and threatening the overall nuclear inhibition. Diplomatic manoeuvrings, with the threat of inimical action, are thus central to this approach to strategy. A threat realised, in a sense, indicates a strategic failure, rather than a success. It loses its utility. And it also poses the problems of *effective* action in a concrete form once it is put into practice.

The dimension of threat is largely psychological with the imponderables—the possibility of bluff, and credibility—acting as a check on precipitate action on the part of the threatened state. This uncertainty strengthens rather than weakens the force of the threat, since the onus for action is placed on the adversary. The threatened state cannot be certain either of the strength of will or of the effective capability of the threatener to implement the threat. However, once the bluff, if bluff it be, is called, then a different situation arises since the threatened state clearly is either driven into a corner having no alternative but to fight or surrender, or sees some prospect of success in the context. The principle of a golden bridge is as relevant to strategy conducted by threats as by action.

Although this dimension of strategy is especially relevant to the nuclear age, with its inhibition on general nuclear exchanges between the nuclear powers, it is by no means irrelevant to the pre-nuclear period. To refer to an example; Benes bowed to Hitler's threats as did Chamberlain and Daladier and virtually surrendered Czechoslovakia.[7] A year later Beck, supported by the same politicians refused to come to terms and Poland suffered invasion and conquest. In one case the struggle was deemed hopeless and in the other not. In *military* terms the two situations were very similar, with Czechoslovakia and Poland isolated and incapable of offering serious resistance to the German army. In political terms the will of the Allies had hardened in the intervening year and the counterthreat, not of military support for Poland, but a total war, was made to Hitler. He found it incredible and accepted the challenge believing he could win the contest, as indeed he did. He did not win the war that was eventually fought but then neither did his opponents.

The implications of threats as a coherent strategy will be examined in the context of bargaining theory. The point here is that strategic prescriptions which rely on threats of inimical action, not merely military in character but including sanctions of various kinds, are significantly different from those which are concerned with the problems of achieving battle-field victory. They are most closely tied up with the achievement of political objectives and are removed from the more obvious aspects of the use of violence as a political instrument. But although removed they are not unconnected and contemporary strategy offers a spectrum of forms of action designed to achieve compliance. That the more overtly military is relatively subordinate to less direct forms of violence, is a reflection of the strategic impasse imposed by parity in nuclear weapons between the major nuclear powers. The problem for strategic theory is how to make violence under nuclear conditions effective as a political instrument, and at the same time to limit and control it. Attempts at prescriptions of this kind will be examined later in this chapter and in the next.

Before examining them the theoretical construct most central to strategic reasoning—rational action theory[8]—should be considered. On the practical level almost all purposive action is postulated on the premise of expectations of proper action on the part of others. No action designed to achieve an end in a social context can ignore the possibility of responses and some estimate of their appropriateness. This is particularly true of strategy and its attempts to prescribe effective action. The status and nature of these expectations as represented by rational action theorists will be examined in this chapter. The notion of rationality is bound up with what counts as an appropriate action or appropriate response. Rational action theory is primarily concerned with establishing a case for appropriate or instrumental action under conditions of risk or competition. It postulates a means-end relationship in terms of conditions for success relative to some explicit criterion such as economy, or simplicity. Rationality therefore consists of making a *correct* choice.

There is some ambiguity in the concept of rationality as was seen in a previous chapter. To call the choice of appropriate instrumental action *rational* is merely to make an external judgement. The question of the grounds for appropriateness—the theoretical basis for the choice—is left open. However, we are not concerned with justifying theory; its justification lies in whether it does in fact support practice by prescribing effective action. But rationality is also conceived of as acting in accordance with rules and principles or acting in accordance to some normative values. Assessments of rational action on this basis are clearly evaluative and justificatory and do not imply any reference to theoretical explanation. There is confusion often between establishing a rational basis to action, in the form of an adequate theory independent of the reasoning of the actors, and the assumptions of a common rationality operating in the world of practice and derived from the assumptions of the actors themselves.

Since we are concerned with instrumental action and with prescriptions relating to instrumentality, rationality as a normative judgement is irrelevant to our purposes. In this context expectations of proper action relate not to social conceptions of what is appropriate, based on norms and values, but to predictions based on a validated theory. The successful outcome—the achievement of the ends sought—should be in principle predictable on the basis of the specification of the conditions, necessary and sufficient, and the governing law. It may be the case that this turns out to be a theory of rationality as much as a theory of action, but whatever its explanatory focus, it constitutes a theory and not a form of evaluative judgement innately subjective and culturally related.

Rational action theory has a number of synonyms, being variously called preference theory, decision theory, utility theory, conflict resolution theory, etc. The common denominator is what von Mises called *praxeology*,[9] that is the set of conditions that govern the choice a rational agent would make in a given situation. This corresponds to the Popperian notion of the 'logic of the situation'[10] discussed earlier. A basic stipulation is a fixed set of preferences or ends with one preferred outcome. The set of preferences may be ranked according to various criteria. A range of optional courses of action is open to the agent in inducing the desired state of affairs. What governs his choice of strategy depends on reference to a governing condition. Such conditions are various; cost is an obvious criterion and the optimal course of action that produces the result with economy is preferred. There are others such as simplicity, speed, and control. Given the human context of decision with its uncertainties and variables a simple plan carries less risk than a complex one. It is also more easily understood by an adversary and, as we shall see, communication is an important element in contests of this kind especially under nuclear conditions. Speed may also be important especially when exploiting relative advantages beteween states as well as reducing costs. Control over each state of the plan is a necessity, especially where threats rather than implementation are the prime instrument of policy.

But control also means the restriction of the strategy to the ends sought without the means changing the ends or impinging on other areas of policy. The choice of means should not have consequences unforeseen or uncontrolled for the domestic and international environments of the actors. Finally, conformity to the value system of the actor may be a limiting condition of the adopted strategy. This is particularly relevant where ideology is an important component of the political system represented by the actor. It will be seen from this that cost is the only quantifiable element and even this is misleading. Everyone knows that Pyrhhic victories are no victories at all, but how can the costs of Fabian tactics be assessed? Equally, given the finite nature of material resources, expenditure on one course of action precludes another. For example, it was a matter of considerable controversy during the Second World War that resources spent on Bomber Command deprived the army and navy of supplies and equipment necessary to the achievement of the common aim—battle-field victory.[11] At the military level bombing German cities did not produce the desired result. Indeed towards the end of the war when the problems of peace and the achievement of a desired *political* result assumed prominence, such bombing was seen as counter-productive.[12] The air force, for its part, insisted that if resources given to the army and navy had been diverted to their service and a full scale bombing strategy adopted, the war would have been won earlier with less cost.[13] The point here is that relating costs in terms of the requisite resources to produce a desired state of affairs is not the precise calculation it is sometimes represented to be. This is equally true when weapons systems are the subject of choice and attention is concentrated on their performative qualities rather than on the circumstances of their actual use.

A basic assumption of rational action theory is perfect information. A knowledge of the range of options open both to the agent and to the adversary is a necessity if the adopted strategy is to be effective. This leaves open the grounds at this state for determining what constitutes an effective means. Whatever these may be, complete knowledge of all such means must exist if an optimum choice is to be made. Equally the range of response open to the adversary must also be known in advance of making such a choice. Apart from the fundamental problem of determining instrumentality, there is the obvious difficulty of acquiring such information. Secrecy and deception are central to the use of threats, and uncertainty not only as to intention but also as to capability is actually promoted by states.[14] This is perhaps more true of the pre-nuclear period and of actual violent conflict itself. In the nuclear period with its heavy emphasis on defensive deterrence the credibility of the threat is dependent on its demonstration in material terms. Hence an acceptance of surveillance and a tolerable level of espionage is characteristic of relations between the nuclear powers. This is not true however of the sub-strategic level, and one element of NATO strategy is the active promotion of uncertainty of Allied response to Soviet aggression; as we shall see, there are special difficulties in applying deterrent strategies to protect allies.

Information is essentially an apprehension of all the relevant facts appertaining to a contested situation. This poses a problem of what criterion of relevance to adopt prior to action. As we have seen earlier in discussion of capability and power, a knowledge of these is either based on a generalising theory that relates capacity to action so that, given prior necessary and sufficient conditions and a law, a specified result obtains, or is derived *ex post facto* from action itself and supports expectations that may or may not be realised in practice. Knowledge of an opponent's capabilities thus has two possible grounds, and only the first can sustain a scientific strategy.

The problem is compounded when the 'facts' include the intentions of the adversary. Given the complexity of the context of reasoning, that includes a reciprocal element in that the actor's putative reasoning is also incorporated in that of the adversary and vice versa, it is difficult to stipulate fixed intentions. In practice the problem of establishing intentions either fixed or changing as the contest develops, is avoided, either by stressing material capabilities as a substitute for reasons and indulging in worst case analysis, or by making basic assumptions that are both general and relatively stable allowing for continuity of planning. Colin Gray for example asserts a permanent Soviet threat.[15] Indeed this has been a basic postulate of Western strategy, foreign, and defence policies, since the late 1940s. He based this postulate upon a number of assertions about the nature of the Soviet political system. They are normative. The Soviet Union is a police state, centrally controlled from Moscow and the Soviet people, largely hostile to the regime, are kept under control by repression and force. The Soviet state is imperialist in character and controls Eastern Europe through force and intimidation. Further expansion is desired both in Europe and in Asia and a variety of means of achieving this are espoused, including war itself. Even nuclear war comes into this category.

There is an inherent circularity in this argument. The postulate of Soviet intentions is based upon capability. But this capability is in turn the product of the postulate. Reducing inter-state relations to the level of what each state is in principle physically capable of in terms of inflicting damage on each other, produces a situation of constant threat. And of course, actions taken to guard against 'the present danger' exacerbate this threat. Indeed the only logical way out of this situation is to implement the threat and to fight and win a nuclear war, as Gray argues.[16]

The Clausewitzian notion of instrumental violence with its associated rationality as a controlled means of achieving political objectives is abandoned in favour of a mechanical relationship between destructive capabilities. This is the consequence of conceiving of threats not in terms of intentions but of capabilities. It could be argued that this is a product of the perceived military weakness of the democracies in the 1930s and the appeasement of Hitler that led directly to an unavoidable and barely winnable total war.[17] If this is the case, it is based on a tendentious interpretation of events, that bears little or no relationship to the nuclear situation. Why the Soviet Union should want to *use*, as apart from counter-threaten, its nuclear weapons, or directly challenge the territorial integrity of its neighbours, is an unexamined and unresolved question. It is assumed too readily that a belief in Marxism-Leninism, or whatever passes for it in current orthodoxy, directs action. It is perhaps significant that when accommodation is sought with the Soviet Union and genuine negotiations undertaken, the ideological element in statements of policy tend to be minimised or disappear altogether. And this is equally true for the Soviet Union. It may be the case of course, that this form of ideological expression is designed to persuade citizens to accept the material sacrifices of defence provision rather than serving as genuine grounds for motivation.

At any rate this interpretation of Soviet intentions is heavily subjective, as is its counterpart in the USSR. It is, however, convenient through its very simplicity as a basis for 'rational' defence and strategic planning. In an actual contest, rather than as a means of avoiding the difficulties of planning for war in the long term development of weapons systems in relation to a threat lacking in empirical specification, the problem of *intention* is highly important. The case of the Cuban missiles crisis which will be discussed later, illustrates this. As important, is the question of will or the determination to pursue or defend interests. This again is not a factor that lends itself to quantification or to precise statement. It is directly associated to the actual contest and not something that can be predicted in advance. Yet knowledge of how important an issue is to an adversary and what costs, both human and material he is willing to accept, is a necessary part of the information factor in planning a successful strategy. This element is clearly related to the character of the political system, to factors such as morale, and to perceptions of the consequences of surrender. A contrast between the collapse of the Russian war effort in 1917 and the acceptance of the heavy casualties of the 'Great Patriotic War' illustrates this point.

This leads on to another basic assumption of rational action theory, adherence to common value systems. In the light of what was said earlier this seems paradoxical given the incompatibility of Marxism-Leninism and liberal-democratic ideologies. An ideological conflict can only be resolved by total war, by conversion, or the abandonment of the struggle. Wars of religion tend, as Clausewitz would put it, to the extreme, and so are inherently irrational. Under nuclear conditions it is hard to visualise success in such a context. However, if we accept the basic assumption that coexistence is precluded between states that differ in their political systems and ideological preferences, then all conflicts between them are fundamentally insoluble. No negotiation can be viable and no agreement binding. This is akin to the attitude taken towards Hitler by Britain after the German occupation of Prague and the breach of the Munich Treaty. War then becomes inevitable since negotiations are nugatory.

That this is not the case in practice can be demonstrated by numerous agreements that have been negotiated between the Soviet Union and Western States and the common acceptance of a range of non-political regulations and rules that govern the conduct of states. Despite accusations of bad faith and of breaches of agreement made by both sides this has not prevented attempts, often successful, in reaching further agreements. Neither side has in practice opted out of the *diplomatic* system since the end of the Cold War in 1955.[18] However, it is clear that they do not share a common *value* system.[19] And if this is the case it is hard to see how preferences for outcome can be evaluated within the framework of rational action theory. This is equally true for assessing the choice of means and related costs.

Nevertheless, some adherence to a common framework of rules and values must be postulated if rationality is to have definition. It may be the case that where states enter into negotiation they have a common interest in bringing it to a successful conclusion even where they are seeking relative advantages. In violent conflict or in making threats this minimal consensus is lacking except where explicit limits are stated by the contenders. Prescriptions based on threats of violence to be effective in producing the desired result, must be able to stipulate the adversary's value preferences in assessing his likely responses. As we shall see where escalation is discussed this is not an easy matter. In short a common rationality presupposes common ends and mutual acceptance of relevant means in relationship to those ends. It need hardly be said that worst case analysis and an emphasis on capability nullifies this approach.

Finally, control and communication are necessary conditions. In effect this means not only effective control over capability—the means—and the ability to communicate at all levels of the command and operational structures, but also making clear to the adversary what is at stake, what is being threatened and the range of possible further actions. This is especially important within the context of nuclear weapon systems, given their unprecedented accuracy, destructive capacity, and the very short operational time factor. The link between the political dimension and that of technology is very close in the nuclear age. This was not the case in the pre-nuclear period. For example, Hitler could regard the threat contained in the British and French ultimatum in 1939 as unsupported in military terms.[20]

A further dimension of communication is the problem, particularly for the democracies, of controlling political dissent or inducing assent in circumstances that cannot be fully divulged to the public. This aspect of political constraint will be discussed in a later chapter but in effect governments operate at two levels of communication; with the adversary (another state), and with the electorate. In a critical international situation, often heightened or sensationalised by the media, a difficult bargaining situation may be made more difficult by the necessity to achieve a consensus between political factions. Any appearance of weakness in this respect is open to exploitation by the adversary. The Suez crisis in Britain and the Vietnam War are examples of this problem[21] while the Cuban Missiles crisis was an example of successful manipulation and control over the media on the part of the US government. Arms control negotiations in particular are prone to this kind of problem, when displays of strength or the development of weapons systems for purposes of bargaining are misunderstood or exploited for political purposes by domestic factions. Governments are forced to respond to these pressures, since while succeeding in its tragedy is one goal, so is staying in power an overriding goal!

To sum up the basic stipulations of rational action theory; there must be a fixed set of preferred outcomes or states of affairs, sometimes termed goals; a set of capabilities or optional courses of actions that can secure these objectives; perfect information as to what these are for the adversary; adherence to a common set of values and the rules governing the contest; and complete control over operations and perfect communication internally and externally. These are the basic elements in formulating an appropriate strategy, that is, the choice of an optimal course of action that leads to a desired result according to some related governing condition such as economy. The central theoretical postulate is the relation between means and ends—between capability or action and the achievement of the objective. The central thesis is one of a common rationality shared by the actor and his adversaries. Without this, however rational the action may seem to the actor, it will not be so considered by those whose behaviour he is trying to influence. Their response may be contrary to the expectations of the initiator and so render the intiative ineffective.

The question before us is, is this a form of practical reasoning characteristic of a certain culture and incapable of providing a ground for prescriptions that carries any more authority than tenacity of beliefs? If this is the case, given the inherent ambiguity of the basic postulates and the difficulty of making clear empirical references, either to situations or to observable conditions, there are likely to be a variety of competing and contradictory 'strategies'. Choice therefore becomes an arbitrary matter. Alternatively, is rational action theory theoretical? By this is meant, does it provide a method of determining *effective* action through a knowledge of its governing conditions?

According to one writer at least, Michael Nicholson,[22] rational action is based on a principle of choice causal in character. It can be deduced what an actor will do under certain specified conditions. He argues that choice can be analysed so that under specified conditions X, actor Y wishes to obtain Z with A (where A constitutes a limiting condition such as economy, profit, ease, simplicity, etc.). A range of options or courses or actions B C D E, etc., are open to the actor. Of these only one, say B, will obtain Z with A. Therefore Y will do B. This choice is a necessity and is causal rather than merely rational. In his view goal-directed theories follow the standards of hypothetico-deductive explanation—covering law theory—except that 'some of the initial postulates involve statements which assert goal-seeking behaviour'.[23]

In his treatment of causation Nicholson argues that in the case of goal-directed behaviour, the goal which is the 'cause' of the action actually succeeds rather than precedes the act. It is the end state of the means adopted. The choice of action however precedes the action and therefore constitutes its cause. His construction of choice under risk consists of (1) an initial set of conditions (2) the definition of each possible consequent state of affairs (3) a numerical value of utility for each of these (4) a statement of probability for the occurrence of each such state of affairs. The optimum choice of action depends upon the multiplication of (3) by (4). Thus the actor has a set of preferences and a set of perceived likely possibilities. The one that reflects his preferences is the actual choice of action. Given this the actual choice can be predicted by an observer.[24]

There are a number of points to be made about this. First, it will be seen that what is asserted as predictable is the choice an actor makes, not whether it will in fact induce any particular state of affairs. The problem of *effective* action is not addressed. The prediction of choice is itself based upon a postulate of rationality and not causation as claimed. The agent is not in fact compelled to make this choice—on the argument it is simply a *rational* choice. This is not to deny that if it can be known in advance what actions under certain circumstances will be taken by an adversary this will be very useful to the strategist. It will provide a ground for expectations of proper action.

But the argument turns on probability and not prediction. The initial possibilities latent in a situation are turned into probabilities through the analysis of past experience. But this is an inadequate basis, as we have seen, for projections into the future. While the actor may be indeed have intentions that reflect preferences and an estimate of probabilities based on his historical view, these do not entail any action at all. As we have seen, reasons are not causes and no actions are entailed by them. Treating intentions as causes is mistaken unless in turn they are explained causally and incorporated into a general behavioural theory. But the notion of choice implies a measure of free will. Thus while we can explain action in terms of the actor's reasons, this form of explanation does not entitle either generalisation or the assertion of a governing principle of rationality. We may regard, as representatives of western culture, rain dancing (or praying for rain) as irrational, but this is not the case for those who practice it and reference to *their* reasons certainly explains their actions.

What is required, if we are to have a genuine theory, is some explanation as to why specific courses of action can produce a specific state of affairs so that replication of the relevant conditions and selection of an appropriate means can induce what is desired. In other words we need to establish a ground for claims relating to effective action, not grounds for evaluating behaviour as rational or irrational on the basis of some normative principle.

If, for example, we look at the problem of the rationality of ends there are three distinct positions. The assertion of rational ends may imply a principle of rationality which is normative in character, the pursuit of happiness, liberty, or the maximisation of satisfaction. This is culturally derived and related to ethical or social norms. Empirical references will be multifarious and non-generalisable. Secondly, a rational end may simply be one that is attainable in terms of the satisfaction of specific preconditions. This implies a theory, causal in character, that allows us to determine what is, and what is not, attainable in the light of our knowledge. Once the conditions have been satisfied, the end, or state of affairs, is the inevitable result. Finally, we can conceive of a rational end in terms of attainment, but only on the basis of probability through reference to practical experience. This is non-theoretical in character and incapable of supporting prediction.

To illustrate these distinctions, Hitler had a clearly defined end in wanting a colonial empire in Europe.[25] He believed that this was attainable, given the satisfaction of certain conditions, namely; German unity, the defeat of opposing states, and racial purity. His reasons for wanting such an empire were not rational in that they were based on a false racist theory, a belief in the application of natural selection to nation-states that could not be demonstrated, and an economic theory of autarchy that was not cost-effective. The grounds for these beliefs were demonstrably false. But showing that these beliefs were false does not make the end he sought irrational. The conquest of Europe was attainable. In this sense it was a rational end. Taking another example, the rationality of landing human beings on the moon is irrelevant to the question as to whether a moon landing is a rational goal in terms of its practicality. The possession of a grounded and adequate theory enabled a landing. Discussion as to whether this was a rational act turns into discussion about justification and not about instrumentality.

So the larger question as to whether the end is rational or not turns on whether it constitutes a state of affairs which in principle is attainable. This implies that a course of action—a means—exists which is instrumental in achieving this. To hold an end without this connection is to possess an aim or an aspiration. In short, rational ends are conditional upon the existence of an instrumental means and not upon ulterior reasons which are assessed for their rationality. It is clear from this that only the last two distinctions are relevant to strategy.

Turning to the question of the rationality of means, or more specifically, of the means-end relationship, we come to the problem of determining what constitutes an appropriate course of action. Taking the previous example, while Hitler's reasoning was fallacious, his choice of method was alarmingly successful, at least, in the initial stages of war. In assuming the reasons for success and for failure we are in fact advancing a theory of instrumentality that establishes what constitutes the best of the options or strategies available to the actor. But if what concerns us is determining amongst a number of choices relative to an actor's preferred ends, on what criteria can we determine their relevance? To talk of options is to talk of alternative courses of action which will produce a desired state of affairs conditional on the satisfaction or non-satisfaction of certain criteria, such as economy, etc. One of these courses of action will be optimal, according to the criterion employed. Clearly, this depends on the actor's own preference and on what he thinks are options open to him. The observer or commentator therefore, in asserting a list of options and prescribing one of them as optimal, must justify his selection in terms of rationality. And this turns on whether or not he has an adequate theory that provides a basis for stipulating effective action. Without this then the context of preference is part of the *actor's* reasoning. The options perceived by *him* are relevant to any analysis of his actions, and not those imposed on him by an external observer.

Secondly, and related to earlier discussion on theory, to talk of options implies alternative courses of actions effective in achieving a result, but not necessarily in conformity with the stipulated governing condition. The adage about killing a cat springs to mind. But on what grounds are options options? What provides the basis for the assertion of instrumentality? Is there in fact a theory? All this is prefatory to the following examination of examples of theorising in the field of strategic studies. All those who have contributed to this genre believe that in some way they are helping to provide a rational basis for choice in the field of strategy. Some of them indeed have acted as advisers to governments and have been deeply involved in the world of practice.[26]

Bargaining theory, games theory, systems analysis, crisis management theory, theory of interdependent decision, and so on, are all variants of rational action theory. They assert a method of choosing an optimal strategy that will produce a desired result in an adversarial situation.[27] As such they are relevant not only to the use or threat of violence in contests between states but to a wide variety of situations, including those where there are substantial areas of agreement between the contestants, as in the negotiation of business contracts, or economic treaties within the framework of national or international and regional institutions. In this context I am concerned with the dimension of violence. This dimension is omnipresent in international relations and underlies all negotiation. The military capabilities of states have a relevance, however remote this may appear in the conduct of diplomacy. This is as true of economic negotiations, especially where these have a bearing on manufacturing and technology within a national context,[28] as of overt military treaties and combinations.

Bargaining theory is thus concerned with winning a contest using the capacity of the state for violence as its main instrument. Creating such a capacity in the form of what is euphemistically called a defence policy is directly linked to promoting the chances of success in an inherently competitive world. The ultimate contest is of course general war and some conception of the form this might take enters into every defence policy however small and vulnerable the state. Although not a likely protagonist, a small militarily weak power may occupy a pivotal position *vis-à-vis* other moe powerful contenders in terms of its geo-political position or perhaps mineral wealth.[29] Given that the possibility of a general war acts as a parameter for all states and that alliances and alignments formed under the aegis of the major powers provide an opportunity for the smaller powers to bargain, this opportunity exists in a myriad of situations in international politics. The use or threat of force is not a prerogative of the major powers and to a greater or lesser extent it exists, latent or actual, in all inter-state relations.

Bargaining theory is thus not a matter which concerns only the Super-powers but is applicable to all states or agents whatever their absolute capacity for violence. In the main however, bargaining theorists, in so far as they have referred to actual practice, have confined themselves largely to the prevailing contest between the Soviet Union and the United States and their allies. Other contests between smaller powers, such as for example, between India and Pakistan, have been treated either in terms of their relevance to the larger contest or as irrelevant.[30] The point here is that whatever the empirical reference, if bargaining theory is to have a genuine application to human action it must have universal qualities and not be confined to what is in historical, if not in human terms, a limited temporal contest.

Having said this, bargaining theorists, although concerned with general war, have in the main confined themselves to limited contests within the framework of an inhibition on general war imposed by nuclear parity between the major powers. Only comparatively recently has attention turned to major war-winning strategies.[31] However, the controlled use of violence related to the achievement of a limited objective is the most characteristic aspect of a bargaining theory scenario. Acceptance of tacit ruls of engagement and an element of accommodation in conflicts are basic assumptions. Total war is precluded since it constitutes a contest decided only by the elimination of an adversary, and bargaining ceases to be of significance in such an apocalyptic struggle. Although, as we shall see, this does not preclude the *threat* of such a war in a bargaining strategy. And even in total war, as both major wars in this century have shown, bargaining is not totally absent either between enemies or allies where questions of relative national advantage are perceived. The principle of unconditional surrender was devised to avoid divisions in the alliance during the Second World War and was not altogether successful in this.[32] Whether bargaining could take place under conditions of total nuclear war is unknown, but it cannot be excluded *tout court* and indeed the notion of winning such a contest implies some advantages in victory.

Turning to specific examples of this genre, T. C. Schelling[33] has stated the main assumptions most clearly. According to him they are first, the presumption of common interest that is the basis of any bargain; secondly, rationality in the form of an optimalising or value-maximising behaviour; and thirdly, 'an explicit and mutually consistent value-system'.[34] The bargain sought is not what is termed mini-max, that is total gains for the victor and total losses for the loser but 'gaining relative to one's own value system'[35] through mutual accommodation and the avoidance of mutually damaging behaviour. The use of the *threat* of force rather than its actual implementation is central to this approach. As he puts it.

A theory of deterrence would be in effect a theory of the skilful non-use of military force ... the best course of action for each participant depends on what he expects the other participant to do. The deterrence concept requires that there be both conflict and common interest between the parties involved; it is as inapplicable to a situation of pure and complete antagonism of interest as it is to a case of pure and complete common interest.[36]

Bargaining is thus conceived of as entailing a measure of agreement accompanied by a measure of coercion. The main constituents of a bargain are, a definition 'of the essentials of the situation and of the behaviour in question'[37]; a mutual value system; mutual communication; rationality; credibility of the threat; and the capability to enforce it. Bargaining power is derived from the capacity to inflict damage on an opponent. Schelling distinguishes this from force, where superiority in the physical means of violence precludes bargaining and political objectives may be formulated and pursued without fear of countervailing action, since this can be overcome at an acceptable cost. In a typical bargaining situation the use or threat of force is minimised or strictly limited and compliance when faced with a threat of inimical action is not surrender. A balance must therefore be sought between the level of threat and the object sought. This is of course very similar to the Clausewitzian notion of the rational use of violence when the means and the ends must be in a commensurable relation.

According to Schelling 'the power to hurt is bargaining power. To exploit it is diplomacy.'[38] Violence is always a factor in inter-state relations and its calculated use one of the means open to the state for the fulfilment of political objectives. This is, however, at a sub-strategic level. Given the limitations set by his restrictions on use we can see that security considerations do not enter into it. Contests that raise the question of security are in principle unlimited, entailing as they do the very survival of the state. So although the world of states is seen in this approach in realpolitik terms there are overall limits placed on the use of violence: within them violence can be instrumental. Again this echoes Clausewitz's view that the tendency of war to develop to the extreme is aberrational. The normal form of war is limited war.

Much therefore depends upon control over the form and use of a threat of violence as a diplomatic ploy. What in practice are these controls and constraints? If we are to have more than a definition of rationality in the use of violence it is essential that conditions relating to control are stipulated and capable of empirical reference. As we saw earlier this was a question largely ignored by Clausewitz. Schelling attempts to state these; it is necessary for the state seeking to employ 'the diplomacy of violence',[39] to know what is important to the adversary state in terms of priorities and preferences; it must be capable of threatening them and of showing that this threat is credible: the opponent in turn must be aware of what the threat of inimical action is related to and what constitutes an adequate response; and finally the threatened state must have relative freedom of action so as to be able to make this response. An effective threat, to sum up, exists where it is credible in terms of the capability of the threatener; where the threatened action is commensurable with the end sought, where this nexus is understood by the threatened state; where the losses on the possible implementation of the threat are seen to be certain and where they are greater than compliance with the desired course of action (on inaction) would produce.

Although this approach to strategy is primarily concerned with the use of the threat of force at the sub-strategic level, it will be seen that it is also relevant to defensive deterrence. This will be discussed later, but the point here is that security enters into the situation where a state is concerned with inducing restraint or deterring forms of inimical action directed at important national interests. The United Kingdom, for example, at one level is concerned with deterring a major nuclear attack through its riposte capacity and at another is concerned to counter blockade or commerce raiding. Consequently the creation of a counter-blockade force is seen as having a strategic priority. It could be argued that the limits set on violence by the constraints of deterrence actually increase the risk of limited threats of this kind, making them not merely possible without the prospects of their development into major nuclear war, but attractive as a means of applying pressure on a state. It has been argued that the growth of the Soviet Navy is a response to this view. The whole subject of constraints and limits on violence in inter-state relations will be considered in a later chapter. Nevertheless, the point may be made that the sub-strategic level may be extremely important to a state, so important as to risk nuclear war over it.

This is particularly relevant to another variant on the bargaining approach to strategy. This is the escalation theory of Herman Kahn[40] and its emphasis on what is called the rationality of irrationality. Escalation is a process of graduated and controlled responses in a conflict. Kahn is concerned with a strategy which will bring success through the conscious and controlled use of risk-taking at various levels of threat. As he puts it, he seeks to clarify, 'relatively general principles, more or less true for all the interactions of escalation and negotiation in which a fear of further escalation and a desire not to set undesirable precedents or to weaken desirable restraints are present'.[41]

Thus both contending states operate in a common milieu sharing common values and a common rationality. The contest is limited in character and governed by tacit rules understood by both parties. Although violence both in use and as a threat is the chief instrument of manipulation, it is strictly controlled and limited. The chief strategem employed is to force the opponent to face a higher level of inimical action if he persists in adhering to his position, thus placing the onus on him to 'escalate' the contest. He then has a choice between facing the costs of this higher level of action or accepting the costs of compliance. The assumption is that both sides wish to avoid a general nuclear exchange, given its inherent irrationality. Nevertheless, the state able to demonstrate its willingness to move closer to this risk is likely to succeed in intimidating its opponent and thus gaining its object.

In appearing to threaten what is essentially an irrational action—a suicidal nuclear war—the state that does so is employing a 'rationality of irrationality' ploy. As Kahn puts it 'There is a rational advantage to be gained from irrational conduct or from the expectation of irrational conduct'.[42] This presupposes a common rationality as well as the possession of a capability for violence which is both effective and controllable. Control over the development of the contest is also essential using a technique of graduated response clearly communicated to the adversary placing the responsibility for the next level of action on him. The issue at stake must also be clearly indicated. This reverses Clausewitz's dictum that means-ends should be commensurable, for the imbalance postulated between means and ends might well result in an out-and-out nuclear exchange for which no rational end could be stated.

There are many imponderables about this strategic approach which seems extremely dangerous. Although Kahn produces a list of possible actions arranged hierarchically in ascending order of destruction, there is little indication of the empirical circumstances in which this ploy would succeed. Given that no state actually wants to commit suicide it would seem that irrational risk-taking is unjustifiable for any conceivable political objective short of the preservation of the territorial integrity of the state. If two states employ this strategem then the highest rungs of the escalation ladder will be reached very quickly and produce an impasse. The assumption that one state will back down is both dubious and perilous.

There are a number of objections to this approach and indeed to all bargaining theories which will be considered shortly. To complete this survey let us turn to game theory and systems analysis[43]—the former a fairly abstract and formalised technique and the latter a much looser and historically related form of practical reasoning. Like all approaches within the context of rational action theory, game theory postulates a common rationality. It is concerned with maximising gain in a conflict and the simplest form is mini-max where the winner in effect takes all. This is achieved by choosing an optimal strategy based on a quantified set of preferences for both contenders and a delimitation of the possible courses of action open to them. Ends and means are thus related in a quantified scale and the course of action that maximises 'satisfaction' in the light of the probable reactions of the adversary, is chosen. In this respect its chief distinction from other forms of rational action theorising lies in the use of mathematics in quantifying preferences and options and their relations. But like the others it relies heavily upon estimates of capability in terms of effective action and not on any sophisticated knowledge of adversarial intentions. The 'game' is static rather than dynamic, in that each such contest is assumed to be finite with a clear result and isolated from other contests. These are unreal assumptions when referred to international politics, and cases such as the Arab-Israeli conflict or the continuum of the East-West struggle in the post-war period. However, to be able to quantify and analyse in this way they are assumptions necessary to the theory.

Moreover, they are linked to the past in that empirical experiences of previous contests provide a basis for assumptions made about both options and capabilities. Although treated in abstract terms and analysed mathematically this does not alter the fact that subjective interpretation enters into the argument. Expectations of proper action are derived from past behaviour and not from the theoretical dictates of the analysis. In short there is no theory. What is presented is at best a technique that might be useful to a practitioner, although in the absence of evidence this is dubious, in clarifying his preferences without being able to satisfy them.

Systems analysis is another technique, and one which is extremely vague in character.[44] It is perhaps the least conceptually clear approach to strategic theory and the most extensively used. It consists of the construction of idealised situations or scenarios as possibilities with certain rationally based outcomes. As we shall see, deterrence in all its forms constitutes one such scenario. Contingencies are formulated in terms of possiblities in which certain courses of action and certain weapons systems are both relevant and effective in achieving the desired result out of a set of preferences. This analytic approach is not concerned with formulating ends. As one proponent argues, 'no amount of research or analysis can provide the policy maker with simple guides to action on the muddy normative issues of high policy.'[45] Systems analysis is merely a guide to action not a basis for prescription. Only the policy-maker can determine his priorities. Nevertheless the approach is concerned with options in the form of courses of action that lead to results. These are mainly in the operational area where various methods are under consideration within a common framework of policy assumptions.

However, to quote the same writer, 'Systems analysis sought to consider more than the use of particular weapons in a specific operational context, and generally attempts to take into account all the relevant factors affecting a complex problem under investigation.'[46] 'A 'system' in this context can mean a new weapons system and all the interrelated economic and strategic considerations associated with its development.... Or a 'system' can refer to the broader and more elusive concept of a total constellation of military forces and political constraints that may govern the implementation of a broad strategic objective.'[47] In the area of 'high' policy, systems analysis can, under conditions of uncertainty identify, 'the costs and consequences of different courses of action'. It will be clear from this that systems analysis is highly speculative, and an aid to policy-making dependent upon the priorities of the policy-maker rather than prescribing what these should be. Where these involve the concept of security there are, as we shall see, serious problems in using techniques as imprecise as these.

At this stage an example of the application of the rational action approach to a specific contest will illustrate some of the points made above. In an unusual and interesting study, Graham Allison has examined the Cuban Missiles crisis of 1962 in the light of the rational actor model.[48] He is concerned with explaining this contest through selecting 'the relevant important determinants of the occurrence'.[49] It is important to note that *explanation* is his goal. It was argued earlier that explanation is a necessary basis for strategic prescription. To prescribe *effective* action, strategic reasoning needs to be grounded on a testable theory. Does this emerge from Allison's study?

In applying the rational actor model he asserts that the analyst has explained the event, 'when he can show how placing the missiles in Cuba was a reasonable action given Soviet strategic objectives. Predictions about what a nation will do or would have done are generated by calculating the rational thing to do in a certain situation given specified objectives.'[50] He accepts that at the core of this approach is a rationale, normative in character, on which appropriate action is based. The assumption is that there is a *best* strategy that will achieve the desired outcome. It can also be retrodicted from the action itself what the associated rationale was. Probability rather than theoretical prediction supports this rationale. The expectation of a particular course of action is based on the following factors: a nation's relevant values and objectives; perceived courses of action as alternatives; estimates of consequences of choice of options and net valuation of each consequence. This is related to the governing condition of cost. Options that are economical in terms of cost are preferred to those that are not. Cost is treated somewhat eccentrically as a reduction in *value* of the consequences of an action, or a reduction in its probability.[51] The value-maximising choice is the preferred option.

This schema, little different to those considered earlier, is, however, referred to a criterion of verification. Choice between strategies that assert different value-maximising options is determined by reference to evidence.

This constitutes public statements made by decision-makers, details of behaviour, government papers and other manifestations of purpose. Armed with this material, Allison considers three hypotheses concerning Soviet intentions in installing missiles in Cuba.[52] The first is that they intended to use this as a means of bargaining with the United States over its own installations in Turkey. Secondly, the Soviet intention was to provoke the United States to take action against Cuba and so provide an excuse for Soviet action elsewhere, possibly in Berlin. Thirdly, the Soviet intended in fact to do as they actually said, that is provide the Castro regime with protection against a more competent Bay of Pigs expedition.

Of course all three postulated intentions are compatible and, it could be argued, simultaneously pursued. However, it is interesting that Allison seeks to do more than ascribe 'motiveless malignity' to the Soviet Union and actually tries to examine intentions in terms of evidence. Unfortunately this is scant. Even if it were both copious and reliable it could not support any general hypothesis about Soviet behaviour that could be incorporated into strategic theory. As we have seen earlier, evidence about an agent's reasoning supports an explanation of his actions. Indeed action cannot be explained in any other way. No generalisation can emerge from this and all we have explained is the action itself.

The publicly declared intention of the Soviet Union was that it was concerned to protect Castro from a repetition of United States intervention designed to destroy the regime. This is disputed by Allison who,[53] abandoning his laudable concern for evidence, argues that the Cuban armed forces were more than sufficiently able to defend Cuba against a 'discreet attack', that in any case the presence of Soviet troops in Cuba would deter overt operations on the part of the United States; that if defence was the aim, the emplacement of relatively long ranged missiles rather than tactical weapons was excessive; and that the numbers to be emplaced were more than were necessary for defensive deterrents. Two further hypotheses are then put forward, firstly, that the ploy was intended as a probe into US intentions and to destroy American credibility as to the military defence of foreign commitments; and secondly, to improve the overall strategic position of the Soviet Union. It must be said that all conjectures rationalise rather than offer a concrete rationale for Soviet actions. There is no way of submitting them to empirical test by reference to evidence.

If we look at the development of the crisis it was clear that in the initial stages both the Soviet Union and the United States were anxious to avoid any misinterpretation of position that would lead to a nuclear exchange. Although strategic parity had not been reached then, the Soviet Union was capable of retaliating to any American strike on its territory. The United States did not possess first strike capability, that is, the capacity to destroy the Soviets' means of retaliation. Placing medium range missiles on Cuban territory did not enhance the Soviet's strategic position which was based, as was that of the United States, on *defensive* deterrence. Kennedy himself had recognised that forward based missiles made no contribution to the basic deterrent and was planning to withdraw missiles from Italy and Turkey. For its part the Soviet Union insisted that their move was not designed to secure strategic advantages for them but was intended to protect Cuba. Given their military weakness in the Caribbean, and indeed the range of military options considered by Kennedy as viable against Cuba, the only physical guarantee of Cuban integrity lay in the possession of nuclear weapons.

The outcome of this crisis was the withdrawal of Soviet missiles from Cuba and a guarantee made by the United States that it would not violate Cuban integrity.[54] Although this pledge was later withdrawn on the pretext that the missiles were not removed under United Nations supervision, it was a reversal of American policy towards Cuba that had sought to destroy the Castro regime. A communist Cuba, with all its implications for Latin America and the promotion of revolution, was there to stay. This cannot be called a victory for Kennedy however much his success in getting the withdrawal of the missiles was publicised. If the Soviet intention was to maintain the Castro regime in power then it succeeded.

How was the withdrawal of these missiles brought about? Given that they were never actually installed and made operational, Kennedy had a number of military options open to him. He could destroy the missiles sites by air or even missile attack. He could directly threaten important targets in Cuba and use punishment as a means of achieving the removal of the missiles. He could invade Cuba. It is possible that these moves would have had the result not merely of removing the putative menace of medium range missiles threatening the eastern seaboard of the United States, but of removing Castro too. In the event Kennedy settled for the mildest of the measures open to him by blockading Cuba and threatening to intercept the freighters carrying the missiles and so forcibly prevent them from completing their mission. The Soviets responded by recalling them and agreeing to the dismantling of the sites. It was clear from the discussions between the American decision-makers that resort to any extreme measures that would directly affect the Castro regime was likely to have counter-productive consequences. Although the American position was strong in the Caribbean area this was not the case elsewhere, in Berlin and in Indo-China, for example. The Soviets were themselves in a strong position in these areas and might well respond in kind to heavy American pressure on Castro.

In what sense is this contest explained by rational action theory? If we take the necessary condition of a list of outcomes ordered by preference and linked to effective courses of action governed overall by considerations of cost, ease, simplicity, etc., we can see that this was not possible at the outset of the crisis. A distinct preference for avoiding a nuclear exchange existed on both sides. Uncertainty on this possibility precluded early decision on action. When it became clear that this fear was shared the crisis could be said to have limits and this could be constructed as adherence to rules, a mutual value system or a common rationale. Whatever it was it could not simply or safely be assumed.

A clear ordering of preferred outcomes was not possible until the crisis developed and the strength and purpose of Soviet commitment to missile emplacement could be assessed. What could be evaluated was the range of possible coercive actions. Here the United States possessed advantages from its military capabilities and geographical location. If a military contest was confined to the Caribbean then it was reasonable to suppose that the United States would be successful. But of course very much more was involved than the postulate of battle-field victory. Excessive use of force might produce a contest with the Soviet Union in which the issue was not missiles in Cuba but the preservation of spheres of influence abroad and perhaps survival itself. Political survival was also important for both leaders. Whatever action was chosen it must itself be limited to securing the removal of the missiles and no further object. And success in this depended on accommodation with the Soviet Union in the form of a quid pro quo. This was tacit acceptance of the Castro regime, something which had not been conceded before and which had actually been contested by the United States.

Thus it was important to detach strategic from the sub-strategic level so as to avoid nuclear confrontation. Exchanges between the leaders did not immediately clarify this and communications were decidely vague. However, once it became clear that the context could be so limited Kennedy was relatively free to choose a course of action that was sufficiently threatening yet not so provocative as to force the Soviet Union into a corner. While rationality prevailed a bargain could emerge. We can see here that the rationality of irrationality or escalation strategy has no relevance to this crisis. If uncertainty as to willingness to use nuclear weapons was allowed to prevail then both sides risked a nuclear exchange. The issue at stake whether it was Kennedy's domestic political position, or Castro's, was hardly worth that.

It could be said that certain lessons were learnt from the crisis. The most important of these was the necessity to detach crisis of this kind from the level of strategic security competition. The Cuban Missiles crisis occurred at the point when strategic parity in nuclear weapons was just emerging between the two major powers. The consequences of this was a form of minimal defence termed defensive deterrence. The implications will be considered later, but the point here is that it implied the inability of nuclear weapons to provide deterrence at their sub-strategic level. Castro was not worth an Armageddon. The credibility of a threat was bound up in recognition of such limits.

Clear and direct communication was seen as an important pre-requisite in resolving contests of this kind. Uncertainty of purposes and ignorance of capability were too dangerous to be allowed to prevail. A hotline was installed between Washington and Moscow after the crisis.[55] Information as to fail safe devices was also passed by the United States to the Soviet Union. The factor of control emphasised by the rational action theorists, or at least those lacking a preference for the game of chicken, was also understood by the politicians. Although domestic pressures were perhaps not a factor for Krushchev, Kennedy showed considerable astuteness in manipulating the media and in preserving freedom of decision. He had perhaps also learnt from his previous unfortunate experiences.

It was also an important lesson that precipitate action based on military capability was counter-productive without some knowledge of the intentions and will of the adversary. Responses or initiatives should be related not merely to the issue but to the whole policy context. A balance between means and ends should be sought, so that the latter did not radically change through an injudicious choice of the former. This is, of course, Clausewitzian rationality. In the case of this crisis a degree of mutual accommodation was seen as necessary. A golden bridge was made for the Soviet Union, together with the implicit threat that if this route was not taken more direct action might be levelled against Castro. In the event this threat was never more than implicit. The seizure of Soviet ships on the high seas did not occur either. It is interesting to speculate whether the subsequent spectacular growth of the Soviet navy was not a consequence of a perceived weakness in this area during the crisis.

In short, while we can see reasoning in this crisis, although lacking in evidence, particularly on the Soviet side, such reasoning supports only a very limited form of explanation. It cannot support the attempt of generalisation offered by rational action theory or indeed any kind of strategic prescription. The crisis in this respect is *sui generis*. Allison asserts 'we should ask not what goals account for a nation's choice of an action but rather what factors determine an outcome.'[56] But this is to assert a theory of action determinist or causal in nature. We are entitled to ask where is it? Substituting rationalisation for reason-giving, or defining rationality, are not answers. If a causal theory is implied, and on my argument it must be if we wish to make authoritative prescriptions for effective action, then it must be clearly stated and its conditions satisfied. But this is not done. An account of the Cuban missiles crisis turns on the perception and understanding of the principals in the contest. This properly belongs to a different explanatory form and is not capable of extension into theory.

Kahn recognises this when he said, 'It is clear that the exact action we took in response to the particularly [sic] Soviet action could not have been pre-planned; it depended on the special circumstances of a major shipment of "offensive weapons" being in transit. This is probably typical of most crises; the particular tactics to be used are likely to depend on details of the particular circumstances and it will not be possible to determine them.'[57] Circumstances do indeed alter cases.

To return to the theoretical claims of scientific strategy, the classical school, as we have seen, stresses the importance of a commensurate relationship between means and ends. This is the basis of the instrumental character of violence between states. Scientific strategy, however, appears to be more concerned with the question of means, defined as capability. The problem of ends and their viability and character is not examined very closely but rather taken for granted. This perhaps stems from the fact that what is desirable is itself a subjective matter. It is easier to treat the means to such an end more objectively, in terms of the satisfaction of material conditions, and the adoption of an effective course of action. The end itself is thus left unquestioned. Of course what constitutes a rational end depends upon whether it is reasonably attainable; that is, upon a notion of viable means. To desire the unattainable is perhaps the lot of the romantic poet and relevant to the politician only when he seeks political support by enhancing the expectations of the people. But the formulation of political ends generally takes place within the framework of capability; either as it is supposed to exist, or as something to be created. This is especially the case for defence policy. Capability thus becomes the focus of attention—the means rather than the ends. Defence itself as an end is rather a cloudy notion.

Such a focus, if it is to be a basis for prescription, depends upon a precisely formulated theoretical statement of capacity as a set of necessary and sufficient preconditions, together with the law that governs them. Rationality, or rational behaviour, consists of applying this theoretical statement to practice in the form of action. If strategy is to have a scientific base then this is an entailment that must be satisfied. Capability is the central concept of such a formulation. It is equivalent to instrumentality. Options based on it are deemed to be effective in achieving the purpose for which they were designed. Choice between options is not so straightforward, since such objective factors as political expediency, value, cost, economy, simplicity, etc., enter into the rationale. But all options, to be options at all, are considered to be equally effective as instruments. When this notion is applied to bargaining theory with its dimension of threat, we can see that problems of credibility become relevant. For a threat to have effect it must be credible. What is the basis for this belief where capability cannot be demonstrated? As we shall see in a later chapter this is extremely important where deterrence is central to strategy.

Now bargaining theorists assert capability as a condition; it as assumed rather than analysed. In reality, contending states dare not make this assumption without examining the evidence on which an asserted capability is based. This is not an easy exercise and much of the difficulty in pre-nuclear conflicts lies in assessing the nature of the threat in terms of the potential effective use of violence. At the time of the Munich crisis in 1938, for example, Chamberlain was concerned for British weakness in the air. An estimate of the damage from enemy bombing (although later found to be very much exaggerated) emphasised the importance of air forces and led him to assume British vulnerability to the Luftwaffe.[58] It had a weakening effect on his negotiating position. The assumption by bargaining theorists of the existence of effective and controlled capability is facile if the conditions for its existence are not stated. Where these conditions include credibility this is not a matter simply of quantitative but of qualitative judgement. The question as to whether or not an effective capability exists is central to any dispute between states, indeed in many cases, it is what the dispute is about. And in terms of strategic theory the effective use of force in terms of the capabilities of states is its major concern. In order to formulate prescriptions relating means to ends, the appropriate empirical conditions for effective capability, and the governing principle for the relevant situation, must be stated with precision.

Past practice is no guide, and certainly no basis, for a scientific strategy. Links between putative courses of action and their consequences in the past, and present practice, must be established a-temporally and not a-historically, taken out of context. Capacity, or its synonym, power, as we have seen earlier, is a product of a validated theory, that stipulates precisely defined conditions, an associated process, and its consequence. This type of theory, scientific in character, is not in fact developed in 'scientific' strategy, nor indeed do the advocates of this approach claim that this is their goal. Nevertheless, if any authority is to be claimed for their analyses and prescriptions it is this sort of theory that must support them. In its absence their apparent precision and logicality are merely spurious.

In any case the rational action mode with its variants assumes a rationality based on a common perception of factors, conditions, capabilities, intentions, and objectives, that exists, and indeed must exist, for all the contenders. An appropriate strategy depends not so much on a theoretically derived notion of capability as on what capability is perceived to be by those engaged in conflicts involving violence or its threat. Thus the social and psychological dimensions are crucial to this schematised strategic reasoning. In other words we arrive back at the level of 'expectations of proper action' and its associated rationality, when constructing an appropriate strategy. From whence is this derived? If this is based on an idealised rationality that forces the logic of the situation on the contenders, then it can only be derived from a theory of rationality causal in nature. If, however, what is rational is derived from practice itself, that is, as an extrapolation from the actual perceptions of actors in the past, then this has no theoretical relevance to any postulated future mode of thinking and related actions. Such projections have little or no value in serving as a basis for prescription. Again we come to the dichotomy between adequately grounded theoretical postulates and those derived from subjective impressionism disguised as rigorous analysis.

A social theory is thus implicit in this strategic approach, as a political theory was implicit in the Clausewitzian analysis. In both cases these theories are not developed or subjected to close scrutiny. In particular the assumption of a common rationality precedes the analysis rather than being derived from its empirical application. It is indeed a necessary assumption to strategic thought, but one that emerges from practice itself rather than standing as a theoretical postulate. In short, it may have an historical, but not a theoretical, basis. The value systems that coexisted in the inter-war period, for example, with liberal-democratic, communist, and fascist, political systems in conflict, hardly constituted a collective rationality in terms of ends, although all recognised the mediating effect of threats of violence. Combined with the ambiguities of extant weapons, neither the intentions nor the capabilities of the contenders were easy to interpret. As we shall see in a later chapter serious miscalculations were made by all the belligerent states, and the war they actually fought was far from being the war they set out to fight.

The diplomatic manoeuvres that preceded the war indicate the complex nature of bargaining between states. France and Britain were anxious to limit Hitler's ambitions in Europe but without going to the lengths of general war. When confrontation was eventually sought over Poland, neither state believed that total war would be the result. Hitler would fall from power as a consequence of economic blockade and defensive strategies. The Soviet Union, anxious to stiffen democratic resistance to its dangerous near neighbour, turned to compromise when it became apparent that it was expected to bear the brunt of any armed challenge to Germany. Hitler, himself, concerned to avoid a prolonged war which he did not think he could win, hoped that the Molotov-Ribbentrop Pact would deter the British and French from intervention. None of this manoeuvring makes the kind of rational action theory central to scientific strategy particularly relevant.

It is however, nuclear weapons and a compelling concern to avoid, rather than provoke war, that has stimulated interest in 'scientific' strategies, designed to achieve relative advantage within the framework of an inhibition on general war imposed by nuclear deadlock between the major powers. Ideological issues, adventurism, imperialism and militarism itself, are removed as influences inducing war. In their place is a common rationality shared by the nuclear powers towards the appropriate use of war. It is not so much shared values as shared fears that impose constraints on the instrumental use of violence between states. Thus bargaining theory appears to have come into its own, given this concern for imposing limits and control over war that is the consequence of the nuclear stalemate. It seeks to re-introduce the Clausewitzuan notion of war as policy by other means. But as we have seen earlier, whatever the political objectives sought by states using violence or its threat as a means, there must be no involvement of security in the contest. It is at the sub-strategic level that this theory operates. Limited war is thus both rational, given that it remains limited, and capable of producing success. But this is merely to make the same sort of distinction that Clausewitz made, i.e., to produce a definition of rationality without being able to state its empirical conditions and laws. No amount of strategic analysis can take it further without an adequate theoretical basis. And the overall constraint on general nuclear war that makes limited war both possible and rational is based on the mutual perceptions and consequent military provisions of the major nuclear powers. This cannot be said to be immutable. Nor can it be said to depend upon theoretical postulates.

The tendency in scientific strategy has been to concentrate on limited scenarios, or idealised situations, where the technical capacities of weapons systems become predominant. The lack of historical precedents for nuclear use is the main reason for this emphasis on the physical properties of weapons. As we shall see, this was equally true for weapons innovations in the pre-nuclear period. But as with their predecessors, there is a considerable gap between theory and practice. Even though the destructive effects of nuclear weapons under experimental circumstances can be established there is no guarantee that these will be replicated in actual use. Accurate delivery entails the perfect performance of a missile, both in terms of its own engineering, launch and flight, but also in terms of the defensive and countering measures adopted by the opponent. Estimates of capability, even in strictly technical terms, assume operational success. If this is broadened to include the effort on the will of the enemy, and imponderables such as the level of acceptable damage, it is even more difficult to equate technical performance with military success, or military with political success, even at the sub-strategic or limited war level.

It has also been helpful to the development of the scientific school of strategy, very largely an American product, that the broad policy assumptions of the United States over a long period of time have been both consistent and simple. The Soviet Union has been treated as the main potential enemy. It has not seemed necessary to question this assumption, and this is consonant with the tendency of this approach not to analyse political ends too closely. American policy-makers and strategists have thus been able to concentrate on the problem of resource allocation and the matching of material capabilities, rather than on the intentions of the adversary. The consequence has been the predominance of quantitative rather than qualitative analysis. The possibility that this assumption is something of a self-fulfilling prophecy producing equivalent Soviet reactions does not seem to have been considered. This aspect will be examined in a later chapter, together with the problem of arms control. The point is that in the absence of a properly grounded theory the scientific school has, perforce, concentrated on means, seen largely as capabilities. This has meant adopting very simple covering assumptions, such as the performance of arms competition, an adversarial framework of international politics, and an emphasis on weapons technology. This last and its effects will be considered in the next two chapters.

NOTES AND REFERENCES

1. See Uri Bialer, *The Shadow of the Bomber: fear of air attack and British politics 1932*–1939, Royal Hist. Soc., London, 1980, p. 27.
2. See Giulio Douhet, *The Command of the Air*, Faber and Faber, London, 1943.
3. Basil H. Liddell Hart, *The Strategy of the Indirect Approach,* Faber and Faber, London, 1946.
4. Favourable auguries might have done as much for soldiers' morale as church parades!
5. Jomini.

6. This was not always the case: Sun Tzu was a major advocate of the strategem and of winning without fighting. The use of strategem was a major element in the invasion plans for both Husky (Sicily) and Overlord (Normandy) but in these cases it acted as an adjunct to the direct battle—field confrontation which was actively sought.

7. For an account of this see John Wheeler-Bennett, *Munich: Prologue to Tragedy,* Macmillan, London, 1948.

8. See as an example of this genre Bueno de Mesquita, *The War Trap,* Yale University Press, New Haven, 1981.

9. Von Mises.

10. Karl R. Popper, *Objective Knowledge, op. cit.* p. 179.

11. See the comments of Maj-Gen. Sir John Kennedy, *The Business of War,* Hutchinson, London 1957. pp. 323–5.

12. Even Churchill's enthusiasm for area bombing waned after Dresden. See Martin Gilbert, *Road to Victory: Winston Churchill 1941–1945,* Heinemann, London, 1986 p. 1257.

13. A defence of Bomber Command's policy is made in Dudley Soward, *op. cit.*

14. See in particular Anthony Cave Brown, *Bodyguard of Lies,* W. H. Allen, London, 1976, for an account of the deception plans preceding major Allied operations in the Second World War.

15. See Colin Gray, *The Soviet-American Arms Race,* Saxon House Lexington Books, 1976, p. 66. The alleged contrast between the realpolitik of the Soviet Union and what he calls the moral politics of the West is a particularly specious piece of special pleading.

16. See also Colin Gray, *Strategic Studies, op. cit.* p. 29.

17. It is curious how successive American Presidents including Reagan, have regarded negotiation with the Soviet Union as appeasement. A parallel between the USSR and Nazi Germany is implicitly made.

18. I take the successful negotiation of the Austrian State treaty of 1955 and the consequent withdrawal of the occupying powers as the end of a hiatus in inter-state relations. The Cold War constituted a breakdown in diplomacy and the end of an attempt to reach a negotiated settlement between the victor powers. From 1946 both sides pursued unilateral policies that resulted in an armed confrontation between two groups of allies. Although the United States and the Soviet Union have pursued adversarial policies since 1955 this has not precluded normal diplomacy, negotiation and agreement.

19. The persistent attempts to persuade the Soviet Union to adopt Western human rights practice illustrates this. While making good propaganda and serving as a bargaining lever, it is hard to see the relevance of this issue either to national security or to world peace.

20. There is a precedent for this in the Kaiser's notorious reference to the British Expeditionary Force in 1914 as a 'contemptible little army'.

21. The earlier case of Munich also illustrates this and both Chamberlain and Daladier were under considerable political pressure to avoid hostilities. It is not appreciated by latter-day critics how popular the Munich agreement was with the general public in both Britain and France. And both were democracies.

22. See Michael Nicholson, *The Scientific Analysis of Social Behaviour,* Frances Pinter, London, 1983.

23. *Ibid,* p. 69.

24. *Ibid,* pp. 151–67.

25. See A. Hitler *Testament, op. cit.* pp. 43–6.
26. Paul Nitze is a good example.
27. Examples of this genre are found in Herman Kahn, *On Escalation,* Praeger NY, 1965; T. C. Schelling, *Arms and Influence,* Yale University Press, New Haven, 1966, and *Strategy of Conflict,* OUP, 1960; William Kaufmann, ed. *Military Policy and National Security,* Princeton University Press, Princeton, NJ, 1956; and the pioneering study by Wohlstetter A. J., Hoffman F. S., Lutz R. J. and Rowen H. S., *Selection and use of Strategic Air Bases,* RAND r-266, 1 April, 1954, declassified 1962.
28. The United States has placed an embargo on the export of computers and computer technology and this has affected nominal allies such as France as well as formal adversaries such as the Soviet Union.
29. The Low Countries have long served as a battlefield given their position on the Rhine and Scheldt. The existence of Belgium and the Netherlands as sovereign nation states owes a great deal to the 'imbalancing' policies of the major European powers and the inconclusive nature of the wars fought.
30. Within the framework of great power competition, smaller powers have pursued their own interests and engaged in bargaining and the use of threats as much as their more powerful exemplars. The Arab-Israeli contest; the activities of Vietnam in Indo-China after the American withdrawal, and the Iran-Iraqi conflict, are cases of localised conflict that are both dependent on and independent of, the major powers.
31. It must be said that this phenomenon is closely associated with the electoral strategies of President Reagan and his supporters. The apparent radical departure from the strategic doctrines associated with Macnamara may however only be illusory. The Committee on the Present Danger may be convinced that there is indeed a danger to American security but it has yet to be demonstrated in terms of action that the Administration shares this belief. It has served more as a vehicle for the election of Reagan than as a genuine source of strategic doctrine.
32. President Roosevelt announced this during the Tehran Conference without apparently consulting his allies. In the closing stages of the war it was clear that Stalin believed his allies to be negotiating a separate surrender with the Germans, as the Berne incident indicates. While the negotiations with the German forces in Italy were inconclusive it was certainly the case that the United States took the initiative in concluding hostilities with the Japanese and in deciding terms.
33. See T. C. Schelling, *Arms and Influence,* and *The Strategy of Conflict, op. cit.*
34. *Strategy of Conflict, op. cit.* p. 4.
35. *Ibid,* p. 6.
36. *Ibid,* p. 8.
37. *Ibid,* p. 13.
38. *Arms and Influence, op. cit.* p. 2.
39. *Ibid,* p. 2.
40. See Herman Kahn, *On Thermo-Nuclear War,* Princeton University Press, 1960.
41. *On Escalation, op. cit.,* p. 25.
42. *Ibid,* p. 57.
43. See John von Neumann and Oskar Morgenstern, *The Theory of Games and Economic Behavior,* Princeton University Press, NJ for the original application of this type of mathematical analysis to human action. For a

critical discussion of game theory in international politics see M. Nicholson, *op. cit.* and Nigel Forward, *The Field of Nations*, Macmillan, London, 1971, pp. 24–52.

44. There is a huge literature on systems analysis, a primary if deeply flawed work is Morton Kaplan, *System and Process in International Politics, op. cit.*
45. See Bruce L. R. Smith, *The R.A.N.D. Corporation*, Harvard University Press, Cambridge, Mass., 1966.
46. *Ibid,* pp. 161–2.
47. *Ibid,* p. 162.
48. See Graham T. Allison, *Essence of Decision*, Little Brown, Boston, 1975.
49. *Ibid,* p. 4.
50. *Ibid,* p. 5.
51. *Ibid,* p. 34.
52. *Ibid,* p. 48.
53. *Ibid,* p. 49.
54. See Robert Kennedy, *Thirteen Days*, Pan Books, London, 1969, and Elie Abel, *The Missiles of October*, and A. Schlesinger, *A Thousand Days*, Mayflower Dell, 1967.
55. This marked the beginning of arms control negotiations between the USA and the USSR and the recognition of a strategic balance between them.
56. Graham T. Allison, *op. cit.,* p. 255.
57. H. Kahn, *On Escalation, op. cit.* p. 259.
58. See Neville Chamberlain, *In Search of Peace, Speeches 1937–1938* ed. A. Bryant, Hutchinson, London.

5 Weapons and Strategy—Conventional Practice

Wars are fought with weapons. Defence in peacetime is seen as a function of weapons and their relative national distributions and capabilities. I come now to the attempt to prescribe specific courses of action based on the capabilities of weapons and their relation to success in war or in the procurement of security in peace. If, as Clausewitz argued, rationality in war consists of a commensurable relationship between means and ends, how is this possible in practice where the means constitutes the use of certain weapons systems? Clausewitz did not face the problem of radical innovation in weapons. His strategic vision did not encompass the major changes in weapons technology that at present place the existence of states and their populations in jeopardy.

Can the preconditions for success through the use (or non-use) of weapons in war or peace be established on any rigorous basis? What is meant by success? Is it defined purely instrumentally as the achievement of battle-field victory, at the tactical level as it were, or is it the attainment of clearly defined *political* objectives? To restate the distinction made at the beginning of this study, strategy consists of a course of action designed to achieve pre-stated objectives, whether these are related to the offensive or the defensive, i.e. as an initiative or as a response. Violence or its threat is thus instrumental to policy; whatever its form or character, it constitutes a means and not an end in itself. The level of tactics operates within that of strategy and is directed towards achieving local advantages *vis-à-vis* an opponent which will induce him towards conceding the issue in contention. Clearly in total war where the objective is the complete submission of an enemy in all respects, the two levels are virtually synonymous. Defeat and victory are total in the sense that submission is complete and virtually any objective can be realised at the expense of the defeated. Politics begin at the point of defeat, and the translation of battle-field victory into political success presents new problems to the victor powers. Indeed the defeated powers may well be saved from a draconian fate through the quarrels of their victors, as was the case for Germany and Japan after the Second World War.

The political point of such wars however, is subordinate to military exigency, and they may be regarded as wars of contested hegemony—imperial in character. The instrument—violence—is paramount in such contests and strategic debate is largely concerned with achieving the necessary military victories. The only objective that makes total war political in character is the achievement of security.[1] As we have seen earlier the security dilemma created by a combination of geo-political factors, extant military technology and differential national capabilities for organised violence, can be resolved through an imperial hegemony imposing peace. Of course only the hegemonial power enjoys security, supposing that it is successful. Past precedents indicate that such regimes operated within limits where isolating factors, economic, geographical, and technological, prevailed. The Roman, Chinese and Islamic hegemonies offer examples of this kind of imperium.

In the modern age neither the Napoleonic Wars or the two World Wars of this century resolved the security dilemma posed by the existence of competing nation-states. Total war has not provided a solution. These two World Wars can be seen as attempts to establish hegemony in Europe by France and Germany. Supported by allies who did not, or could not, share this ambition, neither state succeeded in its aims. Britain and the United States were unwilling to aggrandise France at the expense of Germany at the end of the First War, while at the end of the Second War Germany was needed to offset the enhanced power of the Soviet Union. France, eclipsed by defeat, Britain through the cost of the struggle, and Germany through partition and occupation, were in no position to dictate European politics. For its part the Soviet Union, thrice invaded in this century, and deeply concerned with unresolved security problems posed by radical innovation in weapons technology and the commanding position of the United States both in Europe and the Pacific, found no solace in its victory. The security dilemma continued, but as we shall see, in a new guise.

If total war, as Clausewitz recognised, is the epitome of violence for its own sake, limited war is concerned with retaining the relationship between political and military objectives so that the latter do not determine the former. Whatever limits are observed in the scale of the war and in the adoption of a strategic approach, they preclude the development of the contest into total war. In short, the objectives sought, and the means adopted, are such that failure is accepted as a possible option. Success is not to be bought by the extension of the conflict and the abandonment of the original objectives for ones which entail a war of life and death for the contending states. Consequently the tactical level and the military goals do not dominate the adopted strategy. A decisive victory is not the prime objective where victory constitutes the complete defeat of the enemy state. Military decisions in the context of the successful use of force are subordinate to the overall political control and negotiation is always a possible option, indeed an inevitable conclusion to the struggle. Such a war balances the use of violence and the use of diplomacy and depends upon a nice calculation of forces. At no point is the existence of the contending states at stake. The capabilities of the weapons employed are defined, controlled, and utilised, accordingly. This is of course to assume what must be proven, namely that the means—i.e. the capabilities of weapons—are both known and capable of control. And so far limited war has been defined but its empirical preconditions and method of control not stated. What this entails is the subject of this chapter and the next.

It is in some senses easier to calculate and theorise at the sub-strategic level since weapons have physical properties and a quality lacking in the more abstract realms of grand strategy. Things are more tangible than ideas. Troops and weapons can be counted; the Pope's lack of divisions noted. Where new weapons come into existence their significance and relevance to the art of war become the subject of controversy and debate among strategic theorists and politicians. But whatever the substance of the claims of the latter it is important to establish the relation between such weapons and the overall strategic purpose of the state, whether this be the preservation of itself as a political and territorial entity, or the pursuit of national interests in the world of states. The capabilities of these weapons must be appraised on some ground common to all contenders in order to clarify the implications of the threat or use of violence in inter-state relations. Short of total war where reasoning is subordinate to maximum effort, common perceptions of threat and of related capability are essential in using violence as policy by other means. As will be argued later, so-called conventional weapons are highly ambiguous in this respect. At the level of threat their value is indeterminate. They are very imprecise as instruments of diplomacy. No one before the event could determine, for example, whether or not a highly mobile armoured force could defeat a much larger but less concentrated mechanised force in a relatively strong defensive position. The utility and significance of the major innovations of the pre-nuclear period—the tank, poison gas, aircraft, the submarine, etc.—could not be pre-determined, although as we shall see, there were various attempts at doing so. At least in the case of these weapons there was a body of practice that provided a basis, however imperfect, reference for the strategic theorists.

With ballistic nuclear missiles, while there is no such reference, their destructive effects can be established with precision. At present there is no effective defence against them. They are accurate, very destructive, and long range. Whether this has any significance at the strategic level will be discussed later on. At the sub-strategic level it is clear that the damage these weapons can inflict on their target can be assessed far more precisely than has ever been the case in the past. The conclusions of the Strategic Bombing Surveys[2] at the end of the last war can be matched with the aspirations of Bomber Command and the discrepancies between theory and practice established *ex post facto*.[3] But in the case of a nuclear attack there is little room for speculation; annihilation, and not damage to morale through terror, is the consequence, although, as we shall see, terror may have some value at the strategic level.

If the primary condition of rational or limited war is control over the means employed, then the capabilities of the weapons to be created and used are highly important. But as has been pointed out earlier, capability does not constitute simply the performance of weapons under battle-field conditions. It constitutes effectiveness in terms of the political objective pursued, whether it be national security or the pursuit and protection of lesser national interests. It is the relationship between weapons systems and this context that is important. What is at stake is not the development of an adequate tactical theory, but a knowledge of the preconditions for the successful use or threat of violence as a means of persuading an actual or potential opposition to concede the issue in question. Knowing these in advance permits effective prescription and, from this, a definition and fulfilment of the objectives sought. In short, tactical theory must be formulated within a body of strategic doctrine and cannot be treated separately. Those who advocate specific weapons systems or who urge a particular tactical usage, must relate their advocacy to the larger issues involved in using violence to achieve political objectives.

In historical terms there has been a level of debate surrounding the introduction of new weapons. This debate involves not merely the defence establishment with its political, military, and industrial components, but also takes the form of academic commentary that occasionally impinges on political decision-making. It is instructive to compare two such periods of debate, that concerning the significance of armour and its supporting weapons in the period immediately before the Second World War, and that concerning the significance of different nuclear missiles systems in the contemporary period. The security dilemma in both periods was radically different, for reasons which will be discussed later, and I am concerned at this stage of the discussion with what I have termed the sub-strategic level. In examining them in this chapter and the next, I am concerned with the question on what grounds can prescriptions about weapons procurement and effective use be authoritatively based? This leads to the larger question of the relationship between arguments of this kind and those concerned with grand strategy.

I have used the term sub-strategic as virtually a synonym for tactics. The latter is generally, and narrowly, taken to mean the methods of combat—air, sea and land—employed at the level of actual engagement with the enemy. Weapons procurement policies reflect this preoccupation and constitute a kind of theoretical tactics. Naturally enough the military practitioner tends to dominate discussions at this level, although given political control over expenditure there is a common denominator in terms of arguments about cost-effectiveness and cost-benefit. Nevertheless the final decisions both as to purchase and as to use are political in character and it is this nexus between procurement, instrumentality and the objectives sought that is the focus of this chapter. Where these objectives are distinct from the minimal preservation of territorial integrity they are sub-strategic. Such a distinction is difficult to make in the pre-nuclear period given a weapons technology that did not lend itself to precise definition of function. It is a different case in the nuclear age given the doctrine of defensive deterrence. If this doctrine is accepted by political practitioners, then outside its limiting conditions there is scope for debate at the sub-strategic level, that is for relating violence to relatively limited political objectives. In the pre-nuclear period the two—strategic and sub-strategic—tended to merge in the form of total war, although even here, as we shall see, a distinction between them can be maintained.

My view of tactics as being sub-strategic, in the sense of using violence for the achievement of political objectives which fall short of security, is broader than in military usage. It is not so much the mechanics of winning battles, as the context for battle-field victory, that stipulates what sort of victory it is. It is the relation between military practice or postulated practice and its theoretical or hypothetical basis and the political dimension, that dictates its character. Generals, like economists, tend to argue that political practice vitiates their theoretical success,[4] but this is to have a rather one-sided view of the enterprise! It is the political level that is responsible for the overall deployment and use of forces, whether this is constituted by a Fuehrer or a Churchill—a single leader, or a combination of allied politicians and their parliamentary base.

Perhaps an example might serve to make these distinctions and their implications clearer. The Normandy landings of June 1944 were the consequence of a major strategic decision to defeat the German forces in France and prosecute a land war in NW Europe. Battle-field victories were sought. The reasons for this decision were both complex and conflicting and will be discussed later on in this study.[5] It was however, a political decision taken at the highest level, reluctantly accepted by the British, but deemed necessary in default of American agreement to pursue other strategic directions, in order to prevent the Soviet Union from claiming sole credit for the defeat of Nazi Germany and thus strengthening its negotiating position in terms of the post-war settlement. The composition and disposition of the forces employed, together with the plan of attack and the associated deception plan, correspond to the purely military conception of the tactical level. The battle was expected to develop into a mobile mechanised combat with artillery and tanks the dominant arms. There were disputes over the appropriate tactical roles of the air force, the army wanting close tactical support, with the air force, notably Bomber Command, being reluctant to divert their forces from the strategic bombing of Germany.[6] Speed was very important in view of the German capacity for reinforcement and this latter was impaired by a number of measured; these included the deception plan designed to make the Germans believe the main assault was to come in the Pas de Calais area;[7] the use of the resistance to reinforce this view and to sabotage communications; the Transportation Plan[8] involving the destruction of rail centres and repair facilities through bombing; and the coordination of a major Russian offensive to prevent the withdrawal of panzer forces from the Eastern Front.[9]

The need for speedy decision on the battle-field was not, however, purely a function of the relative preponderance of German forces in the field over

Allied forces operating from beachheads and the consequent logistic difficulties. Britain with its overstretched resources and overextended manpower could not afford a war of attrition. The military defeat of Germany, however desirable, could not be purchased at the cost of political emasculation through a severe bloodletting of her armed forces. If Britain was to influence the peace and secure political objectives, it could not afford to assume the major role in combating German forces if this meant a decimation of its forces. The United States with its superior manpower could afford to take the major part in the offensive and this was equally true of the Soviet Union. This meant that a conservative attitude towards the expenditure of British troops in combat was an element in the tactics adopted.

The Battle of Normandy did not develop according to plan.[10] It initially developed into what was basically an infantry battle. The Germans, having proved unable to prevent the acquisition of beachheads, did not withdraw, regroup and fight a battle of manoeuvre as expected, but held their positions around Caen and fought it out, reinforcing as they did so. Montgomery was unable to force the issue without committing many more troops and thus accepting a higher level of casualties. The problem was exacerbated by the expectation of a mobile battle, and the composition of the forces was imbalanced leaning towards armour and artillery rather than to infantry. He thus lacked the flexibility and the manpower[11] to press home attacks such as *Epsom* and *Goodwood* and thus force a breakthrough at Caen. Instead he adopted the tactic of holding down as many German forces in that area, especially the panzer units, in order to provide an opportunity for the American forces to break through on the western flank. This they eventually succeeded in doing.

The point here is that it is this mixture of political and military factors that constitutes the sub-strategic level. On the face of it the actual planning and conduct of operations appear to be a-political but this is certainly not the case. What could be called strictly tactical was the brilliant improvisation and subsequent exploitation of a means of extricating armour from the confines of the *bocage* restoring mobility and the use of tanks to the battle-field.[12]

The same point can be made about the Transportation Plan deemed necessary by the army to prevent rapid panzer reinforcement, although not by the air force which claimed to be unable to bomb with the necessary accuracy, and in any case did not want to divert bombers from German cities. The problem was that bombing railway centres entailed inflicting high casualties on French and Belgian civilians. It was argued that such casualties would affect political attitudes in those countries and make them inimical to British influence in Europe. This was an important consideration given the potential for political instability and chaos and the fact that much of the resistance in both countries was organised by left wing and communist groups.[13] Winning the Normandy battle would be counter-productive in political terms if the result was the alienation of France and Belgium in the face of an extension of Soviet influence in the

East. This was equally true of area bombing in Germany if post-war political developments meant that German reconstruction was a necessary part of an anti-Soviet front.

Similarly, nuclear weapons at the sub-strategic level cannot be considered in terms of their capabilities as a superior form of artilllery. There are political aspects to any tactical plan that envisages their use in 'friendly' territory as a means of achieving battle-field victory over Soviet forces. Limited nuclear strikes, as we will see later on, may be considered relevant as a sub-strategy designed to achieve specific political objectives, but not in the context of a conventional war on allied territory. For states in this zone such a war would be total in effect.

Both grand strategy and the sub-strategic level are concerned with the overall result, or rather with the production of a victory that produces a desired state of affairs, or peace. The sub-strategic level operates where security questions are not directly involved, but where they provide a context that may act as a restraint or an inducement for an expansion of the conflict. As we shall see, the former is the case in the nuclear age, but the latter is more characteristic of the pre-nuclear period. For example, the German-Polish war of 1939 and the Finno-Russian war of 1940, could have been treated as limited conflicts, presenting no threat to British and French security. From their geo-political position and given extant military technology, Poland and Finland were remote from their frontiers. Moreover, these conflicts brought Germany and the Soviet Union into closer contact and made military confrontation more likely. Finland was virtually a German ally at the time. Poland had disappeared from the European map for over a century before it was reconstituted as a state by the victor powers after the First World War. Indeed had the Tsarist Empire survived the war it is doubtful whether this resurrection would have taken place, given the partiality by which the principle of self-determination was observed by the victors.

However, Britain and France saw the violation of Polish integrity by Germany (although not by the Soviet Union) as a *causus belli*. They were even prepared to invade the Scandinavian countries in order to aid Finland against the USSR.[14] These contests were seen as part of a larger war whose *raison-d'être* was the preservation of national security. Unlike Germany they were fighting a total war, although the paradox is that the means they adopted were both inadequate and incommensurate with the ends sought, while the reverse was the case for their opponent. Hitler believed himself to be fighting what was essentially a political war, akin to those of the Eighteenth Century in that battle-field victories were a means of changing the European map. Such victories and consequent changes would be endorsed by negotiations. Although certain of the newly created small states of Europe would come under German hegemony, he did not believe that he was fighting a security war—a war that threatened the integrity of Britain and France. But while there was some ambiguity in the *drôle de guerre* period his opponents refused to accept the consequences of these limited contests and turned the conflict into a total war by making it an issue of security. If Hitler was operating at the sub-strategic level, his opponents were pre-eminently concerned with grand strategy. For Germany the war did not become total until the failure of the invasion of the Soviet Union to achieve a quick victory. For his surviving opponent, Britain, it became total with the defeat of France.

The consequence of these assumptions for weapons procurement and assessments of the capabilities and relevance of weapons systems were profound. Both Britain and France were unprepared to counter the kind of war Germany was planning. Britain, with its imperial interests and consequent concern for naval power, and its limited manpower, traditionally maintained a small land force. The heavy involvement in land fighting and the consequent losses was seen as an aberration in the British conduct of war that should not be repeated. The new factor in warfare that emerged during the inter-war period was air power. This, if anything, intensified the close interest that Britain took in changes in continental politics that seemed likely to produce a dominant power capable of controlling the Channel coastal states, particularly Belgium and the Netherlands. The Anglo-German naval arms race that preceded the First World War produced a parallel in British concern for the growth of the Luftwaffe and the apparent desire on the part of Germany to change the European map, by force if necessary. Air power presented not merely a strategic threat directed at vulnerable population centres, but also at the sub-strategic level nullified British naval superiority. It was realised that expensive capital ships that could not be replaced quickly were either exposed to attack or had to be conserved and defended in such a manner as to make them a military liability rather than an asset.

There were two problems that confronted British policy-makers in the 1930s; how to provide security through countering this new development and how to provide teeth for a foreign policy designed to preserve the European status quo. The answer in terms of weapons provision was not an easy one. It was beyond British resources to match division for division German forces and deploy and support them on the Continent. Any contemplated army was one designed to support an ally and needed to be equipped accordingly. Conscription and mobilisation in this arm can be seen as a political and not a military gesture, indicating commitment to the French alliance and to the position adopted *vis-à-vis* German demands.

The navy could not be expanded rapidly for obvious reasons, and in any case had a global as well as a regional role. It was not a good instrument for supporting foreign policy, although before the advent of aircraft it provided a more than adequate defence of Britain, given the absence of any major naval rival. It was also a means of checking attempts at economic blockade. But it had now become extremely vulnerable, although the extent to which this was the case was still unknown.

It was in the air that the chief expansion took place.[15] But even given this priority there was confusion between the tactical—or sub-strategic—role of aircraft and their strategic role. A bomber force was seen as the main threat to open cities and countering this could be done in two ways; firstly by developing an equivalent bomber force and thus presenting a defensive deterrent to the enemy, exposing *his* cities to attack; or alternatively, creating a fighter and anti-aircraft force capable of destroying any incoming attacker. Given adequate resources both expedients could be adopted and both offensive and defensive deterrence would then exist for the first state able to do so. Given the British predicament, starting late in this field of development compared with the Germans, and with the French even later, such a policy was long-term, and could only be directed towards fighting a security war. In the immediate circumstances of the late 1930s a defensive posture was all that was viable and this meant allowing Germany to fight and win its limited contests. The strategic dominated the sub-strategic.

It is within this context that we should examine the development of the tank and of theories of mobile armed warfare. We can see that for Britain, but not for France and Germany, the tank was a peripheral weapon given the strategic assumptions of the day. Before going into the implications of this let us look more closely at the new weapon. There is some ambiguity in discussing weapons in terms of their purpose. Their early designers, and to some extent their proponents, were concerned with technical performance as related to the fulfilment of certain tasks in combat. Weapons are tools designed to do particular things. But they are also non-specific in strategic and sub-strategic terms; that is, they permit a wide variety of uses, and theories stipulating utility and effectiveness mould them to their precepts rather than vice-versa. Such theories may in turn stipulate their specifications. I will return to this subsequently. In the case of the tank a wide variety of conflicting and often confused argument concerning their use in battle existed in the inter-war period, often misleadingly represented as armour versus the horse. In fact the debate was a good deal more sophisticated than that. But no consensus had emerged even in Germany about the most effective way to use the tank, nor on what form the tank should take. Some weapons had been purpose designed—the Stuka divebomber, for example, with its 30 feet accuracy in bombing, was one of them, but this was not the case for armour.

Paradoxically the most notable characteristic of the tank is not its armour—static positions could be more heavily protected—but its mobility relative to infantry and animal and wheeled transport. A tracked vehicle is able to move on most kinds of terrain off roads, although mud, dust, swamp, and certain types of sand, can restrict it in this respect. With armour it was impervious to small-arms fire, and being mobile presented a difficult target for artillery and anti-tank weapons, although it was vulnerable to the air. It was versatile as a weapons carrier and could carry a variety of guns, both anti-tank and anti-personnel, and thus had greater fire power than infantry and more varied roles than artillery. With the appropriate type of gun it was a particularly effective form of mobile artillery. But its main role was against infantry.

The early tank had been battle tested under the trench conditions of the First World War and was given an infantry support role. In the later 'open' stages of the war the mobility and capacity of the tank to penetrate and infiltrate static positions was noted. By the end of the war the British, the pioneers of this new weapon, had some thirty-five tank battalions in the field.

The main characteristics of the tank, its mobility and cross-country capacity, the security offered by its armour and the enhanced fire power it was able to deliver, were all variables each of which could be developed at the others' expense. A highly mobile fast tank, for example, could not carry as much armour as a heavier tank, but would have more range and manoeuvrability. Increased armour meant more fuel consumption and shorter range but more protection, and so on. The optimal balance between these factors very much depended upon battle-field contingencies and what Guderian called *operativ*,[16] that is, the mix of logistical and operational elements that operate at the sub-strategic level. The British light tank developed in the 1930s was what Fuller called a 'mechanical mouse'[17] and was actually geared down so as not to outpace the infantry. If tanks were to act as infantry support then there was little premium in mobility, armour and fire power then became important if the tank had to deal with heavily defended static positions and engage in positional warfare.

Tank development in Britain was extremely conservative. The Vickers Medium rank remained for sixteen years after the First World War the sole medium tank in the Army. It was not until 1937 that the first mechanised division was formed but even this was equipped with light tanks. The major assumption governing war preparation[18] once the ten year rule had been abrogated[19] was that a small expeditionary force was to be the main army contribution to a continental war. The bulk of any British war effort was to be concentrated not in the army, fighting a continental land war, but in the navy and the airforce. The notion that the army would play a peripheral role in any European war exacerbated the tendency to treat these three services as quasi-autonomous, and encouraged the special pleading associated with each service. As we shall see the absence of a common strategic aim and the consequent indecision in terms of weapons procurement stemmed directly from political rather than military decisions. The question of the composition of such a small army and its tactical or sub-strategic role was thus an academic one. Whatever the potential of the tank in this respect, so far as the British were concerned, it was irrelevant. The achievement of battle-field victory through the application of blitzkrieg methods was not an appropriate course of action.

The same was true of aircraft. Little or no consideration had been given to tactical cooperation with the army, mechanised or not. Priority in the period up to Munich had been given to the production of bombers, reflecting their use as a cheap form of colonial policing and fears of the vulnerability of British cities to bombing. At this time Britain had in total less than 100 modern fighters, and this included only one squadron of Spitfires. After March 1939 the priority was given to fighter production but this was a response to parallel German production and the existence of some thousand German bombers. As such it was a defensive measure at the strategic level and had no relationship to the tactics of land warfare. In principle, either a large bomber or a large fighter force could provide defence through deterrence—the former by threatening retaliatory or reciprocal destruction and the latter by preventing it.

The French, being a continental land power and sharing a frontier with a more populous and industrialised state, developed the largest land army in Europe over the inter-war period.[20] By 1940 it possessed the best tanks in terms of armour and firepower. The Germans considered these to be superior in all respects save that of speed. The first armoured division was formed in 1934 and two more armoured divisions were authorised in 1938. By 1940 the French had as many tanks as the Germans and they were superior in quality. But although the tank had been accepted in the French army as an important weapon there was a proliferation of types and formations that precluded any coherent battle-field role. This again reflected political confusion. The prime role of the French Army was defensive, with the Maginot line central to French strategy. The tank was therefore used as a mobile fortress to stiffen resistance rather than to aid a breakthrough and promote a strategic offensive. It related to tactics that essentially responded to enemy initiatives rather than promoting any of its own. Tanks were thus dispersed throughout the French army as support to infantry formations.

Similarly, the French air force had a considerable range of aircraft that included dive bombers and a fighter superior in some respects to the Spitfire. This diversity was the consequence of a number of factors that included the relatively late start in matching the Luftwaffe; the disorganisation of French industrial production; the vulnerability of French aircraft production centres to German attack, and political indecision. The prime weakness[21] was the lack of a system of mass production designed to replace losses in action. This last was the consequence of political decision that envisaged a protracted and defensive war that allowed time for both aircraft type and production to be determined at a relative leisure. In any case close cooperation at the tactical level with the ground forces was not considered to be important.

Turning to the German forces, a very different picture emerges over the 1930s. With Hitler's decision to break the demilitarisation clauses of the Versailles and Locarno Treaties, came an opportunity to design new weapons in terms of purpose rather than indulge in the adaptations and compromises forced on his rivals through an unwillingness to scrap existing weapons at a time of economic stringency. Moreover these weapons could be battle tested. The Spanish Civil War provided an opportunity for both tank and aircraft performance to be assessed. It is true that the rapid expansion of the German armed forces after 1935 presented problems. A debate ensued as to the proper role of the tank.[22] Some tank formations were designed as support units for infantry, while others were permitted an independent development. The main point here is that the adoption of an offensive role permitted much more flexibility in devising tactics than was the case for France and Britain. This decision was of course a political and not a military one.

In 1935 three panzer divisions were created. The main battle tanks were the PzIII and PzIV; the former weighing 20 tons and the latter 25 tons carrying 3.7 and 7.5 calibre guns respectively. Both had a crew of five, the PzIII cruising at 25 mph and the PzIV at 18.5 mph. Both were equipped with radio. The earlier smaller tanks the PzI nd PzII continued in production and by 1939 the balance between these and the heavier tanks was highly disproportionate, some 2159 PzI and PzIIs to 361 PzII I and PzIVs with 400 Czech tanks of 35–38 tons armed with 3.7 guns and capable of 25 mph. By May 1940 heavy tank production had succeeded in modifying this imbalance to the extent of 628 PzIII/IV as against 1478 PzI/II with a leavening of some 334 Czech tanks. Armoured vehicle production of all marks was less than 200 a month.

By 1940 the German Army consisted of some 156 divisions; of these ten were panzer divisions and six motorised infantry divisions. The total number of tanks was 2,600 but this figure disguises the fact that only 962 were modern heavy tanks and of these a third consisted of Czech tanks. What was to be the *operativ,* the role of these panzer divisions, and what were the conditions deemed necessary for them to fulfil it in the coming campaign against France? Guderian had stressed three years previously, 'only movement brings victory'.[23] The chief property of the new weapon was its mobility. This was not an absolute but a function of relative performance when compared with opposing weapons. As he put it 'the effectiveness of a weapon is a relative quality depending on the effectiveness of the counter-weapons employed against it'.[24] The tank was a means of finding and exploiting the weakness of the opposition and opening the way for mobile infantry. It was necessary to have the necessary support, both tactical and logistical, and this must be as mobile as existing technology could make it. Tank formations must be protected from the air and anti-tank defences destroyed quickly, and this required close tactical support by aircraft designed for the purpose and deployed with this priority. Tanks by themselves could not achieve battle-field victory but rather created the opportunities for it. Speed was essential since this deprived the enemy of initiative and the chance to regroup and force the fighting into positional warfare.

It is clear from this summary of Guderian's argument that the tank organised into panzer divisions was an opportunistic weapon. It did not and need not constitute the major part of land forces. It relied on enemy weaknesses. It should not be so specialised a weapon as to preclude a variety of uses on the battle-field. Optimal flexibility was to be encouraged—speed, armour and fire-power should be balanced. This flexibility was to be encouraged through the use of radio and close command by the field commanders, operating at the point of contact with the enemy and appraising and reacting to the tactical situation as it developed.

The absence of inter-service rivalry also helped. The army was central to

German strategic thinking, and although the Luftwaffe was accepted as a separate arm its role was closely tied to support for ground forces. The prime instruments for this task were the Junkers 87 dive-bomber and the Junkers 88 twin engined bomber, acting as a kind of aerial artillery. Bombing operations were closely related to ground operations, destroying enemy communications and supplies in order to frustrate counterattacks and to create maximum confusion. Close cooperation with forward formations was encouraged through liaison and wireless communications. The aim was to preserve the momentum of the forward drive of the mechanised forces. Like the tank formations, the air tactical support element was only a small proportion of the total; there were only some 350 Ju 87s out of a total of nearly 2000 bombers by September 1939.

The whole purpose of such an *operativ* was to achieve quick decision. But the relevance of such a modus operandi depended on the satisfaction of political as well as military conditions. Hitler wanted a quick and decisive war, given the longer term aims he sought, and the relative imbalance of resources enjoyed by his opponents. Moreover, the use of tank formations in this way depended upon both surprise and the existence of an opportunity to be exploited. In the context of the opening stages of the Second World War neither could be induced by military means alone. Hitler benefited enormously by the assumptions and decisions made by the Allies.

Before looking at these and the strategies actually adopted by the contenders in 1940, let us look at the theoretical debate surrounding these new weapons. It should be stressed that the same debate, in kind if not in content, surrounds the relation of nuclear weapons to strategy and politics in the contemporary period, as we shall see later. The difference between this debate and that of the inter-war period, is that the latter could be referred to a body of practice in which the new weapons had actually been used. With the exception of the bombing programme of August 1945 there has been no precedent for nuclear war. My concern here is with the questions, is there any valid prescriptive basis that can be applied to weapons procurement and use at the sub-strategic level, or is this really a matter of luck combined with intelligent pragmatism at the command level? On what grounds can the potential of new weapons be translated into effective use?

Guderian, the successful panzer commander in the Battle of France, whose views on tanks have been discussed above, acknowledged Fuller as a pioneer in this field and as an early mentor. Colonel Fuller first stated his views on the importance of armour in modern warfare in a series of lectures on *Field Service Regulations, Vol II (Operations)* in the winter of 1929/30.[25] The new factor in modern warfare produced by the tank was mobility. This factor was not solely the function of the tank but was derived also from the aeroplane. Indeed, he regarded the major revolutionary change in the machinery of warfare emanating from the First World War to be aircraft and not tanks. He was remarkably prescient in arguing that the weapon of the future was 'the manless flying machine—

the true aerial torpedo'.[26] He said, 'when such a weapon is invented the whole form of war on land and at sea may once again have to be recast.'[27] He was certainly right in this, although his prediction was no more than an inspired guess, given the technology of his day.

It is perhaps in his insistence that tanks and aircraft are complementary that his main contribution to tactical theory lies. He argued that, 'in future warfare cooperation between tanks and aeroplane is likely to prove far more important than cooperation between tanks and infantry. So important that we may see tanks and aeroplanes forming one force and infantry a completely separate force.'[28] Both tactical aircraft and ground forces should come under one command. The precedent for this was set in July 1918 when 8th Squadron R.A.F. equipped with 18 Armstrong-Whitworth planes was attached to Tank Corps and given reconnaissance, strike and tank support roles.[29]

The novelty of the tank lay in its ability to provide firepower whose effectiveness and defence was provided by mobility combined with armour. Fuller insisted on the importance of speed and on a variety of tank types, each designed to perform a specific function such as crossing water, bridge-laying, mine-clearing and so on. He envisaged two main types of tanks—the light reconnaissance and the heavy or main battle tank, fairly heavily armoured and carrying a combination of guns and machine-guns. Command and control are stressed, although not surprisingly, given the time these lectures were given, the use of radio is not mentioned. The importance of the commander being at the point of contact with the enemy is continually emphasised. As he put it, 'the general will be *with* his fighting troops, he will be *in* the battle and not outside of it.'[30]

The tank should have a special role in warfare quite independent of that of the infantry. It should not be used for infantry support. He argued, 'To combine tanks and infantry is tantamount to yoking a tractor to a draught horse.'[31] This role was offensive in character. It was the means of forcing a decision using the mobility of the tank to deprive the enemy of the initiative and to open a gap at a point of weakness, sowing confusion and preventing counterattacks or effective defence. This is the negation of positional warfare. Armoured formations were free in their choice of tactical objectives, given their mobility and flexibility, as infantry formations were not, tied as they were to a slow pace of advance, relatively immobile artillery support with short range, and a huge tail of logistical support. With tanks the elaborate supply system necessary for setpiece battles was no longer needed. Given the possibility of a quick decision this not only released resources but also preserved the element of surprise. The complex and lengthy preparations and dispositions for positional battle were readily detected through aereial reconnaissance and gave time for counter-measures.

Surprise was an essential condition for success when facing an opponent either partially or equally mechanised. There was of course little problem in dealing with an enemy lacking in armour. But since the whole point of having armour was to be able to force a decision, there existed some difficulty when engaged with an opponent sharing this objective. Surprise was the only means of breaking the deadlock. How this was to be achieved was clearly an imponderable although an important condition for success. In principle, without it, opponents evenly matched in armour and aircraft could not resolve their disputes through battle-field victory. Lightning campaigns would then be transmuted into wars of attrition dependent for their resolution on the balance of resources possessed by the contenders. The great virtue of the tank thus seems to lie in monopoly.

Fuller recognised this problem by stressing the element of surprise as important where the contenders are evenly matched in armour and aircraft, but also in realising the difficulties of tank-to-tank combat.[32] There was no precedent for this in the First World War and the tactics of tank battles were a matter more of practice than of theory, although he made a valiant attempt to resolve some of the problems. Thus while the advantages of tanks and aircraft in combination could be depicted in comparison with the alternative positional warfare of the previous World War, it was more difficult to relate these to a recipe for success where opponents were evenly matched. In theory tanks and aircraft could be seen as a means of quick battle-field decision simply by contrast with the painful *via dolorosa* of positional trench warfare. But this begs the question of an adequate tactical theory as a basis for armoured warfare between comparable opponents.

This point is reinforced by the ambiguity with which Fuller treats the role of the infantry. He is very vague both about its composition and its use with armour. He gives the impression that battles are won with tanks and aircraft alone, leaving the infantry with the residual role of policing conquered territory. This reflects the traditional British predilection for a maritime strategy with a small professional army and avoiding major military commitment on the European continent. The First World War with its huge consumption of manpower was an aberration to be avoided in the future. Mobile armoured warfare was thus seen as an alternative to the mass slaughter of the trenches, economical both in life and in resources. But this desirable form of warfare had to produce results in the form of battle-field decisions that in turn produced a political settlement. The latter was the concern of the politicians, but armoured warfare was a means to this end. Essentially it was offensive in character. If it led to a quick decision then indeed it was both economical and rational in the sense of rationality argued earlier in this work, that is relating means and ends in a balanced and commensurable manner. But what if it did not? The consequence would appear to be a different kind of war. In any case as we shall see, neither Britain nor France sought a quick battle decision in 1940. The use of armour and aircraft for this purpose was thus irrelevant to both states. In the case of Britain, still obsessed with a global as opposed to a continental strategic posture, it was even more irrelevant.

However, the point here is that whatever the advantages in comparing forms of warfare—mobile, as opposed to positional, operations—the comparison, if it is to lead to effective prescription, must be based upon a full statement of the necessary and sufficient empirical conditions for operational success. General principles are insufficient for this purpose. Fuller himself understood the essential political character of war, and, echoing Clausewitz, stated that 'the aim of strategy is to clinch a political argument by means of force instead of words'. The true object of war is 'to establish a *more perfect peace*'.[33] It was thus counter-productive to embark on a form of war unlikely to achieve this because it led directly to mass slaughter. A rational war was not a total war where the national capacity to destroy was translated into action to the utmost limit.[34] In his view armoured warfare was a limited form of war and operated at what he called the moral level, directed at the rationality of the contenders. The ideal he aimed at was equivalent to that of warfare in the Eighteenth Century, when victories and defeats were conceded and the point yielded, without any descent into the abyss of total war. While the use of tanks and aircraft at the tactical level may be seen as limited exercises in violence the political dimension is not so limited it is not the weapon but the will that determines the character of war. Fuller may well have been right in eliminating the infantry from its primary role in battle, and indeed the chief casualties of the Second World War, unlike the First World War, were civilians rather than soldiers, but this was not the consequence of the new weapons but of political decision. It is perhaps ironic that the most perfect example of his idealised war took place in a virtually uninhabited desert.

In the main, however, Fuller concentrated on the machinery of armoured warfare rather than on the relationship of the lightning offensive to the overall strategic and political purpose or end. The new weapons provided, under unspecified conditions, a means to speedy and economic battle-field victory, but what this victory was intended to achieve is left unexamined. That it might leave more problems for the politician to resolve is left unconsidered. He was more concerned with tactics and the sub-strategic level than with strategy.

It was Liddell-Hart[35] in this period who sought to combine the new weapons within the framework of a general strategic approach. Fuller believed that the tank and its supporting tactical air force was a means of quick battle-field decision. Liddell-Hart, however, although recognising that both tank and aircraft were innovatory weapons, and that mechanised warfare was superior to positional warfare with its huge drain on resources, came to very different conclusions. He understood, far more than Fuller, that the aim of war is not victory in battle but the defeat of the enemy and this could be achieved by a variety of means without recourse to the direct confrontation of armies, armoured or other otherwise. Like Fuller, and equally following Clausewitz, he realised that defeat was a matter of will as much as material damage. In this he was indulging, as was Clausewitz, in assumptions of common rationality belonging more to the Eighteenth than the Twentieth Century. The enemy should be presented with a dilemma that cannot be resolved through military means and his consequent demoralisation leads him to concede the political issue at stake. This indicates that whatever this issue was, it was not one of security in its fundamental sense, and so did not entail total war. Limited war was the postulate of this form of strategy. The end dictated the means.

The strategy of the indirect approach, as Liddell-Hart called it, was not offensive in character. Analogies are always suspect, but a comparison with bull fighting illustrates the principle. The relative imbalance between the adversaries—the bull and the matador—is offset by a progressive weakening of the bull and the use of the bull's own strength to produce the kill. Time is not on the bull's side. Liddell-Hart saw the indirect approach as a 'law of life',[36] as a universal principle operating on all situations of conflict regardless of their immediate circumstances and conditions. Decision, as opposed to battle-field victories, is obtained through the operation of what is essentially a defensive strategy directed at the enemy's resources rather than directly at his armies. The end sought was not the decisive battle, although in certain circumstances this may constitute the means, but the state of affairs desired by the actor. It is rarely the case that battle-field victory produces this. Again, following Clausewitz, he argued that the means adopted and the ends sought must be in balance. Ideally, he argued, 'the perfection of strategy would be therefore to produce a decision without any serious fighting'.[37]

Liddell-Hart did not attempt, any more than did Clausewitz, to produce a rigorous theory. Instead he produced a number of maxims derived from experience. These were not dogmatic rules but 'guides to practice.'[38] They were universal in the sense that they applied to all organised uses of violence for political ends regardless of their context. They constituted a rational framework for war. There were eight of them; six positive and two negative.[39] Success in warfare could be achieved by adjusting ends to means, i.e. seeking only what is possible; the end must predominate over the means adopted; surprise is an important condition; weaknesses in the form of the line of least resistance should be the focus of effort; flexibility in operations by maintaining alternative courses of action of options is important, and finally, there should be a willingness to adapt to changed circumstances. The two negative principles consisted of not putting the main effort against the principal enemy dispositions, since defence has the advantage over attack, and not reinforcing failure.

As he put it, 'the essential truth underlying these maxims is that for success, two major problems must be solved—dislocation and exploitation. One precedes and one follows the actual blow which in comparison is a single act. You cannot hit the enemy with effect unless you have first created the opportunity, you cannot make that effect decisive unless you exploit the second opportunity that comes before he can recover.'[40] In short manoeuvre and the adoption of tactics designed to push the enemy off balance, thus creating opportunities to be exploited while preserving an overall defensive posture, constituted the recipe for strategic success. The indirect approach thus 'aims at an eventual decision by sapping the opponent's strength and skill.'[41] Not surprisingly he regarded the Dardanelles[42] operation, albeit unsuccessful, as a more appropriate means to the end sought than the positional battles of the Western Front. It is even less surprising that he became an adviser to Winston Churchill.

Fuller in his advocacy of the combination of tanks and aircraft in highly mobile and flexible warfare, saw no further than battle-field victory. This combination was offensive in character and a means of achieving quick military decision. The overall political purpose served by such a decision is ignored. Liddell-Hart came to opposite conclusions in reviewing the changing character of warfare and the role of the new weapons. Rather than strengthening the offensive he believed that they made the defensive superior. The crucial factor was not the tank but aircraft. Even so it was not the revolutionary effect of a new weapon, measured in terms of its capability to inflict damage that was significant, but the relationship between this and the political objectives sought by Britain. It was this political dimension that established the framework for the assessment of innovation in weapons.

Writing in 1939 he made a number of specific prescriptions.[43] The first priority should be given to aircraft production. An air umbrella should be created over the British Isles. The Royal Air Force, followed by the navy, should have priority over the army. He saw the impending war with Germany as primarily an economic rather than a military contest. Instead of seeking victory on the battle-field, Britain should direct the main effort at curtailing the supply of some twenty basic minerals and commodities through blockade. The overall aim was not the defeat of Germany but an appeal to a common rationality by demonstrating the impossibility of a German victory. As he put it 'Our objective is fulfilled if we can convince the enemy that he cannot conquer.'[44] This could be done by adopting defensive rather than offensive measures.

From his study of the First World War and of the use of the new weapons he believed that, 'in sum the soldier's dream of the lightning war has a decreasing prospect of fulfilment'.[45] He recognised that this belief was not shared by the Germans whose military literature is 'lit up with the theme of the blitzkrieg—the lightning war'.[46] He accepted that against an unprepared opponent the use of armour and aircraft is likely to succeed. But with adequate preparation this could not be the case. He urged 'It is thus our responsibility to disassociate our allies from endangering their defensive prospects by pursuing an offensive strategy.'[47] Here he had in mind the almost disastrous early moves of the French in 1914. The most appropriate strategic posture for Britain was securing the base by providing a deterrent against bombing in the form of fighters, assisting the continental ally in defence, adopting economic blockade measures, and countering similar attempts by the enemy.[48]

So far as the use of armour is concerned, Liddell-Hart thought that a fully mechanised tank force supported by motorised infantry and artillery would serve as a counter to the newly formed panzer corps.[49] Their role was defensive, although they could exploit mistakes made in the offensive by the opposition. The initiative rested with the enemy but, given the superiority of the defence over the offensive, this did not matter. He was to be encouraged to exhaust himself by fruitless attempts to break the defence. The primary role in frustrating enemy attack was given to the French army. The British role on the continent was to act as support and to provide a reserve. It was appropriate therefore to make British land forces, although small in number, as mobile as possible with a relatively large armoured component.[50]

Before looking at the relation of these strategic ideas to practice, a comment on the method used as a basis for their formulation would seem appropriate in the light of discussion in earlier chapters. Both Fuller and Liddell-Hart, and especially the latter, devoted time to the analysis of past cases of military action to support their assumptions and generalisations about the proper conduct of war. There were difficulties in applying this analysis where new weapons were concerned, but neither of these writers believed that they were so revolutionary as to make past wars irrelevant to future practice. Fuller accepted the validity of past classical precedents for armoured warfare, while Liddell-Hart based much of his argument on a lengthy examination of campaigns from those of Alexander to those of the Nineteenth Century. The weaknesses of what might be called the historical method have been noted elsewhere.

A more insidious danger existed in their attempt to avoid what they conceived to be the mistakes of the First World War. If generals and politicians in preparing for the next war are concerned to refight the last war, but more successfully, this is certainly not the case for the strategic theorists and policy-makers of the 1930s. They were united in seeking to avoid the huge costs in men and materials of positional trench warfare. On the French and British side the solution as we shall see, was to adopt a defensive strategy. The Germans following much the same reasoning adopted an offensive strategy.[51] Strategic theorists, if their advice was to be even considered by the politicians of these countries, had to address themselves to the problem of avoiding a repetition of the First World War. This war thus exercised an influence, albeit negative, on strategic thinking.

The problem was that instead of focussing on war aims, that is on the relation between ends and means in terms of an appropriate form of warfare, the emphasis was placed on means alone, that is on warfare itself. The First World War was a disaster, not only in the destruction it inflicted on the contenders, but also and more importantly, in its failure to resolve any major political question, especially that of security. Battle-field victory was not translated into a peace that was acceptable to all the European states or provided any of them with security. Fuller, in concentrating solely on the sub-strategic and tactical levels, was concerned only with the achievement of battle-field victory in a manner radically different from the bloody battles of attrition of the previous war. Liddell-Hart, however, was concerned with strategy proper. His notion of the indirect approach avoided confrontational battles but also avoided military decision itself. He appealed to a level of rationality that set limits on war. No political end could be achieved by total war. His war of feint and manoeuvre was designed to achieve relative advantages that would be recognised by all the contenders. But could this method be so controlled and limited as to prevent its degeneration into total war? Attention was given more to the fact that it was an alternative to the horrors of trench warfare than to the political ends it might serve. In this sense the experience of the First World War and its use as a source for bad or good or good examples—Cambrai as against the Somme—exercised a malign if subtle influence on the strategic reasoning of the day. Experience in this sense is a bad guide to practice. Nor is it a good basis for theory.

Perhaps the important critical point to be made about these apparently competing strategic views—the blitzkrieg and the indirect approach—is their empirical vacuity. Depending on circumstances and an associated political analysis, they can be made relevant to almost any politico-military contest. They are not rivals. It is true that machine warfare is really a tactical form, but its implications in planning for war are extreme. A relatively small professional army, the creation of an integrated tactical airforce, and an emphasis on mobility through mechanisation, is a formula suited to fighting quick wars limited in scale with clear political ends. Hitler found it attractive, not because he was convinced by the idea of Guderian and Manstein, themselves influenced by Fuller and Liddell-Hart, but because their proposals fitted in with his political ambitions and his need for quick victory. Their proposals coincided with the kind of war he wanted to fight. But it was not the war he actually fought.

His lightning victories in the early stages of the war made him believe that he had discovered the secret of success in war. In seeking the same kind of victory in the Soviet Union he was encouraged by these successes. He ignored the fact that his political ends had not been achieved. Such was his optimism that he actually divided his armoured divisions, increasing their number but not their strength, in order to pursue the same tactical plan depending on mobility and the envelopment of superior forces. Failure to achieve the victory he sought was disastrous. Germany found itself fighting a war of attrition faced with superior resources, while deploying armoured forces designed for quite different purposes. The quest for quick decision was replaced by a struggle to regain the initiative—a struggle lost after Stalingrad.

The primacy of the tank and supporting aircraft and of blitzkrieg tactics so far as Hitler was concerned, ended in the winter of 1941/2. The recall of Guderian on 20th February 1943 as Inspector General of Armoured Troops saw an attempt to return to this formula. New types of tanks were to be introduced to counter the superior Soviet T34 and overall production increased. Guderian actually referred Hitler to Liddell-Hart's arguments in his effort to convince him of the primacy of the tank.[52] It was recognised however, that the initiative had been lost and that 1943 would see only limited offensives. It was to the next year that Guderian looked for the launching of large-scale attacks designed to wrench the initiative from the Red Army. Success could only be achieved through surprise and concentration. How this was to be achieved, given the situation after Stalingrad, was far from clear. Instead of one side being able to exploit the weakness of the other, the position was one of huge attritional battles, positional in character, between evenly matched contenders. The difference between them was largely a question of resources, both manpower and tanks. The failure of the last major attempt to check the Russians—operation *Zitadelle,* with its double envelopment tactics, was the death blow to the use of armour as a means of forcing a decision on the battle-field. Thereafter it became largely a defensive weapon as a kind of mobile artillery. It is fair to say that although Guderian had no operational responsibility, he actually opposed *Zitadelle*[53] since he realised that the German armoured forces were inadequate both in type and in numbers. Moreover, the element of surprise was missing given the repeated postponements of the operation.

If blitzkrieg was a flawed tactic both in military and in political terms, what of the indirect approach? Hitler needed a blitzkrieg since time was not on his side. The Allies on the contrary, given their relative unpreparedness and their conception of political ends, sought delay. They desired no battle-field decision. The doctrine propounded by Liddell-Hart that war had passed onto the defensive since the defensive possessed all the advantages,[54] fell on ready ears. Like Hitler's belief that the cabinet wars of the Eighteenth Century could be re-fought so that politics dominated the battle-field, the Allies' own variety of wishful thinking was based upon expediency. Neither side had prepared for the war that was to be fought. Since the British and the French believed that they could not seize the military initiative with any great hopes of initial success, a defensive strategy aimed at removing Hitler and his regime was the answer.[55] The war was thus seen to be a long one, at least three years, during which the Allies would hold the Western Front, plugging the gap in the Maginot Line with their best land forces. Opportunities would be sought using sea and air forces to force dispersal of effort on the Germans. An economic blockade was to be mounted with the intention of depriving the German people and so undercutting support for their Fuehrer. Air forces were to be strengthened, providing both a bomber force capable of attacking key German targets and a lighter force to prevent or deter counter attacks. Britain was to provide the naval and air forces and a small, but highly equipped, land contingent. The British were to mount the blockade and to provide diversion as opportunity occurred, while the French were to frustrate any German attempt to force the initiative on land. Although Poland had been lost, since it could only have been saved by adopting offensive measures, this was only a temporary loss, and another restoration of Poland would ensue on the fall of the Nazi regime.

This strategy was the product of the traditional reluctance of Britain to become involved in major continental land operations, especially given the precedent of the First World War, and of the French reluctance, on the same precedent, for another blood-letting. It can be seen why the advocates of machine warfare got a poor hearing in their own countries while being greeted with enthusiasm in Germany. In the event Fuller was right in 1940 and wrong in 1943 and Liddell-Hart continued to prevail in

British thinking at least until the 1944 landings. The penchant for the 'soft under-belly' in Churchill's strategic reasoning was a recognition of the paramountcy of politics in formulating military operations. In this instance it reflected as much a concern for Russian as for German expansion.

The lightning victory in 1940 did not however, much to Hitler's chagrin, lead to political recognition of battle-field success. Britain did not accept negotiation, even on his generous terms,[56] and in spite of the indications of the Hess mission that Hitler desired a negotiated peace. Blitzkrieg tactics could not work against Britain given the existence of the Channel and the difficulty of achieving surprise. Nor was Hitler capable of bringing about British defeat through the air. Contrary to British pre-war expectations the Luftwaffe was designed not for strategic bombing but for tactical support. It was not capable of inflicting sufficient material damage such as to force Britain to the negotiating table. Neither did the assault on the British fighter force known as the Battle of Britain solve the problem. This tactic may be regarded not as a preliminary to an invasion but, in combination with the operation *Sea Lion*, as a form of pressure designed to induce the British towards negotiation. In the event it was a failure.[57] Yet it can be seen as evidence of Hitler's own unpreparedness, since he clearly believed that with the defeat of France through blitzkrieg he would attain his political object—which was a free hand in Europe and the acquisition of *lebensraum* in the East. The refusal of Britain to accept defeat and its political consequences meant that the war changed its character. By implication it became a total war since the only result acceptable to the British government was German defeat.

In turning to the bombing of British cities and mounting a submarine campaign as well as accepting the British challenge in North Africa, Hitler tacitly acknowledged this. The solution was to be found nevertheless in another blitzkrieg, this time against the Soviet Union. Success here should surely bring about the British acceptance of German dominance in Europe. The failure of this move confirmed the war as total with all that that entailed. The war had moved into the realms of irrationality. The only objective sought was unconditional surrender. But this is not what had been intended, either by the use of blitzkrieg tactics, or by the strategy of economic warfare. Both sides sought to fight a limited war that produced a favourable political settlement. From the Allied side they had shown themselves willing to accept changes in the European map by negotiation. When it became clear that negotiated settlements were regarded as temporary expedients by Hitler after his occupation of Prague and his breach of the Munich Agreement, they were forced to look at German military *capability* rather than his intentions. Nevertheless they did not wish to fight a total war with the destruction of Germany as its main objective. The removal of the Hitler regime was a more limited aim and an appropriate strategy was devised to achieve it. But neither did Hitler want total war and he was baffled by the refusal of his opponents to come to terms with him after his military successes. He came too to regard the removal of Churchill as a main condition of negotiation. After all this had been the case with the defeat of France, and the Petain government had thereafter proved amenable. But were the means adopted commensurate with the ends sought? In the event changing a political system meant a direct and total assault on the state.

To return to the problem of the appropriate strategy and the use and procurement of new weapons, we can see that choice is a function of a complex of factors—geographical position and topography; national resources and economic structure, population, technology; political control and objectives, and the immediate political and military circumstances at the time of crisis and decision, as these are perceived and interpreted by governments. Such a choice is rational within this framework of decision. It was entirely rational of Britain in 1940 to temporise given her commitments and military preparedness. This was equally true for France. Neither state had any territorial ambitions in Europe nor were they *necessarily* committed to the Versailles system. In choosing to go to war, their main political objective was to contain Germany by checking the unilateral threat and use of violence as a means of forcing changes in the political status quo. They wanted to demonstrate to Germany that this was not a viable policy. Since restraint through negotiation had proved a failure an ultimatum threatening war seemed the only alternative. The German political objective was to force such a change since it was very unlikely that this—*lebensraum*—would be conceded through peaceful diplomacy. Hitler was therefore compelled either to give up the policy or counter the Allied threat. Both sides adopted different means to their end. The blitzkrieg came into conflict with the defensive strategy of the indirect approach. Both strategies implied different applications of the new weapons. Tanks and aircraft could be used both in the defensive or the offensive. The consequence of this clash in 1940 was what neither side had expected—a total war.

The point to be stressed here when considering the influence of the new weapons on strategic reasoning, is that the relation between means and ends—the sub-strategic and the grand strategic levels—cannot be stated with any precision. The tactics of the blitzkrieg were highly successful in 1940. But battle-field victory did not produce political success. Nor could it be argued from this victory that it could easily be repeated. There were a number of highly variable factors involved in the Battle of France. The element of surprise was a central condition; and the contributions the allies made to their own defeat through their troop deployments in the Low Countries; their inability to perceive and respond to the early German moves; the ease the terrain gave to the passage of tanks after the Meuse crossing; the relative sophistication of the road system; the ample supply of civilian petrol available to the invaders; the panic flight of the refugees, encouraged by the strafing of the Luftwaffe, that clogged the roads and hindered Allied movement, etc., were all factors that contributed to the success of the blitzkrieg, but could hardly be repeated. Yet even if blitzkrieg theory could be considered as a recipe for tactical success, the essential point for the strategic theorist and the political decision-maker is to establish the link between military and political success. The rationality of the battle-field has to be translated into the rationality of the political contest. A concentration on method alone precludes this. With the advantages of hindsight we might conclude that if Hitler made the mistake of concentrating on means, his opponents in pursuing the indirect approach were equally mistaken in concentrating on ends. Neither sought a proper relationship between ends and means within a framework of a common rationality. Given their cross-purposes and the ambivalent nature of extant weaponry it is hardly surprising that the war turned out as it did.

This point is brought out most clearly in the development of two weapons and their political and strategic rationale. The bomber and the landing craft (both tank and infantry) afford a contrast in terms of their relationship to policy. Rather than the planned development of a technical means to a clearly defined strategic purpose, producing a desired political end, they illustrate a haphazard and often irrational approach towards strategic planning. They appeared at times to have more relevance to inter-allied disputes over strategy and its relationship to conflicting political goals, than to the struggle against the common enemy. In this sense they had a political rather than a military role.

On the face of it the bomber appears the more obvious strategic weapon. Very early on in the inter-war period claims had been made for its revolutionary influence on war.[58] These claims had been accepted, in part at least, by the politicians, who feared for the vulnerability of their densely populated cities. It was realised in Britain for example, that air power was both a direct threat to population and industrial centres and also to the navy, reducing its value as the ultimate defence of the homeland. As was noted earlier, the question of a deterrent airforce—whether in the form of a fighter screen or a retaliatory bomber force—was central to the defence debate of the 1930s. The Battle of Britain revealed the effectiveness of air defence but gave no indication how to turn it into an effective offensive. The blitz, significantly, had not proved as devastating as was first supposed. Instead of drawing conclusions from this, however, attention was diverted to making similar attacks on German cities.[59]

With the exception of operations in the North African theatre, an air offensive of Germany was the only viable form of attack open to Britain after expulsion from the Continent. The technical resources and productive capacity for building large bomber forces already existed and could be utilised without making excessive demands prejudicial to the overall war effort. Such a strategy fitted in with the general strategic approach, which precluded a direct assault on Nazi-occupied Europe. It made no radical departure from that adopted before the Battle of France. The loss of the main continental ally only emphasised the defensive opportunism characteristic of British strategic thinking. The acquisition of another ally—the Soviet Union—did not change this attitude. The British saw their main role as diversionary, forcing the Germans to disperse their forces over a number of theatres and thus relieving the pressure on the

USSR. This was the purpose of the North African campaign and later the Italian campaign. No direct confrontation with the main German forces was to be sought. As with France, these last were to be held in check by the Soviet Union. This was in essence an indirect strategy using the air force and the navy as its chief instruments.

The more positive aspect of this indirect approach was the air offensive.[60] What was the nature of this offensive and what were its aims? The main target of what were to be thousand bomber raids was the civilian population of Germany. This was not planned deliberately but was a consequence of extant military technology. The relative short range of fighter escorts and the effectiveness of fighter defence, together with the vagaries of the weather and the limitations of existing radar systems, meant that bombing was less costly at night. Night bombing, however, was inevitably inaccurate. Purely military or industrial targets could not be attacked with precision except by daylight and with air superiority. The consequence was what was called euphemistically *area bombing*. Blast damage through the dropping of high explosives, accompanied with incendiaries, produced under optimal conditions fire-storms more destructive even than the effects of atom bombs later. The principal victims were civilians.

The rationale for this strategy was consistent with the indirect approach. The Chamberlain governments had concluded as we saw earlier, that rather than seeking a costly battle-field victory the overthrow of the Hitler regime was a more rational goal. It was presumed that the hold the regime had on the German people was necessarily tenuous and would break when they were faced with sacrifices. They hoped to accomplish this through economic blockade and a defensive strategy.[61] Nazi domination over Europe after the fall of France precluded this. Churchill, however, after the experience of the Battle of Britain and the Blitz, did not fear German retaliation as his predecessor had done, and decided to adopt a bombing offensive. Civilian morale was therefore the major target. This illustrates the point that for Britain it was the regime in Germany and its expansionist policies that constituted the problem and not the German state itself. This was, of course, not the case for either France or the Soviet Union, who had cause to fear Germany as a major continental land power regardless of its political system. It was no victory for Britain to destroy the state of Germany as well as its regime, with the consequence that its neighbours become dominant powers in Europe. If the regime could be ousted without going to the lengths and sacrifices of total war so much the better.

The bomber was thus to be used to persuade the German people to repudiate its leadership. In attacking the home front, German morale, both civilian and military, would be sapped to the point when the will to continue the war would be destroyed or weakened so that a negoiated peace might be possible with a non-Nazi government. The problem for Britain, apart from actually realising this goal through the method of area bombing, was that neither of her two allies, the Soviet Union and the United States, had any interest in the survival of Germany as a political

.entity or of preserving some sort of balance in Europe. For them the war was total and could end only with the complete surrender of Germany. This could only be achieved through battle-field victory in direct with the German armies. Churchill perforce, although not until after a long struggle to persuade his allies otherwise, was obliged to accept this. Indeed it is doubtful whether without the principle of unconditional surrender the alliance could have been maintained. In any case it was highly unlikely that, as the junior partner in the war, with the Soviet Union, and later the United States, carrying the major burden of the effort, the British view could prevail.

The use of the bomber and its strategic rationale was thus condemned to be irrelevant almost from the beginning. It became another instrument of total war destroying largely for destruction's sake. The bombing offensive served as a demonstration to the Soviet Union, and to the United States, that Britain was making a contribution to the war and as a means of evading demands for a Second Front. This was a far cry from the hopes expressed by Churchill when he said as early as July 1940 'When I look round to see how we can win the war I see that there is only one sure path. We have no continental army which can defeat the German military power. The blockade is broken and Hitler has Asia and probably Africa to draw from. Should he be repulsed here or not try invasion he will recoil eastward and we have nothing to stop him. But there is one thing that will bring him back and bring him down, and that is an absolutely devastating exterminatory attack by very heavy bombers from this country upon the Nazi homeland. We must be able to overwhelm them by this means without which I do not see a way through'.[62]

While this may have been Churchill's hope in 1940 at a time when Britain was isolated and prospects looked hopeless, the policy of strategic bombing remained unaltered for the duration of the war. In spite of the acquisition of allies, and the mounting pressures to adopt a strategy of direct confrontation with the main German forces in Europe, this remained a consistent strand in the British approach to war. On the 9th July 1941 the Air Staff directed the C. in C. of Bomber Command to attack the weakest points in Germany; these lay in 'the morale of the civilian population and the inland transportation system'.[63] The main effort of the bomber force 'was to be directed towards destroying the morale of the civil population as a whole, and of the industrial workers in particular'.[64] The goal set for Bomber Command was a force of some 4000 heavy bombers, to be achieved late 1943 or early 1944. The C. in C. wanted a 1000 bomber force especially charged with the destruction of German cities. An early operation, code-named Millennium, was an attack on Cologne designed, 'to annihilate one of Germany's main industrial centres by fire'.[65] This raid on 30th May, 1942 was intended to gain support from the political leadership for this ambitious bombing programme. Harris stressed that 'strategic' bombing of this kind would win the war without the necessity of mounting a cross-Channel invasion. The principal condition was a 'sufficient bomber force' with an absolute priority in terms of the allocation of resources and production.[66] The programme was 'to raze substantially to the ground 30 to 40 of the principal German cities'. Again the point was stressed in January 1943 that the aim was 'the undermining of the morale of the German people to the point where the capacity for armed resistance is fatally weakened'.[67]

On the 10th June 1943 a new directive, Pointblank, taking into account the new factor of American participation in 'strategic' bombing, was issued. The bombing of Hamburg, code-named Gomorrah[68] (sic), over the period 24th July—30th July 1943, produced a fire-storm which killed 41,800 people and injured 37,439 others. By comparison, the total number of people killed by German raids on Britain was 63,000. It is estimated that 500,000 were killed in Germany by allied raids. Area bombing dominated the air strategy until the Overlord programme began to short priorities towards tactical support in the form of the Leigh-Mallory Transportation Plan and ground support after D Day, such as the bombing of Caen. This diversion was resisted by Bomber Command, as they had resisted the use of bombers in the campaign against submarines during the Battle of the Atlantic.

Some attempts at precision bombing were made, notably the attacks on the ball-bearing and aircraft factories at Schweinfurt and Regensburg.[69] These raids were costly. They were also ineffective. They left the important machinery largely undestroyed and dispersal proved a relatively easy means of preserving and maintaining productive capacity. The admitted inability of Bomber Command to bomb with precision where fighter cover was absent, and experience, such as these raids, reinforced the policy of area bombing. Attempts to introduce a policy of bombing industrial bottlenecks, or even to give tactical support to the main battle effort, were countered with assertions that these were not the proper or effective use of heavy bombers.[70] The war would be won, with economy, by bombing German cities. Indeed, from considering forty cities as the optimal target, Harris now revised his figure to sixty to be attacked systematically by a 1000 bombers at the rate of two a month.

The bombing of Dresden[71] by British and American bomber forces 13th–15th February 1945 was probably the ultimate futility in the strategy of area bombing. Nominally this target was attacked because it was an important communications centre. It was thus a tactical and not a strategic target. As the Germans had strafed civilian refugees during their blitzkrieg on France in 1940 in order to maximise panic and thus confuse and delay allied counterattack, so the purpose of attacking Dresden was 'to cause great confusion in civilian evacuation from the East and hamper movement of reinforcements from other fronts'. Even Churchill baulked at the consequent carnage. In a letter to Ismay, he said, 'it seems to me that the moment has come when the question of bombing German cities simply for the sake of increasing the terror though under other pretexts should be reversed. Otherwise we shall come into control of an utterly ruined land ... the destruction of Dresden remains a serious query against the conduct of Allied bombing.'[72] It was by this time, and indeed from the time

Overlord became an agreed and serious programme, clear that the war would not be won by area bombing. Churchill now became conscious of the possibility, as indeed he had done with the adoption of the Transportation Plan, that this strategy was likely to present problems once the war was won. The same civilian populations who were its principal victims were needed to cooperate with post-war settlements.

I am not concerned with the morality of this bombing offensive, this aspect will be considered in a later chapter; but with the question of its effectiveness. Was it an adequate instrument for its stated purpose—the destruction of civilian morale as a means of achieving German defeat? Or was it simply an expedient—a surrogate for action conceived of at a time of impotence in military terms, becoming a programme that ecaped control while becoming increasingly irrelevant to the main war effort? Was it an alternative to a strategy that actively sought battle-field victory maintained by Churchill as he sought to persuade his allies to accept his views on an indirect approach? A distinction should be made between the claims of those charged with the conduct of area bombing operations and whose who authorised them. The former—Bomber Command—were strongly committed to the principle of strategic bombing without questioning very closely its aim. It was assumed perhaps too readily, that the level of damage inflicted by mass bombing was sufficiently devastating at least to retard German war production and, if intensified, to break German morale and so win the war. As we now know, in fact German war production actually increased during the most intensive phase of the bombing. Civilian and military morale, although affected in the short term, never wavered in its support of the Nazi government. Dissatisfaction amongst the senior military leadership was not reflected lower down. Germans fought with tenacity even though they must have known their efforts were sacrificial. On the home front civilians worked to repair the ravages of the raids and restore production. Bombing, rather than destroying morale, seemed to intensify it. The Nazi government manipulated the feelings of patriotism stimulated by both the bombing and the demand for unconditional surrender made by the Allies. Given the prior experience of the Blitz and of the invasion scare, this might have been expected by British policy-makers. Given the intelligence sources available to the Allies, reactions to the bombing could have been monitored and its value as a 'strategy' properly evaluated.

Why then was the bombing pursued so tenaciously in spite of the change in direction in allied strategy and its ineffectiveness in achieving its stated aim? It is true that German resources were placed under pressure through constant attack. The Germans had to produce fighters, use scarce fuel, train pilots, manufacture anti-aircraft guns, and divert manpower, to meet the aerial threat. Yet they could do this and still maintain their prolonged struggle against their opponents. It cannot be shown that the diversion of resources to counter the bombing offensive had a decisive effect on their war effort. Decision came only through the mounting of a cross-Channel invasion coordinated with a major Russian offensive. It would appear that the heavy bomber was used mainly because initially it was the only means of attacking Germany directly. Revenge for the Blitz and a tangible form of attack was good for British morale. After Soviet entry into the war it was a means of staving off Soviet demands for a Second Front. It was argued that strategic bombing sapped German resources and took some of the strain off Soviet troops. It compensated in some measure for British inability, combined with reluctance, to seek direct confrontation with the main German forces. And it fitted in with Churchill's predilection for an indirect strategy. However, once the bombing programme was endorsed and the production of large quantities of heavy bombers under way, it appeared to take on a life of its own. The only option once strategy broadened with Russian and American participation in the war, was its abandonment. Continuing the programme seemed a preferable course of action. It was preferable because it could be represented as an important British contribution to the Allied war effort and because it was compatible with Churchill's own preference for an indirect approach in strategy that was more likely to produce a favourable post-war situation in Europe for Britain. The bomber was thus a weapon whose utility waxed and waned as political and strategic exigencies changed. It is difficult to see, with hindsight, evidence of a rationally developed strategy in the bombing offensive.

If the bomber was a weapon that appeared to have a life of its own, the landing craft was intimately linked to a developing debate between the Allies. If we look at this debate after the invasion of Sicily,[73] we find a growing division in terms of strategic objectives between Britain and the United States. Neither Roosevelt nor his Chiefs of Staff wanted any further postponement of a cross-Channel invasion. From their point of view the correct military solution was a classic concentration of forces, both Soviet and Anglo-American, against Germany. Decisive battle-field victory was the main strategic aim. It should be noted that the brunt of the war against Japan was borne by the United States and, given the priority of the war against Germany, some impatience with delay in achieving decision in this theatre was clearly felt. The political end of victory was not over subtle; it was not the aggrandisement of either Britain or the Soviet Union. Nor was the United States interested in establishing or endorsing spheres of influence in Europe. The United States was to act as a political arbiter encouraging neither state in the fulfilment of what were seen as territorial aspirations. The longer battle-field victory was delayed, the stronger the Soviet position in Eastern and Southern Europe became, and this was also the case for the British position in the Mediterranean. The indirect strategy urged by the British, making the Balkans and Italy the focus of operations, not only prolonged the war against Germany but was seen as designed to promote British imperialism, securing the Eastern Mediterranean and routes to SE Asia and the Far East, an area seen as exclusively an American sphere of influence. The United States was not prepared to see a restoration of the pre-war status quo nor aid the British to recover their position. The longer victory over Germany and Japan was delayed, the more likely it was that British aspirations would be satisfied in this respect. The thrust of American strategic thinking was thus towards a cross-Channel invasion at the earliest moment.

For Britain such an invasion seemed not only costly in lives—British lives—but politically undesirable. Assuming that defeat for Germany was only a matter of time, the important question was what political consequences followed from this? The problems of mounting such an invasion were not insuperable, but it could be stalemated and lead to a war of attrition. This could only benefit the Soviet Union, who once confident of success on the Eastern front, could view with equanimity the progressive weakening of a state far from friendly towards Soviet aspirations and most capable of checking them in Europe. It seemed to Churchill that an advance in Italy and the Balkans through the Ljubjana gap, if successful, would allow the entry of the British troops into Vienna and give Britain a substantial military and political presence in Southern Europe, thus preventing a Soviet monopoly. On the presumption that the United States would withdraw from Europe soon after the defeat of Germany, some accommodation with the Soviets appeared inevitable; it was better to negotiate this from a position of strength. Moreover, his predilection for an indirect strategy reinforced this view. Only the Soviet Union and the United States would benefit from direct confrontation with German forces in Western Europe.

It is not possible to enter into the complex negotiations between the Allied leaders that ensured after the success of the invasion of Sicily (Husky). In the event the United States (and the Soviet Union) won the strategic debate. Control over the landing craft proved the decisive factor. Overlord and the supporting operation Anvil were to go ahead according to plan. Churchill succeeded in keeping the Balkan option open but the German decision to fight in Italy proved conclusive. Overlord was effectively delayed until 1944 because Britain, so long as it was both a necessary springboard and maintained more forces than its ally, held a veto. This was used to push the North African and Mediterranean strategy. Once, however, the American contribution to the joint war effort became preponderant, British influence on strategy waned.

The United States had more leverage on strategic decision than did Britain. A threat to switch priorities to the Pacific continually hung over the British. If they proved too recalcitrant it might be implemented. Moreover, the Soviet Union could be used as a bargaining lever. It was a more important ally in the Pacific than Britain. It could engage Japanese troops on the Asian mainland. And its cooperation was necessary if political stability in China was to be achieved. The British with their colonial possessions were competitors in the Pacific. Unlike the Russians they possessed a major navy and, when recovered from the Japanese, major naval bases. If the British were worried over the prospect of the Pacific becoming the main theatre of operations, they were horrified at the possibility of the United States and the Soviet Union coming to terms behind their backs. This fear was consciously used by Roosevelt to obtain a more cooperative attitude towards the American notion of strategy.

It is the place of the mundane landing craft in this strategic debate that illustrates the political as opposed to the strictly military importance of weapons. A cross-Channel invasion was a most complicated operation necessitating the coordination of the three main arms designed firstly to seek a beach-head, and secondly, to fight out of it and win a decisive battle. Landing craft were clearly central to the initial phase, although once the beach-head had been secured they diminished in importance. Equally all operations that involved crossing water—as was the case for the Mediterranean strategy, and indeed for the Pacific theatre, required them. The production of these quasi-amphibians was crucial to these operations. This fell mainly on the United States. At the time when the decision was taken to embark on their manufacture in quantity it was not appreciated how crucial they were in terms of control over strategy. It was readily assumed that they would be available for whatever strategy was adopted. So long as it was assumed that the United States would fall in with British strategic thinking it was expected that landing craft for a Balkan strategy would be provided. The British thus fell victim to their own decisions on war production. Now while Churchill had reluctantly accepted the priority of Overlord he still believed that this did not pre-empt all landing craft and so prevent operations in the Eastern Mediterranean. Success in the latter area could be used to shift Allied strategy in the direction he wanted. The bulk of Allied forces in that area was under British command. They were useless to him, however, if he lacked landing craft.

The United States was well aware of this difficulty and, tantalisingly, while approving in principle operations in this area, imposed conditions and a time-tabling of movement of landing craft, that precluded them. Their chief strategem was Anvil. This operation entailed landing forces in Southern France in August well after the D Day landings. It required substantial numbers of landing craft. It was thus not possible for Churchill to use landing craft no longer needed after the initial phase of Overlord for his ventures, so long as the plan for Anvil was still in being. Paradoxically, Overlord was secured by Anvil, for no diversion of landing craft could be made so long as Anvil followed Overlord and this reinforced their commitment to Overlord. Churchill thus, while supporting Overlord, made strenuous objections to Anvil.[74] Neither the United States nor the Soviet Union were prepared to compromise on this issue. Landing craft freed from Overlord could not be diverted to suit Churchill. All that was conceded was a delay in their transfer to allow the Anzio landings (Shingle). All hopes of an alternative strategy faded as the Anzio operation failed to fulfil expectations.

It should be said that Churchill's strategic hopes were essentially opportunistic, lacking any clearly formulated operational plan. Much depended on the tenacity with which the Germans held ground and the speed of the Soviet advance. It was no part of his plan that Allied forces be bogged down in Western Europe or in Italy, while the Soviet Union effectively occupied the rest of Europe. The time for strategic decision was late in 1943, and the German defence of Italy, combined with American pressure in favour of the main effort being made in Western Europe, were decisive in this respect.

It was the denial of the crucial landing craft however, that prevented Churchill from seeking tactical success in his preferred theatre and turning it into a thrust that pre-empted Allied strategy. Roosevelt and his Chiefs of Staff understood this very well and used this denial to check his strategic ambitions.

So far, I have been concerned with analysing the relation of weapons to strategic decision and policy in terms of actual experience. We have seen that very often the link between the sub-strategic level and the political objectives sought, is either fortuitous or not clearly established. Success at the sub-strategic level did not necessarily lead to the achievement of desired political ends. Weapons were inherently ambiguous in this respect. The bomber, for example, pounding away at German cities, served no clear political purpose, nor was the relationship between the tactic and the goal sought ever closely monitored or even examined. In this case the military purpose of the heavy bomber—its destructive capacity and use against cities of 'areas'—was its only rationale. It appeared to escape political control and even ran counter to the policy ends sought in the closing stages of the war.

Such weapons and their use not merely run counter to the Clausewitzian principle of the commensurability of means to ends, but become ends in themselves. The point was made earlier that it was not the weapons that gave war its character but the will of the contenders. From the opening stages of the Second World War in its *drôle de guerre* phase, through the blitzkrieg, to the final stages of total war, culminating with the use of the atomic bomb, there is little evidence that control over weapons produced a consistent and rational relationship between the means of violence and the ends sought by its use. The simplest solution, both in dealing with the enemy and in dealing with allies, appeared to be to allow the means of violence to dictate the ends sought. The demand for unconditional surrender and total war were the results. Both weapons and will merged to create virtually an a-political conflict—the negation of rational violence. In the next chapter the new phenomenon of nuclear weapons will be considered. In analysing these in terms of the rational use of violence we cannot draw on experience in order to derive strategic lessons. Perhaps this is as well.

NOTES AND REFERENCES

1. Of course this does not preclude politics between allies, especially when national interests are related to strategic ends, as was the case in Churchill's preference for a Mediterranean and Balkan strategy in the face of opposition from the United States dubious about the promotion of British imperialism. Nor does it preclude the politics of revolution and resistance when the question of a post-war political order became relevant with the imminence of victory.

2. Both the United States and the United Kingdom conducted studies of the effects of the strategic bombing of Germany. See Sir Charles Webster and Noble Frankland, *the Strategic Air Offensive Against Germany*, Vols. I–IV, HMSO, 1961.

3. See Herman Kahn, *On Thermo-Nuclear War, op. cit.*, p. 376. He says that pre-war calculations were fifty casualties for every ton of explosive dropped, eighteen of which were expected to be fatal. A large number of associated psychic casualties would also result from bombing. In the event this was a gross over-estimate.

4. In the Second World War both Churchill and Hitler were criticised by their generals for their strategic pretensions. See Kennedy, *The Business of War, op. cit.* p. 336 and Guderian, *Panzer Leader, op. cit.*, p. 378.

5. See Mark A. Stoler, *The Politics of the Second Front*, Greenwood Press, Westport, Conn, 1977.

6. See Lord Tedder, *With Prejudice: War Memoirs*, Cassell, London, 1966, pp. 521–9.

7. Anthony Cave Brown, *Bodyguard of Lies, op. cit.*

8. See Sir John Kennedy, *The Business of War, op. cit.* p. 343.

9. See Albert Seaton, *Stalin as War Lord*, Batsford, London, 1976, p. 217.

10. For an account of the Normandy battles see Carlo D'Este, *Decision in Normandy*, Pan Books, London, 1984.

11. The manpower problem was particularly acute for Britain see, Carlo D'Este, *op. cit.* pp. 252–70.

12. *Ibid*, p. 155.

13. See Martin Gilbert, *Road to Victory, op. cit.*, p. 727.

14. Llewellyn Woodward ed., *British Policy in the Second World War*, Docs, Vol. 1, *op. cit.* pp. 42 and 75.

15. For a discussion on the British defence debate at this time see Uri Bialer, *the Shadow of the Bomber, op. cit.*; Robert Paul Shay, *British Rearmament in the Thirties*, Princeton University Press, NJ, 1977; and Keith Middlemas and John Barnes, *Baldwin*, Weidenfeld and Nicolson, London, 1969, esp. Chapter 13 and Chapter 27.

16. H. Guderian, *op. cit.* p. 22.

17. J. F. C. Fuller, *Machine Warfare*, Hutchinson, London, 1941. p. 13.

18. See the discussion of the Defence Policy Requirements Committee especially the Ideal Scheme proposals and their fate, Shay, *op. cit.* p. 56.

19. The Ten-Year Rule made the assumption that no war was likely in the next ten years. It was abrogated in March 23rd 1932. It had restricted weapons procurement and defence provision severely while it was in force.

20. These were the Somua S53 and the Char B1 bis. Guderian commented on these, "the French tanks were superior to the German ones both in armour and in gun calibre although admittedly inferior in control facilities and in speed." He considered the French possessed the "strongest forces for mobile warfare". *op. cit.* p. 94.

21. See Paul Reynaud, *In the Thick of the Fight*, abridged and translated by James D. Lambert, Cassell, London, 1953.

22. Guderian, *op. cit.*, pp. 25–6.

23. For an account of Guderian's theory of tactics see *ibid*, pp. 39–46.

24. *Ibid*, p. 42.

25. Published as *Armoured Warfare*, by Eyre and Spottiswoode, London, 1932.

26. *Ibid*, p. 28.

27. *Ibid*, p. 28.
28. *Ibid*, p. 25.
29. Cited in Fuller, *Machine Warfare, op. cit.* p. 40.
30. *Ibid*, p. 53.
31. *Ibid*, p. 85.
32. *Ibid*, p. 32.
33. *Ibid*, p. 41.
34. *Ibid*, p. 12.
35. For a discussion on Liddell Hart's ideas and influence see 'Liddell Hart and the French Army 1919-1939'. Andre Beaufre; and 'Liddell Hart and the British Army 1919-1939', Sir Fred Pile; in Michael Howard ed., *The Theory and Practice of War*, Indiana Press, Bloomington, 1965 and, 'Three People— Liddell Hart'. in Michael Howard, *The Causes of War, op. cit.*
36. See *The Strategy of Indirect Approach*, Faber and Faber, London 1946, 1st Published as *The Decisive Wars of History*, in 1929 and later published as *The Way to Win Wars*, 1951.
37. *Ibid*, p. 161.
38. *Ibid*, p. 178.
39. *Ibid*, pp. 179-80.
40. *Ibid*, p. 180.
41. *Ibid*, p. 213.
42. *Ibid*, p. 211.
43. Basil Liddell Hart, *The Defence of Britain*, Faber and Faber, London, 1939.
44. *Ibid*, p. 42.
45. *Ibid*, p. 42.
46. *Ibid*, p. 101.
47. *Ibid*, p. 113.
48. *Ibid*, p. 22.
49. *Ibid*, p. 210 and p. 267.
50. *Ibid*, p. 206.
51. This accounts for the interest shown by Guderian and Manstein in the writings of Fuller, Liddell Hart and de Gaulle (Vers L'Armée de Metier, trans. as *The Army of the Future*, Hutchinson, London: as compared with the relative lack of interest shown in their home countries.
52. Guderian, *op. cit.* p. 295.
53. *Ibid*, p. 309.
54. Liddell Hart, *The Defence of Britain, op. cit.* p. 27.
55. See Maurice Cowling, *op. cit.* pp. 357-65.
56. In the circumstances of the defeat of France Hitler's terms were generous. As expressed in his Reichstag speech of the 19th July 1940 they were 1) the removal of Churchill from the government, 2) British recognition of German hegemony in Europe, 3) the restoration of Germany's former colonies. In return Hitler offered a 'guarantee' of the British Empire and recognition of the primacy of British interests abroad. These were confirmed by Hess on his mission in May 1941.
57. One of the reasons why this pressure failed to secure British compliance in a negotiated peace was that Churchill knew from his Ultra intercepts that Sea Lion was a bluff. He was so confident that Hitler would not invade as to feel able to send key armoured units to North Africa. In this context it is interesting to cite John Colville's diary entry for Friday July 12th 1940—'He [Churchill] emphasised that the great invasion scare (which we only ceased to

deride six weeks ago) is serving a most useful purpose: it is well on the way to providing us with the finest offensive army we have ever possessed and it is keeping every man and woman tuned to a high pitch of readiness. He does not wish the scare to abate therefore, and, although personally he doubts whether invasion is a serious menace, he intends to give that impression, and to talk about long and dangerous vigils, etc., when he broadcasts on Sunday.' This was certainly more efficaceous than the distribution of white feathers or the Derby Scheme in encouraging general conscription into the armed services and into war work.

58. See Douhet, *op. cit.*
59. See Colville, *op. cit.* p. 311.
60. For an account of this from the point of view of Bomber Command see Dudley Saward, *op. cit.*; for a criticism see F. S. P. Veale, *Advance to Barbarism*, Mitre Press, London, 1968, first pub. in 1948.
61. See Stoler, *op. cit.* and also Gilbert.
62. Cited in Colville, *ibid*, p. 186.
63. See Saward, *op. cit.* p. 108.
64. *Ibid*, p. 108.
65. *Ibid*, p. 145.
66. *Ibid*, p. 148.
67. *Ibid*, p. 186.
68. *Ibid*, pp. 209–11.
69. See Martin Middlebrook, *The Schweinfurt-Regensburg Mission,* Penguin, Harmondsworth, 1985 and Albert Speer, *Inside the Third Reich,* trans. R. and C. Winston, Avon Books, NY, 1970, pp. 371–4.
70. See Saward, *op. cit.* pp. 227–30.
71. *Ibid*, pp. 278–301.
72. *Ibid*, pp. 290–1.
73. For a discussion of Churchill's views on strategy see Martin Gilbert, *op. cit.* Chapter 43 and 44; also A. C. Wedemayer, *Wedemayer Reports*, Devis Adair, NY, 1958 and Mark Stoler, *op. cit.*
74. See Martin Gilbert, *op. cit.* pp. 814–31.

6 Weapons and Strategy—Nuclear Theory

If we turn to the nuclear age we find the same basic dilemmas facing the post-war powers. The problem of security had not been resolved with the defeat of the neo-imperialist powers—Germany, Italy and Japan. Britain had prevented at enormous cost the domination of Germany over the European continent, but now faced the Soviet Union presenting the same threat. The United States, too, found that hemispheric defence and non-involvement in European politics were prejudicial to its security. The Soviet Union, primarily a victim of pre-war European politics, found itself facing on a global scale a potential enemy, indeed a consortium of enemies, possessing vastly superior military capabilities. The immediate conse-quence was a political realignment in the form of opposed alliances and spheres of influence. However, parallel with this development was an arms race. The consequence of this arms race was to have a profound effect on world politics.

This chapter will be devoted to a consideration of this competition and of the introduction of the new weapons and their effects on the sub-strategic and strategic levels. Six main developments of varying significance will be considered; the atomic bomb; the hydrogen bomb; the inter-continental ballistic missile; the development of anti-ballistic missile systems; 'theatre' and limited range nuclear weapons; and counter-ballistic missiles based on space stations and new technology such as lasers. The basic dilemma is that of reconciling the use of violence to provide security for the state with its use in promoting other national interests, without placing the state in jeopardy. The enhanced destructive power of these weapons makes this a particularly acute problem. As we have seen, in the pre-nuclear period the pursuit through the use or threat of violence of what initially were non-security objectives led to security or total wars. Weapons procurement and the ambivalence of extant weapons technology exacerbated this progression. Is this the case in the nuclear age? What is the rationality underlying weapons procurement programmes?

Before looking at specific weapons let us look at the grounds for choice in general. There are broadly two main objectives that weapons are intended to serve; the primary one is the provision of security for the nation-state, minimally conceived of as the preservation of its territorial and political integrity; the other being the preservation and promotion of interests beyond the nation-state that may or may not relate to the well-being and welfare of its citizens but do not directly involve security. Involvement in world politics reflects both these concerns and violence is directly relevant to them. They are not unrelated and may be consonant or conflicting. Extant weapons technology for example, may provide a rational basis for imperial policies designed to provide a global base system for the exercise of sea power.[1] Whether trade follows the flag or the flag follows trade, it is clear that economic and security interests may in this instance be closely related. A change in technology and this link may be broken and the empire then becomes a danger to the state rather than a source of security. Such changes in technology, as we shall see, may not be rational in that the consequences of their introduction nullifies the purpose which they were intended to serve, and create a new rationale.[2]

As was argued earlier, rational action at its basic consists simply of possessing reasons that through citation allow explanation. In strategic thought however, the reasons are related to action so that a specific means can be shown to achieve specific ends without any change in this relationship. In the case of weapons procurement the decision to research, develop and deploy particular weapons systems is often only remotely connected to this level of reasoning. It may be directed to purposes very different from those stated in declaratory policy as security based. Moreover in discussing choices of weapons, especially where competing weapons systems claim partisan advocacy, attention tends to be focussed on technical performance rather than any overriding strategic aim. Strategic use cannot simply be extrapolated from technical performance.

A rational choice of weapon is thus related to the fulfilment of a specific state of affairs through its threat or use; an end realisable through its means. It must be seen as being both capable and credible, not merely to its possessor but also, especially where the level of threat is paramount, to the target state. Any appraisal of the grounds of choice must contain some estimate as to its effectiveness in this respect. As we shall see, this is not a simple matter where nuclear weapons are concerned, in spite of the ease compared with conventional weapons of estimates of technical performance. A nuclear weapons system may provide security through offensive or defensive deterrence but seriously compromise the fulfilment of other objectives through the use or threat of force. Equally, it may provide a means of using force on a limited scale but jeopardise security at the strategic level. The pursuit of strategic security through acquisition of both offensive and defensive deterrent capacity may provoke an arms race with counterproductive results. Whether the end is to create a desired state of affairs, or to protect it by countering an opponent's weapons systems, or pre-empting future developments in weapons technology, the milieu is essentially competitive. The introduction of new weapons or modification of existing weapons must include some evaluation of responses and reactions on the part of competitors. This postulates some common rationality as a basis for choice.

There are other considerations. Cost enters into choice where alternative means exist. A more sophisticated, and expensive weapon, is not necessarily the best choice where the objective can be attained by a variety of means. Here again, although relative performance is what is usually considered to be the basis for choice, the overall purpose of the competing weapons should be paramount if they are to have any strategic purpose. The point here is that producing weapons without any clearly defined role is not merely a waste of resources but may disrupt the common rationality that is an essential condition for strategic effectiveness. A further reason that qualifies this point but strengthens the condition of mutual rationality, is that weapons may be functional in inducing an opponent to accept a particular negotiating position. The politics of arms control, as we shall see, offers a number of examples of this ploy. The significance and utility of this manoeuvre are not confined to negotiations at the strategic level, but are linked to the pursuit of non-security aims such as the preservation of political relationships with allies. To pre-empt later discussion, the Sentinel/Safeguard anti-ballistic missile system for example, introduced by President Nixon,[3] was not simply a means of inducing the Soviet Union to accept a ban on such systems but was also intended to persuade the Soviet leadership to aid the United States to extricate itself from Vietnam. Arms control negotiations are not solely confined to questions of arms control but are linked to a variety of political issues not necessarily related to security.

Other reasons for the choice and introduction of new weapons systems not directly linked to strategic purpose, exist. These include the demonstration of technical ingenuity designed to impress a domestic audience for electoral reasons. Such weapons may also be a surrogate for action. They may indicate firmness of purpose and qualities of leadership in a situation where prudence dictates inaction, or where a genuine impotence in promoting interests exists. As we shall see, the stalemate produced by mutual defensive deterrence inhibits decisive action in a variety of areas even where the material capacity for violence exists. Declaratory policy intended to induce support for increased armaments expenditure through the use of rhetoric, arouses expectations that cannot in practice be realised without producing Armageddon. The introduction of new weapons is thus an alternative to action. Such considerations, of course, are more relevant to democracies where techniques of persuasion are necessary to obtain the finance and support for defence. It is a problem as well as an advantage for policy makers in democracies that defence is largely a secret subject. Given that one of the conditions for defensive deterrence is a common rationality entailing mutual understanding, both of the capabilities of the weapons possessed by both sides and of their purpose, the need for secrecy is perhaps less important than formerly. Nevertheless, where negotiations are continuing it would be unwise for a negotiator to reveal his position prematurely. In the case cited, President

Nixon came under heavy criticism for seeking an anti-ballistic missile system. He obtained Congressional assent only very narrowly. The criticism assumed that this intent was serious and raised valid objections against the development. He could not reveal to his critics that it was a bargaining device without alerting the Soviet Union.

The competitive nature of industrial production in non-planned economies also influences the choice of weapons. Inter-service rivalry in alliance with manufacturers may press the claims of a particular weapon that lacks any clear strategic *raison-d'être*.[4] Political inertia or the existence of an active lobby may result in its introduction. It needs no conspiracy theory or presumption of a military-industrial complex to see that the context of decision-making in the area of defence may include such pressures. Their relevance and effectiveness is perhaps peripheral to mainstream strategic procurement. The continued survival of the manned long range 'strategic' bomber for example, owes more to the desire for insurance through the maintenance of the strategic triad than to the career interests of the air force and the success of its lobby.[5]

The point being made here is that the basis of choice for new weapons is not necessarily strategic rationality. If we look at the first of the weapons under consideration, the atomic bomb,[6] we can see that it was developed without any clear conception of its strategic use. The main impetus lay in the fear that Germany might develop it first. The success of the Manhattan project came too late to affect the war itself. Germany was defeated by conventional means and Japan was already suing for peace. The use of the bomb on Japan was dictated by almost entirely political reasons.[7] A negotiated peace was rejected in favour of unconditional surrender. The difficulty for the United States, and to a lesser extent for Britain, was how to obtain this without involving the Soviet Union. Until the atomic bomb was successfully tested the Soviets were needed to contain the Japanese forces on the Chinese mainland. They of course, had a price for entering the war against Japan and this included a share in the occupation of Japan.[8] With the bomb and a quick end to the war, the Soviets would no longer be needed and the United States would have virtually exclusive control over the defeated Japan. The bomb was therefore used not to bring about an inevitable defeat, but to exclude the Soviets from the consequent peace.

Although the atomic bomb appeared to be a revolutionary weapon its strategic significance was masked by its dependence on long range aircraft as a delivery system.[9] The monopoly enjoyed by the United States was useless without a capacity to use it. This depended on the creation of a ring of forward bases giving it global reach extending the range of its bombers. Victory in the Pacific gave the United States such an extension. It was able to convert the Japanese strongholds in the Pacific into 'strategic trusts' that could be used for atomic tests.[10] Possession of Okinawa, of the major Pacific island bases, and sole occupation of the main Japanese islands, together with the huge peacetime naval forces, including the biggest carrier fleet in the world, gave the United States a commanding strategic position in this area. It was an extension of American military strength unprecedented in the pre-war period. The close association with the Nationalist government in China reinforced this position. The strategic position gained through Japanese defeat was relatively uncomplicated by political factors. Neither domestically nor internationally had the United States pursued isolationist policies towards the East.[11] It was generally accepted that in terms of security the United States had a compelling interest in this area. The collapse of the European empires, of Japan, and the continuing civil war in China, gave the United States an opportunity to exercise its military strength without opposition at home or abroad. A challenge to this position came only with the success of the Chinese communists in 1949 and the appearance of national liberation and revolutionary movements supported by the communist states. Even this produced no major challenge to the American position. Korea, and later Vietnam, were contests on the periphery of American strategic interests.[12]

The position was very different on the European continent. It was in Europe that the two World Wars had begun. It was here that the major industrialised nations were concentrated, carrying the greatest potential for a challenge to American security. The Japanese war although vexatious did not present nearly so dangerous a threat to American security as the possibility of a German New Order in Europe.[13] The defeat of Germany did not provide the same political eclipse and consequent opportunity as did that of Japan. Germany was 'shared' by three other powers, France, the USSR and Britain. These states too had security interests and a voice in the eventual post-war settlement. If security competition was not an immediate factor in the Pacific, given the clear dominance of the United States, it was central in European politics. The main argument used by the Soviets in demanding that any future Polish government should be pro-Russian, that is effectively under Soviet control, was that of security.[14] Similarly the British involvement in Greece and Italy was designed to protect British imperial interests through control of the Eastern Mediterranean and the Suez Canal. All, including France, were concerned that Germany should not be allowed to recover its position as it had done after Versailles and make yet another challenge to its neighbours.

It is not possible here to go into the complexities of the origins of the Cold War.[15] I am merely concerned with the security dimension and its relation to the new weapon, the atomic bomb. If cooperation with the Soviet Union was rejected and a four power resolution of the German problem deemed possible, then there were a number of important consequences. From the Soviet point of view a defensive glacis of Eastern and Southern European states was necessary on the grounds of security. They had been attacked with land forces three times in this century.[16] The route had been across Poland. The weakness of the small powers of Europe provided an opportunity for manipulation by their more powerful neighbours at the expense of Russia. Romania, Hungary and Bulgaria had been allies of the Third Reich and the former two countries had fought in the Soviet Union.[17] The greater distance that had to be crossed by land armies before being able to attack the USSR, and the less opportunity for political manipulation, then the more secure was the Soviet Union. The problem was now compounded by the development of airpower and the appearance of the atomic bomb. The spatial relations of the major powers and this new technology reinforced the need to create distance between a potential belligerent possessing the new weapon and Soviet targets. If relaions, for whatever reason, broke down with the United States, and the latter state sought a permanent presence on the European continent, then a temporary solution had to be sought in providing this distance and a permament solution found in acquiring the new weapon. The Iron Curtain and the arms race were the consequences.

From the United States' point of view, while the Soviet Union presented no security threat, although it could be conceived of as a threat to the new economic order they sought to establish, the potential threat existed.[18] If the Soviet Union dominated Europe and possessed the atomic bomb, something considered likely within a few years, the United States would be dangerously isolated. Moreover, without forward bases it could not exercise its atomic monopoly since effective use depended on the bomber. Such bases in turn depended on both a political agreement and the political stability of the governments and their political systems making the agreement. In short, if seeking a political framework for security provision was important to the United States, the quid pro quo for potential allies was security provision for them. This was provided through American bomber bases in Britain[19] and elsewhere that gave the United States the global reach *vis-à-vis* the Soviet Union it otherwise lacked, and at the same time protected under the nuclear umbrella the European allies. A solution of the German problem was also provided by a merger of the three western occupation zones, and the creation of a new state, rearmed and incorporated within the alliance structure. The new Germany was both policed and policing.[20] This assuaged the French and British fears of a German revival and of the threat posed by the Soviet Union's expansion westwards. The alliance itself was underpinned by economic aid from the United States, the promotion of European economic cooperation, and a regulated world market system that precluded economic nationalism and the revival of divisive protectionist policies that promoted the political crisis of the 1930s.[21]

While in this post-war period a community of interest appeared to exist within the alliance, based upon security provision by the major American ally, and largely directed towards a putative Soviet threat, two of the bigger members of NATO, France and Britain, did not regard this as being immutable. It could not be assumed that in this respect American and European interests would always be in harmony. Moreover, the key decision as to the threat or use of the new weapon was in American hands. They therefore decided to make the new weapon.[22] In effect an arms race was in being from the moment it was clear that the United States possessed an atomic bomb. But no coherent view existed as to a rationality of use or of its threat. The new weapon while posing a threat by reason of its very destructiveness and its monopoly, could not be fitted into any clear strategy serving political purposes. Certainly, providing the United States kept a monopoly both of the bomb and of its delivery system and forward bases, it was supremely secure. But this did not enable it to pursue sub-strategic goals easily. Neither changing the political status quo—'roll-back'[23]—or maintaining it—the 'global containment of communism'[24]—could be achieved simply by rattling an atomic sabre. And the very security it enjoyed challenged that of all other states. It could only be maintained by destroying their political integrity and assuming world hegemony. Even her closest ally, Britain, realised this and was pursuing a parallel policy designed to preserve her independence. The initial success of the Soviet Union in testing an atomic weapon in 1949, of Britain doing the same in 1952, France in 1960 and of China in 1964, did not radically change the overall strategic situation. Neither did the American decision in 1953, followed by all her competitors, to manufacture thermonuclear weapons. Again the successful testing of an H bomb by the United States in November 1952 was followed by that of the Soviets in August 1953 with the others eventually doing the same. This new development had no clear strategic purpose. It was more destructive that the atomic bomb but still depended on the same delivery system—the long range, but by now, jet, bomber.[25] The jet bomber had a longer range that is propelled predecessor and with air re-fuelling was less dependent on bases. The basic strategy however, was the same—the possession of global reach designed to strike with impunity at Soviet targets.

Without such reach an equivalent bomber force was useless. Merely developing a strategic air command the size of that of the United States would not help the Soviet Union out of its strategic trap. Acquiring the necessary bases was denied them, partly by geography, and partly by the policy of containment. The hydrogen bomb itself changed nothing and can be regarded as an early case of technological momentum, that is, as a demonstration of technical expertise rather than serving any rational purpose.[26]

It was the inter-continental ballistic missile that produced a revolution in strategic thinking or at least gave it a focus. Ever since the Germans first demonstrated a cruise missile—the V1, and then a ballistic missile—the V2,[27] in the closing stages of the Second World War, missile technology was being developed in the Soviet Union and the United States. It was a matter of time before a missile was completed and deployed that had inter-continental range. The significance of such a missile was that it largely nullified the need for forward bases; in principle, global reach could be obtained from the homeland. This had no immediate consequence for the extant system of alliances so long as the United States possessed a monopoly of the new delivery method. The Soviet Union remained vulnerable to attack, whether from Strategic Air Command, or from missiles, was immaterial; while the United States could still maintain a nuclear umbrella over its allies. These states however, became more vulnerable and more exposed to American pressure as their territory became less relevant to American security.

When *both* major powers possessed a viable inter-continental missile capability, the strategic situation and related security underwent a radical transformation. It is important to stress that nuclear parity was a wholly unintended consequence of the arms race. The United States had set the technological pace in its weapons development and had sought at the very least to maintain superiority, providing security both for itself and for its allies, and protecting its global interests. The policy of the global containment of communism was the political corollary of global reach. But now the new weapons had created a very unusual situation in international politics—a security stalemate. This was to have profound repercussions for the states directly involved in the arms race and for their allies.

Before looking at these, let us consider the doctrine of deterrence that emerged from the stalemate. Again it is important to point out that this doctrine came after the event and, in part, was a realisation that rationalised what had already happened. The deadlock was not intended as a rational goal of strategic reasoning and of weapons procurement policies. It was the consequence of an undirected security competition between the United States and the Soviet Union, with the lesser allies responding as they might. Not only did Britain and France seek to compete in the nuclear arms race but so did China. While this chapter is mainly concerned with the relation of new weapons to the sub-strategic level, the deadlock at the strategic or security level has profound implications for the promotion of non-security interests and for relations with allies. As we shall see the ideas of extended and enhanced deterrence stem directly from the overall strategic deadlock.

Turning towards the notion of deterrence we can see that the idea of preventing inimical action on the part of another state (whether nominally friendly, or explicitly hostile, is immaterial) through threats or acts of denial or punishment, is central to the rational or instrumental use of violence. Inimical actions in this context extends from direct aggression on the homeland to the competitive promotion and protection of interests of all descriptions, economic, military, political, etc., in the world at large. All states to a greater or lesser degree have possessed some form of deterrence and exercised it from time to time. The cost of invading Switzerland, for example, is raised to the maximum level possible by the Swiss government, through planned demolitions and universal military training. Nuclear attacks are precluded in the belief that the consequent destruction would nullify any conceivable advantage sought. In this the Swiss enjoy the advantages of their geography, political significance, and their utility in providing facilities for international negotiation and secret banking.[28]

Practising deterrence, dependent as it is on the existence of a common rationality based on a shared set of values, was by no means easy, even where the deterring state possessed overwhelming military superiority. The United States for example, in spite of its nuclear monopoly, was unable to achieve victory in Korea[29] and was forced to a humiliating stalemate by an opponent economically, and technologically backward. In general, however, the United States was able to provide for security and to defend its main interests, as it defined them, during the period of its atomic monopoly it possessed, and could demonstrate that it possessed, offensive deterrence. Offensive deterrence thus consists of a capability for violence that can be used for a variety of ends, including security provision, with a fair prospect of success. But on the principle that 'one can do anything with bayonets except sit on them' this does not confer success in all circumstances. Indirect threats to the political status quo, such as, civil war, insurrection, national liberation movements, dissent and subversion, could not easily be countered by superior military strength.[30] The familiar problems of relating means to ends, of the use of violence to achieve political objective, was always present in the policy of containment.

Whatever these practical difficulties of application, offensive deterrence entailing threats or acts of direct violence ceased to be relevant or credible when the Soviet Union succeeded in achieving nuclear parity. Defensive deterrence became the basic strategy doctrine in the mid-1960s[31] and it is still the prevailing orthodoxy, especially in the West. What are its theoretical and practical conditions? In principle, the cost of making an attack on the territorial integrity of a state is made so high as to nullify any conceivable purpose in making such an attack. Such a cost must be both certain and credible. There are four basic conditions for defensive deterrence; the states in an adversarial relationship must have vulnerable territory; an invulnerable retaliatory force; observe a moratorium on radical innovation in weapons technology; and accept a common rationality relating to the use of their weapons and their relevance to the objectives sought. They must also possess political and technical control over their weapons systems.

The deterring threat is based on a retaliatory capacity that can inflict unacceptably damage on a state initiating an attack. This need not necessarily entail complete annihilation. Nor does it deter only nuclear attacks. Any attack upon the deterring country, conventional or nuclear, would invite an appropriate retaliation and so prove irrational as a means of fulfilling political objectives. It should be stressed that the only objective served by the possession of a defensive deterrent capacity is the preservation of the integrity of the homeland. No other objectives can be secured under conditions of nuclear parity. A threat of violence in relation to a lesser objective would be lacking in credibility because of its suicidal implications. As we shall see later, this poses problems for allies.

In practice this has meant the creation of a missile force capable of inflicting such a cost. Any strategy or related technological innovation directed as eliminating an adversary's retaliatory capacity is seen as an attempt to obtain offensive deterrence thus, in the jargon as 'de-stabilising'. Similarly, any defensive measure that effectively protects territory or potential targets, carries this implication by denying success to an opponent's retaliatory capacity. Guarantees against pre-emptive attack or a first-strike, designed to eliminate retaliation, are provided by making the military targets difficult to detect or destroy by a variety of means, including underwater launching, mobility, protecting launch sites by counter-ballistic missiles or hardened silos, multiplying both missiles and their warheads, using diverse launching methods such as long-range bombers, and non-ballistic drones or cruise missiles, and by developing effective control, communication and command facilities. The gathering of intelligence is also extremely important.[32]

All such technical developments have increased the sophistication and accuracy of nuclear weapons and indeed considerably increased their numbers and types. Nevertheless, such advances since the defensive deterrent deadlock first appeared over twenty years ago have not challenged its basic rationale. The retaliatory capacities of the contending states remains intact, credible, and effective, in respect of providing a defence of the territorial integrity of the homeland. This of course is a matter of belief and not of empirical demonstration. That such a belief and its associated rationality exists, can be shown by reference to the exercise of restraint by the nuclear powers, their negotiation of arms control agreements, their basic weapons procurement programmes, and their declared policies. Clearly such beliefs and such a situation are not immutable. However, the essence of defensive deterrence lies in mutual recognition of the inutility of making an attack for whatever purpose, on each other's territory. This recognition may be based upon different reasoning. The United States has engaged in an open strategic debate for most of the nuclear period, although this is often tempered on occasion by attempts at political manipulation by various Administrations.[33] The doctrine of defensive deterrence is, however, largely western in origin. For its part the Soviet Union, while publicly professing to treat deterrence as if it were wholly offensive in character and relating it to the policy of encirclement pursued in the days of global containment, has in fact largely accepted its conditions, both in its own weapons procurement policies and in arms control negotiations.[34]

It will be seen from this necessarily brief exposition of the deterrent argument that the relationship of invulnerable missiles capable of inflicting a devastating blow upon an aggressor, regardless of what that aggressor does, to security, is highly unusual in the history of warfare. It is not the character of the weaponry as such—the hordes of Genghis Khan could be said to have much the same effect on the peoples whose territory they invaded—but it is the reciprocity of action and the mutual recognition of its inhibiting effect on the use of violence for political purposes, that has produced this unique situation. For the first time national security can be given a precise definition and a precise statement of conditions. Security consists solely of preserving the home-territory for attack by posing a threat of equivalent retaliation that cannot itself be prevented. The effects of such retaliation can be exactly measured in terms of destruction. This could never be done in the pre-nuclear period when a variety of factors, domestic, political, geographical, technical, demographic and so on, made one state's security another state's insecurity. Nuclear weapons, unlike other weapons, can be assigned a role without ambiguity or provoking a competition leading to security or total wars. It is of course true to say that this form of security is enjoyed only by those states able and willing to create and fulfil all the conditions of defensive deterrence. Outside the nuclear club the same relative anarchy prevails,[35] although mitigated by the restraints imposed on local and regional conflicts by the major nuclear powers. The overall inhibition on general war between the major powers both prevents their extension and reduces the rationality of involvement in limited war. Whatever their rationale they have little relevance to security.

However, it is beyond my brief to examine the effect that weapons have had on the general state of international politics. The point here is that the advent of the inter-continental ballistic missile[36] and the resultant arms race produced a wholly unexpected outcome. This was a solution to the problem of security. It is a solution only in so far as it is recognised to be one, that is, by a mutual acceptance of the rationale of defensive deterrence and the fulfilment of its basic conditions. The relationship between the means—violence—and the end—security—depends on a common rationality observed by the contending states, and so long as this prevails then so long does the associated peace. It is thus a matter of belief and not of some demonstrable empirical truth. It is also dependent upon the possession of weapons with a clearly defined function. The main requirements of defence—the provision of security—would thus seem to have been met so far as the major nuclear powers are concerned.

Defence however, constitutes more than the protection of the territorial integrity of the state. The point here is that however it is conceived, it cannot involve extensions of the defensive deterrent posture without compromising its rationality. The implications of this will be examined later when security provision for allies and intermediate nuclear forces are considered. Apart from the inherent ambiguities of the concept of defence, there arise problems of weapons procurement stemming from attempts to seek relative advantage in arms control negotiations as a consequence of domestic political pressures. As was pointed out earlier, there are a number of factors affecting the choice of weapons systems external to the basic requirements of defensive deterrence. The defence debate, particularly in the democracies, contains numerous hypothetical arguments derived from the technological capabilities of security provision through defensive deterrence. This is of course, generally true of all weapons in their initial stages; the original purpose of the atomic bomb was far from clear, as was that of the hydrogen bomb. Although it is true that the technological capability—or performance—of weapons is subordinate to the intentions behind their postulated use, this is obscure at their research and development stages, especially given the volatility of the domestic and international environments. Where domestic politics are hostile to the introduction of new weapons or where arms control negotiations are at a crucial stage, strategic debate and political decision often appear to be at variance with the logic of deterrence. Bureaucratic, factional and political competition, produce rationalising arguments that are advanced more for their political effectiveness and persuasive power than because they genuinely relate to a strategic programme.[37]

An example will perhaps clarify this point. The case of what is termed 'throw-weight'[38] is a good illustration of this genre of argument that has little or no bearing on strategic purpose or reality but is introduced into the debate for strictly political purposes. 'Throw-weight' is defined as the destructive power of a missile, constituting its warheads and their post-boost and defensive devices. Using this as an index, a distinction can be made between types of inter-continental ballistic missiles depending upon their respective 'throw-weights'. The Soviet SS 18 for example, carrying six warheads, has nearly three times the 'throw-weight' of the US Minuteman 111. This reflects the different procurement policies of the two countries; the former producing missiles of a high megatonnage, initially to compensate for their relative inaccuracy; the latter with a technological advantage in miniaturisation and in computers, producing smaller but more accurate missiles. However, with the increased accuracy of Soviet missiles, this disparity in 'throw-weight' has been represented by some as conferring an advantage on the Soviet Union, enabling them to strike and destroy hardened Minuteman missile silos. The Soviet emulation of the American MIRV programme meant[39] that many—up to ten—warheads could be fitted to their heavy missiles, thus compounding the problem. This argument has been used both to justify the introduction of a new missile system—the mobile MX[40]— and to press the Soviet Union in arms control negotiations to make concessions by reducing the number of their heavy missiles.

However, within the context of mutual defensive deterrence, the kind of distinction made by measuring comparative 'throw-weights' is irrelevant if the overall stability is not affected. Stability lies in the mutual possession of an invulnerable retaliatory capacity capable of inflicting unacceptable damage on an aggressor.[41] The hypothetical capacity of the Soviet Union to destroy hardened missile silos does not affect the strategic balance, for the United States still retains its retaliatory capacity through SLBMs and aircraft, the other two legs of the strategic triad.[42] What gain could be postulated for the Soviet Union making such a strike, yet being unable to counter or inhibit retaliation? Moreover, given the proximity of some missile silos to centres of population such a move would be counter city as much as counter force, making retaliation that much more likely. In any case the destructive effect of a heavy missile compared to that of a relatively light missile is not qualitatively different, the target is completely destroyed in both cases.

Yet arguments that stress the disparity between the respective 'throw-weights' of the two national missile forces treat the issue as if it were a substantive one. The deployment of the MX mobile missile system was urged as a means of closing a 'window of opportunity'.[43] The putative strategic role of this new weapon was to counter the Soviet threat to the Minuteman silos. But this adds nothing to the stability of the overall balance nor has it any strategic rationale. Mutual defensive deterrence is maintained not by developing weapons of this kind but by preserving the invulnerability of the retaliatory forces, thus making any act of aggression fruitless both in contemplation and in execution. The decision to deploy the MX is really an exercise in political maneouvre rather than a contribution to the fulfilment of any security objective. Nevertheless, it can be seen as a means of achieving a political objective and as such falls within the definition of strategy used in this study. In this context, as we shall see in a later chapter, the MX programme is designed as a means of strengthening a negotiating position. Even so the point of the bargain sought if it is to have any rationality, should be the achievement of a specific political goal, or the enhancement of security, or both. Whether this is actually the case will be considered later. Similarly while the maintainence of public confidence in political leadership is important as a condition of maintaining the credibility of the defensive deterrent posture, particularly in democracies, the fortunes of a political faction may override the interests of the state in certain cases.[44]

The introduction of the MX weapons system with all the problems of making it credible as a mobile system, capable of surviving, and thus inhibiting, a pre-emptive first strike, can be seen not as a rational response to a changed strategic relationship but as an appeal to psychology. It appeals on the one hand, to the desire of a domestic political audience for strong leadership in the world of states and thus to nationalist sentiment, and on the other hand, to the desire of the Soviet leadership to avoid wasteful and fruitless competition in the development of weapons systems. As such this weapon may serve political purposes even if these are removed from security provision, and it cannot therefore be summarily dismissed as an irrational development in the strategic arms race. The question thus becomes whether such ploys are effective or counter-productive.

The case of MIRV referred to earlier illustrates this problem. Multiplying the number of warheads existing missile systems could carry seems on the face of it an attractive idea. Given the American lead in miniaturisation it was an easy and inexpensive means of increasing missile forces and countering a possible anti-ballistic defence that might be developed by the Soviet Union. Such a system could be saturated by large numbers of incoming missiles. Although anti-ballistic missile systems were precluded by treaty, the United States decided to deploy MIRVs, reaching the stage when each warhead could be independently manoeuvred onto independent targets. Again this did not serve any specific strategic purpose nor did it make any qualitative change to the overall mutual defensive deterrent posture. Inevitably, however, the Soviet Union followed suit, with the difference that they MIRVed much heavier missiles, leading to the situation described above. It is difficult to think of this kind of competition as serving any strategic purpose or having any rationality. Nor can it be seen as a negotiating ploy although *ex post facto* it may become so. I will return to this aspect of weapons procurement when I discuss the so-called 'star wars' project.[45] For the moment let us consider the development of intermediate nuclear weapons (INF). These are explicitly given a sub-strategic role. In what sense do these weapons have a genuine strategic purpose? In what way are they related to the overall strategic balance?

If, as has been argued, the basic problem of security has been resolved for the major nuclear powers, what of other interests that are served by the development of the means of violence? The implications of mutual defensive deterrence are far reaching. As was pointed out earlier, the threat of violence is relevant only in countering an equivalent threat.[46] Only the national territory is protected by this means. Even in this strictly limited sense of deterrence the postulates of control and of effectiveness are not easy to establish and maintain. A complex communication system capable of identifying the nature of an attack and immune from disruption, is but one of the prerequisites. Evaluation is of supreme importance if a response is to be controlled. Given the risks it is hard to postulate any rational ground for a limited war or token strikes made by one nuclear power upon the territory of another nuclear power. But whether, by miscalculation or by intent, this actually occurs, the response must be controlled to avoid a nuclear exchange that results in the same stalemate but at greater cost. The point here is that whatever the ostensible issue at stake, short of national security in its most basic sense, nothing could be gained by such an exchange. It would be inherently irrational, lacking any relation between means and ends.

If defensive deterrence provides security for the major nuclear powers by making violence between them irrational, can this deterrence be extended to provide security for their allies? Both the Soviet Union and the United States maintain alliance systems whose rationale was derived from before the strategic deadlock. Are their allies defensible? The premise underlying collective security is that the territory of the ally is as sacrosanct as that of the major nuclear ally. Any kind of assault, nuclear or conventional, upon this territory is deemed as equivalent to an attack on the major ally. The inhibition on aggression imposed by defensive deterrence is thus extended[47] to include an inhibition on aggression on the minor powers.

If this assumption is challenged as lacking in credibility because it is unlikely that the major nuclear protector would be willing to become involved in a suicidal nuclear war on behalf of a minor power, then there are certain problems for alliances. Formally, both NATO and the Warsaw pact are indivisible. Iceland (or Berlin) stands in the same regard for security to the United States as does Bulgaria to the Soviet Union. Certainly no one can foresee in the event of a crisis affecting a smaller power what attitudes will be adopted by the major contenders. Nevertheless the desire of Britain, France and China[48] to have independent control over national nuclear forces, is an indication that some allies have serious misgivings as to the commitment of their major ally to their protection against another nuclear power. China withdrew from an alliance to confront her former ally, France withdrew from the military commitments of her alliance, although formally committed to its terms, and Britain has a highly equivocal relationship to her alliance. All of these three states pursued nuclear programmes independently of their security arrangements with other powers. It appears from this that these states at least, and until recently this has been regardless as to which government was in power,[49] do not believe in the credibility of extended deterrence. A Soviet, or American attack upon a non-nuclear ally is regarded as unlikely to produce a counter-strike between each other. National suicide is not conceived of as a rational response to the destruction or invasion of an ally. If this argument is accepted, then defensive deterrence cannot be extended to provide security for allies.

Their security is provided in other ways than through the threat of nuclear retaliation. Firstly, although their nuclear protector is inhibited in threatening direct retaliation, it can credibly do so against an opponent's non-nuclear allies. Threats levelled against each others' non-nuclear allies—Roumania in exchange for Italy, or West Germany for Czechoslovakia, for example, inhibit attempts at changing the political status quo in Europe through violence. Such threats are credible as they do not involve the major nuclear powers in nuclear exchanges, suicidal in character, and indeed limit any war to third-party non-nuclear states. This possibility clearly motivated Britain, France and China. The result of such ally-swapping, however, could hardly be described as victory in any meaningful sense for the major powers. Nor does the security provided for the non-nuclear states in Europe seem very secure. Their fate lies entirely in the hands of the major nuclear powers. And so far as these last are concerned, the state that possesses fewest allies, or holds its allies in least regard, would seem to have an advantage! The degree to which a non-nuclear ally is deemed expendable would clearly be relevant to any contest between the major nuclear powers. The level of violence postulated by this argument would be limited to the pursuit of relative military advantage in non-nuclear territory without the slightest involvement of the major nuclear contenders in terms of their security.

If this reasoning is accepted, then there is clearly a major change in alliances and their relation to security. Their non-nuclear members have a tenuous defence depending on their relative value to their major protectors. Invading the West or East would result in equivalent losses for both sides. Only if the Soviet Union and the United States actually wished to devastate non-nuclear Europe, would such a move be rational. Given the economic value of their non-nuclear allies and the political advantages of a stable status quo in Central Europe, this appears unlikely. In this respect the two major contenders would appear to have more in common that would appear in view of their rhetoric. The point here is that such ally-swapping, whatever its rationale, takes the form of limited war; a war by proxy in effect, that does not directly affect the security of the major nuclear powers, however grievous their losses might be in economic terms. Such a war would be irrelevant to their security. This must be borne in mind when we examine the various forms of intermediate nuclear weapons systems associated with the defence of Europe.

Secondly, the defence of Europe may take other forms than the threat of an inutile proxy war discussed above. At its most fundamental level it consists of raising the costs of invasion to an unacceptably high level. It is assumed by neutral countries, Sweden and Switzerland for example, that,

possessing no means of attacking a major nuclear power, their security
from invasion lies in the fact that their nuclear destruction would be
pointless, firstly, because they do not constitute any threat to the security
of the potential aggressor, and secondly, such an attack would be counter-
productive since it would destroy the assets or resources that the aggressor
presumably coveted. A conventional invasion is therefore the most likely
kind of threat, being the most rational, and this must be made as costly as
possible. This is of course a deterrent policy of sorts. It is also heavily
dependent upon the initiatives of a potential aggressor. Nuclear blackmail
in the form of threats of strikes against selected targets could not easily be
countered. Domestic political pressures constitute an imponderable factor
in this respect. There are precedents, for example, in Hitler's treatment of
the leaders of small European countries and his often successful
intimidation.[50]

At another level there is the provision of a major defensive capability in
the form of a concerted effort through conventional forces against
conventional invasion. Checking and containing such an invasion, or
demonstrating a capacity to do so, is another form of deterrence.
Assuming that the point of such an incursion is to achieve concrete gains,
the cost of such an adventure is raised by the degree of effort needed to
achieve success. But given the geo-political distribution of allies in Europe
it seems clear that the initiator of aggression will have the advantage in a
number of ways. First, he can pick his time and place and hope for
surprise. Secondly, the kinds of armies that currently exist are highly
mechanised and mobile and therefore capable of deep penetration.[51]
Thirdly, the necessary logistical support will be deployed across protected
areas and fourthly, the actual fighting will take place in the invaded
territory. By the time any check to the invasion occurs, the aggressor is
likely to be in a better bargaining position than the defenders. There is a
precedent for this too; although Germany did not succeed with the
Schlieffen Plan in 1914 she was in possession of Belgium and part of
Northern France, thus precluding the possibility of a negotiated
settlement.[52]

If we relate this to the case of the two Germanys; any Soviet or
American thrust in its initial phase will be likely to penetrate into East or
West Germany with the consequence that victory need only be defined as
the holding of sufficient ground as to force a renegotiation of the *de facto*
agreements which created the two states. If such a conflict is seen purely as
a limited conventional war then the defending forces, however strong they
may be in terms of holding off military collapse, will always be at a
disadvantage in political terms, since they will be obliged to cede territory
without being able to reverse the situation by extending the war. Only if it
is both able and prepared to counter-invade would there be any real
prospect of a political as opposed to a military victory. With the initiative
in the hands of the aggressor, and with total war precluded by the nuclear
stalemate this is an unlikely prospect.

However, it is the next level, that of the use of nuclear weapons, that introduces a complicating factor. If nuclear weapons are introduced at an early stage then all the advantages possessed by a conventional invader are nullified. Nuclear exchanges, however limited, would preclude any advantage in a surprise invasion. Indeed the prospect of their early use would constitute the most effective check on military adventurism.[53] The corollary of this argument is that major conventional forces are not only irrelevant to security provision, but exercise a de-stabilising effect in that their relative ineffectiveness and ambiguity might offer opportunities for the pursuit of relative advantage to the contenders. There is no clear opportunity for an aggressor to mount a lightning war in the hope of gaining the advantage over opposed conventional forces, if any advance meets with immediate nuclear retaliations. Once nuclear engagement occurs the net result is a loss to both sides, nullifying whatever opportunities may be conceived in making an attack in the first place. Again the damage and the risk are limited to the non-nuclear allies, whose destiny in this case is placed in the hands of their major nuclear ally.

The final level is that of the provision of a defensive deterrent that operates in the same way as that of a major nuclear power. If European countries possess an invulnerable retaliatory nuclear power capable of inflicting unacceptable damage on a potential aggressor, then security is provided for on the basis of the deterrent argument. Such a deterrent cannot be provided for in the form of a collective security alliance on the preceding argument. It is clear why Britain and France have chosen this path, with nuclear weapons firmly under national control. This is the basis for their security, not the NATO alliance.

From this we can see that the creation and deployment of intermediate range nuclear forces in the European theatre constitutes a political or psychological, rather than a strategic, commitment. Their function is to assure the non-nuclear allies of a commitment to their defence. In strictly strategic terms a threat of nuclear or conventional attack upon these countries can be deterred by posing a nuclear threat from inter-continental ballistic missiles outside the European theatre. Such a countering threat is levelled at the non-nuclear allies of the potential aggressor who stand in the role of hostage. Limited range missiles, i.e. those whose range does not extend to the principal targets in the United States or the Soviet Union, are irrelevant in military terms. Their presence corresponds to that of the presence of American troops, that is, as a physical symbol of commitment. They may also have some use as bargaining counters in the constant search for relative advantage in arms control negotiations.

Once having made these gestures towards allied solidarity however, it is difficult to withdraw them without alarming the allies they are intended to reassure, and encouraging adventurism on the part of the opposing nuclear power.[54] Commitments of this kind can produce expectations that breed a logic of their own. They are made largely because of what might be called the German problem. One solution to the security dilemma of Western[55] Germany would be to follow the British and French examples and provide it with nuclear arms. On the rationale of defensive deterrence this would provide it with an effective counter to any Soviet threat. However to do this would not only alarm the Soviet Union but Germany's European allies as well. The Soviet Union has consistently opposed the nuclear arming of Western Germany and, to counter it, has threatened to conclude a separate peace treaty with Eastern Germany. This would effectively confirm the division of Germany and close the prospect of future re-unification. Berlin too would remain a hostage in Soviet hands and a means of leverage. Nor would nuclear arming be popular with Germany's western neighbours, especially France. A resurgence of military independence in Western Germany in the light of the past would be seen as an inimical development. Western Germany is perhaps the only ally whose defence policy and military forces are completely integrated within the NATO command and, in effect, under American control.

There are political reasons for this, as indeed for the permanent presence of foreign troops in the Federal Republic. As was remarked earlier, Germany is both policed and policing. Emplacing intermediate range nuclear missiles on West German territory and in Western Europe, is a tangible means of reassuring the Germans as to a continuing commitment to their defence without alarming other European countries, both in the East and in the West, by giving the Federal Republic military autonomy. All this indicates the political rather than strategic role of these weapons. Intermediate range nuclear weapons have no strategic purpose. They are, in this context, irrelevant to the overal mutual defensive deterrent situation. They do not, and indeed, cannot, extend this deterrence to the non-nuclear allies and so provide for their security in the same way. Their security is provided through the mutual exchange of hostages, or, as I have put it, ally-swapping.

At the battle-field level the very short range nuclear weapons designed for tactical use have significance only if conventional war on a limited scale is envisaged. Their function is thus not strategic but designed to produce an early check on any invading force. Their use however, would inevitably be on 'friendly' territory and thus contribute to the devastation. While it can be argued that their very existence precludes any chance of success for an aggressor if his aim was conquest, and so acts as a deterrent of sorts, they would be effective if the aggressor has some other purpose. Their contribution to the security of the non-nuclear states in Europe is thus marginal and must be seen within the larger context of ally-swapping, involving the punishment of the aggressor's own non-nuclear allies. The larger scale INF weapons then become relevant.

It is clear from this that the major nuclear powers could fight a limited war in the non-nuclear areas of Europe. Such a war would not directly involve their security although it would affect non-security interests. Damage to the European nuclear powers would also occur through radioactive fallout. However, given the guarantee of security they possess through mutual defensive deterrence and the relative balance that prevails in nuclear weapons, it is hard to see any rational ground for such a context, and easier to see the military balance as supporting a mutually acceptable political balance in Europe, with recognition of spheres of influence and of an acceptable solution to the German problem. Nuclear weapons at this sub-strategic level thus have symbolic rather than military significance. An important distinction was made earlier between offensive and defensive deterrence. One of the conditions for holding the latter stable is the vulnerability of potential targets, whether these are nuclear forces or civilian population centres. Paradoxically, mutual exposure to attack preserves the stable balance between the major nuclear powers. If one state unilaterally succeeds in making its territory invulnerable through a perfect defensive system, then it has succeeded in acquiring an offensive deterrent capacity, allowing it to use, or threaten to use, its nuclear weapons, or indeed any weapons it possesses, without fear of direct retaliation. Similarly, damage limitation schemes, such as an extensive civil defence, may restrict the scale of enemy retaliation and so reduce it to an acceptable level.[56] If this were the case then it would be rational and credible to use, or threaten to use, nuclear weapons, in the pursuit of national interests. Security would lie in immunity from attack and at the same time the relationship between violence and the attainment of non-security objectives would be restored to the foreign and defence policies of the first state that succeeded in making its territory invulnerable. It is true that making this relationship rational would pose the same problems associated with the rational use of violence in international politics as in the pre-nuclear monopoly. Nevertheless a number of options would be open that are currently closed. Such a state of affairs would, of course, place all other states not possessing such a defence in jeopardy. It would restore the protective element in alliances where the major ally is able to extend its defence to cover its allies. It would also remove the necessity for allied possession of independent nuclear forces, assuming that this position of superiority could be maintained indefinitely.

Having said this, the earlier precedent of the possession of offensive deterrence by the United States is not very encouraging. Although Western Europe was secured the guarantee for Berlin was equivocal. Moreover, bayonets were not easily sat on outside Europe. More significantly, the direct consequence was an arms race that resulted in the unexpected stalemate that constrains the present nuclear powers. It would appear very likely that if some nuclear power sought such an advantage, its major nuclear rival would seek to counter it. The consequence, if this were successful, would be another stalemate but one with a difference. If both major nuclear powers succeeded in making their territory invulnerable then they would have produced the paradoxical result of making nuclear weapons redundant so far as their strategic relationship was concerned. Neither could attack or threaten to attack the other with such weapons. There would be a high premium on developing alternative weaponry in order to resolve this dilemma. In other words the security problem would be as acute as in the pre-nuclear period. Violence in all its forms and ambiguities would be restored to the world of states without the clear distinction that can now be made between security and other ends that can be rationally pursued through its means. So-called conventional war on a total scale would be restored to the national repertoire of means.

There is also the danger that in this new arms race a situation might develop in which one state possessing relative advantage might have to translate this into action for fear of losing it. In other words pre-emptive war would be a rational course of action for the state that enjoyed a lead in the development of 'defensive' weaponry.[57] Indeed the only point of such an arms race is to achieve superiority and this implies maintaining it. War itself thus becomes instrumental in creating a condition of absolute security. As was argued earlier in this study, this leads to a hegemonial form of politics in international relations.

All this is implicit in attempts to find an alternative to mutual defensive deterrence through the development of new weapons systems. The first such attempt once the nuclear stalemate came into being was the appearance of anti-ballistic missile systems. It was the Soviet Union with its Galosh system between 1961 and 1964 that first took this path. In the context of American qualitative and quantitative superiority this was probably purely a damage limiting measure rather than an attempt to achieve offensive deterrence. When balance between the rival missile forces was achieved later in the decade, the need for this form of defence was removed. However, as was noted earlier, the potential for a new and highly unstable arms race existed with the anti-ballistic missile system. If incoming missiles could be destroyed this conferred offensive deterrence on the defender.

Although the initial response of the United States was the production of MIRVed missiles designed to saturate and thus counter a missile defence, Sentinel—an American ABM system—began development in 1967, to become Safeguard in 1969. Clearly what was being threatened was an arms race whose consequence was either a new stalemate with some of the paradoxical effects noted earlier, or the achievement of superiority, and hence offensive deterrence by one of the contenders. This, given superior technology, would probably be the United States, although given past precedents in weapons development its lead would be limited. In the event both sides accepted an arms control agreement that tacitly acknowledged the stalemate of mutual defensive deterrence with all its political ambiguities. From that point on the Soviet Union increased in strength and influence as opportunities for the exercise of power occurred in the volatile field of international politics. The period of global containment and its associated enforcement through offensive deterrence was over and the dying phase of the Vietnam War symbolised this.[58]

While the possibility of a new arms race seeking a qualitative change in the strategic balance was checked with SALT I and the constraints on anti-ballistic missile systems, the problem for the United States remained. How could a position of minimal deterrence, that depended on tacit and formal agreements with an ostensible adversary, be extended to provide security for its non-nuclear allies? How could Soviet influence in the world be checked without disrupting the overall strategic balance? The answer was a combination of bluff and threats. The bluff consisted of making apparently tangible commitments to Western Europe in the form of intermediate range nuclear weapons (INF) and cruise missiles. These last are relatively short-range low-flying sub-sonic drones that carry nuclear warheads and are capable of penetrating radar defences.

The so-called strategy of flexible response left the exact nature of an American reaction to Soviet aggression in doubt. This was deliberate. Ambiguity of response disguised the inherent irrationality of making or threatening to make, nuclear attacks on the Soviet Unions as a means of defending the security of the non-nuclear European allies. It also tried to compensate for the conventional military imbalance between Warsaw Pact and NATO forces, and the geographical and logistical advantages enjoyed by the Soviet Union.[59] The disparity between the means—direct nuclear attacks on the Soviet Union—and the ends—the security of minor allies— was blurred. This may have reassured the allies and confused the enemy, but the main point was that political debate, both internal, and within the NATO alliance, on this issue was thus avoided. The debate shifted to concern with arms control and to the terms acceptable to the United States in return for removing the missiles and weapons it had placed in Europe. As was noted earlier the INF debate is irrelevant to the overall strategic relationship. Both Pershing and the cruise missiles are political rather than military weapons.

So far as the second dimension of American concern for protecting non-nuclear allies is concerned—that is the level of threat—the strategic relationship is directly involved. The strategic defensive initiative taken by President Reagan in 1983 is a revival of the anti-ballistic missile issue. Without recapitulating the arguments relating to the significance of creating a perfect defence and thus restoring offensive deterrence, it is clear that the SDI carries these implications. The context of this proposal was one of reaction to the Soviet emplacement of SS20[60] missiles in Eastern Europe. In doing this the Soviets made it clear that in theatre nuclear terms they could match the West. At the same time they enjoyed a measure of superiority in conventional weapons. The immediate consequence was the plan to deploy Pershing and cruise missiles to reassure West Germany and to counter the psychological effect of the Soviet move. As was argued earlier, neither the Soviet or the American emplacement of intermediate range nuclear weapons in Europe had any strategic significance—their respective spheres of influence could be defended by the inter-continental ballistic missile forces they both possessed and which were held outside Europe.

If the intention behind the employment of Pershing and cruise missiles in Europe was to persuade the Soviet Union to withdraw its SS20 missile force, it failed. Arms control will be considered in a later chapter, the point here is that the introduction of these weapons has political rather than strategic significance. In any case they did not threaten the basic position of mutual defensive deterrence. The SDI however, directly challenged its stability. Not only did it involve radically new technology and so opened the door to innovation in weapons—another challenge to the stability of defensive deterrence—but it served notice on the Soviet Union that the United States was seeking strategic superiority. The first state to achieve a defence against ballistic missiles would be in a position to use them. It would possess offensive deterrence. While it would enjoy security it would place the security of all other countries at risk.

The SDI programme by itself could perhaps have been treated as a bluff or as a bargaining ploy if it were not for the context in which it emerged. Debate in the American strategic establishment, especially in that part that actively supported the Reagan Presidency, had become concerned with developing a 'war-winning' strategy. The relative impotence in terms of the protection and promotion of non-security interests in the world of states produced by mutual defensive deterrence, had helped to create a climate of opinion in the United States that desired remedies. Attention therefore turned to alternatives. If, it was argued, the United States could limit damage to an acceptable level after suffering all that the Soviets could do in retaliation and still keep a nuclear reserve, then a nuclear war could be 'won'. The United States could then threaten nuclear war with credibility. Such a war need not go to its limit once the Soviet Union realised that it would suffer more in a continued contest that the United States. Hence the war could be graduated and limited in order to achieve the desired response from the adversary.

This strategic thinking bears more than a close resemblance to the theory of escalation discussed in an earlier chapter. The main point is that given the appropriate weapons system, the cost of a nuclear exchange could be made higher to the Soviet Union than to the United States. Violence, or rather its threat, could thus be restored to diplomacy. As one of its principal proponents, Colin Gray, puts it,

'The pursuit of a "win the war" posture need reflect neither strategically atavistic thought, nor a confidence that the arms race could indeed be won in a militarily definitive sense. All that such postural pursuit need reflect would be a determination to induce reasonable if ambitious Soviet leaders to reconsider the cost-effectiveness of the foreign policy that drives their arms programmes.'[61]

It will be noted how this argument appeals to a common rationality. This suggests a commonly accepted scale of values and recognition of the balance between means and ends in terms of any particular contest. Nevertheless, the presumption is one of ultimate American superiority in terms of their military capacity to prevail in the event of such a contest being pressed to the point of war. Such a condition is a reversion to the offensive deterrence possessed by the United States in the post-war years. Clearly this would constitute a direct threat to Soviet security and one that would be entirely unacceptable. In short any attempt to achieve such a position for the purpose of promoting and protecting non-security interests would intitiate an arms race whose main concern would be security provision. This would seem to be paradoxical if the main intention was simply to improve bargaining power and achieve relative advantage in areas of lesser importance. *Inter alia* it would mean using arms control as a means of establishing this superiority or abandoning it altogether. As a means of stabilising mutual defensive deterrence its utility would lapse as that strategic posture lapsed.

At the time of writing[62] it is not clear whether the threat to make radical innovations in weapons technology and so break one of the conditions for maintaining the stability of mutual defensive deterrence, is serious. It may be, as was the case with the earlier Safeguard programme, another negotiating ploy, designed to persuade the Soviet Union to accept limits on its nuclear deployment at the sub-strategic level in both Europe and Asia. In effect, this would mean threatening to destablise the strategic balance in order to achieve relative advantages in an area not directly involving American security. At face value this is an irrational threat. The issue of West European security is complex, given the existence of British and French nuclear deterrents, the equivocal status of West Germany, and the American presence, but if its only guarantee is seen as the achievement of American strategic superiority, then a new arms race is being threatened with unpredictable consequences. Should another stalemate be the result then the situation regarding European security would be as before.

It may be the case that the nature of the threat is not in fact a challenge to the overall strategic balance but a means of forcing increased expenditure upon armaments by the Soviet Union at a time of economic difficulty, in order to extract concessions relating to the sub-strategic level in arms control negotiations. The problem here is that in spite of the American superiority in technology in a contest of resources, a democracy such as the United States with its political system, might paradoxically find a greater difficulty in obtaining appropriations for this purpose than a one-party state with its centralised leadership like the Soviet Union. Previous experience has shown that the Soviet Union, however relatively backward in technology and stretched in economic terms, has always been able to match the United States in armaments. However, in the short term the threat of such a competition might make the Soviets more amenable to making concessions at the sub-strategic level rather than incur the cost of competing in the new weaponry. A genuine competition at the strategic level carries as much risk for the United States as for the Soviet Union, and if offensive deterrence is not actually sought, achieving an expensive stalemate would be irrational.

Given the enormous technical difficulties in creating an effective defence for the population of the United States from missile attack the SDI might, *inter alia*, be a means of providing for what is called enhanced deterrence. This would take the form of an anti-ballistic missile defence of existing missile silos thus closing the so-called 'window of opportunity'. This would not adversely effect the existing balance. Indeed it would strengthen it by removing doubts about the invulnerability of American retaliatory capability. The problem here lies in existing treaties inhibiting the development of such systems. Such constraints would have to be unilaterally rejected and this would inevitably have consequences for arms control negotiations. However, the point here is that if the purpose of the SDI is to protect the civilian population by providing an effective defence of United States territory this would, if it was achieved unilaterally, confer offensive deterrence upon the USA. If it is intended in declaratory policy terms to coerce the Soviet Union into being more amenable about American interests at the sub-strategic level, and in real terms to strengthen retaliatory capacity, then the situation remains as before—that is a mutual defensive deterrence. This, of course, leaves the non-nuclear allies still exposed in terms of their security, supposing that the bluff is called by the USSR.

This discussion perhaps has been unduly Eurocentric. Both the United States and the Soviet Unon have interests in other parts of the world, although these are not incorporated within formal alliance systems with a security rationale such as NATO and the Warsaw Pact.[63] The Soviet Union has a neighbour, China, that is a growing nuclear power and eventually will enjoy the same relationship of mutual defensive deterrence *vis-à-vis* the USSR as that state does with the USA, assuming no radical changes occur in the overall strategic situation. This will have similar results in the region so far as non-nuclear allies are concerned, as in Europe. Similarly, the United States is closely involved with Japan and has sought to extend deterrence to that state, with the same difficulties as in Europe. However, the Pacific unlike the European theatre, favours the United States, given its naval preponderance and the geo-politics of the area. The hostility of China to the Soviet Union has also been favourable to the maintenance of American influence. The point here is that, whatever the global interests of the major nuclear powers, they are dissassociated from security and can only be pursued within the constraints imposed at the strategic level. The difficulties of pursuing national interests through violence and threats of violence remain as in the past, but unlike the pre-nuclear period are prevented from developing into major military confrontations since security is not at risk. Whatever form limited war takes it cannot turn into total war without destroying those who fight it. There is no prospect of success in seeking victory at this level whatever sense it made in the era of conventional war.

To return to the technology of war and weapons, a point that is frequently overlooked through excessive concentration on the technical performance of weapons is that control is essential. A rational strategy using nuclear weapons must be based upon the intent behind their use or threat and this must be clear to both sides. As we have seen, the only credible threat of use under conditions of mutual defensive deterrence is one of retaliation. This is a minimal guarantee of security and is understood by both sides. The use of limited strikes to attain purposes that fall short of security—defined as the preservation of the territorial integrity of the homeland—is not only incredible but difficult to control. Now that missiles can carry up to ten multiple independently targeted war heads it becomes extremely difficult to evaluate an attack. Given the limited warning of a strike the appropriate response must be decided in the knowledge of the nature and purpose of such an attack. An inappropriate response could be disastrous. Yet it cannot be known what an incoming missile is actually carrying or, except in its final phase, where its warheads are targeted. Those who devise strategies based on the limited use of nuclear weapons tend to ignore such human factors as the problem of making quick decisions under conditions of stress and where knowledge is limited. This is of course true for both sides, both the attacked and the defender. It is difficult to conceive of a political issue, short of security itself, that warrants this sort of risk-taking.

If then an effective and rational strategy is one that has a commensurable relationship between means and ends so that the latter are fulfillable at an acceptable cost, a major problem exists for the proponent of limited nuclear war. He must establish this relationship in the face of such imponderables as the intention behind the threat, the evaluation of the threat and the appropriate response to it, when the former are unknown and unassessable. The point is that intentions are what really matter in strategic reasoning. An emphasis on worst case analysis as a basis for weapons procurement leans heavily upon the capabilities of weapons, and neglects the intentions of their potential users. Yet strategic reasoning, as we have seen is primarily concerned with the use or threat of violence to persuade an opponent to concede the point at issue. Outside basic security—obtained as was argued earlier, by observing the conditions of mutual defensive deterrence—it is essential to understand the values and intentions of the nominal opponent.

It is even more essential to divorce such issues from security. The means adopted, to be effective and rational, must be in balance with the ends sought from both sides. This puts a high premium on communication and information. If this is not the case then either the contest becomes a costly and futile struggle, as was the case in Korea and Vietnam, or the prospect of an apocalyptic nuclear war becomes a distinct possibility. Strategic theories that derive their rationale from the technical performance of weapons and ignore the psychological dimension are highly dangerous and likely to be ineffective. Wars are indeed fought with weapons but weapons are merely tools whose effective performance depends on the purposes they are ultimately designed to fulfil. These are rather more than mere destruction. They are political in character. If limited war is the only rational form of war under conditions of mutual defensive deterrence, the limits and the purpose it is designed to serve must be clearly understood and observed by both sides. At the same time universal premises postulating inevitable conflict between incompatible political systems as a basic policy assumption, lead directly to open-ended commitment and unlimited conflict.[64] Such premises blur the distinction between the means of providing security for the state based upon a rationality common, or intelligible, to all states, and the means of promoting and protecting state interests in the world of states. It was the blurring of this distinction that made both World Wars of this century total wars. A total war in the nuclear age would be a catastrophe.

NOTES AND REFERENCES

1. For the significance of sea-power see Admiral A. T. Mahan, *The Influence of Sea Power upon History 1660–1783*, Sampson Low, and *The Influence of Sea Power upon the French Revolution and Empire*, London, 1890, 2 vols, Sampson Low, London, 1870.
2. Technical advancements such as changes from sail to steam, and from steam to turbine, have resource implications that impinge on security. Such improvements generate competition not only in matching technologies, but also in commanding the appropriate resources.
3. This system began development in 1966.
4. For an account of an early example of this rivalry in weapons development see Michael Armacost, *The Politics of Weapons Innovation—the Thor-Jupiter controversy*, Columba University Press, NY, 1969.
5. The history of the B1 bomber illustrates this. A new bomber known as the Stealth bomber designed to penetrate radar and other defences is currently being developed by the USA.
6. For an account of its development see Lawrence Freedman, *The Evolution of Nuclear Strategy*, Macmillan, London, 1981, and also Maurice Mandelbaum, *The Nuclear Revolution*, Cambridge University Press, 1981.
7. For a somewhat tendentious account see the revised edition of Gar Aperovitz, *Atomic Diplomacy*, Penguin Books, Harmondsworth, 1985.
8. This was the Far Eastern Agreement made at Yalta between the United States and the Soviet Union. It stipulated that;
   Russia would enter the war 2–3 months after VE.
   S. Sakhalin be returned to the USSR (lost in 1905).
   Dairen be internationalised.
   Port Arthur leased to USSR.
   Chinese Eastern Railway south Manchurian Railway to be operated jointly by the USSR and China with Soviet Rights.
   The Kurile Islands to be handed over to the USSR.
   The concessions on the ports and railways required the consent of Chiang Kai Shek as was the case for the status of Outer Mongolia; the USA contracted to obtain this consent.
   The USSR for its part contracted to conclude a pact of friendship with KMT government.
   The Heads of the three great powers have agreed that these claims of the Soviet Union shall be unquestionably fulfilled after Japan has been defeated.
9. The B29 Bomber.
10. Unlike the other former territories and colonies of the Turkish and German Empires that had been made into Mandates under League of Nations supervision and then into Trusts under the United Nations, the Marianas, Carolines and Marshall Islands were created 'Strategic' Trusts, under the supervision of the United States. This unique form of trusteeship enabled the United States to build military installations, to deport the inhabitants and to conduct nuclear tests. The welfare of the inhabitants, unlike those of the other Trusts, was subordinated to these purposes.
11. For an account of pre-war policies in this area see Whitney Griswold, *The Far Eastern Policy of the United States*, Yale University Press, Newhaven, 1964.
12. This was tacitly recognised by Dean Acheson when he made the so-called 'green-light' speech in which he implicitly excluded Korea from the sphere of

American interests in the Far East. This apparent exclusion was supposed to encourage the communists to 'invade' South Korea. The United States took little interest in Indo-China until 1950; indeed the attitude adopted opposed French colonialism. This radically changed with the Korean War.

13. The United States had much closer economic ties with Europe than with China or Japan. The attempt made by Hitler to create a closed economic system on the Continent was as much a danger to American economic interests as the military consequences of German military domination of Europe.

14. See my *Theory and Explanation in International Politics*, Martin Robertson, 1973, p. 126 and Chapter 5.

15. There is a large and growing literature on this. See Joseph Siracusa, *The American Diplomatic Revolution*, Open University Press, Milton Keynes, 1978.

16. Without going into the question of justification, the invasion by Germany in 1914 following Tannenberg, and the attempt at Brest-Litovsk to truncate Russia, as well as the period of intervention by Britain, the United States and Japan, the invasion of Poland in 1920 and the gains made by the Peace of Riga, together with the German invasion of 1941, gave Russian leaders sufficient precedents of direct threats to security as to warrant a deep concern for their western frontiers.

17. Spain and Italy had also provided military contingents fighting with the German forces in Russia.

18. The compatability of the Soviet economic and political systems to the economic and financial institutions of the United Nations, the International Bank for Reconstruction and Development (IBRD), and the International Monetary Fund (IMF), was a source of concern. The issue of reparations and the economic treatment of the defeated Germany were vexed questions in the immediate post-war period together with the problem of war debts and balance of payments.

19. The attitude of the United States towards its own security can best be judged by its unilateral breach of the Hyde Park agreement with Britain on sharing atomic technology. This was only revised when, in 1948, an agreement was reached over the stationing of six squadrons of B29 bombers on British territory, thus enabling the United States to strike at Soviet targets. Similarly, the United States sought to lift the UN proscription on Fascist Spain when bases on Spanish territory were being negotiated.

20. It was the only member of NATO to have its military forces entirely integrated under what was effectively American command.

21. Marshall Aid and the European Recovery Programme.

22. For an account of British policy on this issue see Margaret Gowing, *Independence and Deterrence*, Vols. I and II, Macmillan, London, 1974.

23. 'Roll-back' was a rhetorical phrase indicating a commitment of the United States and, by implication, its NATO allies, to push the communists out of Eastern Europe thus 'liberating' it.

24. On the notion of containment see G. F. Kennan, *Memoirs*, Vol. 1 1925–1950, Little Brown, Boston, 1967 and 'The Sources of Soviet Conduct (Mr. X)' in *Fifty Years of Foreign Affairs*, ed. Hamilton Fish Armstrong, Praeger, NY, 1972, pp. 188 (ff). Containment in practice differed from his more elastic and ambiguous notion and led to commitments with foreign governments and alliances that Kennan deplored. It became global, that is extended beyond

Europe, through commitments such as the SEATO, Anzus Treaty, and the Japanese Peace Treaty, negotiated by Dulles during the first Eisenhower Administration.

25. The B47.
26. See Freedman, *op. cit.* pp. 65–8.
27. The A4, see A. Speer, *op. cit.* pp. 464–81.
28. This would not have protected them from Hitler; he intended to invade Switzerland and probably Sweden before his plans went awry in the Russian campaign; vide his remarks, 'A state like Switzerland, which is nothing but a pimple on the face of Europe, cannot be allowed to continue' ... 'As for the Swedish vermin, they must be swept away like the Danish vermin in 1848', pp. 660 and 661, *Hitler's Table Talk*, ed. by Hugh Trevor-Roper, Weidenfeld and Nicolson, London, 1953.
29. The barest hint that the United States might use the atomic bomb against China brought Attlee to Washington to check this development. Macarthur, who was publicly advocating its use, was sacked by Truman in spite of what appeared to be popular support for him and consequent electoral damage.
30. The case of Cuba is a good illustration of this. Attempts by the United States to destroy the Castro regime ranged from economic embargo, economic sanctions, support for military intervention to plans for assassination. They all failed. But there have been successes such as, for example, the coup against Allende in Chile and his subsequent murder, but in general it has proved difficult to protect friendly regimes by means short of direct military and political intervention.
31. For some reason this has been associated with Macnamara, deriving from his speech at Ann Arbor in 1962. See Laurence Martin, ed. *Strategic Thought in the Nuclear Age*, Heinemann, London, 1979; Henry R. Rowan, *The Evolution of Strategic Nuclear Doctrine*, p. 148 and William, *The Macnamara Strategy*, pp. 114–15.
32. Surveillance is extremely important given the speed of ballistic missiles. It is necessary to know the nature, source and direction and targeting of any launch in order to formulate an appropriate response. The consequences of an inappropriate response do not bear thinking about. Given the time factor and the technical complexity entailed both in monitoring and formulating a response, the possibility of human error increases at an exponential rate. As more states possess ballistic missile capacity this problem can only intensify. It is also important to know accurately the technical performance and size of all nuclear forces in order to preserve the conditions for a specific balance. Hence a non-proliferation policy pursued by existing nuclear powers is designed to protect themselves in this respect. Finally, maintaining arms control agreements also requires adequate surveillance.
33. Or potential administrations, as the allegation of a non-existent missile gap by Kennedy and his supporters indicates.
34. For an interesting exposition of the official view of the Soviet Union on deterrence see Study on Deterrence Report of the Secretary-General of the United Nations, 41 Session 7 General Assembly item 64(g) A/41/432/23rd July 1986, since printed as *The International Politics of Deterrence*, ed. by Barry Buzan, Frances Pinter, London, 1987.
35. It must be admitted that this confines this aspect of the study of the rationality of violence to some five countries. Nevertheless, most large-scale wars in the past have involved the major powers and it is these states in effect that set

limits (or otherwise) on the scale of violence, if not its incidence, in the world at large.

36. The first missile capable of reaching targets more than 1500 miles was the consequence of the decision taken in 1955 by the USA to maintain nuclear superiority over the Soviet Union. This was the Atlas missile. Intermediate range missiles were in development and production. These were Jupiter and Thor and they required, as did the extant jet aircraft, forward bases to be effective against their Russian targets.
   The Soviet Union demonstrated its own capacity to produce ICBMs in the launching of Sputnik in October 1957. The American response was to give the Polaris programme top priority in January 1958.

37. See for example on the contemporary debate in the United States, Strobe Talbot, *Deadly Gambits*, Pan Books, London, 1985.

38. *Ibid*, pp. 214–18, and pp. 303–11.

39. The American MIRV programme began in the 1960s and was deployed in 1970. It was not included in any arms control agreement. The USSR followed suit deploying MIRVs on ICBMs in 1975 and on SLBMs in 1978. More than any other development in missiles it created a quantum jump in the number of warheads, complicating the problems of arms control and of maintaining strategic stability between the two adversaries.

40. Mobility being one means of escaping destruction from a saturation attack.

41. This has been calculated by American planners as one fifth to one third of Soviet population and one half to three quarters of Soviet industry. See Michael Mandelbaum, *The Nuclear Revolution*, Cambridge University Press, 1981, p. 118.

42. The Triad consists of (1) hardened missile silos launching ICBMs (Minuteman) together with MX mobile ICBMs (2) underwater launched ICMs (Poseidon now Trident) and air-launched cruise missiles and (3) bombs (launched by a variety of aircraft but the main force consisting of long-range bombers now the B1).

43. See Warner R. Schilling, 'US Strategy Nuclear Concepts in the 1970s', pp. 204–208 in Steven Miller ed. *Strategy and Nuclear Defense*, Princeton University Press, NJ., 1984.

44. Of course a political faction can identify its political features *with* the interests of the state.

45. This is the Strategic Defense Initiative (SDI) announced by President Reagan in March 1983.

46. For the notion of equivalence see Benjamin S. Lambeth, 'The Political Potential of Soviet Equivalence', pp. 255–72 in Steven E. Miller ed., *Strategy and Nuclear Deterrence, op. cit.*

47. The notion of extended deterrence is simply the application of defensive deterrence based on mutual assured destruction (MAD) to non-nuclear allies. Nuclear allies possessing their own defensive deterrents are in no need of this 'nuclear umbrella'. It is claimed that the United States has foreign interests that must be defended through strategic means. Hence extended deterrence is one way of indicating a level of threat that in security terms appear irrational. Per contra the notion that the Soviet Union has similar non-security interests in the world is denied legitimacy, see Gray, *The Soviet-American Arms Race, op. cit.* p. 75.

48. The Nassau Agreement of 1963 which conferred the Polaris missile system on Britain, was concluded only after strong representations from Macmillan.

Although Polaris was nominally placed under NATO it could be used where British interests were deemed paramount. The French, although offered Polaris under more stringent conditions, preferred to manufacture their own system. This they succeeded in doing in spite of non-cooperation and indeed some obstruction from the United States. It appears that one of the reasons for the Sino-Soviet split in the late 1950s was the refusal of the Soviet Union to help the Chinese in their nuclear programme.

49. Although in opposition the Labour Party rejected the independent possession of nuclear weapons, in office it has endorsed them. Harold Wilson, for example, before the 1964 election declared that if he won it he would abolish 'the so-called independent, so-called deterrent'. In fact he completed the programme. Similarly, the modernisation of the Polaris system—Chevaline—was undertaken by a Labour government (Callaghan) in spite of the presence of two opponents of nuclear weapons, Wedgewood Benn and Michael Foot, in the Cabinet. Perhaps this accounts for the secrecy of the programme. More recently, before the 1987 election, the Labour Party announced its intention of cancelling the Trident programme. Since it lost the election there is no means of testing the sincerity of this declaration.

50. See John Wheeler-Bennett, *Munich: Prologue to Tragedy*, Ovell Sloane and Pearce, NY, 1948.

51. The unfavourable balance after the Battle of the Marne resulted in a military stalemate and was a factor in making this war total. A military solution was sought instead of seeking some form of negotiation largely because the German government held the advantage in territory,

52. It is unlikely that such a consequence would occur after a general nuclear exchange and the threat of a limited nuclear attack in the European theatre is designed to frustrate adventurism in the form of a bid to occupy territory and then negotiate.

53. It is for this reason that the United States has resisted a ban on the first use of weapons proposed by the Soviet Union.

54. In current jargon this is termed 'de-coupling'.

55. Although the West Germans have specific allocation of Pershing 1A missiles for their 'defence' the warheads are effectively controlled by the United States. The West German government has recently agreed to their removal (Sept. 1987).

56. This is equally true of methods of protection for missiles and the notion of 'enhanced deterrence' has appeared in recent strategic discussion in the United States reflecting the use of anti-ballistic missiles systems to protect strategic missiles sites.

57. A case for this has been made by one strategic analyst. See Colin S. Gray, *Nuclear Strategy: the case for a Theory of Victory*, in Steven E. Miller, *op. cit.* pp. 23–56.

58. Global containment, that is, the policy of confining the Soviet Union to its immediate post-war sphere of influence was predicated on American military superiority. The implicit threat that countered Soviet expansion was based on American nuclear forces. When this threat lost credibility in 1968 with the appearance of strategic parity, then the policy collapsed coinciding with both the acceptance of failure in Vietnam and the beginning of the negotiation of SALT I. The Western allies were forced upon traditional means of diplomacy, negotiation, bluff, and threats, to maintain their relationships with other countries in which they had an interest. In this they had mixed results and

since the end of the 1960s the Soviet Union has succeeded in breaking out of the attempt to force isolation upon it.

59. While the geographical advantages enjoyed by the Soviet Union in both Europe and Asia when compared with the United States, are beyond dispute, the actual imbalance in conventional force levels is a matter of controversy. The arithmetic depends upon which forces are counted, both in situ and capable of being deployed. A further complication exists if qualitative factors such as training and equipment are included in the equation. It is claimed for example, that Soviet armour is inferior to that of the West. Past experience does not lend credibility to this kind of argument.

60. SS20. These are mobile missiles capable of hitting most European targets but not reaching the United States.

61. See Gray, *The Soviet American Arms Race, op. cit.* p. 168.

62. 1987.

63. The United States has attempted in its arms control negotiations on INF to extend the ban on SS20s and the deployment of these weapons to the world at large thus protecting Japan (and China).

64. It is disheartening to the contemporary historian who is also a citizen to hear the same Cold War rhetoric as that which preceded the present nuclear stalemate being used to justify strategic postures and weapons procurement that have no clear rationale. For example, Colin Gray talks of the 'facts' that, 'The Soviet peoples as a whole have no self-evident affection for, as opposed to toleration of this political system of their individual political leaders.... The Soviet Union, quite literally is a colonial empire—loved by none of its non-Great Russian minority peoples.' Love is a potent force in human relations but this kind of argument is not merely superficial but highly dangerous where nuclear war is a possibility. Regardless of the character of the opposed political systems, or of the values they purportedly represent, their differences pale into insignificance in the face of a possible Armageddon.

7 Reasons and Violence

War has been considered up to this point as organised violence between states in pursuit of their interests. We come now to a form of violence deemed equally functional, but factional in character. If war and its threat are related to a struggle for control within the world of states, factional violence, and its threat, is about power within the state. The two often are parallel or complementary, one emanating from the other. In the Second World War, for example, many of the national resistance movements were not so much concerned with fighting the German occupiers of their states and helping the Allies, as with the question of power and the nature of the political system after their departure. There were a number of civil wars within the greater war.[1] All resistance movements, to a greater or lesser extent had political objectives and engaged in violence to this end. In most cases their struggle was pre-empted by foreign intervention, as in Italy, Greece, France and Belgium, and in Eastern Europe; while in others as in Yugoslavia and China, a bloody civil war ensued.

War, of course is only one occasion for promoting radical political changes within states, although it is significant that all the major revolutions in the recent past have occured with foreign intervention as a factor. Defeat and governmental impotence are potent elements in encouraging political challenge. However, political changes through the aegis of violence have occured without general war, and while the latter provides an opportunity, it is not considered essential by revolutionary theorists. The struggle for power within the state is thus the central focus of this form of violence; although, as we shall see, larger claims are made for revolution than merely transferring power from one faction to another.

Violence is conceived in this context as the use of threat of physical force and restraint towards human beings whether directly through the infliction of pain or death, or indirectly, through deprivation of food, shelter, clothing and status, and restrictions on the ability to have and seek pleasure. It is the imposition of a sanction consciously conceived by the perpetrator and consciously perceived by the victim or potential victim. As such it is related to the enforcement of one will against another's. It presumes a common rationality.[2] As with war I am concerned here with the nature of this rationality, that is with the use of this kind of violence as a means to an end. I am not concerned with the question of its justification or legitimacy although these question enter into the political debate. They are also related to the impact and strength of the sanction in that a challenge to values is part of the threat as well as the material damage inflicted. This is central to terrorism. But the moral connotations of justification are beyond this study.

There are three aspects to factional violence; the first is its use to achieve a different socio-political system through revolution or people's war. The second is the counter to this, as the defence of the existing system through what is termed counter-insurgency or the promotion of internal security. Both these aspects concern civil war, insurrection, dissent, terrorism and violence within the state over the question, who rules? As was argued earlier, violence is an essential part of politics in that its legitimised use by the government in maintaining law and order is a basic element of the modern state. The state has a monopoly of violence operating with the rule of law. Citizens may be deprived of life, liberty, property and rights, by the state, according to procedures and rules generally recognised as legitimate, constitutional, or legal within it.[3] Civil war or revolution is not concerned so much with challenging these rules as with challenging the right of the government to implement them.

Capitalist governments according to Marxist critics, are merely instruments of one exploiting class and the particular rule of law with which they are associated is simply a means of promoting sectional interests. Property has a higher value than people. In its place they would put a rule of law based on 'socialist legality' or people's law. Similarly, democratic government, according to fascists, is a means of promoting the interests of particular factions, whether those of labour, or those of capital, over the interests of the nation as a whole. Such governments, in effect, wage war against the people. Their monopoly of violence is used to maintain sectarian interests. Revolutionary violence, as Lenin pointed out, is designed to counter state violence exercised on behalf of the bourgeoisie.[4] Once in power the abuse of the monopoly of violence enjoyed by the capitalist state would be corrected by a new revolutionary polity. Thus while the monopoly itself is not in question, what is challenged is the form of government that exercises it and the political system associated with it. And this challenge, of necessity, takes on a violent form. Violence is met with violence. This argument will be considered later.

The third aspect is the conscious use of this factional struggle by other states in order to achieve political objectives, either limited in character, or as an element of national security. While the promotion of dissent in other countries has always been a conscious political manoeuvre on the part of the states, it assumes a particular importance given the nuclear stalemate and its inhibition on the use of other forms of violence between nuclear states. This form of intervention, including state terrorism, does not endanger the state engaged in it, nor can its cost be said to be excessive.

Such manipulation, fashionably called de-stabilisation tactics, may be directed simply with a view to disrupting political control generally, as a means of weakening an opponent's security posture. Domestic pressure groups objecting to weapons procurement policies may be encouraged;[5] and indeed, support given to any faction that challenges the political will of the opposing government. Dissent and opposition in an opponent's allies and in third-party states where the opponent has a major interest, are also encouraged as a general tactic.[6]

A challenge to the authority of a government that controls nuclear weapons is not only a challenge to its effective rule, or the legitimacy of a particular political system, it also constitutes a weakening of its deterrent posture. This, as we have seen earlier, depends on the credibility of a specific threat. Credibility, in turn, is bound up not merely with the material capacity to inflict damage upon an opponent but upon the will to do so. A government wracked with internal political crisis, or incapable of effective rule, is unstable and unpredictable. It is also exposed to pressures operating from within that are susceptible to manipulation from outside. In short, there is a security dimension in that challenges to the authority or legitimacy of governments controlling nuclear weapons can be exploited, indeed invite exploitation, by their rivals. At the least, dissent over weapons procurement can be exploited to support a position in arms control negotiations favouring one particular country. Such support, and indeed such dissent, need not of course entail violence.

Under conditions of nuclear stalemate it could be argued that it is more important, so far as the nuclear powers are concerned, to minimise the possibility of political instability in each other's polities, since they all have an interest in survival. Only if a pre-emptive attack is being considered, and military victory sought, would it make sense to seek to induce and exploit political instability in a nuclear adversary. The risks are obvious. Exploiting dissent through sub-terrorist uses of violence designed to provoke specific reactions, may be successful in the short term, and for limited objectives, but becomes counterproductive if security becomes directly involved. Incumbent governments tend to frown on this kind of activity although there have been exceptions.[7] As we have seen, the command and control aspects of nuclear deterrence are in any case insulated from the political process, whatever its nature. But the risks of irrational behaviour, irrational in terms of maintaining the basic conditions of mutual defensive deterrence, are too high for any nuclear power to encourage adventurism of this kind.

It is, of course, a different matter when open civil war occurs, and few states have resisted the temptation to exploit collapse in another country to their advantage. Non-intervention is a dubious concept without the means of enforcement. The Spanish Civil War stands as a supreme example, although there are many others. In this particular case, in refusing to supply arms to the Republican government, the Western states, in effect, supported the Franco Nationalists, who were able to obtain not only arms, but the direct intervention of Italian and German forces on their behalf.

Only the Soviet Union, directly, and the French government, indirectly, helped the Spanish government. Neither non-intervention nor involvement were pursued as policies for altruistic motives and all these nations had reasons for their stance on the issue, that reflected national interests.[8]

While the deterrent relationship precludes war between the nuclear powers, this places a premium on indirect forms of violence as a means of securing political advantages for non-security interests. Security itself as we have seen is achieved through mutual defensive deterrents. The main focus in practice has been in the non-nuclear states. Proxy wars and violent intervention, state terrorism and covert operations, are all in the main directed at Third World countries and have been concerned with maintaining or changing regimes deemed friendly or inimical to the major powers. It is true of course, that these small relatively weak countries have not only engaged in such tactics themselves, but have also employed open war as a means of promoting their own interests. Some wars, such as those of the Middle East have an alarming resemblance to the Balkan Wars of the past.[9] The main difference being the restraints on major patron states from settling the issues involved through their own resort to war.

However, before considering the theoretical and prescriptive aspects of low-intensity operations,[10] counter-insurgency, and state terrorism, I want to examine revolutionary violence and its associated theories. An important point in interpreting the analysis of proper use of violence by revolutionary writers, is that they were for most part not only engaged in it but were very successful at it. Lenin, Mao Tse Tung, Giap, Che Guevara, etc., were successful revolutionary leaders.[11] They were actively engaged in making command decisions and in formulating strategy. They were also engaged in politics, not merely the political ends for which their strategies were a means, but in achieving and maintaining control over their followers and rivals. Theoretical analysis was not only an explanation of the necessity for a particular action or tactic, placing it within a coherent conceptual framework, but also a means of conferring authority on a policy identified with the leadership. The policy adopted had to be successful, but it also had to be ideologically right. Theory and practice must be united in the leadership.

Doctrine thus had to be flexible enough to allow on the tactical level as much room for manoeuvre as changing circumstances dictated. The revolutionary leader could not afford to become a prisoner of doctrine, or relegate his freedom of action to doctrinal precepts capable of being used by his rivals as a weapon against his leadership. 'Right' or 'left' deviationism was to be condemned, and the 'correct' line established by the leader, to forestall any challenge to his authority.[12] He was not merely concerned with being successful against his nominal opponents, but also with maintaining his position within the faction. The consequence in terms of revolutionary doctrine is theoretical ambiguity and contradiciton. Prescriptive analysis—the relation between theory and practice—is constantly being modified and revised according to the incidence of factionalism or changes in fortune. As might be expected, the greatest ambiguities occur in times of adversity when challenges to the leadership reflect success or failure. On the revolutionary upswing the leadership enjoys support and so there is little need for the kind of theoretical justification typical of the period of adversity. In this respect at least revolutionary politics seem little different from bourgeois politics!

It is not possible to undertake an examination of the relationship between doctrine and politics in the context of revolutionary struggle, fascinating though such an exegesis would be. I am primarily concerned, firstly, with establishing what kind of theoretical argument supports the use of violence for revolutionary purposes, and secondly, with appraising in prescriptive terms the rationale that emanates from it. It is theoretical content *per se* that concerns me, not the element of political opportunism and circumstance that undoubtedly permeates it. The point here is that interpretation of the theoretical argument must take this element into account.

I have confined myself to the many variations of Marxism in this examination of revolutionary doctrine and the instrumental use of violence. I am, however, aware that the right too has a concern with violence. In a previous work[13] I examined the relationship between theory and practice in the context of the Third Reich. National-Socialism, or rather Hitler's version of it, postulates a form of Social-Darwinism that has as its central thesis the existence of permanent struggle—a war of all against all. The theory of a racial hierarchy and its correlate of racial purity, is one that preaches not merely the existence of violence in human relations as a permanent feature, but its necessity. Conflict between nation-states induces a process of natural selection. The fittest nation emerges victorious from the struggle. A racial-state, that is one purged of its non-national and racially impure elements, is one best fitted for survival. But the incessant struggle is also necessary to keep the state at its highest pitch.

In a sense a strategy is derivative from this sort of theory, dictating racial purgation, but Hitler was no more anxious than left-wing revolutionary theorists to bind himself with dogma that might prove inconvenient as support, opposition, and circumstances, changed. The 'theory' he espoused was justificatory, rather than a basis for prescriptions, authorising his policies, rather than dictating them. It was not programmatic. *Fuehrerprinzip* justified his position in power and this was derived from dogma, but it did not entail any accountability as 'democratic centralism' did for Marxist leaders. And this was equally true for other fascist leaders such as Mussolini, Franco, and Salazar,[14] who also kept dogma at a distance. Neither am I concerned with fascist or other theorists of the right such as D'Annunzio who were not engaged in practice in the same way. In short the link between theoretical argument and practice that exists for Marxist and left-wing revolutionaries does not exist for right-wing radical leaders.

Marx and his followers had as their central concern the achievement of power within a framework of capitalism. Their analysis of capitalism was crucial to their practical programme. Revolution or a revolutionary situation was a product of capitalist contradictions. No less opportunistic than fascist political leaders, they had a structured and coherent analytic framework that related abstract principles to concrete practical action. The pragmatism and opportunism was largely a question of timing. The end was revolution and this depended on a correct interpretation of the processes of capitalism. Characteristically, the theory looked no further than this. The nature of the polity that followed a successful revolution was left in a theoretical and prescriptive void. The remnants of the bourgeois state would wither away after its collapse. It was revolution, the promotion of this collapse, that was the focus of attention, and the revolutionary process was reactive to, and contingent upon, the analysis of capitalist society and its politics. Without capitalism there could be no revolution. Changes in the capitalists system necessitated changes in the Marxist analysis, as Lenin well understood. Revision was inbuilt in the theoretical postulates.[15] Tactical pragmatism was the consequence.

Fascist theory was more concerned not with the method of achieving success but with the nature of the fascist state. Revolution was merely incidental although important as a first step in changing the state of its fascist mode. Violence was thus a means to an end but it lacked the kind of theoretical relevance characteristic of Marxism, operating as it did within an analytic framework of capitalism. The theoretical element was synthetic rather than systematic, and took the form of a world view normative in character. Its relevance was more as a set of aspirations that inclined to an ideal state and mode of human relations, idealising such entities as the 'nation' or the 'family'. In the event, Hitler's racial state and its imperium were never realised, and, ironically, the main reason for this was military defeat. His use of violence had as its theoretical basis the same sort of strategic prescriptions and rationality as that utilised by his non-fascist opponents, as we saw earlier. But the political system he sought to create and the war he fought were not revolutionary in character.

Before turning to revolutionary violence and its theoretical referents the point should be reiterated that there is no necessary connection between belief and action so that the latter is entailed by the former. Having beliefs does not constitute a cause for a specific decision or act, although they may provide reasons. The relationship between theory and action—in this case the theoretical basis of guerrilla war, terrorism, and revolutionary violence—is prescriptive in character. As we shall see, much of what passes for theory in this context is justificatory, and is concerned with legitimising particular courses of action. This is important from the point of view of eliciting support and maintaining solidarity when external and internal pressures on revolutionary groups are, of their nature, acute. But while prescriptions concerning the *effectiveness* of propaganda are relevant, it is the instrumental use of violence that is important. What is the theoretical basis of effective action? In what sense are prescriptions a derivative? What makes them authoritative? In this respect the advocate of revolutionary violence is no different from those involved in the kind of strategic thinking considered so far.

The necessity for violence in making the transition from capitalism to socialism is taken for granted by both Marx and Lenin. The bourgeoisie with its command over the apparatus of the state, including the police and the armed forces, will not surrender its privileged position without a struggle. The practical use of violence required the recognition of a revolutionary situation and the adoption of appropriate tactics. Marx provided the general conceptual framework, or strategy; Lenin the prescriptions derived from it, or the tactics. This is something of an oversimplification since, as we shall see, Lenin also embellished the theory. His analysis of capitalism led Marx to believe in the inevitability of revolution arising, as he argued, from its inherent contradictions, notably the incompatibility of labour and capital. This was a fundamental cleavage that could not be bridged through compromise and reform. Capitalism itself was driven by the need to derive surplus value[16] from a finite labour supply and impelled into ever more expansion and concentration, deepening and extending class divisions. Such a process was both inevitable and irreversible. It created the 'objective' conditions for revolution. Where capitalism was most developed a revolutionary situation was most likely. Marx believed this to be the case for Germany.

Although Marx provided a theoretical analysis of the capitalist system that included a statement of the necessary conditions for revolution he did not provide a set of prescriptions other than in a negative sense through historical analyses. The conduct of a revolution, as opposed to its likelihood, was outside the scope of his argument. There was little practical instruction for revolutionary leaders other than avoiding the mistakes of the past. It was Lenin who faced the problem of relating theory to practice. But before doing so he revised the theory. According to Lenin, capitalism has entered its highest (and final) stage of development.[17] The imperialist stage, following Marx, was the consequence of the economic drive to realise surplus value. After diminishing returns set in through the realisation of the finite national labour pool, capitalists sought to resolve this problem through international expansion. The quest for economic territory that ensued was based on the same dynamic as described by Marx, but constituted a new imperialism. This was manifest in the wave of later Nineteenth Century colonial expansion and the resultant competition between the European powers. It accounted for the appearance of new financial institutions, what Lenin, taking his argument from Hilferding,[18] called monopoly capital, and new industrial organisations such as trusts and cartels. And finally, it accounted for the phenomenon of world war. In Lenin's view the First World War was essentially an imperialist war in which the real issue was a struggle for economic territory, brought about by the exhaustion of national labour resources and the consequent need for a new labour supply from which to realise surplus value. The inherent contradiction within capitalist countries was palliated by the creation of privileged sections of labour separating them from the main proletarian masses. This was at the expense of the new proletarians in the form of the exploited peoples of the empires and of economic territory.[19] Because each capitalist country was forced to solve its economic problems in this way, a struggle between them for domination over economic territory was the result. Imperialist expansion was necessarily violent, both in its conquest, and in its competition.[20]

What has this analysis to do with revolution and the effective use of violence to attain revolutionary ends? On the face of it, it constitutes a form of description that permits identification of class enemies and progressive forces without any clear prescription as to appropriate action.[22] As Marx argued, revolution is inevitable, but recognition of what is a revolutionary situation is not an easy matter. Lenin believed that the war was the last dying throes of capitalism and revolution was certain to emerge from it. But this was a question of opportunity. No clear programme of action was proposed. Opportunism was characteristic of Lenin's approach to revolution. For example, in an earlier work written after the abortive insurrection of 1905 in Russia, he insists on an eclectic approach to revolutionary violence. 'In this respect', he asserts, 'Marxism *learns* if we may so express it, from mass practice and makes no claim whatever to *teach* the masses forms of struggle invented by "systematizers" in the seclusion of their studies.'[22] Lenin thus asserts that any means are acceptable and what determines choice depends upon 'the concrete historical situation'. Violence may take the form of guerilla warfare in the context of an uprising, but larger engagements and civil war are the only decisive ways of achieving final success. What is appropriate depends upon circumstance, given that the ultimate objective is revolution, that is, a *radical* change in the political system.

This pragmatism reflects both uncertainty and a tautological view of revolution implicit in dialectical materialism. A revolution is successful by definition. When conditions are right, so a genuine revolutionary situation exists, but there is little guidance to the would-be revolutionary, other than the comforting reassurance that it is inevitable, as to how these conditions may be recognised. It is perhaps understandable after the failure to achieve revolution in 1905 that Lenin should be cautious about prescribing in detail a revolutionary programme. The fact that an insurrection occurred at all was encouraging, but its failure also presented a challenge to would-be revolutionary leaders and their factions. The chief lesson learnt by Lenin was that mass support was essential to success.[23] Given this, then it could be led in the right direction. More precise formulations were precluded, both by the absence of this support, and the dangers of becoming wedded to a strategy that circumstances might frustrate and so expose its proponent to attacks from rival factions. His opportunity came with the Russian collapse and the consequent opposition to the war. The war itself thus provided an opportunity for revolution not only because of the consequences of defeat, but because of the cleavages in Russia, engendered by the concentration of power and the sacrifices demanded of the people, the existence of an industrialised proletariat, albeit small, but organised and essential for war production, and their training and incorporation into an army. As Lenin put it, 'a revolutionary class cannot but wish for the defeat of its government in a reactionary war, cannot fail to see that its military reverses facilitate its overthrow.'[24] However wishful this thinking, it seemed clear that violence between capitalist states could be transformed into civil war and revolution.

More specifically, the military collapse and the consequent loss of authority by the government in 1917 gave Lenin the opportunity to put his minority party into power. His tactics were rationalised as two revolutionary phases; the first being that of using the more radical factions under his control to enlist popular support and manipulate the provisional government. Mass support, as he clearly understood, could only be obtained by ending the war and transferring ownership of land to the peasantry. The political changes of March and afterwards, were only superficial and the state apparatus remained intact with the bourgeoisie still in control. What was necessary in order to achieve a genuine revolution was the removal of this class together with its institutions. The programme to be followed in his April theses[25] was to use the Soviets as the main focus of power, encapsulated in the slogan 'All power to the Soviets'; to separate the Soviets in terms of their representation, thus giving the urban proletariat more effective control than the peasants; to obtain a Bolshevik majority in the Soviets, and to 'arm the people', destroying the army and replacing it with a new Red Army. The war itself was not to be prosecuted unless it became revolutionary with parallel collapses in other capitalist countries. And initial support was to be obtained through the confiscation of all landed estates, the nationalisation of all land and its disposal to local Soviets composed of peasants. The major financial institutions were also to be nationalised. This then, was his basic programme of action. While broad support was sought amongst other political factions sympathetic to parts at least of this programme, the underlying rationale was to destroy as much as possible the existing political system, while achieving control over resources and communications. In particular, as he put it, 'The first commandment of any victorious revolution, as Marx and Engels repeatedly emphasised was, smash the old army, dissolve it and replace it by a new one.'[26]

The second phase was that of genuine revolution involving violence.[27] Armed struggle was a necessity, both in smashing opposition through civil war, and in eliminating unorganised opposition through terror. The transitional phase of bourgeois-democratic revolution had to move into the more violent phase of socialist revolution. The first phase was in his view a necessary tactical move designed to transfer leadership and power to the Bolsheviks, ' ... a general Peasant revolution is still a bourgeois revolution, and that without a series of transitions, transitional stages, it cannot be transformed into a socialist revolution in a backward country'.[28] The point of these transitions was to obtain power by manipulating those factions prepared to cooperate with the Bolsheviks but who would certainly oppose them if the full extent of their aims was understood. In this context timing was extremely important, given the numerical insignificance of the Bolsheviks and their need to acquire mass following.

The first priority for Lenin was ending the war with Germany.[29] This was not only a popular move, but it would place a German army between those foreign powers anxious to overturn the revolution and Russia. Making enormous territorial concessions to the Germans removed their support for counter-revolution. In any case Lenin believed that revolution would spread in Germany and the rest of Europe, thus making such concessions irrelevent in the face of a new political order. Similarly, in declaring to the peasants that landlordism and serfdom were dead, he led them to believe that ownership of the land would be transferred to them. Lenin hoped to obtain their support but his long-term plan was to create a new economic system that subjugated the peasants to the urban industrialised centres and their requirements.[30]

Within the framework of this political manoeuvring Lenin organised for civil war. He clearly recognised that force was the only means to achieve a radical transformation of the political system. He believed, 'Not a single problem of class struggle has ever been solved in history except by violence.'[31] He approached the problem pragmatically by organising forces under the command of former Tsarist officers directed by Trotsky. He aimed at fighting the White forces in open warfare. Guerilla war and terrorism were also used; the latter designed to remove actual and potential civil and military leaders from the opposition. But these were peripheral to the main struggle. As he put it, 'We should have but one slogan; seriously learn the art of war, put the railways in order.'[32]

It is important to stress the pragmatism of Lenin's strategy of revolution. The end was clear—power concentrated in the hands of the Bolsheviks and the complete destruction of the old political system and its complex of values, property rights, and legality. This could only be achieved through direct confrontation in the form of civil war;

'Whoever recognises the class struggle cannot fail to recognise civil wars which in every class society are the natural, and under certain conditions, inevitable continuation, development, and intensification, of the class struggle. And the great revolutions prove this. To repudiate civil war, or to forget about it, would mean sinking into extreme opportunism and renouncing the socialist revolution.'

And again, 'The revolutionary dictatorship of the proletariat is power won and maintained by the violence of the proletariat against the bourgeoisie, power that is unrestricted by any laws'. Yet the revolutionary situation was one which, in this case, was created, rather than emerging through the satisfaction of theoretical conditions.

I will examine the relationship between theory and practice in terms of revolutionary violence after Mao Tse Tung and his followers have been considered. For the moment, the central thesis that Lenin argues is the recognition of the revolutionary situation and the pursuit of a directed opportunism, consolidating one position after another, bearing in mind the final goal, the acquisition of an undisputed power. An inspired piece of opportunism for example, was the use of the Soviets as an instrument of control and manipulation of rival factions or potential opposition within the loose coalition that supported radical political change. Lenin did not create these, but he recognised their utility as an alternative to the constitutionalism of the provisional government. The chief mechanism for achieving revolution was, however, civil war.

This was fought on conventional lines between regular military forces. It had, like all civil wars, an element of beastliness, enhanced in this case by the revolutionary doctrine of class conflict. Atrocities and reprisals against civilians were perpetrated by both sides. But terrorism and guerrilla warfare were not encouraged by Lenin. These aspects of political violence will be considered later, the point here is that Lenin regarded them as a divergence from the main effort, that of formal war. Terror was useful in the early stages of revolution, in intimidating potential opposition and eliminating rival leaders, but it was only ancillary to the main war effort. Lenin regarded this form of violence with suspicion since it led to independence of action and encouraged factionalism. It could not be controlled effectively, and Lenin was not simply interested in promoting revolution, he wanted to lead it. His main problem lay in preventing foreign intervention from frustrating it. He also needed to create a Red Army that was effective in the field. The first was essentially a political problem that eased when Germany accepted an Armistice and Allied efforts to keep Russia in the war no longer were relevant. The second was largely a practical and not a theoretical matter.

Mao Tse Tung, far more than Lenin, can be regarded as the theorist of revolutionary violence in all its aspects. Lenin, in his theoretical writings, appears to be more conscious of the political dimension of revolution—the problem of gaining power and the need to consolidate his leadership.[33] Mao appears to be primarily concerned with the mechanics of violence. This perhaps reflects the fact that the revolutionary struggle in China was so prolonged. In many ways it was a paradigm for almost every type of war. Beginning with civil war and the brief coalition of the Kuomintang (KMT) and the Communist Party, in an attempt to defeat separatist movements and factions led by warlords, moving into revolutionary war challenging the quasi-feudal political system, back into civil war combined with resistance against the Japanese invasion and finally from sustained guerrilla war into a war of movement and regular military formations that culminated in Mao's victory. It is not surprising that he developed a thesis of protracted war.[34]

Compared with Lenin, Mao had a much more difficult situation in which to pursue revolution. Tsarist Russia was a more developed and centralised political entity. It was more autonomous as a state, being an Empire, rather than being a victim of imperialism. It had developed bureaucratic, communication, and logistical systems. It was partially industrialised. It had an army and a police force. In his bid for power Lenin had the advantage of military and political collapse in Russia in 1917, together with the fact that those states that might have frustrated him were themselves engaged in fighting each other. Indeed, Germany in sending Lenin to Russia, actively assisted him in his revolutionary effort, seeing this as a means of breaking the alliance. Perhaps the only clear similarity between the two cases of revolution is that both Russia and China had broadly-based peasant economies. Even this is distorted by the social and religious character of their respective communities and by the fact that the Chinese economy was directly influenced by foreign interests.

Although the fall of the Manchu dynasty in 1912 was regarded as a revolution, its effect on the political system was nominal. The first phase of the struggle to create a new China constituted a confused civil war that continued through Japanese invasion and occupation to its end in 1949. Lenin succeeded in consolidating his position in just over five years. It took Mao from 1927 to 1949 to do the same. Once the revolution began in 1917 Lenin had little leisure for theorising and was largely concerned with practical matters. Mao had on occasions ample time to contemplate both his and the revolution's future. This is reflected in their respective contributions to the theoretical basis of revolutionary violence.

Mao himself was well aware that Chinese circumstances were different from those which prevailed in Russia in 1917. In his analysis of the situation in Hunan in 1927, he wrote of unique conditions, producing what he called a red enclosure in a white area.[35] There was, he said, no direct imperialist rule. The imperialist powers, although having interests in China, had succeeded in preventing each other from achieving an imperialist monopoly. The white regime itself was also divided, with factions vying with each other in a confused and indeterminate civil war. Warlordism was rife. The economy was localised and peasant in character. Working within these conditions was a party that had a nationwide basis with no parochial or factional affiliations. It was strongly and centrally organised with its own military forces. This was the Communist Party and it possessed a coherent ideology and could engage in political education operating through a system of ever-expanding revolutionary cadres working closely with the peasant population. In his view these were all necessary conditions for the revolution. And they were unique to China.

In the first phase of civil war between 1927 when the break with the KMT occurred and 1936, when relations were restored and a united front policy against the Japanese invasion was adopted, Mao's strategic doctrines were related to survival rather than victory. Although, as he acknowledged, the loss of the southern bases after the fifth encirclement campaign of the KMT with its blockhouse tactics, was a major reverse, nevertheless the Long March[36] and the establishment of new bases in the north meant that the revolutionary process was still in being. Defeat was not a lost battle or campaign, but, 'the total extinction of the Red Army', and that had not occurred. The Long March was a genuine strategic retreat in spite of the huge losses, and the new strategic base was more easily defended and, significantly, bordered Soviet territory, preventing a further encirclement. The Long March was thus not a political defeat.

Mao's analysis of the revolutionary struggle up to 1936 should be interpreted in the light of a leadership contest. At Tsunyi, and in this specific work,[37] he was concerned to discredit those whom he deemed responsible for the debacle of the fifth encirclement offensive, and the defeat at Kuangchang in April 1934, that led to the abandonment of the base in Kiangsi. The mistakes of both 'right and left opportunists' were analysed in detail. The 'right opportunism' of Chen, T'hsin, who was expelled from the party in 1939, was associated with the breakdown of the CCP alliance with the KMT in 1927, while the 'left opportunism' of Li Li-san was 'corrected' in September 1930. However, Mao was more concerned with what was called the 'new left opportunism' of Po ku, the current chairman of the Politburo and the Military Commission, who was responsible for the defeat of 1934. Wang Ming, and possibly Chou En Lai, were associated with this group and the policy adopted before the Long March. It was at this Tsunyi Conference[38] that Mao established his leadership and much of his literary effort between 1935 and 1936 was devoted to refuting his opponents in the party and urging his views on strategy. His attacks fell on those party leaders who had been closely associated with the Soviet Union. His exhortation, for example, that those who advocated a slavish imitation of the Soviet examples were 'cutting the feet to fit the shoes'[39] is not so much a reflection of his own pragmatism as a condemnation of that faction of his party most closely associated with Moscow and the Comintern, and which challenged his claim to leadership.

Looking more closely at his critique of his rivals' mistakes we can see certain consistent elements in Mao's thinking on what constituted an appropriate strategy for revolutionary war. What had gone wrong? he asked his audience in this post mortem after the Long March. On the strategic level, he argued, there had been a failure to place the revolutionary focus on the countryside and the peasants. A mistaken policy was adopted of seeking (on classic Marxist terms) to unite the urban proletariat and ferment revolution in the cities. Not only were the urban workers unwilling to give mass support to the Communist Party, they were peculiarly exposed to intimidation and corruption by the KMT, which also had claims to be a nationalist and revolutionary party. But the problem was more fundamental, stemming from the fact that China was predominantly a peasant society with a quasi-feudal economy. Even if the CCP was able to dominate the cities the peasants would still have to be brought into the revolution. On the purely military level the defeats in the cities, and the necessity for defensive small-scale warfare, made the countryside even more important in any long-term strategy. On the political level, an emphasis on purely military aspects ignored the point that battle-field successes were useless if they were not accompanied by an increase in popular support.[40] The Red Army[41] was not simply a military force, it was an instrument of revolution. Political education was essential if revolution was to be promoted. A doctrinaire view of revolution that emphasised its urban focus and that took a universalist approach, ignored the importance of proceeding stage by stage, consolidating support from the peasants, and gradually expanding in 'waves'.[42]

Equally, overemphasising the class struggle following 'leftist' interpretations of Marxist-Leninism derived from the European experience of revolution was inapposite for China. It was important, Mao urged, to distinguish poor from rich peasants, sympathetic gentry and small merchants, from rural magnates and major entrepreneurs, the petty bourgeoisie from the rulers and warlords, and to forge a common front with the former in each case. The first stage of the revolution had to be a bourgeois-democratic stage. In stressing the peasant basis of the struggle and in urging a policy of common front with all 'progressive' forces, Mao was following a pragmatic and non-doctrinaire line in the light of China's unique conditions.[43]

In his purely tactical considerations, he revealed an equally opportunistic disposition. He opposed what he called 'guerrillaism' or 'roving rebel bands'.[44] Guerrilla warfare was important, indeed, at the present time,[45] it was the only viable form of armed struggle open to the party, but it could not serve as a substitute for open warfare nor should it be conducted in isolation from the political programme. Like Lenin, Mao was afraid that irregular warfare would escape his control. A conventionally constructed Red Army was essential to final revolutionary victory and guerrilla operations should be treated as a means of creating cadres for larger forces through recruitment and seizure of material from the enemy, and proseletysing in the countryside. It gave valuable experience in combat and training for war. Where possible, however, these small scale operations should be phased in with major actions and designed to dislocate the enemy communications and divert or disperse enemy formations. They were also useful for information gathering and reconnaisance.

The main military effort was to come from the Red Army. When circumstances permitted it, the principle of concentration on classic strategic lines should be employed, with the object of gaining a quick and decisive success. Prolonged campaigns should be avoided and contact broken off when enemy forces concentrated themselves. Strategic retreats and diversions should then be mounted, ceding territory when necessary, to buy time, or to work for a more advantageous position later. This reflected the reality of the numerical inferiority and scant resources of the revolutionary forces and the fact that a defensive strategy was the only viable policy. All resources that could not be captured from the enemy had to be obtained from the peasants. It was totally counterproductive, however, to alienate them by forcible expropriation. Only the rich peasants and the landlords were to be dispossessed. This was to be done in a rational and organised manner, sharing the proceeds with the peasants and redistributing the land in their favour. Purely military considerations could not be allowed to override the paramount need to win and keep their support.

Mao also stressed the importance of establishing major secure base areas serving logistical and training functions, as well as being a refuge. They also served as a demonstration of revolutionary ideas, with land reform and political education encouraging those outside them to participate in the revolution. Gradually, with sustained military successes, these bases could be extended, thus expanding the revolution. Ideally they should be remote from attack so that their sacrifice did not become a major revolutionary setback as had happened with their Kiangsi base.

Such a programme was argued not merely as a counter to those who had led the party into its debacle, but as a practical response to the situation the party found itself in after the Long March. Although the Long March had provided a safe refuge the cost had been very high. In later party mythology it became a symbol for the revolution, but in fact it was a major military defeat and the badly disorganised and demoralised party needed a sense of purpose and direction. This Mao was at pains to provide. But the programme outlined above was followed fairly consistently throughout the struggle. It became known as a theory of protracted war.[46] Mao eschewed theoretical justification and the abstractions of Lenin's own attempt to persuade his followers, and laid emphasis upon circumstances and factors that could be readily appreciated by those who would physically carry out the struggle. In particular he placed great stress on morale. It was a soldier's rather than a revolutionary's morale however.

Protracted war was essentially a policy of attrition directed at the morale of enemy troops. Operations were based upon a combination of guerrilla forces and regular formations. The former were dispersed but were used in conjunction with regular forces, concentrated to achieve local superiority, but avoiding setpiece battles. Such warfare is mobile rather than positional and is designed to achieve quick victories damaging to the enemy's morale but not to his main forces. The aim of such operations is not decisive victory on the battle-field but limited successes. Time and not territory is the objective sought. They are intended to demonstrate the inability of the enemy to achieve a decision, or indeed any tangible results, in spite of their numerical superiority and command of resources. Such protracted war is thus designed to have political rather than military consequences.

Mao's insistence on tactics in his reports, lectures, and writings, was intended to maintain tight control over this programme, especially as such a sustained struggle had its effect on his own forces' morale. They, too, looked for results. The constant reiteration of the ground rules for combat and the immediate objectives sought, was intended to reassure his troops as well as providing a check against local adventurism. In essence, protracted war is defensive and opportunistic, leaving the main initiatives to the enemy and exploiting his weaknesses in deployment.[47] Success is thus dependent on favourable circumstances and combat is avoided as much as actively sought. Under these conditions problems of morale and of maintaining the revolutionary momentum are clearly important. Political education thus assumed a major role in the strategy. Violence itself, as terrorism or 'roving rebel bands', or in the form of concentration on purely military aspects (militarism) was to be deplored. Where it is limited and directed to a specific target, as in the killing of landlords or opposition political leaders, or as part of a concerted campaign with psychological as much as military objectives, then it fitted into the overal strategic approach. The individual soldier and commander was thus made aware of his contribution to the struggle and the importance of concerted as opposed to individual action.

Revolutionary violence thus has a dual role; it is designed to meet and counter that of the opposing forces and in this aspect is defensive and conservative in form. It is also designed to secure a radical political order. It operates as the instrument of a state within a state. This calls for much more discipline and control than is the case for military operations between national forces where this political element is absent. Defeat and victory are seen in purely military terms by the combatants, if not by their governments. But a military defeat for revolutionary forces does not entail a political defeat. The revolution can survive military disaster, as Mao himself had demonstrated with the Long March. This partly explains the difficulty of meeting such a threat by the incumbent political authorities through conventional military responses. The so-called 'hearts and minds' campaign in the Vietnam War illustrates this. It is yet another example of the problem of adopting an effective strategy based on assumptions of common rationality. In a revolutionary struggle such rationality is not to be found in the form of a set of common assumptions purely military in character.

Protracted war is thus *political* war. The end was the overthrow of the existing political system. There could be no compromise or limit set on this. In operational terms as Mao constantly pointed out, it was possible only where space for deployment, retreat and manoeuvre, existed. Support, both political and material had to be obtained from the inhabitants of this space. It was important therefore not to alienate the peasants. Strict discipline was imposed in terms of personal conduct. Levies were paid for. In areas more or less controlled by the communists, land reform policies were introduced, which, in striking contrast to Lenin's policies, redistributed the land into peasant ownership. Like Lenin, Mao intended to nationalise the land but, unlike Lenin, he needed explicit support from the peasants. The Soviet armed forces were mostly raised from the urban proletariat and in any case the Russian civil war was not a prolonged one. Taxation and expropriation was thus directed at the richer peasants and landlords by Mao. Even this policy was relaxed during the period of united front tactics after the Japanese invasion.[48] Mao justified this ideological laxity in terms of a two-stage revolution much in the way that Lenin did, and for much the same reasons.

The main significance of Mao's strategic approach is that, like Clausewitz,[49] he sought to relate the level of armed struggle and its tactics to political ends. Revolutionary war, of course, epitomises the purely political form of violence more than any other kind of war. The end is the total overthrow of a political system and not the achievement of any lesser political objective, including that of preserving the territorial integrity of the political entity in which it is fought. Lenin was prepared to sacrifice huge areas of the Tsarist Empire in order to secure power. Military defeat was encouraged.

So far as the means were concerned, almost any tactic was permissible provided it did not compromise in any fundamental way the revolutionary purpose. The continuance of the struggle was a basic condition for the achievement of power, although this did not preclude the adoption of popular front or united front tactics, depending on their expediency as circumstances changed. This of course was in the defensive phase of the struggle. Ultimately, when the party was strong enough in military terms, direct confrontation with opponents was sought. Before this point could be reached, however, a long process of gradual preparation is necessary. Military operations in the early defensive phase of the revolution were subordinated to the need to obtain mass support from the peasants. Allies or associates who were nominally class-enemies were useful and were actively sought, but it was support from the peasants that was crucial. Obtaining this dictated the adoption of land reform schemes and low taxation designed to demonstrate the superiority of communism and to break the grip of the landlords, and check alternative bids for their allegiance. At this stage, as Lenin himself found, nationalism and nationalist sentiment had much less appeal than immediate material benefit so far as the peasants were concerned. The next stage in the process was political education and the formation of revolutionary cadres. These acted as intermediaries between the higher echelons of the party and the peasants, transmitting instructions, obtaining consent and generally acting as a catalyst for the revolutionary programme. A new social system, based upon the traditional peasant community but with new organisational features and political cohesion, was to be created, serving as a basis for expansion and as a contrast to the licensed anarchy and injustice of the areas controlled by the KMT or by independent warlords.

Once a strong base had been created in this way, the next stage, that of more radical socialist measures, including the elimination of the richer peasants, and further redistribution of land and party control over it, could be adopted. The use of violence, including terrorism, was both instrumental and subordinate to this end. The development of a regular army and a strategy of open warfare was the ultimate goal, but premature resort to this without the sort of political base described about would prove disastrous, as it had done at the beginning of the struggle. Such a programme appears both rational and sufficiently flexible as to accommodate itself to changing circumstances. It can, in fact, be regarded as a rationalisation of the predicament Mao found himself in after the Long March. His own position as a leader was secure but the future of the revolution was far from assured. Invulnerable in his Yenan fastness, he was in no position to take the offensive. Yet he had to present some coherent programme to his followers to keep the revolution in being.

It was the Japanese invasion and its consequences that gave him his opportunity. The initial distraction caused by Japanese imperialism, and the united front tactics pursued by Mao, took the pressure off the revolutionary movement. The eventual Japanese collapse was produced not by the combined forces of the CCP and the KMT, who throughout the war period were more concerned with out-manoeuvring each other, but by the Allies.[50] It left the Communists in possession of North East China and the Red Army the principal beneficiary of the arms of the defeated Japanese armies. From that point on the struggle with the KMT assumed the dimension of regular warfare and the latter collapsed through a combination of its inability to achieve popular support and its own military ineptitude. Communist success was primarily achieved on the battle-field.

Thus the prescriptive aspects of Mao's thinking on revolutionary war are mainly related to the defensive phase of his struggle and concerned with survival rather than victory. As he well understood, his was not a rigorous theoretical programme but a set of principles that could be applied to the peculiar circumstances prevailing in China at that time. It was not a formula for people's war. His method was essentially pragmatic, and reflective rather than theoretical. As he put it, 'All military laws and military theories which are in the nature of principles are the experience of past wars summed up by people in former days or in our own time. We should seriously study these lessons ... We should put these conclusions to the test of our own experience, rejecting what is useless and adding what is specifically our own.'[51] And again he says, 'What is important or decisive should be determined not by general or abstract considerations but according to concrete circumstances.'[52]

Writing in 1936, he showed his awareness of contemporary military thinking in Europe. Dismissing its relevance to Chinese conditions he said 'The military experts of the newer and rapidly developing imperialist countries, namely Germany and Japan, trumpet the advantages of the strategic offensive and come out against the strategic defensive. This kind of military thinking is absolutely unsuited to China's revolutionary war.'[53] The blitzkrieg, using new weapons and seeking quick decision, was not for China. Decision had to be prepared given the circumstance prevailing in China at the time. A political base was essential. A prime condition for the success of any offensive was active support from the peasants. All other conditions relevant to military operations; the suitability of the terrain, concentration of forces, specific weaknesses of the enemy's dispositions, the fatigue and demoralisation of the enemy forces through harrassment and tactical withdrawals, inducing the enemy command to make mistakes through feints and strategems, etc., are secondary to this. In short, given the social conditions that existed in China, a purely military strategy would fail. There could be no formula derived from the past that is relevant to this context. While the destruction of the enemy forces is an aim in all forms of war, 'In a revolutionary war this principle is directly linked with basic political principles.' People were involved. 'Weapons are an important factor in war, but not the decisive factor; it is people not things that are decisive. The contest of strength is not only a contest of military and economic power, but also a contest of human power and morale.'[54]

This individualist approach to revolutionary violence and its effectiveness is little different from that of Clausewitz. It makes no appeal to dogmatic theory or to a general level of explanation. In Mao's terms,

'We admit that the phenomenon of war is more elusive and is characterised by greater uncertainty than any other social phenomenon, in other words that it is more a matter of "probability" '.[55] So although the basis of revolution is war, and 'according to the Marxist theory the army is the chief component of state power'[56] there is no *Marxist* theory of the use of violence by revolutionaries as such. Capitalist violence is explained, as we have seen earlier, but a strategy and tactics of revolutionary violence is left to experience itself. It lacks a theoretical basis. This complicates the problem of determining whether a revolutionary situation exists. For Lenin, following Marx more closely than Mao, the 'objective' conditions existed as a consequence of capitalist development. Few of these conditions existed in China. Even Lenin was forced to supplement the classic Marxist theory with his own revisions, as we have seen. In China, as indeed in revolutionary Russia, it was more a case of creating revolution than fulfilling its conditions. The conditions for revolution, if they did not exist, were to be brought into existence as a consequence of revolutionary action itself. The most effective action was war. But the character of this war, or to be more precise the stages leading up to formal military confrontation, differed from country to country, and from one set of circumstances to another. The exact set of circumstances, and success in meeting them could not be duplicated in every revolutionary situation. Neither the Russian, nor the Chinese revolutions, were for export. As we shall see, the consequences of this pragmatic approach produced difficulties for those who wished to emulate Lenin and Mao. The inability to relate prescriptions to theory in any univeral theoretical form militates against the superiority of any particular revolutionary strategy.

However, before making a full critique of the theory of revolutionary war and its putative link with practice, let us look at some later developments, notably guerrillaism, terrorism, resistance and counter-insurgency. These are all aspects of what might be called informal war and are not necessarily revolutionary in purpose. The theoreticians of revolution in the post-Maoist period have tended to move away from prescriptive analysis and a concern with technique, although there are some exceptions to this. Their focus, in the main, has been the study of later phases of capitalism. In the absence of an active revolutionary situation, and, indeed, the failure of national liberation movements in Africa and Latin America and parts of South-East Asia to achieve more than a change of regime, the emphasis has been on what might be called the contemplative phase of revolutionary promotion. This entails, as in the parallel case of Lenin's exile and activity as a writer on revolution, an outpouring of theoretical speculation rather than an involvement in action. This is the equivalent of Lenin's *Imperialism,* and *The State and Revolution* and attempts to establish a conceptual framework for revolution. The main relevance to practice lies in the indentification of revolutionary targets. While what might be called the orthodox targets of the state apparatus, of the liberal-bourgeois capitalist polity, remain in being, the main emphasis has moved from these to the Third World and the link between the developed and the under-developed states. This perhaps reflects the fact that political change appears to be more common in this area, and susceptible to radical development through revolution. It also reflects the success of Mao's revolution and the consequent belief that peasant economies lend themselves more readily to radical political change.

Economic dependency thus has been the subject of neo-Marxist analysis.[57] The multi-national corporation, for example, has been singled out as the main agency for the exploitation of Third World countries. It acts as an agent of the capitalist powers. Multi-nationals distort their host economies, producing contradictions in them, and class conflict.[58] The blame for social and economic inequalities in Third World states is placed on the operations of these new capitalist institutions and they have replaced the capitalist state as direct exploiters. Similarly, some neo-Marxist thinkers conceive of the cities as sources of exploitation. Andre Gunder Frank,[59] for example, conceives of contemporary capitalism as a system of metropolis-satellite relations within the Third World, and between the developed and the under developed states, that is economic and not political in character. The modern proletariat and the peasants are exploited by a ruling elite operating from the main urban centres; the elite in turn is controlled by foreign capitalists.

It can be seen from this that any assault on any aspect of the state in an under-developed country is a revolutionary act. The notion of capitalist exploitation permeating all activities, political, social and economic, in under-developed countries and operating through a ruling elite, provides a rationale as well as a justification for any kind of violence. De-stabilising the state is a very general objective, fulfilled as much by individual acts of terrorism as by more organised guerilla warfare. The enemy exists in all forms of socio-economic practice as well as in more clearly defined state agencies such as the police, the judiciary and political and industrial leaders. And the principal focus for revolutionary action is the city. The excesses of Pol Pot[60] have this justification in that a genuine revolution is only possible through the destruction of the state apparat and this is exemplified by the urban centres.

There is little in this, however, to provide more than a generalised justification for a generalised violence. There is no concern for a specific strategy in the form of a rational and controlled use of violence in pursuit of specific revolutionary ends. What is effective in this sense, is left to experience itself to determine, on the principle that action itself is educative. It is praxis and not theory alone that produces revolutionary success. Violence thus becomes an end in itself. In short, contemporary neo-Marxist theorising takes two forms; firstly in supporting a generalised violent form of dissent in developed countries as terrorism. This aspect will be considered later. Secondly, and more closely related to revolutionary war, has been the encouragement of guerrilla war on broad Maoist lines in Third World countries which have predominantly peasant or mono-cultural economies.

On the face of it, it is surprising that so much emphasis has been placed on guerrilla tactics in rural areas, and on such dicta as 'power grows out of the barrel of a gun.'[61] Mao himself never wavered in his belief that revolutionary success would come only with conventional military campaigns and battle-field victories. The problem was to create a formal revolutionary army given the initial weaknesses of a revolutionary movement, facing, as it usually did, the resources of the state, organised and deployed against it by its political opponents. Converting a position of weakness into one of military strength was of necessity a gradual process, but not one to be confused with an aimless guerrilla war. As both Lenin and Mao realised, obtaining mass support and exploiting fissiparous forces in the political system, were necessary conditions of success. Circumstances such as the military collapse of governments in inter-state wars, although not created by the revolutionary movement, were nevertheless crucial factors in the revolutionary struggle. They urged a form of directed opportunism in which the end was clear, if not the means.

Nevertheless, in spite of the absence of a prescriptive revolutionary theory in the writings of Lenin and Mao, encouragement and precedent were found in their successes. This may reflect the need to consolidate political control and leadership by placing it within the rubric of revolutionary orthodoxy. Writers such as Giap, le Duan, and Che Guevara[62] were endorsing the revolutionary leadership as much as providing a strategy of the revolution. The seizure of power requires as much legitimising for the left as for any other political faction, lacking, or rejecting, constitutional forms of endorsement. The need to identify with the forces of history in terms of the fulfilment of a manifest destiny is a common political phenomenon. In revolutionary circles it may be a question of life or death. Thus both the Vietnamese and the Cuban revolutions were placed within the Chinese model. Loosely following the Marxist view of revolution, with a genuflexion in the direction of the principle of proletarian leadership, and the class contradictions of a genuine revolutionary situation, le Duan asserts the primacy of the peasants.[63] The first phase of a revolution constitutes an alliance between the 'progressive' forces, including the *petit bourgeoisie* and the intellectuals. Like Mao he welcomed the Japanese occupation of Vietnam since this created an opportunity for revolution. Not only did it break colonial rule and destroy its authority, it also fostered nationalism and make it easier for the revolutionaries to manufacture a united front against the invaders.[64] The ultimate defeat of Japan would thus leave an organised and unchallenged political faction in power, and capable of taking the revolution into its next stage. This was at least partially successful. The defeat of the French in 1954 at Dien Bien Phu was the product not of guerrilla warfare, or of terrorism, although both of these, as in China, were used, but of conventional warfare using regular troops.

In short Giap stressed, as Mao had done, the importance of open warfare in achieving decision.[65] He recognised that this required a combination of circumstances and of long preparation, gaining peasant support and securing safe bases.[66] His success established political control in the North but the Geneva Accords[67] left the South still under foreign influence with the Americans replacing the French as patrons of the regime. The next phase of the struggle was more problematic depending as it did on both American commitment and the existence of self-imposed limits. The campaign fought by the Viet Cong and the North Vietnamese corresponded to the ideas on protracted war propagated by Mao and was designed to avoid direct military confrontation with American forces. The Tet offensive[68] was an exception and was intended to achieve psychological rather than military success.

In the event the combination of guerrilla tactics, terrorism, and short engagements, using regular troops, was based on the principle of seeking political rather than purely military successes. Exhausting the morale of the opposition and exploiting dissent in the United States were the main foci of the war effort. This was essentially a defensive strategy and the final phase of open warfare came only with the departure of the United States. That this departure was achieved as a conscious aim, using what were in the main psychological tactics, indicates a nice appreciation of the political situation by the North Vietnamese, but is hardly a product of revolutionary theory. Nor could any other so-called revolutionary situation be expected to have the same self-imposed limits apply to one of the main contenders. Defensive tactics in themselves, while important in keeping the revolution in being, are insufficient to create a revolution. Only when the combatants are more evenly matched does this become a possibility.

The Cuban case also had its peculiarities. According to Guevara the Cuban revolution followed classic Maoist lines.[69] Beginning as guerilla war, it sought to establish a 'liberated zone' or base area. The strategy endorsed by Guevara, and by implication, Castro, was to pursue the revolution by gradually expanding the guerrilla campaign and 'by strangulation and attrition to promote the break-up of the regime.[70] The peasants were central to this policy. Their desire for land reform was to be appeased by expropriating land-owners and redistributing the land. Food and shelter were paid for and not extorted. Revolutionary justice was demonstrated by the trial (and execution) of deserters,[71] informers and 'bandits' thus reinforcing the idea of a state within a state, as well as having practical value. United front tactics were pursued, seeking an alliance of all 'bourgeois-democratic forces'. This corresponded to the defensive phase of the revolution and was a necessary preliminary to the offensive phase. As he put it 'the fundamental concerns of this phase were survival and the establishment of a guerrilla base.'[72] Once this had been achieved then positional warfare was to begin, aimed at destroying the Batista forces.

Thus the protracted war programme of Mao was compressed into the space of less than three years. This account, particularly of the events of 1958, must be treated with suspicion. It seeks to present Castro not merely as a revolutionary leader with a successful programme but as the heir to the revolution. In fact his political base was far from secure, either within his own revolutionary movement, or in relation to other revolutionary claimants, either in exile in Miami or in the cities.[73] It was not enough to destroy the Batista regime. Political coups, with the support or connivance of the Army, were a common Latin American phenomenon. The undisputed leadership of Castro had to be asserted and maintained. Given the united front tactics adopted, and the necessity to obtain the support of Cuba's urban areas, there was a distinct possibility that while winning the military struggle against Batista's forces, Castro might lose its political fruits. As Guevara wrote, 'Between December 2nd and May 28th [1957] we slowly established links with the city. These relations during this period were characterised by lack of understanding on the part of the urban movement's leadership of our importance as the vanguard of revolution and of Fidel's stature as its leader.[74] The reality of a combination of opportunism, circumstances, and the negative effects of corruption and ineptitude on the part of Batista and his supporters, was masked by an emphasis on the revolutionary programme modelled on that of Mao. Myth-making was more important than a concern for a genuine revolutionary strategy. In this context Castro has more in common with Mussolini than with Lenin or Mao.

Of course, in the sense that violence is directed as much against the will as the body, this aspect of revolutionary violence is not irrelevant to strategy. But guerrilla operations have been treated in the main as adjuncts to conventional war by revolutionary writers. They are part of an overall strategy designed to overthrow a political system and to gain power. Terrorism is perhaps in a different category. It is specifically intended to induce a state of mind in the nominal victims, the real targets, and in the supporters, actual and potential, of the cause it promotes. This is as true of what might be called state terror, whether directed at other states, or at its own subjects, as of private or non-state terror. Its rationale is thus psychological in character, directed, although not exclusively so, at values.[75] This is something of an over-simplification since cost is an important factor in both terrorist and anti-terrorist campaigns. But cost is also related to value since the expense and commitment to countering terrorist threats may preclude or curtail other activities in other areas deemed more important to the state.

A prolonged terrorist campaign is equivalent to a war of attrition, keeping the cause alive and waiting for a favourable opportunity when the opposing government is in a relatively weak position and more inclined to make concessions.[76] 'England's danger is Ireland's opportunity!' This sort of opportunism depends upon circumstances the terrorist does not create or control but which may work to his advantage. For example, Britain fought a long and costly campaign against Chinese revolutionary terrorists in Malaya.[77] It was a successful campaign. But the fact that it was fought at all was not unconnected with the fact that at the time Malaya was a major source of dollar earnings through the export of tin and rubber. In the case of Cyprus[78] when the anti-terrorist campaign resulted in rising costs and the commitment of very large British forces without any clear prospects of success, a political settlement ceding independence was the consequence.

Clearly, Cyprus did not have the same utility as Malaya. Given the disparity in resources between terrorist organisations and their main opponents—governments—an attack on values seems to be more effective than attacks on property or economic assets. Terrorism is an equivocal phenomenon and has moral connotations related to political justification. In general violence against the individual is deemed legitimate where it occurs within the framework of a rule of law, or international law. In other words the state preserves its monopoly of violence and denies the legitimacy, except under strictly curtailed conditions, of private violence. Governments may be repressive or indulge in 'reigns of terror', and, as we have seen earlier, the use or threat of violence is a basic form of conflict resolution and thus political in character. But in general it is bound by rules and conventions and the breach of extant rules is sanctioned by emergency decrees, martial law, or exceptional legislation.

Governments may of course engage in extra-legal terror and use their armed forces, police, or para-military organisations to maintain their rule.[79] Torture, although usually illegal and unacknowledged, is often used as a means of protecting the political system. This can vary from harsh interrogation techniques designed to obtain information, to deliberate and systematic cruelty as a means of obtaining obedience and curbing dissent. Even in states where the rule of law is firmly established there is some ambiguity between citizens' rights and the right of the state. Political expediency tends to erode the former.[80]

Terror is important as a political instrument in inter-state relations, and, as we have seen, the essence of defensive nuclear deterrence is the threat of massive retaliation in the event of an attack on the homeland. Fear is the spur to contemporary defence programmes and the rationale of the strategic relationship between the nuclear powers. We saw also that the indiscriminate bombing of civilians was a conscious policy of inducing terror in order to destroy morale and undermine support for the Nazi government. Similarly, in the context of the Battle of France, attacks by the Luftwaffe on refugees were designed to spread panic and impede Allied troop movement. The blitz on British cities was intended to force the British government to negotiate rather than continue the war. All these are forms of terror. The fact that they occurred within the context of war should not disguise, if it may excuse, their use. The point here is that state terror, whether as a conscious policy of repression, or as an instrument of external policy, exists. The question of its legitimacy is as open to as much special pleading as the more familiar form of political terrorism indulged in by individuals acting against the state.

There are indeed many forms of terrorism ranging from state terrorism, revolutionary terrorism, resistance, and what might be called pressure group or private terrorism. They are distinguished by their aims.[81] These vary from controlling and suppressing dissent and maintaining the prevailing political system; adjuncts to winning wars or promoting political objectives in international politics; overthrowing political systems;

removing foreign occupation, and achieving political identity and autonomy; or obtaining a specific demand or reform within a polity. All these forms of terrorism, while varying in their objectives, have a common means. They use violence, or its threat, against individuals in order to induce a particular state of mind on the part of governments, political factions, state agencies, and functional organisations, such as electoral assemblies, ruling elites, the police, the armed forces and citizens in general. Terrorism is thus a form of psychological warfare. The act of violence and the selection of targets are designed not merely to inflict material damage on life and property, but to create a specific effect in the minds of those whose control and power are most germane to the object sought. As in the war the will of the opponent is central to the strategy adopted. Unlike war it is the weapon of the weak against the strong and is directed against values rather than resources. It has this in common with war: it presupposes a common rationality.

I am not concerned with defining, describing, or establishing a taxonomy of terrorism. It is its rationale that is important in this study of the rational use of violence. In what sense does the use of terror constitute a means to an end? What conditions must be satisfied for it to be effective and rational? Anarchistic and nihilistic terror have as their goal the destruction of a form of order—the state—and its social, political and economic structures. In this sense it is akin to total war. Terror is for terror's sake and means and ends are encapsulated in the action. Given this apocalyptic basis, such forms of terror need not concern us here, except to note that they are inherently negative, having no political programme or end other than the removal of the state. The problem of controlling and using violence rationally after the demise of the state would still remain. Politics and the state are not synonymous.

If then terrorism is to be a rational instrument there must be a clearly defined link between the form of terrorist action and the end result. The latter must be induced by the former. Taking the extreme form of revolutionary terrorism where the ultimate aim is the destruction of the extant polity, it is clear that de-stablisation of the state apparat is a necessary but not a sufficient condition for revolution. There is no bargaining or negotiating element in this context, for the only other party capable of entering into that relationship is itself the principal target. But terror by itself, while possibly an agent of destruction, cannot supply the creative forces necessary to the replacement of one polity by another. It is this negative aspect of revolutionary terrorism that was recognised by both Lenin and Mao. The selective murder of local officials, political leaders, and ideologically designated class enemies, was useful where it promoted the conversion of allegiance from the extant institutions to the revolutionary party, or where it helped the revolutionary war effort. But it was of primary importance to have a viable alternative political system. There must be a revolutionary programme and an associated ideology, or set of prescriptive principles, capable of attracting mass support. Terrorism by itself cannot provide this; it is purely negative. Within the context of revolution it serves as a technique subordinate to guerrilla and regular warfare. It is an aid to, and not an agent of, revolution. In a sense therefore, revolutionary terrorism is a contradiction in terms.

Acts of terrorism of their nature are indiscriminate. Since terror is a weapon of the weak the targets tend to be those who are neither powerful or protected. The same is true of attacks against property, assets and facilities. This tendency is exacerbated the longer the terrorist campaign, as its more powerful opponent deploys its superior resources in counter-terrorist measures. The generation of fear may create attitudes which are non-supportive of the regime, but given the resources commanded by most governments, this is not necessarily effective in weakening the response. It is the state's provision of security for the individual citizen that is the main target of terrorist attack, and almost any action taken by a government can be presented as a defence. The propaganda war can be won by exploiting the indiscriminate nature of the attacks and using the media to generalise the fear. If terrorists seek to be more selective in their attacks, choosing targets more closely identified with the regime, such as the police, or political leaders, this in turn both dissipates the general fear and enables the regime to adopt more effective defensive measures.

It is only where the state apparat is itself seriously weakened, not by terror, but by failure in war, external intervention, internal conflict, or economic collapse, or a combination of these, that terror can become effective in promoting radical political goals. Clearly, such circumstances may provide an opportunity for terrorism but can hardly be said to have been created by it. And, as was argued above, even here it is not the prime instrument of radical change. Thus the more radical the ends sought by the 'revolutionary' terrorist, the less likely he is able to fulfil them in the absence of other factors, that in effect, constitute a revolution. Raising the political consciousness of the masses, de-stabilising the state, or the 'propaganda of the deed', are very imprecise ends and tend to nullify any notion of terrorism as a programme of action designed to be effective. It cannot be stated in advance of a particular terrorist act, or campaign, what the response will be, either of a government, or of the general population. What might be called declaratory terrorism cannot therefore constitute a strategy designed to achieve specific goals. Its ineffectiveness in promoting revolution lies in its inability to relate means and ends with any precision. On the basis of experience *ceteribus paribus* it seems to strengthen governments rather than weaken them.

The same points can be made of resistance terrorism and, to a lesser extent, of terrorism in support of national autonomy. Where the occupying or colonial power is in situ, unpreoccupied by other demands on its resources, local terrorism is generally ineffective. It is dependent on circumstances for its opportunities. In the context of general war it was not until Germany, for example, in the Second World War, was suffering military reverses, that resistance grew in Europe. 'Setting Europe ablaze' through the encouragement of resistance movements was by no means easy, as S.O.E. discovered. Liberation was eventually achieved by armies and not by terrorism, although this last was useful to the Allies as a means of disrupting communciations during the invasion phase. Resistance movements were also used to collect information and to disseminate false information to the occupying power. As such they were adjoints to the strategic planning, operations, and political objectives of the Allies.[82] Liberation when it came often proved illusory. In any case the common end for liberation movements is only nominally that of freeing national territory from alien rule. The questions who rules? and which political systems? are uppermost in the minds of the various factions involved and resistance is only a phase in a complex political struggle. The point here is that terrorism as a strategy is not effective without a combination of circumstances that is really only fortuitous. Such circumstances are beyond the control of any local resistance movement. In the event, with very few exceptions, the intervention of foreign powers decided the political issue.

Colonial liberation is more complex and involves a number of factors, some of which are economic in character. Again, terrorism by itself cannot be said to have been a main cause of collapse of the major European empires. The effects of the war led, as was the case with the First World War, to changes in colonial possession and relationships. This time, however, the changes favoured extending self-determination to the world rather than to certain selected minorities in Europe. It was a gradual process with perhaps the most important single factor being the relative economic importance of the colonial possession, combined with the cost of maintaining a colonial presence. With the establishment of a world market system dominated by the advanced industrial powers it could be said that a formal political relationship was no longer necessary. And it is true to say that with this, the cost of fighting colonial wars, raised by terrorism, was the crucial factor in ceding independence, not terrorism itself.

It is the bargaining or pressure group form of terrorism that is more obviously strategic in character. Here the ends sought are not general but specific and more closely related to the means. It operates within the extant political system and is concerned with revision and reform that in principle, can be accommodated, although resisted by established interests. Indeed it needs the existing political system in order to realise its aims even where it seeks to change it. The use of the media and of publicity in general is crucial since, paradoxically, terror seeks to persuade people and to convince government, through the pressure of public opinion, to concede the issue in question. A terrorist campaign of this kind must not be so indiscriminate as to alienate its potential clientele or support, or to provoke effective counter-measures. It is innately political in that it constitutes a means of resolving conflict by postulating both a cost and an alternative. Concede or compromise the issue at stake and the violence will cease is the message. The use of violence in this form implies both a recognition of extant social and political *mores* and a desire for recognition within that context.

The use of terrorism by agencies affiliated to the P.L.O., for example, is related to the need to gain international recognition as a negotiating body, as much as to the desire to keep the Palestine issue alive in inter-state politics. In this although the destruction of the state of Israel is a cardinal objective, it is not so much a matter of promoting revolution from within through terrorism, as of securing international recognition for the claim to an autonomous Palestine through negotiation. Acts of terrorism seek therefore to cut the umbilical cord that connects Israel to its principal patron—the United States. Conversely, Zionist terrorism was directed at the occupying power—Britain—rather than at the Palestine Arab community, with the intention of breaking the Mandate and forcing partition. But the question of an Israeli state was settled by war and not by terrorism. Once this aim had been achieved the new polity condemned terrorism and at the same time actively engaged in forms of state terrorism. The main form of violence, however, has been formal war between Israel and its Arab neighbours. Such war has not proved effective in achieving its political objectives and the question of the status of Israel remains open.

Given that this form of terrorism operates within a specific socio-political milieu in that its effectiveness depends upon successful bargaining, it is hard to see any theoretical basis for a particular terrorist strategy. The flaws in basing a strategy upon bargaining techniques have been discussed in an earlier chapter. In this case attempts at offering universal generalisations, either about the causes and nature of terrorism, or about its instrumental use of violence, collapse in the face of its essential pragmatism. The same problems exist for the would-be theorist of terror as for the economic or military strategist. It is another case of practical reasoning based upon presuppositions about expectations of proper action with a specific social and political context. International terrorism, that is the extension of pressure-group terrorism to a range of countries and involving cooperation between a number of terrorist groups with different objectives, makes the problem of effective action (and counter-action) even more difficult.

If then political terrorism is a kind of psychological warfare its psychological dimension must be explicitly defined and explained if there is to be a genuine theoretical basis for prescribing effective action. What conditions must be fulfilled for the requisite inducement of fear? Whose fear is relevant? At what point can this fear be controlled and directed to the achievement of specific demands and what are the relevent conditions? Can any level of generalisation concerning the inducement of fear by specific acts of violence be developed? Since the supposed effectiveness of terrorism is through attacking people who are not directly involved in the political process and is thus an indirect strategy, what general conditions linking this to the decision-makers are applicable? What if they are indifferent or prepared to accept it? Calculations of value as well as of political expediency are involved here. It cannot simply be assumed that the terrorist and his target share a common rationality; it must be demonstrated that this is the case.

In practice assessment of likely responses to calculated acts of terror is based upon experience and on trial and error. A behavioural theory is not forthcoming and terrorism has been successful only minimally at the tactical level, that is in maintaining a level of activity and capacity. At the strategic level it has only succeeded in the broader objective of keeping issue alive. Publicity for a cause has been obtained through violence largely directed at people far removed from responsibility for their resolution. Judging from past precedents such issues are resolved not by this form of declaratory violence but by war, either civil, inter-state, or both.

So far, I have been concerned with what might be called private or factional terrorism. But of course governments also indulge in this practice either in pursuit of their own political objectives or as a response to it. In time of war, as we have seen, belligerent countries actively encourage and support insurrection and terrorism directed against their opponents. In time of peace this is equally the case and intervention at various levels in internecine contests is common. It has been argued that this is perhaps the only way of influencing international politics, given the inhibition that exists on the direct use of war as a political instrument stemming from the nuclear balance between the major powers. Thus, the supply of arms, money, food, and equipment, to terrorist organisations and guerrilla groups, takes the place of fighting colonial or limited wars for reasons of state. The encouragement of factions in other countries may not indeed be intended to produce a decisive result, but to create a diversion, or to embroil countries in a struggle that weakens or compromises them in some way. The attitudes of the major powers to the Vietnam War is an illustration of this.

The counter to the American attempt at the global containment of communism through exercising political influence and maintaining close relations with friendly Third World governments, was the Soviet and Chinese encouragement of local dissent. Support for so-called national liberation movements was the result. Hence the Vietnam War was a contest between these two policies and became in effect a proxy war. It cannot be said that the result, the unification of Vietnam under communist rule, was satisfactory to any of the major powers concerned. The United States was expelled from Indo-China under circumstances that had some adverse consequences for domestic politics. Nevertheless, its commanding strategic position in the Far East was not impaired by this expulsion. The Soviet Union, although a major supporter of North Vietnam, did not find its position strenghtened as a result of the latter's victory. the rapprochment of China with the United States was an unwelcome development. China itself became embroiled in hostilities with Vietnam.

The point here is that engagement in covert operations and support for terrorist organisations and violent dissent at whatever level, is as prone to the force of circumstance and is as innately pragmatic, as factional terrorism itself. Governments do not and cannot control all the variables in situations of violent challenge to authority in other countries. They may take advantage of the collapse of political authority, or seek to prevent it in terms of their global interests and the current state of international politics, but however the situation is interpreted, they cannot control it. External assistance thus can only be marginal and where it is limited it is neither risky or costly; whether it is effective is another matter. Any deeper involvement is yet another matter and the intervening state may, as in Vietnam, become a participant in civil war. Seeking to control the politics of another state is not easy. This is true whether the involvement is with governments or opposing political factions. Failure in such interventions can also have a more serious consequence than perhaps malevolent neutrality. The intervening state is necessarily compromised by its association with the defeated party. Through its intervention the contest becomes polarised in two ways. Firstly, from the point of view of the political faction unsupported in this way, it is fighting not only its rival faction but an outside power as well. It naturally turns to find support from other states in opposition to the intervening state. Secondly, the intervening states see the internal political struggle as a proxy contest between them and extend their commitments accordingly to avoid defeat. The result of failure to place or maintain a client in power is alienation and exclusion from future influence. But success, as we have seen in the case of Vietnam, is hardly less problematic since the successful faction may feel little obligation as it pursues national interests that may not be compatible with those of its major supporter. The motives for their association may in fact have no common ground beyond mutual hostility to another power. All this indicates the great difficulty in formulating a rationale that involves more than tactical and temporary cooperation. At the strategic level the ends they seek may radically differ.

If supporting terrorist activities as an instrument of policy in inter-state relations is inherently open-ended and beyond rational control, countering terrorism also has its problems. Counter-insurgency, low intensity operations, policing, internal security, home defence, anti-terrorism, etc. constitute programmes to frustrate the intentions of the terrorist. This is made more complicated by the complexities of international terrorism involving cooperation between terrorist groups pursuing different aims but finding advantages in mutual support. Their use of different countries, both those sympathetic to their cause, and those vulnerable to various forms of pressure, as a means of putting pressure on the actual target country, is difficult to counter. A purely national programme thus is relatively ineffective without agreement between the main target countries on a common response to terrorist demands. The main counter to pressure group terrorism is a refusal to bargain. The problem here is that some countries are more vulnerable in this respect than others. Establishing a common front between governments which have a different relationship to their politics and whose strengths and weaknesses in domestic political terms vary from time to time, is not an easy matter. An astute terrorist group can exploit differences of this kind and focus attention of the weakest government to extract concessions. However, as was argued earlier, pressure group terrorism, apart from the propaganda of the deed, has not been particularly successful in achieving its goals. Those states most able to meet their demands are also those that are strongest in terms of their political stability and their capacity to resist them.

Countering revolutionary terrorism, that directed against the state from within, is a matter of retaining popular support. Terrorism is an attack on the will of governments through a demonstration of their inability to protect their citizens. This practical demonstration is accompanied by an attack on the legitimacy of the political institutions by forcing the government to adopt repressive measures. It then becomes subject to moral obloquy on the grounds that it has lost its moral vantage-point. A counter-terrorist campaign must therefore not forfeit the sympathy of the general public in the measures it adopts. Resisting the tactical extension of actions directed against terrorism, but which affect civil liberties, or which offend social mores, is important in order to preserve the strategic end— the retention of popular support. What appears a rational programme in this respect may be self-defeating if terrorism is taken merely to be acts of physical violence. In a democratic-liberal polity it is the propaganda war this is paramount. That is, of course, not the case in non-democratic polities where repressive measures can be overt but even here, where popular support is absent, their adoption can be disastrous.

Thus while security in the sense of physical protection from acts of violence is important it must be recognised that it cannot be absolute. Some acts of terrorism are either not preventable or are preventable at a political and social cost that effectively concedes to the terrorist his case. There must be willingness to accept the marginal costs of terrorism in lives and in property on the part of the general public. In short a rational strategy is innately political and not para-military in terms of matching violence with violence. In the case of states where radical and dissenting political factions enjoy support, or where the government is unpopular, revolutionary terrorism and political violence generally have more chance of success.

All forms of terrorism and counter-terrorism are essentially pragmatic in their approach to the achievement of their aims. Generalisation collapses in the face of specifics. Each socio-political situation in terms of its norms, values and its political context, both internal and external, is unique in place and in time. The tortuous struggles of revolutionary ideologies to assimilate past experience in their attempts at prescription, illustrate the force of this point. Devising a counter-terrorist strategy is as difficult as making a general terrorist strategy effective. The two are closely related in practice in terms of challenge and response. What local successes terrorist activities have had, have been tactical and in the main defensive, related to fund raising, the protection of operatives, and survival. So far as objectives are concerned, terrorism in all its forms has only succeeded in having a declaratory or rhetorical effect, keeping causes alive. Concrete ends, whether of a radical change in a political system, the achievement of national identity, or obtaining reforms of political concessions, remain unattained. Acts of terror by themselves do not appear to have been particularly effective. The means and the ends are thus not commensurable.

In this respect terrorism is irrational. It succeeds only if it is able to change the rationale of the political system it attacks by persuading or coercing it into its own moral framework. Terror by itself cannot do that, but accompanied by techniques of persuasion and attempts to demonstrate the moral bankruptcy of the extant regime by provoking it into adopting repressive measure, it may succeed in this end. It exploits weaknesses rather than creates them. International or cooperative terrorism has the added disadvantage of operating outside the social context of its target thus reducing any effective exploitation of its prevalent mores.

If terrorism is primarily a technique or tactics rather than a strategy, what of revolutionary or factional violence? Does this have a valid theoretical basis from which authoritative prescriptions governing effective action can be derived? This form of war is innately political. The strategy pursued is not directed simply at military victories, although these are ultimately necessary, but at the creation of an alternative political locus within an existing political system designed to replace it. To this extent the strategic programme pursued is aimed at converting an indigenous population to a political cause and developing political authority while destroying its rival. Fundamentally, this is the implementation of a political programme through violence. Violence is at various levels, including individual acts of terrorism, guerrilla war, and formal positional warfare. These are directed as such at political targets, almost exclusively so in the defensive stage of the revolution, where survival and building a secure base are major priorities. It follows from this that the formulation of a political programme that can serve as the basis for a potentially prolonged campaign is as important as finding tactical and strategic solutions at the military level of the struggle. The object is the attainment of political power within the state. Military must concede precedence to political considerations.

Given this major distinction between revolutionary and inter-state war it is apparent that no theoretical basis for prescribing effective action in the form of a strategy can be postulated. As both Lenin and Mao argued, the theoretical element is designed not to achieve success in action as a ground for the instrumental use of violence, but as an aspect of political indoctrination. It is a means of legitimising the revolutionary struggle, obtaining mass support, a basis for political education and propaganda, and tacitly, a means of reinforcing the leadership and avoiding factionalism. As such, ideology and its related theorising, does not present a programme for action but constitutes a method of creating the necessary political cohesion to make a successful challenge to the political system it wished to replace. It legitimises rather than prescribes action. As such it belongs to the dimension of psychological warfare and is more concerned with persuasion than with force. A contest of wills is thus the central struggle, with the issue determined as much by revolutionary rhetoric and the internal collapse of the political system under attack, as by an appeal to practical reasoning based on expediency, negotiation, self-interest and cost. The latter belong to limited contests with issues that can, through the aegis of violence, be resolved by compromise. Revolution fits the model of total war with the absence of this form of rationality. It ends are extreme and any means may be adopted to fulfil them.

The notion of people's war thus postulates a programme of political conversion as central to strategy. The problem for the would-be theorist is while successful revolutionary war has been accompanied by firm political leadership and the acquisition of popular support, this tells us little about the content of such a programme. *Ex post facto* rationalisations abound, especially as successful revolutionaries are able to re-write history and make their case at the expense of the defeated. The circumstances that produce a revolutionary situation are, as we have seen, largely fortuitous and vary from revolution to revolution. What is effective in psychological terms in persuading people to change their allegiances is not easy to dermine in advance or any general level. It may be true as one commentator puts it,

The relative security of social resources can only be broken by permanently altering the values, commitments, and related patterns of behaviour and socialisation of a mass of people, thereby re-ordering society especially in terms of the fabric of social relations. Should this security be broken, war-will (sic) become a part of socialization not affected by the classical pattern of strategy.[83]

but this remains merely tautologous without a statement of the empirical conditions necessary for this to happen, together with a covering general law.

The appeal of a revolutionary or radical political programme is to a common rationality and a common belief system within a specific social context. The weakness of the extant political system in terms of its popular support is a function of whether it satisfies expectations or aspirations. Circumstances beyond its control, occasioned by inter-state conflict, or some internal breakdown, provide the revolutionary with his opportunity. The ends as we have seen are clearly defined but the means depend upon opportunity and circumstance. There is thus no strategic theory, or theory of revolution, that can provide a prescriptive basis for action. If any means may be adopted provided the end is maintained, there is no notion of a commensurable relation between ends and means in the Clausewitzian sense. The revolutionary programme is innately pragmatic. The real problems for the revolutionary in terms of a rational programme relating ends and means, begin after the revolution. Or to put it another way the real revolution commences after the seizure of power. Violence here plays a part, as we have seen earlier when state terrorism was considered, but this is beyond the scope of this work. The point here is that the relation between theory and practice in which theory informs and directs practice is reversed, with 'theory' emerging from practice itself. Practice, consisting of decisions and actions operating within a context of changing circumstances and associated reasoning, is systematised and treated as if it were in reality a coherent and rational programme. This may well serve as a meas of legitimising the subsequent post-revolutionary situtation, firstly, by incorporating the actual revolutionary record within what becomes ideological orthodoxy, providing a mythology and hagiography for the people, and secondly, by endorsing the successful leadership. Whatever the rationale, it serves as a potent source of myth.

People's war is thus social war, and this presupposes a milieu which is unique; a combination of people and circumstances specific to time, space and the individuals involved. 'Theories' of revolutionary war only make sense when they are located in this context, either historically as a reconstruction of reasoning, or in terms of practical experience. They then, of course, cease to be theories but part of practice itself as an interpretation. They cannot serve as guides to action. At the purely military level it is difficult to see any prescriptive element that is strictly revolutionary in character. The conditions that Mao thought necessary for success are not conditions in any scientific sense but are part of a practical reasoning, the result of trial and error, success and failure, that cannot connect in any rigorous form cause and effect. No precise value can be given to the concepts he employed, such as concentration, dispersion, offensive, defensive, mobility, positional, base, guerrilla area, or to their relational terms outside the context to which they refer. His famous characterisation of the tactics of guerrilla warfare, 'The enemy advances, we retreat: the enemy camps, we harass; the enemy tires, we attack; the enemy retreats, we pursue;'[84] is not a recipe for success. It does not take into account the tactics or strategy of the enemy. Avoiding engagement except on favourable terms is a commonsense precept. But many a general would like to know how this can be determined in practice. In short such a formula is open-ended, lacking a statement of empirical conditions—the conditions that in theoretical terms will bring about a given result when fulfilled. Fleas do not and cannot defeat elephants. Nor in reality did Mao think so. The metaphor is an encouraging one when one is a flea and magnifies the success if it eventually comes, after of course the necessary subsequent transmigration into a larger entity.

NOTES AND REFERENCES

1. See David Stafford, *Britain and European Resistance 1940–1945*, Macmillan, London, 1983, esp. Chapter 6, p. 144 (ff).
2. Where this is lacking as in religious or ideological struggle then, depending on the force of character and depth of belief, martyrdom may be acceptable to the victim.
3. There is some form of judicial review or appeals system, that acts as a check on abuse of power by the state, although this is confined to relatively few states.
4. V. I. Lenin, *The State and Revolution*, Foreign Language Publishing House, Moscow, 1951, first published Aug. 1917 revised 1918, pp. 31 and 41.
5. Soviet support for 'progressive' forces in non-communist countries, including political parties and trade unions, has a long history dating back to the foundation of the Comintern, and of the Cominform and extending to present

support for national liberation movements, etc. But attempts to manipulate public opinion are by no means confined to communist countries. Active lobbying of friendly factions and politicians is a normal feature of international politics. The United States for example, helped to create MRP in France and supported financially the break-way union group *Force Ouvrière*. The CIA provided financial support for the journals *Encounter* in Britain, and *Preuves* in France.

6. There are many examples of this kind of activity; American support for the Contras in Nicaragua, the Chinese and American support for the anti-apartheid movement in Southern Africa, are but two of many instances of such involvement.

7. There is little evidence of Soviet attempts to prejudice the outcome of elections in non-communist countries in recent years. Even if the Zinoviev letter is accepted to be a forgery there is sufficient evidence to link such efforts to policy in the immediate post-war years. The wave of strikes in France in 1948 for example, were directed against the French involvement in the creation and rearmament of Western Germany. They were directly supported by the Soviet Union, which was anxious to try to avert this development. American involvement in French politics as noted above served as a counter. However, given the nuclear stalemate and the consequent need for stable governments to negotiate arms control agreements, this kind of activity is now largely confined to Third World countries.

8. France was alarmed at the prospect of encirclement by fascist (and hostile) states that included Germany and Italy. It favoured the Republican cause and treated the principle of non-intervention rather more leniently than Britain. The Soviet Union was alarmed at the prospect of a further accretion to the number of its ideological opponents. But it was more alarmed at the recrudescence of German military strength. Consequently it provided sufficient aid to the Republican government to keep the Civil War in being thus preoccupying its potential opponents and preventing the formation of any hostile coalition of forces. Germany too saw the advantages of embroiling Italy in the conflict and thus frustrating the possibility of any agreement between Italy and Britain and France. It encouraged Italian involvement and Italy found itself becoming dependent on German resources to continue its efforts. Germany also found Spain a good training ground for its new forces and equipment.
Britain was faced with the dilemma of trying to seek agreement with Italy as a counter to Germany while maintaining relations with France. Non-intervention, or a policy of strict neutrality was thus seen as the only viable course of action.

9. The Arab-Israeli conflict is no nearer a settlement one way or the other. This is largely because of the balance maintained by the Soviet Union and the United States and the consequent frustration of any local military attempt to force the issue. It is interesting to note that the Israelis were forced to abandon their attempt to eliminate the Egyptian 5th Army in the Yom Kippur War of 1973 by the United States, responding to Soviet threats of direct intervention.

10. This is a synonym for policing with a minimal threat of violence.

11. Paradoxically this was not true of Karl Marx who remained a theorist after his abortive involvement in revolution in 1848, see my *Theory and Explanation in International Politics, op. cit.* pp. 95–102

12. On this point for an account of Stalin's road to power see E. H. Carr, *The*

Bolshevik Revolution, Penguin, Harmondsworth.
13. See my *Modes of Imperialism, op. cit.* pp. 124 (ff).
14. None of these fascist leaders allowed their ideological base to be developed as organised parties with a coherent programme and chain of command.
15. See *Modes of Imperialism, op. cit.* p. 69 (ff).
16. Karl Marx, *Capital*, Vol. III, Foreign Language Publishing House, Moscow, 1966 and II Rubin *Essays on Marx's Theory of Value*, Black and Red Detroit, 1972, pp. 63–75.
17. V. I. Lenin, *Imperialism; the Highest Stage of Capitalism*, Progress Publishers, Moscow, 1966 13th ed. First published in 1917.
18. *Ibid*, p. 25.
19. *Ibid*, p. 75.
20. *Ibid*, p. 89.
21. *Ibid*, p. 89, p. 96.
22. V. I. Lenin on Guerrilla Warfare, *Collected Works*, vol. II, 1962, pp. 123–23, first published Sept. 30th 1906, cited in William J. Pomeroy, ed. *Guerrilla Warfare and Marxism: a reader*, Lawrence and Wishart, London, 1969.
23. See *Selected Works*, Vol. II, Laurence and Wishart, London 1947, Marxism and Insurrection, in a letter to the Central Committee of the RSDLP, p. 120, (ff).
24. *Ibid*, Basle Manifesto, p. 25.
25. V. I. Lenin, April Theses, 20th April, 1917, cited in Ben Turok ed. *Revolutionary Thought in the Twentieth Century*, Zed Press, London, 1980, p. 63.
26. V. I. Lenin, *Proletarian Revolution and the Renegade Kautsky Aug-Sept 1917*, in Selected Works Vol. II, p. 120 (ff) 1936, ed.
27. *Ibid*, p. 195.
28. *Ibid*, p. 197.
29. This he eventually succeeded in doing with the Treaty of Brest, Litovsk, March, 1918.
30. *The Proletarian Revolution, op. cit.* p. 190.
31. *Ibid*, p. 269.
32. V. I. Lenin, War and Peace report to the 7th Congress March 7 1918, p. 30 in *Collected Works*, Vol. II. *op. cit.*
33. See in particular, *The State and Revolution, op. cit.*
34. See *Selected Works* Vol. I, How to Study War, Dec. 1946, p. 179 and *On Protracted War*, Vol. II May 1938, p. 113.
35. *Ibid*, p. 65. This was written in 1927. With the Japanese invasion he changed his mind about the inhibiting effect of colonial rule on revolution, see, *On Tactics against Japanese Imperialism*, Dec. 1935, *ibid*. p. 163.
36. For an account of the Long March see Dick Wilson, *The Long March 1935*, Penguin Books, Harmondsworth 1977. It began after the defeat at the Battle of Kuangchang on the Fukien-Kiangsi border in April 1934. In October 1934 the decision was taken to evacuate the main base in Kiangsi. The destination was to be Northwest Hunan, but at the Tsunyi Conference in Jan. 1935 it was changed to Yunnan, Kweichow and Szechuan. When this proved to be militarily impossible the final destination was Shensi province in Northern China. This was eventually reached in October 1935 by some 5000 out of the original number of 100,000, see Wilson, *op. cit.* p. 227.
37. *Ibid*, pp. 39–40 and pp. 89–106. See also *Selected Works* Vol. I 1965 Edition, *op. cit.* pp. 199–200.

222 The Politics of War

38. For an account of the Tsunyi Conference see Dick Wilson, *op. cit.* p. 91 (ff). Most of those involved in the debate were advocates of orthodox Marxism and were closely associated with the USSR and the Comintern. Li Li-san, was a 'Russian' and urged the cities as the main focus for the revolution. The attacks on Wuhan and Chansha he had advocated were failures and he was discredited in 1931. He eventually fled to Moscow. Po Ku, another 'Russian', according to Mao bore the main responsibility for the previous military disasters. Wang Ming, a 'Russian', was the titular leader of the Chinese Communist Party. Chou En Lai was associated with the Whampoa Academy, itself supported by the USSR. As the survivor and victor of this debate Mao Tse Tung may not be altogether an impartial witness but, as he presents it, the debate was between those who had adopted a 'Russian' view of revolution with its emphasis on the urban areas and himself who urged the special conditions in China with its preponderance of peasants, as a basis for a new kind of revolution.
39. *Ibid*, p. 105
40. See *How to Study War, op. cit.* p. 216.
41. Renamed in 1937 The National Revolutionary Army and in 1946 the People's Revolutionary Army.
42. *A Single Spark Can Start a Forest Fire*, Jan 4, 1930. Vol. I, *op. cit.* p. 119.
43. *Selected Works*, Vol. III, *op. cit.* pp. 194–5.
44. *A Single Spark Can Start a Forest Fire, op. cit.* p. 117, 1936.
45. See *How to Study War, op. cit.* pp. 213–16.
46. This was a long held and consistent view. See for example, *Selected Works*, Vol. I, *op. cit.* pp. 64 (ff) and p. 73 (ff) and also Vol. III, *op. cit.* p. 200 (ff).
47. See Mao Tse Tung, *On Protracted War, op. cit.*, p. 119.
48. See *War and Politics*, Vol. 111, *op. cit.* p. 327.
49. He rephrased Clausewitz's famous dictum as 'War is politics with bloodshed' in *War and Politics, op. cit.* p. 153.
50. In his view the defeat of Japan was not brought about by the use of the atomic bomb but by the entry of the Soviet Union into the war, see *Selected Works*, The Third Revolutionary Civil War Period Vol. III, p. 22.
51. *How to Study War, op. cit.* p. 189.
52. *Ibid*, p. 185.
53. *Ibid*, p. 207.
54. *On Protracted War, op. cit.* p. 143.
55. *War and Politics, op. cit.* p. 169.
56. *Problems of War and Strategy*, Vol. II, Nov. 1938, *op. cit.* p. 225.
57. See, for example, F. H. Cardoso and E. Faletto, *Dependency and Development in Latin America*, 1977, T. Dos Santos, 'The Crisis of development theory and the problems of dependence in Latin America', in H. Berstein, ed. *Underdevelopment and Development*, Penguin, Harmondsworth, 1973, and A. E. Emmanuel, *Unequal Exchange: a study of the imperialism of trade*, New Left Books, London, 1972. Gabriel Palma, *Dependency—a formal theory of underdevelopment or a methodology for the analysis of concrete situations of underdevelopment*, Vol. 6, Pergamon Press, Oxford, 1978, pp. 88–912.
58. See Hugo Radice, ed. *International Firms and Modern Imperialism*, Penguin, Harmondsworth, 1975.
59. Andre Gunder Frank, *Latin America: Underdevelopment or Revolution*, Monthly Press, NY, 1969 and also R. I. Rhodes ed. *Imperialism and*

Underdevelopment, Monthly Review Press, NY, 1970.

60. The deportation of people from the towns in Kampuchea by the Pol Pot regime is the logical extension of Mao's cultural revolution with the attempt to destroy the cultural, social, and economic, bases of urban life.
61. Problems of War and Strategy, *op. cit.* pp. 224 and 225.
62. Giap, *People's War: People's Army*, Foreign Languages Publishing House, Hanoi. Le Duan, *The Vietnamese Revolution; Fundamental Problems*, 1970. Che Guevara, *Guerrilla Warfare: Reminiscences of the Cuban Revolutionary War*, trans. Victoria Ortiz, Allen and Unwin, London, 1968.
63. Le Duan, *op. cit.* p. 104.
64. *Ibid*, p. 106, p. 104.
65. *Ibid*, p. 106.
66. Giap, *op. cit.* p. 214.
67. Geneva Accords. Under Articles 16, 17 and 19 no new military equipment could be introduced by a foreign power nor could they establish any military bases. In 1955 Diem repudiated the Accords and the United States became his patron.
68. This offensive was a military failure for the North Vietnamese although they temporarily occupied Hue. But coming as it did at a time when dissent became politically important in an election year in the United States, and after both the Johnson administration and the military had assured the public that success in Indo-China was in sight, it had a devastating effect. If the offensive is treated as a strategem and not as a strategy or tactic then it illustrates yet once more that battle-field success is not essential for the achievement of political objectives through force.
69. Guevara, *op. cit.* p. 102.
70. *Ibid*, p. 208.
71. *Ibid*, p. 92.
72. *Ibid*, p. 199.
73. *Ibid*, p. 208.
74. *Ibid*, p. 196.
75. On this aspect see Grant Wardlaw, *Political Terrorism*, Cambridge University, Press, 1982, p. 35.
76. It could be argued that this is the present position with the IRA in Northern Ireland and with ETA in Spain.
77. The Malayan terrorist campaign was fought largely between British forces and Chinese communists over the period from 1948 to its official end in July 1960.
78. The Cyprus Emergency. This was essentially a struggle for *enosis* or Union with Greece and was at its height between 1954 and 1958.
79. This is a common phenomenon in Latin America.
80. The suspension of the jury system in the so-called Diplock Courts in Northern Ireland is an example of this.
81. On this see Walter Laqueur, *Terrorism*, Weidenfeld and Nicolson, London, 1977. Paul Wilkinson, *Political Terrorism*, Macmillan, London, 1974, and *Terrorism and the Liberal State*, Macmillan, London, 1977, and Frank Kitson, *Low Intensity Operations*, Faber and Faber, London, 1971. There is a growing literature on terrorism.
82. On this see A. Cave Brown, *op. cit. Bodyguard of Lies*.
83. Alexander Atkinson, *Social Order and the General Theory of Strategy*, Routledge and Kegan Paul, 1981, p. 67.
84. *How to Study War*, *op. cit.* p. 213.

8 Reasoning and Violence

The decision to undertake violent action, or make its threat, in pursuit of a political objective is rarely based on considerations of instrumentality alone. Mere capability, however this is assessed, is not the sole relevant factor. There are constraints on the use of violence that extend beyond calculations of its material effectiveness. Such constraints have a moral, ethical, or political dimension. In this respect the Pope has his divisions too. The central concern in this chapter is with the question, is there a rationale of constraint operating on decisions to use, or not to use, violence as a political instrument, or to adopt, or refrain from adopting, a particular form of violence? Previous chapters have mainly been concerned with the rationality of violence in terms of its instrumentality, that is, as a means to an end. But, as we have seen, the definition of ends becomes important in seeking to establish a commensurate (or rational) relationship between them. And ends are related to values. Equally, the legitimacy of the means, as opposed to their effectiveness, is a value-related question. The political practitioner in considering the use of violence acts in a context of values, whether these are adhered to or not. Do these operate as a constraint on action? In what way are they related to decisions and action involving violence? Are they relevant at all?.

The world of international politics is often taken to be amoral in character. Given the multiple and heterogeneous ideological and religious value systems that coexist, the imposition of any one of them, or the assumption that there is common agreement on ethical standards, appears to be unrealistic. While conflicts between states frequently involve beliefs and values, ideological or religious in character, wars of religion are rare. The compromise ending the Thirty Years War in Europe appears to have held, although some have seen the Cold War as a later recrudescence. If attempts to achieve a uniformity of belief in the world of states through violence have been abandoned, the result has not been the adoption of a common rationality based on political expediency. National leaders, while seeking accommodation emancipated from divisive ideological commitments, nevertheless represent their own value and belief systems.[1] In a sense they have a moral constituency. The ends they seek are related to this. Moreover, not only are they representative in this way but they also have a view of the world of states that is essentially normative. Such views may not coincide, or possess common ground for the resolution of differences. As we have seen earlier, the effective use, or threat, of violence is as much dependent on shared values as on perceptions of capacity. A knowledge of what is important or relevant in this respect is necessary when devising an appropriate strategy. Where this element is in doubt, or misunderstood, violence is unlikely to be successful in attaining its object. This of course applied to limited contests. Total war is an exception, for here the end is not conversion to a particular point of view, albeit through force, but conquest and unconditional surrender. This is also the case for revolutionary war where the end pursued is equally apocalyptic.

In short the use of violence as a political instrument depends on a measure of shared perceptions of the nature of inter-state relations and of what constitutes appropriate action. This is a minimal framework for action. The value element in it is not evangelical in character, with each national participant seeking to establish ideological dominance, but consensual. However radical by contrast are the respective belief systems of the contending states, this radicalism cannot be translated into action without transforming the contest into a total war and thus making it irrational. If accommodation is sought, using violence as a means of getting it, then a degree of moderation enters into the intrusion of values. The point here is that although values are relevant and although their extension into world politics as a basis for prescription appears a logical consequence of possessing them, in practice this is not the case, even where violence rather than diplomacy is adopted as a means of conflict resolution. Beliefs neither entail action nor determine the attitudes and responses of states.[2] They are part of the reasoning of practitioners of international politics.

Normative arguments about the nature of the world of states, whether as a Hobbesian state of nature, or as an embryonic international society based on western liberal values, are notoriously inconclusive and incapable of resolution through empirical reference.[3] By selection, 'evidence' can easily be cited to support one normative scheme or another. The existence of war itself, of arms races, military alliances, defence provision, the invention and development of sophisticated and highly destructive weapons, the element of threat in diplomacy, and the dominance of the so-called 'super-powers', all testify to the anarchic model as a true characterisation of the world of states. Conversely, the existence of diplomacy itself, of rules defined through agreement and conventions, non-governmental institutions, alliances and treaties subordinating national independence of action to international supervision and control, arms control agreements, trade associations, etc., all support the thesis of a world, if not harmonious, at least regulated and controlled by agreements that states find it in their interest to keep.

However, broad conceptual frameworks of a normative character cannot constitute general empirical explanations unless they are genuine theories. In the case of the latter they must satisfy logical and empirical criteria and be capable of some form of test before they can qualify as explanations. Such a theoretical explanatory form as I have argued elsewhere,[4] explains in terms of general propositions and constitutes in its causal relations an explanation overriding individual consciousness, reasoning and intentionality. Many attempts have been made to create such a theory but none so far has been successful. Normative theories contain a theoretical lacuna in respect of these conditions. Empirical citation merely illustrates rather than demonstrates their argument. As such, for every instance of political behaviour that supports the general thesis, another can be cited to the contrary. They are really conceptual schemes incapable of refutation, neither true nor false, but ways of looking at the world. In this sense they may be said to constitute, rather than represent, reality.

The normative approach to inter-state relations has tended to be dominated by the western 'realist' view, and the debate polarised between the neo-Hobbesian and the liberal-rationalist arguments. In this context it is the prescriptive aspects of this debate that assumes importance; that is, what practical consequences follow from adherence to one or other of these theses contained in this approach. If, for example, the Hobbesian argument is preferred, then security policies assume primacy in the conduct of foreign policy and state interests are paramount. The liberal approach emphasises international solutions to national security and the cooperative aspects of inter-state politics become central to national policy. The two may of course be combined within regional alliance frameworks such as NATO and the EEC, but, as we have seen, this form of association remains nationally based and there is an uneasy relationship between national and wider interest, with the former usually having priority.

This chapter is concerned with the question as to how far politicians are constrained by normative considerations in relation to the use and threat of violence in international politics. It will be seen that this entails not an imposition of normative schemes upon the political world but a concern for the consciousness of political agents and its relation to a generalised world view. Are their assumptions and their objectives normatively based? Do, for example, Marxist politicians really seek to apply their doctrines to their conduct of foreign and defence policies?[5] Is this the case for liberal democratic or autocratic rulers who base their authority on political or religious belief systems? Are there any general constraints or influences of a normative character on the pursuit of national interests through violence? These constitute general questions, but further questions can be asked involving moral and related influences on political conduct of a more limited nature. Economic constraints, domestic politics and values, pressure groups, interdependent interests, ethical considerations, and so on, provide a context for the decision-maker that may or may not act as a constraining influence upon upon decision and action. The deterrent argument in terms of mutual defensive nuclear deterrence, for example, is an issue that has a number of ramifications of this kind. These are both material and moral in character.

Thus, while I am not concerned with the general debate on the relative merits of broad normative schemes, either as a basis for explanation of the world of states, or as a basis for prescription in order to achieve a better relationship between states, I am concerned with the degree to which normative elements enter into state policy. An important aspect of political decision-making, especially in an adversarial situation, is the assessment of the likely consequences of a contemplated action in terms of countering action. Expectations of proper action are central to the underlying reasoning. What is deemed 'proper' action may have a normative component in that the adversary state may be expected to conform to constraints of a legal, moral, ethical as well as of an expedient, character. This is, of course, applicable only to situations where the contest is limited and where bargaining is an aspect of violence. In short, the use and threat of violence in this context is within a framework of rules that amounts to a common rationale that broadly has a restraining influence. The constraints that hold here, if indeed they do, are normative rather than material.

I am thus concerned with what has been termed the idealist view of the world of states. What influences other than the purely instrumental or the realist, act upon, or are recognised by, states in their formulations of strategies using, or threatening, violence? Concepts such as the rule of law, international order and justice, the just war and the proper conduct of war are central to this inquiry. From this it moves on to broad normative views that allegedly constrain states and their freedom to act, such as the balance of power, or the equilibrium theory of politics. The second part of this chapter will examine the attempts of the state to defend itself and the consequent constraints and inhibitions related to nuclear balance and defensive nuclear deterrence. These include arms control, disarmament and self-limiting agreements relating to various forms of violence. Finally, constraints emanating from the domestic political systems of states on the freedom to use or threaten violence will be examined.

Do rules exist that regulate or influence the conduct of inter-state relations in terms of the use of threat of violence? In formulating a strategy designed to achieve political objectives, whether to provide national security, or to procure some lesser end by violent means, are the formulators and executants constrained in any way by a perception of rules? If such rules are so perceived, are they derived from the social mores of the state, or are they a product of inter-state intercourse itself? Are decision-makers concerned for the consequences of their actions in terms of domestic political reactions, or in terms of adverse and possibly counterproductive responses on the part of other states? These questions are not of course mutually exclusive. We can regard rules in various ways; there are analytic rules, that is those that follow from or are the bases for, conceptual schemes that include such concepts as the state, sovereignty, legitimacy, rights and so on; and customary or social rules that are derived from practice. The main distinction other than their nominal substance lies in whether they are theoretically or empirically derived. By this is meant that logical and conceptual relations and analysis determine the content of the inferred rules or laws in the first case, while conventional or practical relations determine the second category. Rules based on moral laws are justified in terms of their absolute and universal character regardless of their observance. Reference to them is justificatory in character. Empirically derived rules are essentially pragmatic, states recognising or observing them according to motive and circumstance. The former are prescriptive; the latter derived from practice itself, in terms of the consciousness of those making decisions and taking action. They may, of course, refer them as a means of justification to overriding moral rules. In the world of states with its heterogeneity such a reference is of course purely contingent.

The central question here is, are these rules *derived* from state practices or *imposed* on them? If the former then the difficulty lies in separating causes from effects so as to avoid tautology or circular argument. If we infer them from practice, that is from the actual conduct of states, the proposition that it is rule-guided begs the question of the status of the rules themselves. Are they in some way external to the agent whose actions we are assessing? An argument that asserts this entails a conceptual framework independent of the actions it purports to explain. If it merely reifies these actions then it constitutes a form of description subjective in nature, and so adds nothing to our knowledge of why the agent did what he did. If that knowledge is constituted by the agent's own reasoning then the sense in which his actions are rule-guided is dependent upon that reasoning and, while we can derive this from evidence, it cannot constitute a conceptual framework independent or separable from it. In short, the first part of this study deals with the claim that political agents act in conformity to a framework of constraints and inhibitions normatively based, and the second with the level of perceived constraints as understood by the agents themselves. While it is frequently the case in practice that actors face consequences for which they were not responsible, or which were either unforeseen or unintended, these are relevant only in terms of their own reasoning. It is *their* world that is pertinent and not an idealised model imposed on them that seeks to characterise or explain their decisions and actions. There is no more a morality than, as we saw earlier, a logic of the situation, separable from this reasoning.

There is commonly a high degree of moralising and idealistic statement in explanations of policy or justifications of actions and decisions made by political actors. They frequently refer to ethical or moral standards, the innate superiority of a particular socio-political system, the binding force of rules of behaviour, the primacy of peace, or the maintenance of world order and so on. We could of course take this at face value and come to the conclusion that politics and ethics are virtually synonymous. This level of moralising however, is empirically vacuous in that it lacks a statement of conditions that stipulates relevance and appropriateness. Its force and authority depend not upon the application of moral principles and ethical rules to practice in any prescriptive sense, but upon an appeal to shared values. The attempt to universalise these disguises the fact that they are a reflection of national *mores* and can exist and be relevant only in that social context. They are relevant only in terms of the national interest and the interests of its citizens. Only the citizen can understand their appeal and respond accordingly. There are no citizens of the world.

One reason for this element of moralising in declaratory policy is the apparent need for the actor to obtain or retain support from his domestic political audience for decisions and actions that may entail sacrifice or may have a repercussive effect. His problem is thus not only the formulation of a strategy in terms of an effective relationship between means and ends; he has also to justify it. It is a problem that is minimal where communications are controlled and information can be manipulated, as is the case under conditions of total war, or where the regime or political system is repressive. Generally, however, some public support is necessary both for a specific policy, especially where it entails or threatens violence, thus directly involving the citizen, and for a regime, especially where its credibility is linked to the policy. Failure in foreign policy tends to have more disastrous consequences for governments than any other kind of political reverse.[6] This is especially the case when violence is employed. Justification thus seeks to make as wide an appeal as possible to the domestic audience, and this is found in the common denominator of a shared value system or ideology. This is true even of non-democratic systems, where representing action or decision as consistent with ideological orthodoxy is necessary in order to frustrate factionalism and ward off rival bids for power. The point being made here is that statements of policy couched in value terms are essentially manipulative, designed to achieve a particular political effect. They do not represent a genuine motivation. It will be apparent that a stance taken on an issue involving threats of violence between states is weakened if it does not appear to be supported by the general public. One of the grounds for the attack on appeasement in the 1930s was that the British government was either unable or unwilling to demonstrate this support in confronting Hitler.

Establishing whether or not there is genuine ideological motivation, or whether values enter into the formulation of policy, is essentially an historical exercise. This is to say that an investigation proceeds on the basis of evidence of reasoning and is specific to time, place, and the individuals concerned. Given the difficulty of distinguishing between accounts of their motives by historical agents on the basis of evidence of genuine reasoning, any conclusions reached must be tentative. But it is easier to demonstrate radical inconsistencies if the claim is made that such motives are moral in character, than to justify such a claim. In practice this element of declaratory policy appears to be as subject to manipulation as the audience it is directed at. It is noteworthy that where negotiations between states of different ideological persuasion seek to achieve success—that is where genuine accommodation is sought—the rhetorical level is either muted or disappears altogether. This is one indication that it is primarily intended for domestic consumption.[7] The need to manipulate domestic opinion, or to placate it in this way, indicates both the strengths and the weaknesses of domestic political pressure, as we shall see later in this chapter. However, the point here is that the value element in declarations of policy is not necessarily instrumental in the sense of directing and constraining choices of action, but is instrumental in the sense of persuading citizens to accept policies formulated on different premises.

If it is difficult to generalise on the basis of proffered justifications of decisions and actions involving the use or threat of violence in international politics, what of formal agreements on its conduct and control? Nation-states have entered into a number of conventions and regulatory devices relating to the use of violence.[8] Are they constrained by them in any way? Is there a moral or ethical framework that acts as an influence on decisions to go to war, or to use, or threaten to use, particular forms of violence in the pursuit of political objectives in the world of states? We come now to the just war argument[9] and to the alleged inhibitory effects of international conventions and rules designed to restrict and regulate the use of certain forms of weapons. Again it should be stressed that my concern is not with the question as to what states *ought* to do in this context. This is a matter for the political theorist and entails establishing a universal basis for an international moral order. As we have seen earlier, constraints emanating from such a moral system are imposed on, rather than derived from, practice. They are innately prescriptive. Rather, I am concerned with what has been called reciprocal compliance;[10] that is, where mutual restraint on the scale and form of violence occurs out of enlighted self-interest. This may have ethical implications but the principle is more rational than moral. It seeks to limit and control conflict for fear of the consequences of its extension, and it applies as much to deterrence, or threats of violence, as to violence itself. As we shall see, the problem of control is central to moral as well as to rational action.

It is clear that such mutual restraint between opponents is difficult to sustain at the level of conflict. Once hostilities have begun, although both parties might wish to limit their scope and scale, the break down in communications consequent on war with the removal of diplomatic missions, etc., the possibility of misinterpretation, and above all, the fear of defeat and its political consequences, militate against restraint. The *drôle de guerre* period at the beginning of the Second World War, for example, demonstrated the reluctance of the contenders to go to extremes. Neither side wished to violate neutrality, to bomb civilian populations, or to sow mines in international waterways; that they overcame their reluctance was a consequence of the rationale of total war superceding more limited aims at its onset. An awareness of this dynamic stemming from the experience of the First World War, led to attempts to establish a framework of constraints relating to weapons that inhibited states *prior* to hostilities. The problem with this approach is that innovation in weapons is not precluded, and is indeed encouraged by such inhibitions and, as we shall see, it is not the weapons but the intentions of those developing and using them that are relevant, particularly where security is directly involved.

There is in any case a problem in relating moral and ethical judgement to reasoning prior to action. The intention of the actor is to achieve a desired state of affairs. He intends his action to be effective in attaining this. But as we have seen from earlier parts of this work he cannot know in advance whether this will be the case. It is possible, if action is based on a validated theory, to make a rational link between means and ends in that some form of external reference through empirical testing enables a statement of probability to be made that a state of affairs will result from the satisfaction of stipulated conditions. Moral judgements are made about both means and ends, in this context about the conduct of war and its overall purpose. But if the instrumental relationship between means and ends is unknown, that is if we do not know what constitutes a means, then no moral judgement is possible. In this respect at least we act virtually blindly. Only intentions can be subject to moral judgement, not the consequences that stem from action.

An example might clarify this point. The Second World War has been called a just war.[11] In some judgements it was a war against an evil and aggressive state. But it could not have been so described at its outset, or at any point, until it had ended. The intentions of those initiating violence could be assessed in this way, although there is very little evidence that Britain and France, or rather their political leaders, were primarily motivated by ethical or moral considerations. But those responsible for the decisions and actions that historians label 'The Second World War', changed during its course. If we except the Atlantic Charter,[12] a vague and equivocal document signed by a non-belligerent, the United States, as well as by Britain, it was only with victory that the question of justice arose. Victor's justice, embodied in the retrospective legislation of the Nuremberg principles, was primarily concerned with the punishment of the alleged crimes of the defeated. They, as in the case of the First World War, were deemed to be responsible for the war. But retrospective justice of this kind can hardly be said to apply to the intentions of those engaged in waging it.

The point is not that their reasoning was primarily expedient in character, as that no clear explanatory link between actions and consequences can be demonstrated, so as to allow the case for moral responsibility to hold. Moral culpability is, in any case, not the same as criminal culpability, although the concept of intention is common to both. In the absence of a universal moral or legal code such judgements are easy to make and difficult to sustain. What is, or is not, a just war, cannot therefore be determined in advance other than through making judgements of the intentions of those engaged in preparing for, threatening, and using, violence. On this ground none or all of the contenders were culpable. But of course, *ex post facto* descriptions do not enable us to explain the rationale of action itself or determine its moral content. And for our purposes we need to know to what extent, if at all, moral constraints enter into decision-making and action.

232 The Politics of War

The central question of the just war argument is, under what circumstances is it right to use violence against other states? Grotius[13] adduces three main reasons; defence, the recovery of property, and the infliction of punishment. It will be noted that all three are responses to alleged wrongs perpetrated by another state or states. The first is fundamental since it concerns the self-preservation or integrity of the state itself. The others depend on this, and represent the protection of citizen's rights whether through recovery of property, or retribution and reparation. This notion of just war therefore, asserts the primacy of the state as the locus of moral choice. It alone possesses political identity and autonomy. It alone has a monopoly of violence and thus makes the question of war relevant. It alone is responsible for the safety and well-being of its citizens. And finally, it alone bears the responsibility for its own survival as a political entity. No other political agency can perform these functions. As we have seen earlier, a truly universal moral and legal order requires a political basis other than the nation-state. The capacity to perform these functions is, of course, dependent upon a number of contingent factors; these include resources, political integrity and stable authority, population, technological and economic development, and, most important, the context of states and the element of reciprocal action that eludes the control of any one state. The notion of the sovereign equality of states, although an assumption of the just war argument, is difficult to translate into the real world. All these factors are variables.

However, the central question I want to examine here is how the self-preservation of the state—or security—is related to the notion of the just war. Security provision is, *inter alia*, central to strategy. If it is right for a state to go to war to protect itself from aggressions, or acts of violence on the part of other states, what does this entail? It is clear that such a war is absolute, in character, with its object the complete defeat of the criminal state or states. It cannot be presumed that the 'criminal' state will accept a moral defeat or make reparation once it is clear that it cannot succeed in its criminal act. It is more likely that it will persist with all means at its disposal to avoid the material results and the stigma of defeat. There is a contradiction between the instrumental and the moral use of violence in a war with unconditional surrender as its end. Compromise is ruled out since there can be no accommodation with immorality. The consequence is a struggle akin to a holy war between the forces of light and the forces of darkness. A just war is thus a total war. While this may be moral it can hardly be rational in the sense argued throughout this work. The criminal states too are forced to fight for their survival. Their own integrity is placed in jeopardy.

One of the difficulties in applying this aspect of just war to modern political conditions is the absence of any clear reference, independent of political activity, acceptable to all states, that allows a definition of security. If the view is taken that one state's security is another state's insecurity—the basis of realpolitik—then all states are at risk even in time of peace. Indeed, peace is a misnomer since the absence of war depends on the imposition of a system of countervailing threats. Preparations for war, and the threat of war, are thus permanent features of the contemporary international system. The move into actual hostilities in security terms only makes concrete the uneasy and unstable system of threat and counter-threat that constitutes the norm for inter-state relations. States in principle may be peace-loving but in practice find it necessary to respond to threats to their security as they are perceived. Such threats may only be passive in character, existing in the form of relative capacities for war, rather than in any explicit warlike intentions. The state that actually initiates hostilities is thus not necessarily aggressive but seeking to place its security on a better footing. It may be establishing its own right to exist in the light of a perceived threat. The point here is that what constitutes aggression is not easy to determine. In a context where security is based upon competition and where relative advantages are pursued by states, unequal in resources and capacity for violence, and where technological developments in weapons produce differential demands on the environment and on other states, the initiation of hostilities is not necessarily an immoral act.

If, for example, we examine the German invasion of Poland as an act of unprovoked aggression and therefore unjust, there are a number of ambiguities that required examination. Poland itself was hardly innocent in terms of appropriating territory nominally belonging to other states. It had acquired territory from Russia, Lithuania and Czechoslovakia by force.[14] But the issue was not the existence of Poland. It was primarily the question of the security of the major European powers with the smaller states serving as strategic and political pawns. Germany had been defeated in the First World War, disarmed, deprived of its empire, forced to pay reparations, and treated as bearing the main guilt for the war. Subsequently, in 1923, the French occupied the Ruhr in an attempt to enforce reparations payments. The Versailles Treaty, the Tripartite Treaty, the League of Nations, and other treaties, created a security system in Europe that depended on the permanent subjugation of Germany. Despite the withdrawal of the United States into isolationism, the Locarno Pact, and the cordon sanitaire established by France, using the small succession states that bordered Germany, appeared to endorse the system. It depended upon force and not consent.

Yet the states that imposed this system had no clear moral title to their strategic superiority. They were imperial powers and used their military victories to break up their rivals' empires employing the principle of self-determination only where it suited them.[15] Their own imperial possessions were sacrosanct in this respect.[16] The breakup of the German, Austro-Hungarian, Turkish, and Russian empires, was designed to produce a number of manipulable, weak and friendly states that could be used to counter German revival. The point is that the rationale for Hitler's attack on these constraints was the same as that which had created them. He shared the same beliefs about security as did his rivals. He could justify his attacks in the same terms. In short, given prevalent notions of security derived from inter-state competition in arms, and the relation of extant military technology with politics and geography, self-preservation could be used to justify pre-emptive war, intervention, and indeed almost any form of violence or its threat.

If then the end of self-preservation could be used to justify resort to violence, what of the form of violence itself? If it is accepted that a war of self-defence is a just war, ignoring the difficulties of establishing what constitutes security, can such a war be fought justly? There are a number of international conventions and agreements that seek to limit or ban the use of particular weapons.[17] There is also a general principle that civilians or non-combatants should be protected from the rigours of war as far as possible. Much of this is a reflection of experience in violence and consists of a kind of retrospective legislation designed to alleviate some of the horrors of war. Poison gas, for example, was proscribed as a consequence of the experience of the First World War. More recently attempts have been made to eliminate weapons that 'may be deemed to be excessively injurious or to have indiscriminate effects'.[18] These reflect a concern for weapons that are in some way inhumane, as with previous bans on explosive and dum-dum bullets. Nuclear weapons are excluded from this concern. In many ways seeking to ban specific weapons appears to be a surrogate for a ban on certain practices of war. It is not the weapon, particularly not the weapon of yester-year, that constitutes the problem but the way in which it is used. Area bombing with conventional explosives, for example, can match the immediate effects of nuclear attacks if sufficient bombers are used.[19] This does not of course apply to subsequent effects such as radioactive poisoning and genetic damage.

The central point here is that if a just war is a war of self defence then national survival becomes the main end. The war becomes total. It is this that determines how and what weapons are used. The distinction between combatants and non-combatants was possible, and perhaps valid, where military technology and national resources were not closely associated and linked to an apocalyptic end. If a just war requires total effort to bring the 'criminal' states to justice, then civilians are as much part of this as members of the armed forces. In devising means of forcing a result all resources relevant to exploiting relative advantage are deployed. For example, Britain and France were forced on the defensive in 1939 and therefore devised a strategy based on the economic blockade of Germany. The purpose of the blockade was to deprive the German people of the means of survival and so provoke the collapse of the regime. After the defeat of France in 1940, the civilian population remained the primary target, although the means had shifted from economic blockade to area bombing of population centres. The alternative to using such means as existed was a negotiated peace and this, given the permanent challenge to British security arising out of Hitler's dominant position on the European continent, was not an option.

On Germany's part the submarine appeared to be an effective counter to the economic stranglehold that its enemies wished to impose. Although Germany had accepted the principle that submarines should not sink on sight merchant ships, in the 1936 London Naval Protocol, and entered the war with only a small fleet of submarines, it was clear that given the attempt to apply a naval blockade this was highly disadvantageous. All enemy merchant ships radioed enemy sightings and contact and formed part of a surveillance system that enabled successful action against the Germany navy.[20] Quite apart from the contribution their cargoes made to the British war effort, they were in essence, part of the armed forces. The consequent extension of the attacks on merchant shipping was the result. The point here is that a specific act or series of acts cannot be taken in isolation and assessed in terms of their legitimacy, but must be placed in a context of reciprocity and its rationale.

If we accept the minimalist view as expressed in the most recent Geneva convention, that the non-combatant civilan should be exempt from violence so far as is possible under modern conditions of war, what constitutes a non-combatant civilian? In Britain during the Second World War both male and female adults were conscripted into war work. Even agricultural workers assumed a military significance as the unrestricted submarine warfare intensified. Children aged thirteen when the war began were liable to call-up in 1945. The manpower problem was particularly acute in Britain, especially once the Second Front was opened. For Germany, it was crucial, and children were conscripted into the armed forces. If factors such as morale were considered relevant to the determination of the opponent to go on fighting, then even children became legitimate targets. Terror bombing was devised to break civilian morale and undermine allegiance to a regime incapable of protecting the non-combatant population. Total war called for total effort. The distinction between civilian and combatant is thus particularly hard to define in total war, and, as was argued earlier, a just war, of this nature, is a total war.[21] Such a distinction is impossible in the case of civil war, revolutionary war, and wars of resistance, for these too are total in character. The Geneva Convention of 1949 forbids sanctions against civilians in occupied countries, such as the taking and shooting of hostages as a means of ensuring good conduct. Restraints are thus imposed on occupying forces engaging in fighting resistance as well as continuing the overall struggle against an enemy. Such restraints are not imposed on those who resist. They may, for example, be taken prisoner without having the obligation to take prisoners. It is difficult to see how such rules could apply in practice. Blurring distinctions between formal combatants and civilian 'freedom fighters' or terrorists, (depending on one's point of view) is in itself a recognition of the point being made that in total war almost everyone is a combatant.

Some attempt has been made to incorporate instrumentality with an ethical position through the principle of proportionality and the doctrine of military necessity.[22] This is to assert the notion of minimal or moderate violence in achieving a military objective. Clearly these apply at the tactical or battle-field level and refer to specific military actions rather than to a broad strategic area. This is perhaps the corollary of war guilt and general political responsibility for violence, placing the question of culpability at the level of individual decision. Proportionality is the principle of using only so much violence as is commensurate with the object sought. Excessive force is thus proscribed, introducing a damage-limitation element into military operations. Military necessity is the basis for justification of operations in pursuit of the object sought. Violence must be limited to action that is instrumental in military terms. Such criteria of reference in assessing the use and form of violence on the battle-field depend upon relativities and not absolutes. In other words, they depend on the actions of the opponent, and countering this in what is a contingent and changing set of circumstances. To make them effective as basic rules of combat depends on introducing a level of communication and control, internal and external, agreement on what constitutes necessary or proportionate action, and an acceptance of limits on the battle-field. Under conditions of conventional war such control is illusory, although not under those of nuclear war, as we shall see later. Past experience in the form, not merely of total war, but limited wars such as Korea, Vietnam, and the Middle East,23 is not encouraging in this respect.

The principles of proportionality and of military necessity are question-begging. It cannot be known in advance of action whether it will be effective in this absence of a genuine explanatory theory relating the use of violence to the production of desired effects. What is excessive force can only be known retrospectively, and even there is only a partial knowledge, given the inability to make comparison between forms of action in terms of their instrumentality. The bombing of Dresden was certainly excessive but the belief that it was necessary could not be tested *in vacuuo*. Only if the bombing of civilian targets was proscribed by all sides could a clear moral judgement be made. Even here it is effectiveness and not moral argument that is paramount. The bombing was also ineffective if the result was intended to produce a collapse of political authority and an earlier surrender. But this of course is not a moral judgement. What is necessary both in terms of form and scale is primarily a judgement about instrumentality from which moral judgements might stem.

Thus choice between the form and scale of contemplated actions is a matter of what is deemed to be effective in producing the desired result. In the absence of a validated theory, this cannot be based on foreknowledge. A moral judgement thus depends upon a form of empirical knowledge that at present does not exist. *Ex post facto* moralising does not, and cannot, constitute a guide to action or a basis for prescription. The formulation of strategy cannot impart moral notions where the consequences of action are not fully understood. Moral justification and the development of a system of moral or ethical constraints depend upon a knowledge of the consequences of action. Intentions alone cannot constitute a basis for moral judgement since these can be justified on the very general ground that it was the intention to bring the war to as speedy a close as possible thus curtailing the suffering. The apparent brutality and cruelty employed thus only mask the ultimate humanitarianism. Clausewitz himself made this point when asserting that war should be prosecuted with maximum vigour and force.

Where new weapons come into existence there are additional problems in assessing their use and establishing ethical constraints. The use of the atomic bomb on Hiroshima and Nagasaki has been condemned by some on moral grounds.[24] If we take the doctrine of military necessity and proportionality it can be argued that this bombing saved more lives than it destroyed by forcing the early surrender of Japan. The plan to use conventional weapons in invading the Japanese mainland and in defeating the Japanese forces in China, was estimated to cost hundreds of thousands of Japanese, American and Russian lives.[25] The sacrifice of civilians was intended to reduce this cost. Against this it is argued that the Japanese were on the point of surrender and that on any rational ground they had lost the war. While it is true that they were suing for peace through the then neutral Soviet Union, it was equally clear that they were hoping for a negotiated peace that secured some advantages. In a just war, and apologists for the Second World War assert that it was a just cause on the Allied side, compromise with a criminal state is precluded. The Allies sought an unconditional surrender. Japan was regarded as a criminal state, not merely from its pre-emptive attack on Pearl Harbour, but for its defiance of the League of Nations and its invasion of Manchuria and China before that. The rationale of the just war is total war and the atomic bomb appeared not only justifiable in these terms but also conformed with the principle of proportionality and the doctrine of military necessity.

However, while President Truman wanted to end the war with Japan swiftly, the apparent humanitarian motive for desiring this masked a further motive. He wanted to force an early surrender to avoid having to concede to the Soviet Union a share in the occupation of Japan and in the post-war settlement. His concern was primarily strategic in that he had determined that the Pacific was to become an American sphere of influence.[26] American influence in China and in Japan was to become paramount. The former Japanese bases in the Pacific were to revert to the United States and no power in the future was to be allowed to make such a military challenge as had the Japanese. In short American security interests were paramount and these excluded the Soviet Union (and Britain) from having any share in the Japanese occupation. Any prolongation of the war, with the European imperial powers asserting their lost authority in their Far Eastern and South-East Asian possessions, with the Soviet Union extending its influence in Manchuria and China, and with the American monopoly of victory over Japan in dispute, was therefore anathema to Truman. The haste with which he planned the attack on four Japanese cities thus indicated his concern. In the event, the bombing of two of his projected targets brought about the desired surrender. Both his humanitarian and his political objectives were thus fulfilled.

Not only did the United States conceive of the war as just, arising as it did out of the Japanese attack on Pearl Harbour, but as a war free of

238   *The Politics of War*

restraint for this reason. The Pacific War was conducted on both sides with a singular ferocity.[27] The United States sought a complete victory in order to create the security that before Pearl Harbour had been at risk through Japanese naval power. Security too had been the Japanese goal, threatened as they had been by a combination of European imperialism and of naval forces in the Pacific. In short, as with the European War, the chief objective sought by all the contenders was a more complete guarantee of security than had been the case in the inter-war period. This inevitably meant the subjugation of rivals and an uneasy relationship with allies. They all shared the same view of security and its innately competitive base, compounded and complicated by the development of new weapons during the war itself.

It is hard to see any element of moral or ethical constraint observed by states in making strategic decisions. The element of reciprocal compliance in this respect applied only where it was expedient. Neither Germany nor Japan complied with the Geneva Convention on the proper treatment of prisoners of war. During their early military successes there was little inducement to comply, given the imbalance of prisoner holdings. This situation changed with German defeats in North Africa and at Stalingrad. Even so the Russians were particularly badly treated, on the grounds that they were *untermenschen* or because, in typical Nazi contradiction, they were needed as volunteers. Harsh treatment served to induce recruitment.[28] The justification for this was that the Soviet Union was not a signatory of the Convention.

The rationale of expediency related to the object sought, appears to have more influence upon strategic decision than any ethical consideration. Where national security is concerned, in peace or in war, this reasoning is paramount. The pursuit of relative advantage in military terms is the main determinant in strategic decisions and actions. Thus a sea power having chosen this arm through reasons of geography and resources, naturally opposes unrestricted submarine warfare. A land power for similar reasons, seeks to counter naval strength by developing this weapon and, equally naturally, advocates it. An air power, again having chosen and developed this weapon, naturally advocates unrestricted bombing of cities, given the imperfect and inaccurate character of the bomber. A land power, preoccupied with land warfare, and unwilling, or unable, to counter this weapon with an equivalent, attacks its use as terror bombing. And so on.[29] Reciprocal compliance thus operates only where there is no clear disadvantage arising from its observation. Total war, the epitome of the just war, is perhaps the least restrained in this respect.

Limited war, where control is pre-eminent to avoid an irrational extension, sets limits to the use and form of violence and there is more opportunity for the observation of mutual restraint. Even here where the contest is between contenders unequal in resources and in terms of sophisticated and powerful means of violence, the superior belligerent has little inducement to enter into tactical agreements that limits his use of weapons. The proxy wars of this century are in this respect akin to the colonial wars of the past where poison gas, aircraft, massacres of civilians and atrocities, indeed, all the appurtenances of modern civilisation, were used and deemed permissible against uncivilised savages. They, too, were *untermenschen*. Constraint thus depends more on expediency than on ethics. The principal restriction being the relative capacities to retaliate in kind possessed by the contenders. Thus reciprocal compliance in this context constitutes a restraining factor only where parity of resources and capacity for action exists between the belligerents, and where social values are more or less shared. Where there is disparity, and where social values are markedly different, as, for example, where ideologies exercise an influence, then each side finds it possible to deny the rights and the humanity of the other and to pursue violence without restraint.

The rationale of total war, in any case, precludes restraint, on the general ground that self-denial in developing or using forms of violence may lead to disadvantage. The development, if not the actual use, of the atomic bomb, stemmed from the fear that Germany would develop and use it first. This fear of competition is a potent factor in arms races both in peace and in war, and exercises a strong influence on attempts to control and limit weapons development through arms control negotiations. The prevailing rationale is thus based upon security competition, and constraint in the production and use of weapons, where it exists, depends not upon shared ethical or moral values, but upon utility and shared perceptions of the instrumental character of weapons in terms of the interests they serve. Thus so long as security is a central concern, and so long as it is based upon a competitive rationale, no state can afford to accept voluntary restraints that apply to it alone, or forego opportunities to achieve relative advantage. Only where it is clearly seen to be counterproductive will a state abstain from taking action that is nominally unethical. State security is the *ultima ratio*.

On this argument, all wars that involve national security are just in character. And almost any use of threat of violence against other states can be justified in terms of security. Where the conflict becomes a genuine question of national survival, then whatever its immediate cause, the use and form of violence is unrestrained by any consideration short of the achievement of victory. This apocalyptic contest is implicit in the very notion of just war. And it follows from this that a just war cannot be fought justly if its end is the overthrow of a state that resorted to war unjustly. Nor can the threat of an inevitable defeat be made, using conventional weapons, as a deterrent to those willing to resort to war in pursuit of national interests short of national survival. As we have seen earlier, the utility of such weapons is a matter more of practice than of theory and, short of war itself, there is no means of demonstrating their efficacy.

So far, the discussion has concentrated on war in its most extreme form. Before examining constraints on war provision and threats of war in peacetime, particularly those related to deterrence and nuclear weapons, I want to examine the more general notion of world order as manifest in the notion of a balance of power. The present situation of mutual defensive deterrence between the major nuclear powers has been described as a balance of this kind. What is a balance of power, and, should it exist, does it exercise a general constraining influence upon states and their propensity to resort to war or employ particular forms of violence against each other? The previous discussion placed the emphasis on the nation-state and its concern for survival in a world of potentially hostile states. National security was seen in purely national terms. Is there any qualification to this basically anarchic view? Are states constrained by the environment they collectively create and the rules that operate in it? There are two kinds of rules relevant here; constitutive rules that define the system, or set of relations, and regulative, those that direct it. For example, as Kaplan has argued,[30] a balance of power relationship is defined by the operation of a governing principle, such that, when one state seeks to aggrandise itself, the other participating states move to counter it. The regulative rules direct the manner in which they operate, through arms production, combination, and negotiation and diplomacy.

Such rules, if indeed they exist, depend upon recognition and perception by all the states participating in the system. It may have been the case, for example, that the British decisions to go to war with Germany in 1914 and in 1939 were based on the notion of maintaining a balance in Europe, seeking to prevent the domination of any one state. In the event, the consequence of resisting the Central and Axis powers was total war and the virtual destruction of any purely European balance. The point here is that the operation of constitutive rules governing inter-state relations depends on the acceptance of a common rationale by all those states involved. They must recognise the nature of the game they are playing. As we shall see when nuclear deterrence is discussed in the context of arms control, this is of some importance. Uncontrolled violence under nuclear conditions jeopardises the very existence of states.

If constitutive rules are considered to be binding on states in the sense of their operation as laws, as might be the case where a balance of power is seen as akin to a state of nature, tending towards some form of equilibrium between states, then a different kind of argument is involved. If the use of terms such as balance of equilibrium is not merely figurative, then some notion of the operation of forces beyond the direct control of states applies. Those who subscribe to this view must set out the conditions and operative principles that produces such situations in inter-state relations. In essence these would conform to the covering-law mode of explanation discussed earlier in this work. Questions of perception and consciousness are of course irrelevant in this context. Rules in this case correspond to laws that offer no choice; given the appropriate conditions and the covering principle, all states are forced to act and react in a particular way. This is implicit in the argument that a balance of power system operates as a set of compelling and mechanical forces.

Turning to regulative rules, if we accept that the constitutive framework within which they apply is a common rationale generally accepted by states, then the element of choice exists. Rules are not so much binding as related to a form of reasoning constructed around a number of assumptions about the proper, or desirable, (or otherwise) behaviour of states. For example, when the Kaiser realised that the quick victory promised by the Schlieffen Plan was frustrated by the Battle of the Marne he had the option of negotiation. However, his initial successes in Belgium, North Eastern France, and in Russia, meant that any negotiation would proceed with the Allies being at a disadvantage. The alternative was total war and an absolute victory that produced hegemony or dominion rather than a new balance. Similarly, Hitler in challenging the Versailles system, found himself fighting a total war in which the object became the domination of Europe rather than a revised balance of power. The consequence of victory was an armed peace and a division of Europe into spheres of influence, and of Germany into two states. In short, the rationale of a balance of power system is a minimal agreement, not only on what it constitutes in political terms but on the means of changing it through setting limits on violence and with a negotiated settlement as the ultimate goal. Essentially, the politics of appeasement, that is of accepting the revision of the Versailles system, and the reality of German rearmament and its implications, sought to do this. Even the war itself, once it had begun, was prosecuted as a limited contest. It was Hitler's success in defeating France in 1940 that changed the character of the war and made it total. Observing and maintaining a balance of power where there is no general agreement on its terms, not only becomes impossible, but is likely to degenerate into conditions of total war and a radically different rationale.

The problem with relating regulative rules to a conceptual framework such as the balance of power lies in its inherent ambiguity. Almost any policy, decision, or action, taken by a state, can be justified by reference to maintaining or creating a balance between nations. The concept of balance outside mechanics is nebulous, especially when applied to the volatile field of international politics. It tends to become a synonym for the political status quo, however unsatisfactory this may be to some states. This is true also of the concept of power. Does this apply to the potential for violence, to resources and population, the size and character of extant and potential forces, the combination of these in the form of alliances, wealth and economic leverage, relative sophistication of the national economy and its potential, technological superiority, or the political ability to command and deploy any or all of these factors? As I have argued elsewhere, power is as power does,[31] that is, it can only be assessed retrospectively. While all statesmen make some estimation of potential opposition in terms of commitment and capacity, and relate foreign and defence policies to it, this is far from being an accurate science especially in the era of conventional weapons.

Power is usually considered to be related to the postulated capacity to use or threaten force in order to attain an object. It is the latter aspect—the dimension of threat—that is most common in descriptions of balance of power. Once a threat has been implemented, then the balance, whatever it is conceived to be, is destroyed and war ensues. As we have seen in this century, such wars are largely uncontrolled, both in their prosecution and in their political consequences, producing radical changes in inter-state relations unenvisaged by those resorting to war. They are not directed to the achievement of a new and more stable balance between states. This leads to the central problem in using images such as balance of power, both as a description of inter-state politics, and as a basis for prescription. This is the problem of security. Threats of violence, implicit or explicit, are ambiguous in that the consequences of their implementation cannot be known in advance, nor can be confined to limited objectives very easily. They set up a dynamic of response that depends on the level of conciousness of other statesmen and their values and objectives.

This cannot be known or appreciated in advance of action. For example, Chamberlain when faced with Hitler's challenge to Czecho-slovakia in 1938 contemplated the use or threat of force as a deterrent. But he concluded that the Czechs could not be helped by military means. Britain itself was vulnerable to air attack from Germany. A threat of violence was therefore not a viable means of achieving an accommodation with Germany. Whether Chamberlain was right or wrong in this assessment of relative military capacities is a question that can only be argued from hindsight and in any case, as we have seen from earlier discussion, cannot be subjected to any truth conditions. It illustrates two major points concerning security. First, the factor of relativity in technological changes in weapons systems is important. In spite of naval superiority Britain was exposed to attacks on both shipping and territory from the Luftwaffe. Such relativities are equivocal and unstable. They are equivocal in that the operational effectiveness, and so the desired military and political results of weapons systems, cannot easily be predicted, especially where they are radically different. They are unstable in that there is a perceived need to innovate or produce weaponry, in order to match or surpass an opponent, before seeking settlements that are binding and conclusive. This is the so-called policy of negotiation from strength. Chamberlain argued that the Munich agreement bought time for Britain and so enabled a measure of rearmament, especially in the air force, so that Germany could be challenged on more equal terms. But of course arms races and competition in weapons procurement are inherently de-stabilising, particularly where their value as political instruments cannot easily be assessed, as is the case for all conventional forms of weapons.

This leads on to the second point, namely the difficulty of separating security from other national interests. The level of resources devoted to weapons provision as well as being ambiguous in terms of the 'power' it produces, confuses two policy goals—the defence of the state and the promotion of national interests short of this. If we take the example of appeasement again, Chamberlain did not want to fight a total war over the question of the Sudetenland, especially since Hitler appeared to have a reasonable case based on the principle of self-determination, to which the victor powers had paid lip-service in their peace-settlement after the war. Yet he wished to deter Hitler from pursuing policies supported by threats of violence, calculated to destroy the Versailles settlement. Such deterrence could only come from posing an equivalent threat through rearmament and alliance. The cost of continuing the policy of revision through coercion would thus be that of fighting a war. But the threat of such a war was also a challenge, not merely to those inimical policies, but to German security. The issue then became not that of changing the European map and reversing the consequences of military defeat in the First World War, but the very existence of the German Reich. How could Chamberlain so limit his threat as to force Hitler to become more compliant, without turning it into total war? In the event, the challenge was made over Poland and the war that ensued had little to do with the issues with which it began. Both Chamberlain and Hitler became committed to the struggle for reasons that were in part political and related to their own political credibility. But this was implicit in the challenge itself, on both sides.

The problem with the notion of a balance of power is that it is always retrospective. We only know what it was once it has been destroyed. The active pursuit of a balancing policy tends to result in material calculations based on the assessment of relative military capacities and thus introducing, or reinforcing, the element of competition that leads to disruption. Using violence, or threats of violence, to maintain a postulated balance can only be successful where the limits to violence are set and observed, and where there is a reasonable prospect of agreement through negotiation. There must be no explicit threat to security. In the instance cited, it was unfortunate that the states directly challenged by Germany— Czechoslovakia and Poland—were geographically and politically isolated. The ultimatum made to Hitler in his eyes appeared to be unrealisable in practice, and he refused to believe its sincerity since it threatened a total war over a relatively trivial issue. It was incommensurate and so irrational. In this he was wrong.

It is clear that the idea of balance of power owes more to myth than to reality, and accords more with those states anxious to preserve the political status quo. There are no rules, constitutive, or regulative, that can support it in practice. The factor of control necessary to its maintenance is absent. Any element of constraint in situations where threats of violence are made, depends upon effective retaliation and so military deficiencies and relativities determine the course of action and consequent reactions. Violence is thus born of violence and the original political issues become subordinate to the major question of security.

Nevertheless, the idea of balance persists and states actively seek to prevent other states from increasing their power and influence through the development of what is seen as countervailing power. This is seen largely in terms of military capacity and in the context of a rough equivalence in weapons technology related to factor of time and space. Territory and spatial relations are the main determinants of security policy. The abandonment of isolationism by the United States after the Second World

War illustrates this. The advent of new technology with the introduction of nuclear weapons meant that any advantages to be derived from geographical isolation disappeared. In any case, the policy of keeping political options open and avoiding entangling alliances, had meant that the intiative passed into the hands of other states. It was necessary to pre-empt their freedom of action by posing a military threat that not only constrained communism and preserved the political status quo, but also provided the United States with security. NATO thus became a security system that enabled the United States to inhibit the Soviet Union and other states from extending their power and influence beyond the Elbe, while at the same time gave it the necessary global reach for its nuclear weapons. It was yet another change in military technology, as we have seen earlier, that nullified this policy. The inter-continental ballistic missile made both territory and space irrelevant in security terms.

I want to examine this new situation and its consequences for the inter-state system. Does the nuclear stalemate between the major nuclear powers introduce a constraint upon the use of violence as a means of attaining political objectives? Is there a common rationale shared by these states concerning defensive deterrence and its associated inhibitions? What is the relevance of arms control to these questions? If we return to the discussion earlier in this work on deterrence, a distinction was made between offensive and defensive deterrence. Both operate as constraints but in different ways. The former exists only where the deterring state has a monopoly of the means of violence. All things being equal, it is capable of making a credible threat of such magnitude as to provide for both national security and the promotion and protection of other national interests in the world at large. This is to postulate a hegemonial or imperial condition for the world of states, with the monopolist able to exert its will on all other states. In practice of course this is not so easy since, as the adage says, one can do anything with bayonets except sit on them! Nevertheless, a state with a monopoly of nuclear weapons is in a powerful position providing it can deliver them effectively.

Defensive deterrence, however, can be linked with credibility only to the first of these two categories of objective. It can provide security. This is because no monopoly of violence exists and so no credible threat can be made to an opponent possessing an equivalent capacity of violence. Since the destructive effects of nuclear missiles can be precisely evaluated then relative capacities and equations of losses can be measured. No gain can be postulated from the use of nuclear weapons in the form of limited strikes, and resort to total nuclear war would be suicidal for all parties. A distinction can thus be made between a capacity for violence and its object, in a way that was not possible with conventional weapons with their inherent ambiguities. In the case of defensive deterrence, the rationale of threat is to deter any attack on a state which possesses effective means of retaliation. No nuclear state can thus threaten another nuclear state, with credibility, short of this. If this argument is accepted, then means of violence can be allocated to task as was not possible in the period of conventional war. Clearly a good deal depends on all states accepting this rationale.

It should be emphasised that defensive deterrence is not a function of the size of the nuclear arsenal. It depends on the existence of an invulnerable retaliatory capacity capable of inflicting unacceptable damage on a potential aggressor. It might be objected that in a confrontation between major and minor nuclear power (in quantitative terms), the former might be able to intimidate the latter by making limited nuclear strikes on its territory. While to retaliate using its full capacity would be to invite annihilation and so be deemed unlikely, the minor state can still retaliate in kind. The major nuclear power would then be faced with the choice of continuing to the point of a general exchange, in which case it would itself be severely crippled, albeit having destroyed its opponent. Such a process of attrition, while technically possible, lacks political rationality. There are a number of imponderables such as the reactions of the indigenous populations on both sides to the series of strikes. There is also the existence of other nuclear powers, perhaps outside this immediate contest, but willing to exploit weakness on the part of the surviving state. But most important is the fact that the reactions of the minor power cannot be predicted and if it retaliated with its full force the consequence would be as disastrous to the state initiating nuclear strikes, as to its victim. It is hard to conceive of a political objective that merits such a risk, especially since the security of the major nuclear power is guaranteed by its own nuclear forces.

The minor nuclear power possesses only defensive capacity. It could not therefore initiate nuclear strikes on a major nuclear power without risking annihilation. It presents no threat to security. Indeed it is inhibited from making such a threat by the fear of retaliation. This extends to other political levels. It would be equally dangerous, and also irrational, to threaten violence in pursuit of non-security interests, for both minor and major nuclear powers. An attempt to coerce or to force a minor nuclear power into submission on a political issue immediately raises the question of its survival as a state when nuclear weapons are involved. And, consequently, the survival of the aggressor is also involved because of the nuclear level. No rational end can be postulated where survival becomes the issue in a confrontation between nuclear powers.

On this argument national security provision depends on the observations of a set of constraints on the use and threat of violence in the world of states, based on the principle of mutual defensive nuclear deterrence. The threat of violence, implicit in defensive deterrence, is confined to retaliation in the event of aggression on the territory of the nuclear state. Nothing else is deterred. But, whatever interests a nuclear power has in the world at large, they cannot be pursued to the point of using violence directly against a nuclear opponent since this would invoke the deterrent threat. Wars involving nuclear powers are thus limited in scale and confined to third-party territory. Moreover, there is a common interest in establishing rules governing the use of nuclear weapons in the form of arms control agreements. Control over weapons procurement, over the ends new weapons are designed to fulfil, and over the element of competition in this respect, between nuclear powers, becomes extremely important if stability is to be preserved. Given the risks involved, and the consequences of nuclear war, there is a common interest in establishing some form of regulation.

While a definition of security and recognition of some of its conditions exists, there are problems arising out of this rationale for the promotion and maintenance of interests that fall short of this. The two major alliance systems, NATO and the Warsaw Pact, were created during an intensive arms race. As was noted earlier, the major delivery system for atomic bombs during the formative years of these alliances was the long range bomber. Ringed by western bases the Soviet Union was concerned to place as much distance between major industrial and population targets and attacking forces. It was important to create a buffer zone in Eastern Europe, and the Warsaw Pact was a means of doing so, reinforced by political control over the satellite countries. For its part the United States could only reach Soviet targets by using foreign bases in friendly countries. There was both a military and a political quid pro quo in the development of this relationship. The United States, with its nuclear monopoly, was able to provide protection from potential Soviet aggression for members of NATO. And a multilateral economic system was created, using American credit which benefited both sides and which underpinned the political combination.[32] The advent of the inter-continental ballistic missile had a radical effect on this arrangement. The point here is that both NATO and the Warsaw Pact reflect an outmoded weapons technology and an outmoded rationale. Within them political and economic ties have become extremely important, but the link with collective security is seriously weakened by the new development.

Neither of the major nuclear powers can credibly threaten to attack the other on behalf of an ally. Nor are these allies necessary, as once they were, for the security of their major partners. Yet NATO and the Warsaw Pact are alliances designed to provide a collective response to an attack upon a member state. As was argued earlier, this is done under conditions of mutual defensive deterrence by the threat of ally-swapping. This is an indirect response and one which is highly prejudicial to the security of the non-nuclear allies. Until the introduction of medium-range SS20 missiles by the Soviet Union into the European theatre,[33] the preponderant conventional forces of the Warsaw Pact were offset by western theatre nuclear weapons directed against the non-nuclear allies of the Soviet Union. The basic NATO strategy was an initial defensive holding operation at the conventional level, designed to limit Soviet territorial gains, followed by an early use of theatre nuclear weapons. By this means any Soviet attack would be deterred by making it unproductive and costly. Two of the allies, France and Britain, early insured themselves against an extension of the attack to their territory by developing nuclear deterrents independent of the NATO structure. Conversely, the Warsaw Pact countries were defended against Western aggression by the preponderance of conventional forces and by the Soviet Union's own nuclear weapons directed against the nuclear hostages—the non-nuclear powers of NATO. Both major powers clearly hoped to confine the effects of any war to Germany, both the FDR and the DDR.

Now a good deal of this argument is tacit and depends on a level of understanding that can hardly be expressed in a more public manner. The problem is that arms control agreements designed to maintain the stability of the overall strategic balance have an effect on alliance relationships and on the use of violence to promote other than non-security objectives. The security of the nuclear powers is guaranteed through the observance of rules embodied in a number of arms control agreements. They seek to stabilise the strategic balance and endorse the main conditions of defensive nuclear deterrence. As was noted earlier in this work, these are, vulnerable territory, an invulnerable retaliatory capacity, a moratorium on radical innovation in weapons technology, the acceptance of these constraints by the negotiants, and a free exchange of information regarding their nuclear capabilities. In qualitative terms, in spite of the proliferation of weapons systems, their increased destructive capacity, accuracy, and sophistication, there has been no radical change since the appearance of nuclear parity in the early 1960s.[34] It should be stressed that quantitative terms are relevant only in the sense that numbers of warheads have a bearing on survival, and on the infliction in retaliation of a level of damage unacceptable to the nuclear adversary. This can be achieved in principle at a relatively low figure, and the main reasons why nuclear arsenals are so large and so varied are firstly, the need for a plurality of weapons systems as an insurance against the development of an effective counter to any one of them; secondly as a means of enhancing a negotiating position by allowing room for sacrifice and manoeuvre; and thirdly, as a consequence of political momentum, whereby obsolescent and new weapons are retained and introduced as a means of avoiding the charge of appeasement through lack of political will.

For example, the so-called Triad strategy of the United States combining nuclear weapons systems that can be delivered from the air, land and sea is designed to guarantee a minimal deterrent in the event of a Soviet counter being devised against one of them. If hardened missiles silos can be destroyed there remain underwater launched missiles. Multiple re-entry vehicles make the total elimination of a retaliatory attack unlikely, and so on. It is unlikely that a means of eliminating all of these systems will be found by an adversary. Similarly, the creation of the Safeguard anti-ballistic missile system by President Nixon was not intended as a serious contribution to American defence, but as a means of forcing the Soviet Union to reconsider its own anti-missile system development, and to conclude SALT I which preserved the balanced defensive deterrent and avoided a new arms race. Finally, the continued retention of the obsolete Thor and Vulcan missiles of President Kennedy was largely because of the myth of a nonexistent missile gap in his election campaign and his consequent fear of appearing weak or inconsistent. Moreover, although he had decided to remove Jupiter missiles from Italy and Turkey, given their obsolesence, he could not afford to do so in response to Soviet demands that this be done as a quid pro quo for the removal of Soviet missiles in Cuba.[35] They also had another function relevant to this discussion, namely, that their presence, although irrelevant to American security, served as a tangible guarantee of the American commitment to the security of these states. They symbolised the determination of the United States to protect its allies, and any withdrawal, especially under pressure from the Soviet Union, would undermine belief in it. As we shall see, weapons serve other purposes than their nominal role.

There are two broad aspects of arms control; the first is directly related to maintaining the strategic balance and its rationale of mutual defensive deterrence. Any unilateral attempt to convert defensive into offensive deterrence through radical innovation in weapons technology, as, for example, President Reagan's strategic defence initiative (if it is taken at its face value), or as a means of protecting the population and industrial centres, would produce an arms race in which advantages would have to be seized when they occur. For a genuine arms race to be rational, there must be some realisable conception of victory. Arms races must be won if they are to be worth undertaking. But in terms of nuclear weapons what is the end sought? As we have seen in earlier chapters, one of the main national objectives pursued through the use of threat of violence is security, in minimal terms, defined as the preservation of the homeland from attack. Defensive deterrence, provided its rationale is understood and observed by the nuclear powers, offers a guarantee of this.

In this context arms control is designed to reinforce this mutual understanding by limiting innovation in weapons systems, so that unilateral advantages are eschewed in favour of stability. This implies a perception of a common constraint in the field of weapons technology and in the strategic deployment of weapons systems. The 'arms race' under these conditions may lead to the refinement of existing forms of weaponry, but not to any qualitative change in the overall balance. If one side actively seeks to achieve offensive deterrence capacity, that is to attain superiority, then arms control gives way to a contest whose rational conclusion is war. Why is this the case? The reason is that the sole purpose of nuclear weapons is the provision of security. If this is seen in terms of superiority in weapons, that is reverting to the security dilemma of the conventional war period, then the only way to maintain an advantage is to deprive an adversary of its capacity to challenge it. In the context of nuclear weapons, or indeed of any kind of weaponry, this means in practice using violence to enforce and maintain the superiority.

The appearance of ABM systems in the 1960s was such an innovation in weapons technology. Introduced by the Soviet Union, there was a distinct threat that an arms race was in being which could lead to war. If one state perfected a defensive system that could make it invulnerable to nuclear attack, it would then enjoy offensive deterrence. Its security would be guaranteed by its immunity from attack, both nuclear and non-nuclear. It would also enjoy the capacity to use all means of violence to pursue non-security ends with relative impunity. The prospect of this possibility led the United States to introduce a similar system, but the intention of forcing a moratorium in this development through an arms control agreement.[36] It must be said that ABM systems were open to criticism in terms of their effectiveness but, given the incentive to perfect them in the form of competition, as the ICBM emerged out of relatively crude delivery systems, so it can be assumed would be the case for the ABM. Whichever state 'won' this particular development would be compelled to use its advantage in the form of a pre-emptive war, or be forced to accept yet another stalemate.

Paradoxically, if both competing states arrived at a perfectly functioning ABM system simultaneously, then they would have achieved the effect of making nuclear missiles redundant. They would still be faced with the problem of security unresolved. While nuclear war would be precluded, given their invulnerability to missile attack, they would be exposed to other forms of attack. In short, they would have reverted to the pre-nuclear situation of open-ended conventional war, or perhaps alternative technologies in fields such as bio-chemical warfare would be developed. Such a situation would not be a rational end to a programme of weapons procurement designed to provide security. SALT I and its supplementary protocol ensured that this would not happen.

However, since its negotiation, and that of SALT II this prospect has been revived in the form of the strategic defence initiative. As with its predecessor, its practicality has been seriously questioned. Nevertheless, if it is a genuine programme designed to provide an effective defence of the territory and military capacity of the United States, it marks a qualitative change in the arms race. Before examining this it is instructive to make a comparison between the political situation of the late 1960s and the present. The second aspect of arms control is its links with political as opposed to security interests. The Soviet Union has succeeded in achieving parity at the strategic level and this led, as we have seen, to the definition of security in terms of mutual defensive deterrence. There were political consequences that followed from this. Both sides had become enmeshed in alliance systems in which they undertook to provide security for their weaker allies. The rationale for this in security terms stemmed from the relative primitive delivery systems that existed in the post-war period and the existence of an American monopoly, followed by period of superiority in its ability to inflict damage on the USSR. Forward bases were necessary and these were found in Europe and globally. The political divisions after the Second World War were thus endorsed by permanent alliance systems confronting each other, and whose logic was derived from the notion of security that prevailed at that time.

The advent of long range missiles that could be delivered from home territory, from the air, or underwater, made forward bases both irrelevant and dangerous since they could not easily be defended. It was at this point that arms control agreements began to be made and a tacit recognition of the new balance emerged. But the whole network of commitments and relationships was still binding. The problem was that the provision of security for allies became an obligation that, in a number of ways, conflicted with maintaining the conditions for strategic balance. Because of the geo-political positions of the two major powers—one in situ on the European continent and one relatively remote; one more or less imposing its authority on its allies, the other having a more equivocal political relationship, this provision took the form, on the Soviet side, of a large standing army policing Eastern Europe, and, on the American side, of a smaller conventional force supported by theatre nuclear weapons intended to redress the imbalance. Two of the Western allies, Britain and France, stood outside this situation, possessing defensive deterrents of their own.

The implied threat was that any breach of the political status quo on the part of the Soviet Union would be met by an early use of limited range nuclear weapons. Strikes would be made, not on the Soviet Union since, given the existence of parity, this would invite direct retaliation on the United States, but on the non-nuclear Eastern European allies. A limited nuclear war was thus the only rational war that could be fought under these conditions. It would be fought on the non-nuclear territory of Europe. Arms control thus had to take into account security provision for allies based upon this capacity. Yet this did not involve the overall strategic balance between the two major nuclear powers, since this depended on the rationale of mutual defensive deterrence. In the event, what was called detente appeared as a consequence of the agreements at the strategic level. Both parties agreed not to seek any qualitative changes in the strategic balance through the development of ABM systems, or any other innovative and de-stabilising measure. Implicitly, and indeed explicitly, in the form of agreements between Western Germany and its eastern neighbours, detente was an acceptance on both sides of the *de facto* changes in the map of Europe that had been made since the Second World War. The *ostpolitik*[37] of the Brandt government was sanctioned by the United States and endorsed by the Soviet Union. What had been a manifestation of the Cold War and deemed unacceptable by both sides was no longer a matter of controversy. The West German government accepted the loss of German territories in the East and, with East Germany, recognised the abrogation of the Munich Agreement and the new frontiers established at Potsdam. But Germany remained divided, together with its former capital, Berlin.

The point here is that arms control agreements seek to do two things; firstly, to provide stability for the overall strategic balance between the nuclear powers and, secondly, to obtain endorsement of other interests related to non-security issues. In this case a moratorium on ABM systems went hand in hand with agreement on defining sphere of influence in Europe and perhaps elsewhere. It was no coincidence that this coincided with the American withdrawal from Vietnam. However, the problem remained of providing a credible defence of the non-nuclear allies without

251 Reasoning and Violence

jeopardising the overall strategic balance. Moreover, given the existence of foreign interests and commitments, it was tempting to try to relate military capacity, designed to provide security, to their protection. As we shall see, the notion of extended or enhanced deterrence entered American strategic thinking.

The problem of extending deterrence to non-nuclear allies was exacerbated by the introduction of SS20 missiles into Europe by the Soviet Union in 1979. This compounded NATO's problems in devising a credible strategy to counter Soviet attack since these medium range, mobile, missiles neutralised Western missiles while leaving an imbalance in their respective conventional forces. West Germany appeared to be particularly vulnerable. Any attack across the Elbe would be transformed into a nuclear war, limited it is true to non-nuclear Europe, but devastating to those countries in the battle-zone. While such a war would not be relevant to American security, or indeed the security of Britain and France, given the force of mutual defensive deterrence, their economic and other interests would be seriously compromised. The solution to this possibility lay either in the unpalatable expedient of increasing conventional forces to match those of the Warsaw Pact countries, or, somehow, forcing the Soviet Union to withdraw, and preferably, destroy, their SS20 missiles. Destruction was preferable, since being mobile, they could be brought back into Europe or redeployed against China and Japan, thus threatening American interests outside Europe. How could the Soviet Union be induced to do this? Why would the Soviet Union, having emplaced these missiles and matched Western theatre missiles, agree to revert to the former imbalance?

As we saw with the earlier ABM issue, the United States succeeded in coming to an agreement with the Soviet Union that effectively checked an arms race.[38] The implications of instability at the strategic level were not lost on the leaders of both countries. The threat of a parallel development made by the USA was sufficient to produce agreement. But the introduction of SS20s into the European theatre did not present a threat to American security on the strategic level, although, of course, it did present a threat to the security of the non-nuclear states. The initial American response was the introduction of the cruise missiles into Europe. These missiles, although sub-sonic and slow, are not easily detected on radar defences. However, given their relatively limited range they are not a direct threat to the Soviet Union and so in this sense are not de-stabilising. Similarly, the development of the MX missile, an ICBM, with land mobility, did not present any challenge to the strategic balance, being only a further sophistication of existing weapons. It was the strategic defence initiative that appeared to have radical implications.

The form this proposal will take is extremely vague and in terms of rhetoric takes on the force of King Lear's threat,

> 'I will do such things —
> What they are yet I know not — but they shall be
> The terrors of the earth.'

The principle of a complete defence against missiles, if fulfilled, would confer on its possessor both offensive and defensive deterrence. The only constraints on freedom of action would be of the order discussed in the early part of this chapter. No major power could afford to be placed in a vulnerable position due to such an innovation. The likely consequence on precedent is another arms race. The previous arms race moved from atomic to hydrogen or thermonuclear bombs, and from aircraft to ballistic missiles, eventually producing a stalemate and a negative form of security embodied in mutual defensive deterrence. It is unlikely that a new arms race would follow this pattern, since its aims would be to destroy the efficacy of ballistic missiles. In order to do so, existing arms control agreements would have to be abandoned and indeed the whole arms control process would be nullified, thus setting a dangerous precedent for the future by the very abandonment of rules. And there would be a strong incentive to develop alternative weapons systems to missiles and these might include biological and chemical weapons for which there are no precedents. The consequences of the previous arms race were unintended. They were not foreseen. It is highly probable that this will be the case if a new arms race comes into being. But perhaps the most dangerous aspect of the strategic defence initiative is that it is premised on superiority; that is, the aim is to achieve a perfect form of defence unilaterally. If it does not succeed in that then the only achievement is to make missiles redundant without solving the problem of security.

Having said this, it may be the case that the Reagan administration is seeking to do what Nixon did, that is use such a radical threat to force the Soviet Union to make concessions at the sub-strategic level. It may be a bluff. In retrospect it was clear that President Nixon wanted the Safeguard system not as a genuine strategic measure but as a means of threatening the Soviet Union with an expensive and futile arms race if it persisted in deploying its Galosh system. SALT I was the consequence. In this case the object is to use a threat of innovation at the strategic level in order to protect interests at the sub-strategic level. Recent claims for the SDI have reduced its objective from providing a complete defence for the American population, to the provision of enhanced deterrence for existing missiles. The implicit threat exists but the suggestion is made that given the appropriate assurances from the Soviet Union on European missiles it will not be implemented. The intention is merely to strengthen the existing deterrent posture and thus maintain the balance. Its purpose is simply a form of damage-limitation. In other words the SDI may simply be a form of rhetoric and a means of negotiating arms control agreements that seek to insure foreign interests rather than operating at the level of security. The progress made in the negotiations on theatre nuclear weapons to date, seems to support this view. Again it is not the technicalities of such negotiations that are important but the fact of agreement and the consequent endorsement of the political status quo by both sides. It stands as a substitute or surrogate for the peace treaty that was not negotiated at the end of the Second World War and accepts the division of Germany, and of Europe, as a *de facto* settlement.

While states are free to abandon constraints whether in the form of negotiated agreements, or as a tacitly accepted rules, when it appears in their interest to do so, it does not appear to be likely in this instance. Arms control agreements have been kept, although sometimes it appears more in the letter than in the spirit, and the rationale of mutual defensive deterrence has operated for some twenty years, a relatively long time in international politics. This leads on to another form of constraint, that of obtaining the consent and support of the domestic political system. In the case of the Soviet Union this is a matter of speculation since there is little access to decision-making, either by analysts or the general public. The strategic debate is more open in the United States, although much less so in the United Kingdom. A number of important arms control agreements have not been ratified in the USA as a consequence of electoral and political forces. SALT II was withdrawn by President Carter from the ratification process in 1979.[39] The ostensible reason for this was the Soviet intervention in Afghanistan, another case of sub-strategic interests conflicting with the strategic level, since by no stretch of the imagination could this intervention be said to endanger American security or presage an upsurge in Soviet imperialism![40] The Threshold Nuclear Test Ban Treaty, that set a 150 kiloton limitation on underground tests, the Peaceful Nuclear Explosions Treaty that set a similar limit on non-military underground explosions, and also provided for limited on-site inspection, and the convention banning military modification of the environment, all failed to achieve Senate ratification.[41] Since the first Presidential election that placed Reagan in the White House, there has been a vociferous campaign against arms control, alleging changes in the strategic balance adverse to the United States. Pressure groups such as the Committee on the Present Danger[42] have sought to influence strategic decision and promote innovations in weapons development, such as those related to the SDI. Domestic politics in the United States, and politics between allies, constitute a form of constraint that cannot be ignored by political contenders in times of elections, or, given the nature of democratic politics with its bargaining and consensus aspects, at any other time.

If we look more closely at this debate the central argument made by those advocating a change in the American strategic posture concerns the effects of the increased accuracy and destructive power of multiple re-entry vehicles (MIRV). The move towards these sophisticated devices was initiated by the United States at the time of the first SALT negotiations. Given an acceptance of limits on the number of launchers, it appeared rational to increase the number of warheads they could carry. Given the logic of mutual defensive deterrence it is hard to see the point of this development except that it was assumed that the Soviet Union could not easily follow suit. This assumption was invalid and since the Soviets in any case built larger missiles with more powerful warheads because they could not match the accuracy of American missiles, the consequence when they eventually succeeded in both making MIRVs and increasing their accuracy, was that they posed a threat to the Minuteman missile silos in the USA. The result according to some American strategists was that it was possible for the Soviet Union to make a disarming first strike and remove some 90 per cent of American fixed ICBM capacity. The United States would then be faced with the difficult choice of abstaining from counter action or initiating with what was left of its missile and bomber capacity strikes on Soviet cities knowing that the Soviets could retaliate with much larger forces. This was called the 'window of vulnerability' and, it was argued, it should be closed by, *inter alia*, the SDI and the development of mobile ICBMs such as the MX system.[43] In any case arms control should be abandoned altogether, given the Soviet advantage and their alleged cheating.

The argument is a specious one and owes more the rhetoric than to strategic reality. On strategic grounds the fact is that submarine launched missiles are immune from attack and, with the new Trident D5 weapon system, not only possess the range to operate from protected i.e., 'home' coastal waters, but also have the accuracy to strike with precision Soviet silos and 'protected' targets. The United States is thus able to strike, or threaten to strike, the Soviet Union and inflict a level of unacceptable damage as a credible counter to any Soviet threat of attack. This after all is the rationale of the Triad. In any case there are solutions to the alleged vulnerability of the Minuteman silos; such as placing more emphasis on underwater launched missiles, making land-based missiles more mobile; concentrating them and protecting them through fratricide or ABM systems, or increasing their number making it more unlikely that they will be eliminated in an attack. Or, of course, negotiating an arms control agreement that banned or restricted MIRVs and restored the position to some form of numerical balance based on single warhead launchers.

However, the central dilemma for American strategists, as was discussed earlier, is the problem of extending deterrence to protect and promote interests outside the United States in the form of security provision for non-nuclear allies. It is the sub-strategic level and not the strategic level that is their primary concern. This is directly linked to feelings of political impotence generated by the debacle of Vietnam and consequent humiliations in Iran and the Middle East. These have electoral consequences. The problem for American policy-makers is not merely obtaining re-election and political support for measures designed to maintain interests abroad, as that there are genuine limits and constraints on what can be done in this direction. There is no general consensus on an active interventionist policy involving the use on any large scale of American forces in areas where American interests cannot be shown to be central. It is difficult to show that American security is directly at stake in maintaining the political status quo in the world at large. In short there is a constraint in terms of the domestic political climate that inhibits direct interventionist policies. When this is combined with the constraints imposed by the need to observe the conditions of mutual defensive deterrence, it is clear that the scope for action is not very large. It is in this context that the strategic debate in the United States should be assessed. Those who cite the vulnerability of the United States to nuclear attack (the counter-force argument) are in reality urging a position of damage limitation that would extend deterrence to include the ability to engage in limited nuclear war at the minimum level and to win a nuclear war at the maximum level. In other words the notion of actually winning a nuclear war has become current. This means accepting a level of damage providing it was lower than could be inflicted on an opponent. Limiting this damage appears to be a rational policy.[44]

As was pointed out earlier, the successful achievement of a near-perfect defence would confer both offensive and defensive deterrence on the United States. But a large measure of damage limitation would also decrease the risk of using or threatening to use nuclear weapons, and so enable them to become relevant in the pursuit of political objectives in Europe and the Far East. In a sense this debate is not about American security, since this is provided through the rationale of MAD and arms control agreements, but is about the United States' political role in the world. Given Soviet parity or 'essential equivalence' in deterrent capability and its local military and logistical advantages deriving from its geographical position and resources, the American ability to defend its interests through threat of violence is strictly limited and, in the event of their implementation, counterproductive. A limited nuclear exchange in non-nuclear Europe would damage the United States and its allies far more than it would the Soviet Union. It follows from this that arms control agreements that simply endorse the nuclear stalemate without also endorsing the respective spheres of influence of the major powers, have little attraction to the American political leadership. They underline the relative diminution of American power and influence in the world following Vietnam and SALT I.

If we look back at the domestic political context within which SALT I was negotiated, we find a very different situation to that which prevails at present. The Council of Foreign Relations, a strong lobby then, had urged the administration in January 1969 to adopt a *unilateral* moratorium on both ABMs and on MIRVs. The Nixon administration was handicapped in negotiating its way out of Vietnam by the Congressional programme of the phased withdrawal of troops and by the clever tactics of the North Vietnamese. The prevailing political sentiment was in favour of withdrawal, against such foreign adventures, and generally in support of arms control agreements. There was also an undercurrent of feelings of humiliation at the failure in Vietnam and the subsequent need to treat with communist governments.

The American ABM programme began with a proposal by Macnamara in 1967 for Sentinel. According to Kissinger, he realised its value as a bargaining weapon and Nixon urged its development under the name Safeguard. As an indication of political feelings on this issue, Senate approved the programme by only one vote. Testing the MIRV began in April 1968. It was the obvious counter to the ABM since increasing the number of incoming warheads would saturate any finite defensive system. ABMs seemed to most commentators at the time to have radical strategic implications akin to those of the SDI; they were seen as inherently destabilising, as well as, somewhat contradictorily, ineffective on technical grounds. Nevertheless the ABM system was as Kissinger put it, 'at the heart of our SALT strategy'.[45] It was necessary to go against the public mood on arms control so as to counter the Soviet development of ABMs in order, paradoxically, to achieve an arms control agreement that endorsed the stability of mutual defensive deterrence. More than this, it was hoped to link the arms control negotiation with its implicit threat of a new arms race, to the Vietnam problem and to the *ostpolitik* of the Brandt government. Political accommodation in Vietnam and in Europe were linked to accommodation on the strategic level. The Soviet Union would not obtain the formal recognition of the frontiers of Germany they desired unless they helped the United States out of the Vietnam morass. Moreover they were confronted with the prospects of a new arms race in the field of anti-ballistic missile systems with all that that entailed. Safeguard was indeed central to this negotiating ploy. On July 23rd 1970 Kissinger said 'I met with ten key Senators and Congressmen to persuade them to stay with the administration plan on ABM in order to strengthen our hand on SALT'.[46] As was noted earlier it succeeded by only one vote. SALT I and the 1974 protocol effectively checked the development of ABMs for some ten years.

This negotiation illustrates both the limits of arms control agreements and the unforeseen consequences of the actual terms agreed. In this context, that of domestic political constraints, while attitudes of the public and of politicians were frustrating to the Administration, they were not insurmountable. The general public was of course unaware of the detailed course of the negotiations and of the political context in which they were taking place. The very delicate moves towards China in particular were kept secret. The prevalent desire for disengagement in Vietnam and for an end to the arms race, or at least for some tangible agreement on arms control, gave US negotiators an incentive to achieve results in this direction. Unfortunately the limit set on the number of missile launchers encouraged the development of MIRVs. Increased accuracy and the heavy megatonnage of Soviet missiles threatened the invulnerability of the Minuteman missile silos and, as we have seen, instability again became a danger to the overall balance. This illustrates the inherent weaknesses of arms control agreements that concentrate on the technical performance of weapons systems and not on the definitions of security to which they are related or on the political conditions that underlie international stability.

The context of SALT I was one of relative American weakness in seeking an end to the Vietnam war without ignominy, in the face, not only of an apparently intransigent North Vietnam, but of a public opinion strongly in favour of withdrawal, and of a Congress determined to limit the freedom of action of the administration. In the circumstances American negotiators did very well to secure the agreements they did. The SALT II negotiations also proceeded in a period of perceived American weakness *vis-à-vis* their nominal adversaries and, in the event, the agreement was never ratified by the USA. The attempt to tie it to agreements on human rights in the Soviet Union was never particularly successful[47] and the Iranian coup and its consequences proved fatal to the Carter administration. The current phase of arms control negotiation began with the Soviet intervention in Afghanistan and growing instability in the Middle East, that posed a serious threat to Western interests and an opportunity for adventurism on the part of the USSR. The rhetoric that followed and the reluctance on the part of the Reagan administration to pursue the path of arms control, presaged an attempt to negotiate with the Soviet Union from a position of strength. But as was argued earlier, all this manifests a concern for the sub-strategic level and an attempt to link the protection of non-security interests to the overall strategic balance. Maintaining this balance has been more important than pursuing any lesser issue to a bloody conclusion. The rhetoric has stopped short of action.

Thus while the pursuit of relative advantage in international politics appears to be a main concern in arms control negotiations,it is clear that the minimal conditions for mutual defensive deterrence have been observed. Competition between the nuclear powers thus operates within these limits. It is controlled by the fear of a general nuclear exchange. If the thesis that the apparently innovative strategic defence initiative is really only a device, a strategem, to force the Soviet Union to withdraw or destroy its intermediate range nuclear forces (INF) from Europe and from Asia, is valid, then there is a distinct parallel with the SALT I negotiation and the Safeguard programme. The objective is not to upset the nuclear balance, but to link it to the sub-strategic level and so protect and promote Western interests. In principle it would be irrational to destroy this balance by beginning another arms race with unknown consequences.

However, if the Soviet Union is sufficiently intimidated by the prospect of another and more sophisticated and costly arms race at the strategic level, as to accept limits on their own sub-strategic deployment, then such a negotiating strategem becomes rational. There are of course risks attached to it. It is uncertain at the time of writing whether an INF arms control agreement will be successfully concluded or what its terms will be. If it is, and if it results in the Soviets removing the SS20s or destroying them altogether then the overall strategic balance remains intact with the non-nuclear allies being precariously defended through ally-swapping. The gain, if these missiles are destroyed, to the United States, is the extension of this protection to the Far East. As with the Safeguard programme, the Reagan administration has had a measure of success in getting the SDI programme through Congress. Although nothing like a full commitment to it has yet emerged, there is sufficient demonstration of political will to make the Soviet treat it as a credible threat. But this had been obtained, again, as in the case of its predecessor, by treating it as a serious and viable programme. The debate continues, as it must, on false premises. This indicates that the constraints of public opinion can be avoided through manipulation and that they are most effective after the event, and particularly when failure has occurred.

If there is any generalisation about the operation of constraint in peace and war on the use or threat of violence in pursuit of political ends, it is that, whether these are ethical, moral, political, instrumental, or rational, the factor of control is an essential condition. Short of total war there must exist a means of responding to the differential responses, actions and reactions, of those engaged in contests where violence is relevant. Total war without the achievement of total peace is of course inherently irrational since this factor of control is almost entirely absent. Avoiding it where nuclear weapons are involved is a common concern for all nuclear powers regardless of their ideological bent. The pursuit of relative advantage in international politics for whatever end, to be successful, must be accompanied by an appreciation by all the contenders of what is a commensurate relation between means and ends. Losses and gains, potential as well as actual, must be calculated within this framework. It follows that the means of violence must be subject to this calculation and controlled. This was never possible with pre-nuclear military technology. It emerges as a possibility with nuclear missiles. A distinction can now be made between security and non-security ends with weapons whose effects can be measured with precision. It is true that there are imponderables in the absence of any previous experience of their use and in the continuity and force of the reasoning associated with them. There must be a commonly accepted rationale, such as that of mutual defensive deterrence, and an observance of its conditions, for any forms of control to exist. Whatever sources of political or ideological contention exist, agreement on this, and thus on a framework for political action, must be paramount. Relative advantages may then be pursued within such a framework without coming to the ultimate disaster of total war. National survival is not entailed.

So far as ethical and moral constraints on the use and threat of violence are concerned, the prevailing need to avoid general war provides a rational limit to action. The imposition of one ethical system over another, or the assumption of ideological superiority, is not a basis for policy where the contenders are nuclear powers. It is doubtful even before the nuclear balance whether this was a viable policy. The language of ideological commitment is largely a device designed to persuade a domestic audience to accept sacrifice and the direction and leadership of governments, rather than a genuine source of motivation in international politics. The intensity of the rhetoric of the Reagan administration with its castigation of the 'evil empire' of the Soviet Union, was a function of the need to press arms procurement policies through Congress, to rally political support, to reassure allies and generally to restore confidence in American leadership. It was linked to an attempt to place the Soviet Union under pressure in order to make it more accommodating to American interests in Europe. Such moral rhetoric is largely a substitute for action and a tactic designed to free the administration in its weapons procurement and in negotiation with the Soviets from liberal criticism and the imposition of Congressional restrictions. It was decidely muted when genuine arms control negotiations became relevant and an agreement was near fruition. It is significant also that such moralising is partial, extending only to adversaries and not to allies or friendly powers that share the same political beliefs and system as those of the castigated state. It is far from clear that human rights in the Western sense are observed in the People's Republic of China not to speak of the majority of states of the so-called Third World.

A general conclusion might be that in time of war no government has shown itself to be scrupulous or concerned with moral or ethical constraints. The doctrine of military necessity is permissive to the point where almost any action can be justified. As we have seen, total war destroyed most inhibitions on the use of violence. Democracies with their liberal traditions felt able to match in their choice of means of violence anything that totalitarian states did. Indeed they were often at the forefront of innovation in weapons, whose scope and lack of discrimination exceeded all existing engines of destruction. It was Britain and the United States that invented and used the atomic bomb. Dissent was stifled.

Limited wars are no less savage in intensity if not in scope, and what constraints are observed are political and not moral in character. Democracies perhaps have problems lacking in other political systems, in that the factor or political opposition becomes relevant to decision-making. Opposition in its formal parliamentary guise may not be particularly moral but outraged moral sentiment on occasion constitutes a formidable weapon against a regime or government that can be used without scruple by those seeking power. Leading the forces of righteousness can prove profitable in the context of democratic politics. The cases of Suez, Vietnam, and South Africa, attest to this. The objections to the use of force in the first two cases become imperative demands for its employment in the latter case. Governments will or will not be constrained by such arguments, depending on a variety of contingent factors. The restoration of the Falkland Islands by force was justified by the illegality of their original seizure. But attitudes towards the Crown colonies of Hong Kong and Gibraltar in the face of demands for their return to their original owners are more equivocal. As in all things, circumstances alter cases.

We thus return to the kind of rationality discussed in previous chapters where effective action and its conditions are the prime considerations in deciding on the use or threat of violence in international politics. Moral questions become relevant where they relate to justification and so to effectiveness. In a sense the United States administration lost its moral debate over Vietnam, and in losing its will, lost the war. The chief constraint operating on the use of violence lies in perceptions of capability that extend beyond the mere possession of weapons and include the will. The determination to persevere with an objective has a moral dimension in that conviction and morale are important factors. But this is merely to observe that keeping troops and citizens in good heart is necessary in any prolonged and difficult struggle. In essence what has been argued here is a rationalist account of the operation of constraints in this context. Ethical considerations are thus relevant, not in terms of attempts to create or maintain a universal moral order, but when the consequences of ignoring them appear to be counterproductive or reduce the chances of success.

NOTES AND REFERENCE

1. Both the United States and the Soviet Union have ideological commitment written into their Constitutions. The former stresses what are essentially political rights; the latter economic or material freedoms.
2. Having a reason, or intention, does not entail action. Actions are not *caused* by reasons.
3. See for example, Charles Beitz, *Political Theory and International Relations*, Princeton University Press, NJ, 1979.
4. See my *Theory and Explanation in International Politics, op. cit.*
5. Lenin and his New Economic Policy: Stalin joining the League of Nations and apparently converted to the principle of collective security in the 1930s; and Krushchev and his successors advocating 'peaceful coexistence' do not seem to be prisoners of their ideology in this respect. The USSR has been party to a number of negotiations and agreements with its ideological rivals and has generally accepted its contractual obligations.
6. For example, the failure to unite Korea by force wrecked the democrats' chances of re-election; the failure of Vietnam tacitly acknowledged by President Johnson's decision after the Tet offensive not to stand for re-election, had similar effects. More recently, the failure to resolve the hostage issue in Iran had adverse electoral consequences for President Carter. Suez was almost disastrous for the Conservative government and was personally disastrous for Eden. Success in the Falklands War was an imperative for the survival of the Thatcher government although perhaps this is more speculative.
7. The resurgence of interest in arms control negotiations as indicated in the INF agreement of 1987 and the abandonment of rhetoric depicting the Soviet Union as an 'evil empire' by President Reagan, is a recent example of this.
8. Among these are: the Hague Conventions of 1899 and 1907; Geneva Conventions 1929 and 1949; Geneva Protocols 1925; London Naval Protocol 1936. See A. Roberts and R. Guelff eds. *Documents on the Laws of War*, Oxford University Press, Oxford, 1982.
9. See Michael Waltzer, *Just and Unjust War*, Penguin, Harmondsworth, 1978, and Terry Nardin, *Law, Morality and the Relations of States*, Princeton, NJ, 1982.
10. On reciprocal compliance see Charles R. Beitz, *op. cit.* p. 56.
11. This was explicitly stated by the victor powers in their formulation of the Nuremberg Agreements and in charging the Nazi government with conspiracy to aggress.
12. The Atlantic Charter was formulated in August, 1941.
13. Hugo Grotius, *The Law of War and Peace*, trans. Francis W. Kelsey.

14. The Peace of Riga in 1921 gave Poland extensive territories east of the Curzon Line, containing some millions of non-Poles. Vilna was taken from Lithuania during the war with the Bolsheviks and the Versailles settlement had given them German territory with a German population. The collapse of Czechoslovakia in March 1939 was taken as an opportunity to seize Teschen.
15. Self-determination was not used as a basis for resolving the problem of Alsace-Lorraine, although a plebiscite was to be held for the Saar. It was completely ignored in the cases of Danzig and the Polish corridor and in the cession of the Alto-Adige in Italy.
16. The British, for example, felt able to promise the Jews a National Home in Palestine in spite of their obligations as a Mandatory Power. At the time of the Balfour Declaration the Jewish population of Palestine was a very small minority. Mandates in general were treated as if they were imperial possessions, although there were exceptions as in Iraq where a sense of national autonomy was supported by armed insurrection.
17. A recent example of this is the United Nations Convention on Prohibition or Restrictions on the Use of Certain Conventional Weapons 1981.
18. *Ibid.*, see Malcolm Shaw in *Review of International Studies*, (1983) 9, pp. 109–21.
19. The area bombing of Tokyo in 1945 for example, resulted in some 83,000 people killed, more than was the case for either Hiroshima or Nagasaki. Casualties on this scale occurred in the bombing of Hamburg and Dresden.
20. Raeder and Doenitz although found guilty at Nuremberg were not deemed guilty in this respect. See Vice-Admiral F. Ruge, *Sea Warfare 1939–1945*, trans. M. G. Saunders, Cassell, London, 1957, p. 48.
21. The UN Convention defines a combatant as someone who belongs to an organised armed force, with the attribute of a command structure, fixed signs and conducting operations in accordance with the laws and customs of war. There are serious ambiguities in this definition.
22. Article 239 of the Hague Convention of 1907 allows 'necessities of war' to be invoked as an enabling condition.
23. Civilian casualties vastly exceeded those of the military in all of these wars. In addition to those killed and wounded was the problem of huge numbers of refugees.
24. See for example J. Finnis, J. M. Boyle and G. Grisez, *Nuclear Deterrence, Morality and Realism*, Clarendon Press, Oxford, 1987.
25. These were Olympic and Coronet. It was estimated that the Japanese War could continue for some eighteen months after the German surrender. The heavy fighting and self-sacrifices of the Japanese garrisons on Iwo Jima and Okinawa indicated a scale of casualties akin to the blood baths of the First World War in the invasion of the home islands.
26. See Gar Alperovitz, *op. cit.*, for an account of atomic diplomacy. Truman himself in his *Memoirs*, Vol. 1 1945 *Year of Decisions*, New York, Signet Books, 1965, asserted that he had no intention of allowing the Soviet Union to share in the fruits of victory beyond the concessions in the Far Eastern Agreement made at Yalta.
27. See Ronald H. Spector, *Eagle Against the Sun*, Penguin Books, Harmondsworth, 1987, for a concise account of the Pacific War.
28. With increasing manpower shortages the use of Russian and other ethnic 'volunteers' as recruits was actively encouraged by the Germans. A 'volunteer' army was formed under General Vlassov.

29. These contradictions and incompatibilities arising out of different views of national security bedevilled the World Disarmament Conferences of the early 1930s.
30. See for example, Morton A. Kaplan, *System and Process, op. cit.*
31. On power see my critique in *Theory and Explanation in International Politics*, especially Chapter 3, p. 51 and also in *Modes of Imperialism, op. cit.* Chapter 2, p. 19.
32. This was the Bretton Woods system underpinned by the International Bank for Reconstruction and Development and the International Monetary Fund supported by the American dollar.
33. The SS20 was first deployed in 1977 in the USSR and subsequently emplaced in the East European countries.
34. This was not a 'balanced' parity but by 1962 the USSR possessed a few ICMBs capable of hitting the USA. Full parity or 'essential equivalence' appeared in the late 1960s.
35. On this see Robert Kennedy, *Thirteen Days*. With the Congressional elections in the following month Kennedy could not afford to be seen to be weak in his dealings with the USSR. He therefore had to avoid the appearance of making a bargain on equal terms with Krushchev. But this in effect is what he was doing.
36. For an account of the SALT I negotiations see Henry Kissinger, *The White House Years*, Weidenfeld and Nicolson, London, 1979.
37. For an account of the ostpolitik negotiations see *ibid.*
38. The terms of the SALT I Agreement included a virtual moratorium on the development of ABM systems.
39. Although the Senate did not ratify SALT II in 1979 its terms have in effect been kept. Only fairly recently and as part of what is clearly a negotiating strategy have there been minor infringements.
40. This did not prevent it from being interpreted as such by Western political leaders!
41. The Threshold Test Ban Treaty of 1974 set a limit on underground tests of 150 kilotons.
42. The Committee on the Present Danger was set up to prevent the ratification of the SALT II Treaty. It included Eugene Rostow, Paul Nitze, and Richard Pipes.
43. This is the thrust of Colin Gray's thesis. See *Nuclear Strategy: A Case for Victory, op. cit.*
44. *Ibid.*, p. 41 and pp. 54–6.
45. H. Kissinger, *White House Years, op. cit.* p. 536.
46. *Ibid.*, p. 551.
47. Helsinki Agreement.

9 Conclusion

Throughout this study it has been argued that the rationality of inter-state violence, indeed of all political violence, lies in a commensurate relationship between its use as a means and the ends sought. This is as true for the political practitioner as for the strategic theorist. The difficulties that face the latter in specifying the conditions for this relationship have been examined. Strategic theories that turn on the nature of the means only, or emphasise the capabilities of weapons systems solely in terms of their performance, ignore the problem. Equally, theories that posit rationality as some optimal course of action that maximises satisfaction, or, in the jargon, is satisficing, merely posit some normative conceptual framework that implicitly makes claims to a knowledge that is incapable of empirical validation. A spurious expertise enters the debate as to the appropriate strategy, an effective response to an adversary, or the procurement of weapons.

Rationality in practice is a derivative of the perceptions of the policy- or decision-maker, stemming from his notion of instrumentality. In turn instrumentality is a function of a reference to a value-system reflecting the current agenda and its priorities. Foremost in this is the notion of security and its ramifications, both internal and external, held by the state. Such practical reasoning is not made in a void but in a world of states whose politics are, partly at least, a product of shared assumptions, constraints, and expectations of proper action. Only a hegemonial or imperial state can impose its own conceptual systems and its associated rationality on the world and even here, only partially, and with some accommodation. More commonly the world is heterodox in this respect. Success in an adversarial relationship thus depends on a shared rationality. While there is some continuity in historical terms, such reasoning is essentially pragmatic and subject to shifts and modifications as negotiation and bargaining and perceived successes, failures and dangers, in the use of and threat of violence, operate on political judgement. In short the relationship between means and ends in the context of inter-state violence is a product of the reasoning of the actors and their perceptions of the world in which they

264 The Politics of War

act. Rationalising constructs, however intellectually pleasing or logically coherent, cannot stipulate either the means or the ends as being effective, attainable, or desirable. Neither in its rhetorical or in its normative mode can strategic prescription claim authority over those of the practitioner. Through logical and empirical analysis, strategic commentary can point out some of the implications of policy, but not in any sense of the possession of a knowledge superior to that of the practitioner. In the absence of a validated explanatory mode such assessments can only be tentative and suggestive in character. This was the conclusion of Clausewitz and he advocated his own solution to the problem—critical analysis or testing the means employed in terms of its rationality. But he regarded this not as a basis for authorative prescriptions or as emphasising the superiority of strategic thought over practical reasoning, but as a form of intellectual training for the practitioner.

If this notion of the rationality of violence is derived from the reasoning of politicians and from *their* understanding of the world rather than based upon an external conceptual scheme or strategic 'theory' what can be said of such constructs? Have they any value in terms of practice, or are they merely historical exercises? An examination of the assumptions underlying political decisions and actions is of more than passing interest to the citizens who are affected by them. In the past they have had little choice in decisions to go to war and, in peacetime, the paramountcy of national security has excluded them from participation in or even knowledge of preparations for war. Precluded from a genuine knowledge of policy and its assumptions, they fall easy prey to political manipulation. The defence debate in western democratic countries is rigged by governments through a judicious mixture of selected information made available to the public and a bogus appeal to commonly held values and political beliefs. In most countries of course, there is no defence debate, in the sense of any public involvement in governmental decision-making. Citizens are expected to believe what they are told.

A reconstruction of the rationale of defence policy and an examination of its implications, both for the state and the world of states, has a direct relationship to practice, where it informs, rather than directs, political choice. In this respect it is relevant to the citizen as well as to the practitioner. It must not be partisan however, since this presupposes not merely political commitment, but a knowledge superior to that of its subject. As we have seen throughout this book, such a claim, whether made implicitly or explicitly, is inherently flawed. There are no experts on human behaviour. To claim authority for a particular point of view in terms of a postulated course of action, or set of options, that if pursued or adopted will produce a desired state of affairs, is to enter into politics rather than to advance our knowledge. In short, where speculation is grounded upon a construction of actual reasoning, based on evidence, and related to the objectives sought, by those whose decisions and actions we seek to explain, the exercise is not futile or empty. It must be admitted that the problem lies not in justifying the exercise but in actually performing it.

Governments are not only secretive where questions of national security are concerned, but have a vested interest in extending the notion of security to cover a wide range of activities and concerns in order to avoid hostile criticism. Democracies, of their nature, practice adversarial politics and governments seek to govern through persuasion and manipulation. Advocacy and rhetoric are the means generally adopted. It follows that access to evidence is extremely limited and the would-be strategic commentator is forced into more conjecture, in this most conjectural of fields, than he would like.

Quite apart from the need to avoid giving ammunition to critics, democratic, and indeed all governments, have reason to be chary of exposing their reasoning to alien scrutiny. There is a genuine reason to be concerned for security here. The essence of negotiation lies in securing relative advantages within a framework of agreement. As we have seen when arms control was discussed, issues have many dimensions apart from their nominal significance as areas of contention. Exposing one's cards, other than as a bluff or manoeuvre, is rarely a wise practice. The politics of diplomacy in the world of states has a close resemblance to that of democratic politics within the state. If the *ultima ratio*—war—is excluded from the political repertoire, as is the case under conditions of balanced defensive deterrence between the major nuclear powers, then the consequences is a type of politics that relies on persuasion, manipulation and compromise. The notion of power, so often used as a descriptive concept in interpretations of inter-state relations, is misleading, in that it minimises the reality of manoeuvre and bargaining that is more characteristic than the putative ordering of states into Superpowers and the rest. This does not preclude the elements of force and coercion, threats and promises, that are present in all forms of politics, both national and international. If this is accepted as being more characteristic of the politics of the last few decades than apocalyptic and violent struggle, then there is an even higher premium on the use of bluff and threat and the necessity of concealing the truth.

There is a paradox here; economy with the truth[1] on the part of governments while necessary in terms of the domestic audience, can be positively dangerous in terms of the nominal adversary. In all negotiations there is a measure of bluff and manoeuvre, but for genuine agreement there must be some common ground or rationale, clearly understood by all parties. Deception might prove successful in the short run but highly prejudicial for the future. Domestic opinion is notoriously volatile and political memories are short, and in any case responsibility for a stated attitude or policy can be transferred from politician to politician and from party to party. Deception in this context is not especially damaging or prejudicial to future policy. Within the context of inter-state relations, especially under conditions of mutual balanced defensive deterrence, the consequences of economies with the truth might be a disastrous arms race and possibly, war. The stability of deterrence depends upon shared assumptions and shared knowledge. Arms control agreements are important not for what they explicitly ban, control, or limit, but for the tacit agreements that underly them. The use of a short term manoeuvre in the form of the negotiation of a treaty that is not intended to be binding, can be extremely counterproductive as Hitler discovered after his breach of the Munich Agreement. It makes sense to do this only within the context of an anticipated war. The war must be winnable. Under nuclear conditions this is not a likely possibility. The consequence is a greater element of understanding between governments, than between them and the governed, as to the nature and implications of their defence postures.

A world that contains states possessing nuclear weapons, more or less evenly balanced in their capacity to destroy each other, is forced to accept the principle *cuius regio; eius religio*, if it wishes an alternative to this destruction. Ideological differences and the character of the national polity thus have significance only in terms of domestic politics and the manipulation of opinion. Rationality ultimately depends upon common beliefs and values, not in the sense of sharing the same socio-political norms, but derived from rules of behaviour that control and limit war. If domestic values are projected into the international environment in the form of ideological conflict, then the political consequences are not merely instability but a permanent struggle that can find no rational resolution. War cannot resolve it. It is worth quoting the words of M. de Bordeaux, the envoy from Louis XIV to England, who said on 21st December to The Parliament of the Commonwealth: 'The accord which ought to exist between neighbouring states is not affected by the form of their governments; and so, although it has pleased God, in His providence, to change what was formerly established in this country, there has not ceased to be a need for commerce and communication between France and England. This nation may have changed its complexion, and from a monarchy become a republic, but geographical conditions have not changed; our people still remain neighbours, with mutual interests in trade; and the treaties which exist between nations are binding not so much on princes as on peoples, since they have as their principle object the common utility.'[2]

The basis of this utility in modern times lies in defining and controlling the instrumentality of violence as a means of achieving political objectives, including that of national security. Ideologies and the national polities that reflect them are irrelevant to this. The rhetoric of the Cold War paralleled the competitive development of forces of destruction previously unknown to the world. Neither Marxism-Leninism or Liberal-Democracy won this particular contest. It ended in stalemate and a profound fear of nuclear war. The notion of defensive deterrence emerged. Its conditions, both physical and perceptual, were gradually refined. It took the form of a shared rationality that not only defined national security for the first time, but also set limits to the use of violence in pursuit of lesser objectives. In this respect a deep conservatism prevailed. This is not manifested solely in arms control agreements and in accepted limits on arms, their types, production, and deployment. Such agreements are in any case imperfect instruments, given that it is the political will and the intentions, and not the weapons *per se*, that matter. Such matters of perception can more easily be transmitted to a putative adversary than to a domestic audience, which is both ill-informed and open to manipulation. The need to validate agreements poses a problem for political leaders, given their need to use a language of justification that appeals to their potential critics and allies. It is here that the element of ideological rhetoric is re-introduced. Arms control agreements, and the process of negotiation itelf, are presented to a domestic audience in the context of an adversarial relationship. Indeed it is the alleged existence of this contest that is used to justify the arms procurements policies that produced the weapons under negotiation in the first place! The need for their existence and the need for their sacrifice are justified in the same terms.

The realities of the nuclear balance and its limits on national power, fully understood by the political leaders of the nuclear states, cannot be communicated to citizens without jeopardising policy-making and decision, or compromising political positions. Where politicians reveal the rationale of their position on defence and security, as in the case of Robert MacNamara and his Ann Arbor speech,[3] it is usually in the context of a crisis, or where there is a necessity to dampen expectations aroused by prior rhetoric. But in general *national* advantages are expected by the domestic audience in negotiating arms control agreements and it is this aspect, rather than cooperation and reciprocal benefit, that is stressed in their political justification. The tacit agreements are either not emphasised, or are expressed in vague phrases such as *detente*. Allies as well as the electorate must be appeased in this respect. The vulnerability of the non-nuclear allies and their status as hostages to the major nuclear powers are not 'realities' that can be openly debated. The politicians thus must tread a wary path between arousing expectations that cannot be satisfied, or which limit their freedom of manouevre, and revealing relative weakness or willingness to accommodate to an opponent and thus weakening a negotiating position. This is not easy. It was President Kennedy who was alleged to have said that he fully understood the necessity of recognising the People's Republic of China and negotiating with it, but that any move in that direction would result in electoral disaster.

The SDI programme can be regarded as a mixture of threat, promise, and perhaps bluff, directed both at the domestic electorate and the Soviet Union. Explicitly, it threatens an arms race designed to produce a defence against ballistic missiles thus shattering all the conditions of mutual defensive deterrence. If the programme was successful in its putative intent, it would confer on the United States *offensive* deterrence, something it has not enjoyed since the late 1950s. As such it provides a powerful inducement for the Soviet Union to accommodate to the United States on sub-strategic issues, such as the emplacement of SS20 missiles in Eastern Europe and in Asian Russia. It contains a promise in that the American people are given the prospect of a more perfect form of security coupled with a restoration of American world leadership. It has the element of bluff in that no one knows what form it will take, nor whether its continuance as a viable programme is dependent on the Soviet Union accepting specific American proposals. It is also vulnerable to changes in representation in Congress and consequent changes in the degree of political support.

Expectations aroused by the SDI have already been dampened by relating it to the protection of missile sites rather than to the defence of population centres. Damage limitation is not a defence although it may serve to enhance deterrence by introducing a war-winning element. Balanced mutual defensive deterrence depends not only on mutual assured destruction but upon inflicting *unacceptable* damage. Reducing this to the level of the acceptable by one side would thus create an imbalance in which the risks of war are minimised, making its threat more credible. As was argued earlier in this study, this possibility introduces instability in the deterrent relationship and blurs the distinction between a threat of violence designed to guarantee security, and a threat designed to secure some lesser political objective. The rationale of defensive deterrence would thus disappear. There can be no guarantee in a crisis or confrontation between nuclear powers that the state challenged in this way will act rationally. Whatever the scope for damage limitation, it is certain that millions will die and millions more be affected by radiation. It is hard to conceive of any political issue for which this risk is worth taking. National security at present is provided by the rationale of defensive deterrence. Using the threat of nuclear war to obtain relative advantage in international politics is not merely dangerous but also counterproductive. It invites the 'weaker' opponent to adopt countermeasures, and acts as a spur to further weapons innovation and competition. In demonstrating his ability to blockade Cuba, President Kennedy gave a powerful inducement to the Soviet Union not merely to develop ICBMs, but also to build a navy! The phenomenal growth of the Soviet Navy dates from the Cuban Missiles Crisis.

Paradoxically, the move to arms control also stemmed from this crisis. The consequence was the appearance of what appeared to be a stable defensive balance between the two major nuclear powers, with the minor nuclear powers actively seeking their own defensive deterrents. With nuclear parity the Soviet Union was free to erode the commanding world position obtained by the United States in the immediate postwar years, where it could, and freed from the fear of nuclear intimidation. This change in relativities, a change which continues into the present, and which will continue into the foreseeable future, is difficult to reconcile either with a postulated hegemonial role of the United States, either as leader of the 'Free World' or of any other world, or with the notion of a fundamental adversarial relationship with the USSR. Accommodation is necessary under conditions of nuclear parity or 'essential equivalence'. In reinforcing the stability of the nuclear balance through arms control agreements and their tacit acceptance of each others' political interests, a form of recognition of spheres of influence has come into existence. Contests are thus limited in scale and scope by the need to maintain the strategic balance, and this has a controlling effect on the use of violence and interventionist policies in the non-nuclear area.

It is this perception and the tacit acceptance of limits that is most relevant to the notion of control as expressed by the Clausewitzian formula of the commensurability between means and ends where war is 'policy by other means'. Arms control agreements symbolise this rather than dictate its terms. They reflect an international politics that has a striking resemblance to the kind of consensus politics deemed to be characteristic of modern industrialised states. Violence and local instability are present, but contained within a framework of control. In this respect violence is rational. Having said this there is nothing immutable about this state of affairs. The stability of the relatively few extant liberal-democratic and socialist states is neither normal nor of long duration. It emerged out of violent and illiberal social and political practices. But from this point of view both forms of polity have this in common, they are politically stable and violence within them is controlled and rational. On my argument, the same form of politics in inter-state relations is emerging under conditions of nuclear balance. It is true that the beneficiaries are the nuclear powers.[4] They, and they alone, enjoy some sort of guarantee of security in the form of an armed peace. It is a *delicate* balance of terror and rests on mutual perceptions and the acceptance of a common rationale. It could evaporate quickly should these perceptions change. But this is equally true of those which hold states together. In my view it is important not that violence should disappear from human relations, for this I think is a Utopian goal, but that it should be controlled and limited, thus making it rational. This form of violence has a use. It can be beneficial to mankind. World peace is not merely the absence of war but a condition that rests on the consciousness of those who control and direct the means of violence. It must be employed for *specific* reasons; that is, for attainable objectives, where the consequences can be foreseen, and where the effects do not entail more slaughter and waste than is necessary. As we have seen throughout this study, these are difficult conditions to fulfil. But fulfilled they must be if war or its threat is ever to be used as a means of achieving political objectives, including that of providing for our security. We would do well to consider Ogden Nash's cautionary verse

'Consider the auk;
Becoming extinct because he forgot how to fly; and could only walk.
Consider man, who may well become extinct
Because he forgot how to walk and learned how to fly
before he thought.'[5]

NOTES AND REFERENCES

1. All commentators on politics will be eternally grateful to the Cabinet Secretary Sir Robert Armstrong for this illuminating phrase.

2. Cited in Guizot Cromwell Livre III, Paris, 1860.
3. Robert MacNamara, US Secretary for Defense, 1961–8, made this speech in September 1967.
4. But it is also true that an inhibition on general war, while making the non-nuclear powers potential battle-fields, also reduces this possibility through the security guarantee for the major nuclear powers provided by it. The quarrels of the major powers in the past resulted in two world wars, with the smaller states, both in Europe and Asia, suffering disproportionate casualties. The futility of the Korean and Vietnam Wars should not obscure the fact that they were *limited* wars.
5. 'A Caution to Everybody' in Ogden Nash *The Private Dining Room*, J. M. Dent, London, 1953, p. 19.

Select Bibliography

EXPLANATION, RATIONALITY AND HUMAN AGENCY

Allison, G. T. *Essence of Decision*, Little Brown, Boston, 1971.

Anscombe, G. E. M. *Intention*, Blackwell, Oxford, 1957.

Ayers, M. R. *The Refutation of Determinism*, Methuen, London, 1968.

Barry, B. (ed.) *Power and Political Theory*, John Wiley, London, 1976.

Benn, S. I. & Mortimore, G. (eds) *Rationality and the Social Sciences*, Routledge & Kegan Paul, London, 1976.

Binkley, Bronough & Mawers (eds) *Agent Action and Reason*, University of Toronto Press and Blackwell, Oxford, 1971.

Blackburn, S. *Reason and Prediction*, Cambridge University Press, 1973.

Brown, D. G. *Action*, Allen & Unwin, London, 1968.

Buzan, Barry *People, States and Fear*, Wheatsheaf Books, Brighton, 1983.

Carthy, J. D. & Ebling, F. J. (eds) *The Natural History of Aggression*, Academic Press, London, 1964.

Colodny, R. G. (ed.) *Frontiers of Science and Philosophy*, Allen and Unwin, London, 1962.

Davidson, D. 'Actions, Reasons, Causes', *Journal of Philosophy*, LX, No. 23, Nov. 7th, 1963.

Easton, D. (ed.) *Varieties of Political Theory*, Prentice-Hall, Englewood Cliffs, 1966.

Forward, Nigel *The Field of Nations*, Macmillan, London, 1971.

Gallie, W. B. *Philosophers for Peace and War*, Cambridge University Press, 1978.

Gardiner, P. (ed.) *Theories of History*, Free Press, New York, 1959.

Giddens, A. *Positivism and Sociology*, Heinemann, London, 1974.

Hook, S. *Philosophy and History*, New York University Press, 1963.

Hempel, C. *Aspects of Scientific Explanation*, Free Press, Glencoe, 1965.

Hesse, Mary *The Structure of Scientific Inference*, Macmillan, London, 1974.

Hinde, R. A. *Animal Behaviour*, McGraw Hill, NY, 1966.

Lorenz, K. *On Aggression*, Methuen, London, 1966.

Louch, A. R. *Explanation and Human Action*, Blackwell, Oxford, 1966.
MacMurray, J. *The Self and Agent*, Faber and Faber, London, 1966.
Merton, R. K. *On Theoretical Sociology*, Free Press, New York, 1967.
Midgley, Mary *Beast and Man*, Harvester Press, Hassocks, Sussex, 1979.
Mill, J. S. *A System of Logic*, Longmans, London, 1965.
Nicholson, M. *The Scientific Analysis of Social Behaviour*, Frances Pinter, London, 1983.
Oakeshott, M. *On History*, Blackwell, Oxford, 1983.
Popper, K. *Objective Knowledge*, Clarendon Press, Oxford, 1972.
Rescher, N. (ed.) *The Logic of Decision and Action,* University of Pittsburg Press, 1967.
Reynolds, C. *Theory and Explanation in International Politics*, Martin Robertson, Oxford, 1973.
———*Modes of Imperialism*, Martin Robertson, Oxford, 1982.
Richardson, Lewis F. *Arms and Insecurity*, ed. N. Rachevsky and Ernesto Tucco, Boxwood Press, Pittsburg, 1960.
Ruse, M. *The Philosophy of Biology*, Hutchinson, London, 1973.
Ryan, A. (ed.) *The Philosophy of Social Explanation*, Oxford University Press, London, 1973.
Schelling, T. C. *The Strategy of Conflict,* Galaxy, New York, 1963.
———*Arms and Influence,* Yale University Press, New Haven, 1966.
Skinner, Q. *Social Meaning and the Explanation of Social Action*, Blackwell, Oxford, 1971.
Taylor, C. *The Explanation of Behaviour*, Routledge & Kegan Paul, London, 1964.
Taylor, D. M. *Explanation and Meaning*, Cambridge University Press, 1970.
Ushenko, A. P. *Power and Events*, Princeton University Press, 1946.
Von Neumann, J. & Morgenstern, O. *The Theory of Games and Economic Behavior*, Princeton University Press, New Jersey, 1946.
Von Wright *Explanation and Understanding*, Routledge & Kegan Paul, 1971.

NON-NUCLEAR STRATEGIC THOUGHT

Alger, J. *The Quest for Victory*, Cornell Press, Conn., 1982.
Aron, Raymond *Penser La Guerre*, Vol. 1 and Vol. 2, *L'Age Européen Planetaire*, NRF Editions, Gallimard, Paris, 1976.
Bialer, U. *The Shadow of the Bomber*, Royal Historical Society, London, 1980.
Bond, B. *Liddell Hart. A Study of his Thought*, New Brunswick, NJ. Rutgers University Press, 1977.
Butterfield, H. & Wright, M. (eds) *Diplomatic Investigations*, Allen & Unwin, London, 1966.
Clausewitz, C. von *On War*, ed. and trans. Michael Howard and Peter Paret, Princeton University Press, New Jersey, 1976.

————*On war*, 3 vols., trans Col. J. J. Graham, 1st pub. 1874, revised ed. Col. F. N. Maude, 1909, Routledge & Kegan Paul, London, 1949.

Collins, J. M. *Grand Strategy; Principles and Practice*, Naval Institute Press, 1973.

De Gaulle, Gen. C. *The Army of the Future*, Hutchinson, London.

Douhet, G. *The Command of the Air*, trans. Dino Ferrari, Faber and Faber, London, 1943.

Eccles, H. *Military Concepts and Philosophy*, Rutgers University Press, New Brunswick, NJ, 1965.

Gibbs, H. *Grand Strategy*. Rearmament Policy, London, 1976.

Guderian, H. *Panzer Leader*, trans. Constantine Fitzgibbon, Futura edition, London, 1974.

Fuller, J. F. C. *Machine Warfare*, Hutchinson, London, 1941.

————*Armoured Warfare*, Eyre and Spottiswoode, London, 1932.

Howard, M. *The Causes of War*, Unwin, London, 1984.

————*The Theory and Practice of War*, Indiana University Press, Bloomington, 1965.

Liddell Hart, B. H. *The Strategy of the Indirect Approach*, Faber and Faber, London, 1946.

————*The Defence of Britain*, Faber and Faber, London, 1939.

————*The Other Side of the Hill*, Cassell, London, 1948.

Machiavelli, N. *The Art of War*, trans. Ellis Farneworth, Henry C. Southwork, Albany, NY, 1815.

Mahan, A. T. *The Influence of Sea Power upon History, 1600–1783*, Sampson Low, London, 1890.

————*The Influence of Sea Power upon the French Revolution and Empire*, 2 vols., Sampson Low, London.

Paret, Peter *Clausewitz and the State*, Oxford University Press, Oxford, 1976.

Phillips, T. R. (ed.) *Roots of Strategy*, 1st pub. 1940, Greenwood Press, Conn., re pub. 1982.

Rapaport, A. (ed.) *Clausewitz on War*, Penguin, Harmondsworth, 1968.

Roskill, S. *Naval Policy Between the Wars 1930–39*, London, 1976.

Webster, Sir Charles & Frankland Noble *The Strategic Air Offensive Against Germany*, Vols I–IV, HMSO, London, 1961.

NUCLEAR STRATEGIC THOUGHT

Akerman, N. *On the Doctrine of Limited War*, Berlingstra Botryckeriet Lund.

Armacost, M. H. *The Politics of Weapons Innovation. The Thor-Jupiter Controversy*, Columbia University Press, NY, 1969.

Aron, Raymond *Peace and War*, Weidenfeld and Nicolson, London, 1966.

Beaufre, A. *Deterrence and Strategy*, Faber, London, 1965.

Blake, N. & Pole, K. (eds) *Dangers of Deterrence: Philosophers on Nuclear Strategy*, Routledge & Kegan Paul, London, 1983.

Brown, Harold *Thinking about National Security*, Westview, Boulder, Col., 1983.

Buchan, A. *Problems of Modern Strategy*, Chatto and Windus, London, 1970.

Buzan, B. (ed.) *The International Politics of Deterrence*, Frances Pinter, London, 1987.

Carlton, D. & Schaef, C. (eds) *Arms Control and Technological Innovation*, Wiley, NY, 1976.

Catudal, H. M. *Nuclear Deterrence; Does it Deter?*, Mansell, London and New York, 1985.

De Mesquita, Bueno *The War Trap*, Yale University Press, New Haven, 1981.

Freedman, L. *The Evolution of Nuclear Strategy*, Macmillan, London, 1981.

Gray, C. S. *The Soviet-American Arms Race*, Saxon House, Lexington, 1976.

———*Strategic Studies*, Greenwood Press, Westport, Conn., 1982.

Green, P. *Deadly Logic: The Theory of Nuclear Deterrence*, Ohio State University Press, Columbus, 1966.

Jervis, R. *The Illogic of American Nuclear Strategy*, Cornell University Press, London, 1984.

Jones, R. E. *Nuclear Deterrence*, Library of Political Studies, London, 1968.

Kahn, H. *On Thermo-Nuclear War*, Princeton University Press, New Jersey, 1960.

———*On Escalation*, Praeger, New York, 1965.

Mandelbaum, M. *The Nuclear Revolution*, Cambridge University Press, 1981.

Martin, L. *Strategic Thought in the Nuclear Age*, Heinemann, London, 1979.

Morgan, P. *Deterrence and Conceptual Analysis*, Sage, Beverley Hills, 1977.

Miller, S. (ed.) *Strategy and Nuclear Deterrence*, Princeton University Press, New Jersey, 1984.

Smith, L. R. *The R.A.N.D. Corporation*, Harvard University Press, Mass., 1966.

Snyder, G. H. *Deterrence and Defense; Towards a Theory of National Security*, Princeton University Press, New Jersey, 1961.

Talbot Strobe *Deadly Gambits*, Pan Books, London, 1985.

Zagare, F. C. *The Dynamics of Deterrence*, University of Chicago Press, Chicago and London, 1987.

POLICY, PLANNING AND POLITICS

Memoirs and Biographies

Acheson, Dean *Present at the Creation*, Hamish Hamilton, London, 1969.

Berlin, I. ed. Herbert G. Nicholas, *Washington Dispatches, 1941–1945,*

University of Chicago Press and Weidenfeld and Nicolson, London., 1981

Byrnes, J. *Speaking Frankly*, Heinemann, London, 1947.

Churchill, W. S. *History of the Second World War*, Cassell, London, 1956.

Colville, J. *The Fringes of Power*, Hodder and Stoughton, London, 1985.

Dilks, D. (ed.) *Diaries of Sir Alexander Cadogan 1935-1945*, Cassell, London, 1971.

Eden, A. *Memoirs*, Cassell, London, 1965.

Galbraith, J. K. *A Life in Our Times*, Andre Deutsch, London, 1981.

Gilbert, M. *Road to Victory, Winston Churchill, 1941-1945*. Heinemann, 1986.

Hore-Belisha, L. *The Private Papers of Hore-Belisha*, ed. R. J. Minney, Collins, London, 1960.

Jebb, Gladwyn *The Memoirs of Gladwyn Jebb*, Weidenfeld and Nicolson, London, 1972.

Kennan, G. F. *Memoirs, Vol. 1, 1925-1950*, Little Brown, Boston, 1967.

Kennedy, Maj-Gen Sir John *The Business of War*, Hutchinson, London, 1957.

Kennedy Robert *Thirteen Days*, Pan Books, London, 1969.

Kissinger, H. *The White House Years*, Weidenfeld and Nicolson, London, 1979.

Manstein, E. *Lost Victories*, ed. and trans. Anthony G. Powell, Methuen, London, 1958.

Middlemas, Keith & Barnes, John *Baldwin*, Weidenfeld and Nicolson, London, 1969.

Millis, W. (ed.) *The Forrestal Diaries*, Cassell, London, 1957.

Montgomery of Alamein, *Memoirs*, Odhams, Watford, 1958.

Murhpy, R. *Diplomat Among Warriors*, Greenwood Press, Westport, Conn., 1976, 1st pub. 1964.

Reynaud, Paul *In the Thick of the Fight*, trans. and abridged James P. Lambert, Cassell, London, 1953.

Rogow, A. *Victim of Duty*, Rupert Hart Davis, London, 1966.

Saward, Dudley *"Bomber" Harris*, Cassell, London, 1984.

Speer, A. *Inside the Third Reich*, trans. R. and C. Winston, Avon Books, New York, 1970.

Sulzberger, C. L. *A Long Row of Candles*, Macdonald, London, 1969.

Taylor, A. J. P. *Beaverbrook*, Hamish Hamilton, London, 1972.

Tedder, Lord *With Prejudice*, Cassell, London, 1966.

Templewood Viscount *Nine Troubled Years*, Collins, London, 1954.

Trevor Roper, H. (ed.) *Hitler's Table Talk*, Weidenfeld and Nicolson, 1953.

Truman, Harry S. *Memoirs, Year of Decisions*, Vol. 1, Signet Edition, London, 1965, 1st pub. 1955.

Wedemayer, A. *Wedemayer Reports*, Devis Adair, New York, 1958.

Vansittart, Lord *The Mist Procession*, Hutchinson, London, 1958.

Programmes and Actions

Abel, Ellie *The Missiles of October*

Alperovitz, Gar *Atomic Diplomacy*, rev. ed., Penguin, Harmondsworth,

1985.
Armstrong, Hamilton Fish, *Fifty Years of Foreign Affairs*, Praeger, New York, 1972.
Barker, E. *Churchill and Eden at War*, Macmillan, London, 1978.
Baugh, W. H. *The Politics of Nuclear Balance*, Longman, New York, 1984.
Becker, J. *The Decision to Divide Germany*, Durham, 1978.
Boelcke, W. A. *The Secret Conferences of Dr. Goebbels 1939–1943*, Weidenfeld and Nicolson, London, 1967.
Cave Brown, A. *Bodyguard of Lies*, W. H. Allen, London, 1977.
Cowling, M. *The Impact of Hitler*, Cambridge University Press, 1975.
Deane, J. R. *The Strange Alliance*, Indiana University Press, 1946 and London 1973.
D'Este, Carlo *Decision in Normandy*, Pan Books, London, 1984.
Gimbel, J. *The American Occupation of Germany*, Stanford University Press, Mass., 1968.
Gowing, M. *Independence and Deterrence*, 2 vols, Macmillan, London, 1974.
Griswold, Whitney *The Far Eastern Policy of the United States*, Yale University Press, New Haven, 1964.
Irving, D. *The War Between the Generals*, Penguin, Harmondsworth, 1982.
Kaufmann, William (ed.) *Military Policy and National Security*, Princeton University Press, New Jersey, 1956.
Kecskemeti, P. *Strategic Surrender—the Politics of Victory and Defeat*, New York, 1964.
Lash, J. P. *Roosevelt and Churchill 1939–41*, Andre Deutsch, New York, 1977.
Mee, C. *Meeting at Potsdam*, Andre Deutsch, New York, 1975.
Middlebrook, M. *The Schweinfurt-Regensburg Mission*, Penguin, Harmondsworth, 1985.
Middlemas, Keith *The Diplomacy of Illusion*, Weidenfeld and Nicolson, London, 1972.
Milward, A. *The Defence of Western Europe 1945–51*, London, 1984.
Peden, G. *British Rearmament and the Treasury*, Edingly, 1979.
Rothwell, V. *Britain and the Cold War 1941–47*, London, 1982.
Rumble, G. *The Politics of Nuclear Defence*, Blackwell, Oxford, 1985.
Seaton, A. *Stalin as War Lord*, B. T. Batsford, London, 1976.
Schlesinger, A. *A Thousand Days*, Mayflower-Dell, London, 1967.
Shay, R. P. *British Rearmament in the Thirties*, Princeton University Press, New Jersey, 1977.
Siracusa, J. *The American Diplomatic Revolution*, Open University Press, Milton Keynes, 1978.
Spector, R. H. *Eagle Against the Sun*, Penguin, Harmondsworth, 1987.
Stoler, M. A. *The Politics of the Second Front*, Greenwood Press, Conn., 1977.
Theoharis, A. G. *The Yalta Myths*, University of Missouri Press, Columbia, 1970.

Wheeler-Bennett, Sir John *Munich:Prologue to Tragedy*, Macmillan, London, 1948.
Willis, F. R. *France, Germany and the New Europe 1945-1967,* Stanford University Press, Mass., 1968.
Woodward, L. (ed.) *British Policy in the Second World War*, Docs. Vol. 1, HMSO, 1970.

ETHICS, WAR AND INTERNATIONAL POLITICS

Allison, G. T., Carnesdale, A. & Nye, J. S. *Hawks, Doves and Owls: an Agenda for Avoiding Nuclear War*, W. W. Norton, New York, 1985.
Bailey, S. D. *Prohibitions and Restraints in War*, Oxford University Press, 1971.
Beitz, C. *Political Theory and International Relations*, Princeton University Press, NJ, 1979.
Best, G. *Humanity in Warfare*, Weidenfeld and Nicolson, London, 1980.
Bull, H. *The Anarchical Society,* Columbia University Press, NY, 1977.
Clark, I. *Limited Nuclear War: Political Theory and War Conventions*, Martin Robertson, Oxford, 1982.
———*Reform and Resistance in the International Order*, Cambridge University Press, 1980.
Davidson, G. *The Nuremberg Fallacy*, Macmillan, New York, 1973.
Finnis, J., Boyle, J. M. & Grisez, G. *Nuclear Deterrence, Morality and Realism*, Clarendon Press, Oxford, 1987.
Fisher, D. *Morality and the Bomb*, Croom Helm, London, 1985.
Goldblat, Jozef, *Agreements for Arms Control: A Critical Survey*, SIPRI, Taylor and Francis, London, 1982.
Goodwin, F. *Ethics and Nuclear Deterrence*, Croom Helm, London, 1982.
Greenwood, C. 'The Relationship between *ius ad bellum* and *ius in bello*', *Review of International Studies 1983*, pp. 2221-34, Vol. 9, No. 4, Oct. 1983.
Grotius, Hugo *The Law of War and Peace*, trans. Francis W. Kelsey.
Hare, J. E. & Joynt C. B. *Ethics and International Affairs*, St. Martin's Press, New York, 1982.
Howard, M. (ed.) *Restraint in War, Studies in the limitations of armed conflict*, Oxford University Press, 1979.
Kaplan, M. A. (ed.) *Strategic Thinking and its Moral Significance*, University of Chicago Center for Policy Study, 1973.
Laarman, E. J. *Nuclear Pacifism: Just War Thinking Today*, Peter Lang, New York and Berne, 1984.
Linklater, A. *Men and Citizens in the Theory of International Relations*, St. Martin's Press, New York, 1982.
Nardin, T. *Law, Morality and the Relations of States,* Princeton University Press, New Jersey, 1983.
Northedge, F. S. *The Use of France in International Relations*, Faber and Faber, London, 1974.

Nye, J. S. *Nuclear Ethics*, Free Press, New York, 1986.
Osgood, E. & Tucker, R. E. *Force, Order and Justice*, Johns Hopkins University Press, Baltimore, 1967.
Paskins, B. & Dockrill, M. *The Ethics of War*, London, 1979.
Phillips, R. L. *War and Justice*, Oaklahoma University Press, Norman, 1984.
Spaight, J. M. *Air Power and War Rights*, Longmans Green, London, 3rd ed., 1947.
Sterba, J. *The Ethics of War and Nuclear Deterrence*, Wadsworth, Belmont, California, 1985.
Walzer, M. *Just and Unjust Wars*, Penguin, Harmondsworth, 1978.

TERRORISM AND REVOLUTIONARY WAR

Atkinson, A. *Social Order and the General Theory of Strategy*, Routledge & Kegan Paul, London, 1981.
Bernstein, H. (ed.) *Underdevelopment and Development*, Penguin, Harmondsworth, 1973.
Cardoso, F. H. & Faletto *Dependency and Development in Latin America,* 1977
Carr, E. H. *The Bolshevik Revolution*, Penguin, Harmondsworth, 1953.
Emmanuel, A. E. *Unequal Exchange*, New Left Books, London, 1972.
Freemantle, A. *Mao Tse Tung–an Anthology of his Writings,* 1962.
Giap, V. N. *People's War: People's Army*, Foreign Language Publishing House, Hanoi.
Guevara, Che *Guerrilla Warfare*, trans. Victoria Ortiz, Allen & Unwin, London, 1968.
Gunder, Frank E. *Latin America: Underdevelopment or Revolution*, Monthly Press, New York, 1969.
Kitson, K. *Low Intensity Operations*, Faber and Faber, London, 1971.
Laqueur, W. *Terrorism*, Weidenfeld and Nicolson, London, 1977.
Le Duan, *The Vietnamese Revolution; Fundamental Problems,* 1970.
Lenin, V. I. 'The State and Revolution', in *Selected Works*, Vol. II, 1st pub. 1917, Lawrence and Wishart, London, 1936.
Lukes, S. *Power; a Radical View*, Macmillan, London, 1974.
Mao Tse Tung *Selected Works*, Vols I–IV, Foreign Language Publishing House, Pekin.
Marx, K. *Capital*, Vol. III, Foreign Language Publishing House, Moscow, 1966.
O'Sullivan, N. *Revolutionary Theory and Political Reality*, Wheatsheaf Books, Brighton, 1983.
Palma, G. *Dependency*, Vol. 6, Pergamon Press, Oxford, 1978.
Pomeroy, W. J. *Guerrilla Warfare and Marxism: a Reader*, Lawrence and Wishart, London, 1969.
Radice, H. (ed.) *International Firms and Modern Imperialism*, Penguin, Harmondsworth, 1975.

Rhodes, R. I. (ed.) *Imperialism and Underdevelopment*, Monthly Review Press, New York, 1970.
Rubin II *Essays on Marx's Theory of Value*, Black and Red, Detroit, 1977.
Stafford, D. *Britain and European Resistance 1940–1945*, Macmillan, London, 1983.
Stohl, M. *War and Violence*, Beverley Hills, 1976.
Taber, R. *The War of the Flea*, Paladin, London, 1970.
Thompson, R. *Revolutionary War—World Strategy 1945–1969*, Secker and Warburg, London, 1970.
Turok, B. (ed.) *Revolutionary Thought in the 20th Century*, Zed Press, London, 1980.
Wardlaw, G. *Political Terrorism*, Cambridge University Press, 1982.
Wilkinson, P. *Political Terrorism*, Macmillan, London, 1974.
——— *Terrorism and the Liberal State*, Macmillan, London, 1977.
Wilson, D. *The Long March*, Penguin, Harmondsworth, 1977.
Woddis, J. *New Theories of Terrorism*, Lawrence and Wishart, London, 1972.

Index

Action, see rational action theory
Acheson, Dean, 180
aerial bombing, 15, 19, 26, 54, 87. See
    also Bombing Offensive
Afghanistan, 253, 257
agency, see rational action theory
aircraft, 12, 46, 87, 122, 137
air forces, 16, 143
Allende, President, 182
alliances, 7, 10, 20, 67, 79, 169–75. See
    also NATO and Warsaw Pact
Allison, G., 108, 112, 119
ally-swapping, 169–72, 246, 257
Alperovitz, G., 180, 261
Alsace-Lorraine, 261
Alto-Adige, 261
anarchists, 2, 3, 6, 210
anarchy, 6, 9, 80, 225, 240. See also
    power-security hypothesis
anachronism, see explanation
Angell, N., 30
Anglo-German naval arms race 1905,
    127
Anglo-German naval protocol, 235,
    260
Anthropology, 40
anti-ballistic missile defence, 155, 158,
    167, 174, 184, 248–9, 254, 255–6,
    262. See also arms control
Anvil, operation, 149
Ann Arbor speech, 267
Anzio landings, 150
ANZUS treaty, 182
appeasement, 23–4, 97, 117, 229, 241,
    242

Arab-Israeli conflict, 107, 118.
area bombing 117, 126, 234, 238. See
    also Bombing Offensive
April theses, see Lenin
Aristotle, 2, 29
Armacost, M., 180
Armageddon, x, 81, 111, 185
arms control, 99, 156, 175–7, 227, 239,
    244, 246, 248, 265, 268–9
arms control agreements, 164, 171,
    182, 188, 246, 247, 250–3, 257,
    260, 265, 266
Armistice World War 1, 196
armour, 19, 87, 122, 128
arms races, 11, 28, 37–8, 53, 155, 156,
    160, 173, 177, 239, 248, 252, 265.
    See also power-security hypothesis
Armstrong, Sir Robert, 269
Armstrong-Whitworth planes, 133
Aron, R., 84
atavism, 39
Atkinson, A., 223
Atlantic Charter, 231, 260
Atlas missile, 183
atomic bomb, 12, 83, 155, 158–61, 165,
    182, 237, 239, 246, 259
Attlee, C., 182
Austria, 13, 23
Austrian State Treaty, 117
autarky, 8, 13, 61, 101. See also Hitler
Ayers, M. R., 57

balance of power, 7, 40, 79, 227, 240,
    241, 243–4
Baldwin, S., 31

280

Balfour Declaration, 261
Balkans, 20, 27, 148
Balkan Wars, 189
ballistic missiles, 11, 12, 20, 22, 27, 45, 116, 122, 155, 161. See also ICBM, anti-ballistic missiles, and SDI
Barbarossa operation, 18. See also Hitler
bargaining theories, see rational action theory
Barker, E., 31
Barnes, J., 31, 152
Basle Manifesto, 221. See also Lenin
Batista, 207
battle-field victory, 61, 67
Battle of Alamein, 85
Battle of Britain, 46, 141, 143, 144
Battle of France, 46, 132, 142, 143, 209
Battle of the Atlantic, 146
Battle of the Marne, 184, 241
Battle of Normandy, 124-5
Bay of Pigs, 109
Beck, Col., 93
Beitz, C., 260
Belgium, 118, 170, 186, 241
Benes, E., 93
Benn, E., 184
Benn, S., 58
Berlin, 110, 168, 173, 250
Berne Incident, 118
Bialer, U., 116, 152
bio-chemical warfare, 249, 252
Blitz, 19, 46, 143, 147, 209
blitzkrieg, 15, 19, 20, 45, 88, 129, 137, 139-43, 171, 203
bocage, 125. See also Battle of Normandy
Bohemia, 10. See also Munich Agreement
Bolshevik, 261. See also Lenin
Bomber bases, 160
Bomber Command, 88, 95, 122-3. See also Harris
Bombing Offensive, 144-8, 152, 209, 235
bombers:
  B29, 180
  B47, 182
  B1, 180
Bordeaux, M. de, 266

Boyle, J. M., 261
Brandt, W., 250, 256
Brest-Litovsk, treaty of, 181, 221
Bretton-Woods Agreement, 262
Britain, 12, 13, 16, 46, 53, 82, 105, 155, 168, 231, 234, 240
British armed forces, 19, 46, 82
British Expeditionary Force 1914, 82
British ultimatum to Germany, 82
Brown, A. C., 117, 152, 223
Bulgaria, 159, 168
Buzan, B., 30, 58, 182

Cabinet wars, 90
Caen, 125, 146
Caesar, Julius, 49, 90
Callaghan, J., 184
Cambodia, 27
Cambrai, battle of, 19, 139
capability, see rational action theory
Cardoso, F. H., 222
Carter, J., 253, 257, 260
Castro, F., 109-10, 182, 207-8
category mistake, see explanation
centre of gravity, 68
Chamberlain, N., 23-4, 93, 113, 117, 119, 144, 242, 243
Chen T'hsin, 198
Chevaline, 184
Chiang Kai Shek, 180
Chile, 182
China, 149, 162, 178, 185, 186, 198, 214, 237, 251, 256, 267
Chinese Eastern Railway, 180
Chinese Revolution, see Mao Tse Tung
choice, see explanation action theory
Chou en lai, 198, 222
Churchill, W. S., 27, 83, 117, 137, 140, 142, 144-5, 146-51, 153
circular argument, see explanation
civil defence, 173
civilians, 125. See also non-combatants
civil war, 2, 163, 186-9, 235
Clausewitz, Carl von, 4, 14, 30, 42, 61, 62-83, 91, 97, 104, 106, 112, 120-1, 135, 151, 201, 203, 218, 222, 236, 264
critical analysis *(Kritik)* 70-2, 76-8, 89
maxims, 89

Cold War, 98, 117, 159, 185, 250, 266
collective security, 168. See also
    national security
colligation, see explanation
Collingwood, R. G., 56
Cologne, 145
Colville, Sir John, 153
commensurable, 27. See also
    Clausewitz and classical strategy
Committee on the Present Danger,
    118, 253, 262
Comintern, 198
computers, 118
concentration of forces, 68. See also
    classical strategy
conceptual frameworks, see
    explanation
conditions, necessary and sufficient,
    see explanation
Congress of USA, 27, 158, 255, 256,
    258
conjecture, see explanation
constitutive rules, see explanation
constraints, 224–7
contingencies, see scenarios
control, 16, 65, 83, 87, 95, 98, 105, 111,
    178, 188, 236, 258, 269. See also
    arms control
conventional forces, 170
conventional war, 174, 178
cordon sanitaire, 12, 13, 233
Coronet operation, 261
cost-benefit analysis, 123. See also
    rational action theory
cost-effectiveness, 123
Council of Foreign Relations, 255
counter-blockade force, 105
counter-factual conditions, see
    explanation
counter-insurgency, 189, 204, 215
covering laws, see explanation
covert operations, 214
Cowling, M., 31, 153
Crimea, 61
critical analysis, see Clausewitz
crisis management theory, see rational
    action theory
cruise missiles, 161, 175, 251
Cuba, 182, 248
Cuban missiles crisis, 25, 97, 99, 108–
    12, 268

Cuban revolution, 206–8
cuius regio; eius religio, 266
cultural relativity, see explanation
Curzon Line, 261
Cyprus, 208–9
Cyprus Emergency, 223
Czechoslovakia, 9, 13, 23, 30, 93, 169,
    233, 242, 243, 261
Czech tanks, see blitzkrieg

Dairen, 180
Daladier, E., 93, 117
D'Annunzio, 190
Danzig, 261
Dardanelles, 136
Davidson, D., 58
decision-making theories, see rational
    action theory
de-coupling, 184
deductive-nomothetic, see explanation
deductive-nomological, see explanation
defence-coefficient, 37
de Gaulle, General Charles, 153
de-stabilising, 163, 188, 205, 210, 242
D'Este Carlo, 152
détente, 250, 267
deterrence, ix, 3, 7, 22, 26, 46, 92, 96,
    104–5, 128, 156, 157, 162–79, 182,
    188–9, 209, 226, 239, 240, 244–58,
    265, 267–9
Dien Bien Phu, 206
Diplock Courts, 223
disarmament, 13, 25, 227
dissent, 163, 187, 205, 259
Doenitz, Admiral, 261
Douhet, J., 88, 116, 154
Dresden, bombing of, 117, 146, 236,
    261
drôle de guerre, 15, 30, 151, 230
Dulles, J. F., 182
dysfunctional, 39

Eastern Europe, 27, 186
Eastern Front, 24
Easton, D., 58
economic blockade, 19, 46, 127, 137,
    144, 234
economic dependency, 205
economic territory, see Lenin
economy with the truth, 265
Eden, Sir Anthony, 260

EEC, 226
Eisenhower, D., 182
Elbe, 244, 251
Emmanuel, A. E., 222
ends, see rational action theory
Engels, F., 41, 194
Epsom, 125. See also Battle of
    Normandy
essential equivalence, 183, 255, 262,
    268. See also deterrence
escalation, 92, 98, 106–26. See also
    rational action theory
espionage, 96
Esquimaux, ix
ETA, 223
ethology, ix, 39
European Recovery Programme, 181
events, see explanation
evidence, see explanation
'evil empire', 258, 260
'expanding in waves', 198. See also
    Mao Tse Tung
explanation, x, xi, 16, 21, 22, 32, 49,
    51, 72, 73–6, 78, 89
  scientific, 32–6, 42, 69, 74, 87, 89
  subsumption theory, x, 1, 36
  covering law model, 34, 35–6, 43, 44,
    45–8, 55, 74, 94, 99, 240
  deductive-nomothetic-nomological,
    xi, 55, 99
  causation, 1, 17, 19, 20, 32–6, 45,
    47–9, 57, 101, 112, 191, 226, 228
  determinism, 35, 39–41
  conditions-necessary and sufficient,
    11, 16, 22, 47, 52, 94, 113
  verification, 34, 36, 75, 108, 231
  truth, xi, 18, 48–9, 163, 242
  infinite regress, 34
  induction, 34, 37, 45
  statistical generalisation, 37, 55
  prediction 35–8
  probability, 16, 36, 37–9, 45, 55, 99,
    100, 108, 204
  conceptual schemes, 34, 65, 75, 225,
    228
  historical, 19, 22, 23, 52, 56, 61, 70,
    78, 81, 138
  dispositions, 39, 47–8
  situational logic, 38–40, 55–6
  teleology, 40–2, 56
  colligation, 41–2, 55–6

circularity, 22, 23, 34, 45, 76, 97, 228
anachronism, 19, 23, 45, 49, 56, 70,
    81
cultural relativity, 52, 56, 64
tautology, 19, 51
reason-giving, 39, 43, 49, 52, 54, 78,
    112, 191, 226
justification, 22, 48–9, 101, 187, 191,
    228, 229
practical reasoning, 22, 64, 81, 217
normative theory, 3, 39, 48, 54, 57,
    62, 80
intentions, 1, 12, 17–18, 36, 49, 51,
    89, 96, 97, 101, 112, 141, 179, 226,
    231, 236
purpose, 1, 36, 41, 49, 51
counter-factuals, 8, 19
rules, constitutive and regulative, 52,
    54, 89, 94, 98, 136, 227, 240
category mistakes, 44
expectations of proper action, 21,
    38–9, 50, 94, 100, 107, 114, 213,
    227
extended deterrence, see deterrence

Fabian tactics, 88, 95
factional violence, see terrorism
fail-safe devices, 100
Falklands War, 259, 260
Far Eastern Agreement, 180, 261
Fascists, 184, 190–1
fear, 42, 211, 213, 239
Fifth Encirclement Campaign, 197. See
    also Mao Tse Tung
Finland, 126
Finnis, J., 146
fire-storm, 146
first use, 184
first-strike capability, see deterrence
fog of war, 62
Foot, M., 184
Forward, N., 119
France, 8, 12, 13, 16, 53, 83, 168, 172,
    186, 231, 233, 234
Frankland, N., 152
Franco Generalissimo, 190
Franco Nationalists, 188
fratricide, 254. See also deterrence
Frederick the Great, 63
Freedman, L., 180, 182
French armed forces, 130

French collapse in 1940, 8, 16, 19, 234, 241
French occupation of the Ruhr 1923, 233
French Revolution, 65, 80
French tanks, 152
friction, 62, 67, 80
Fuehrer, see Hitler
Fuehrerprinzip, 190
Fuller, J. F. C., 132–5, 137–8, 140, 152

Gallie, W. B., 58
Galosh, 174, 252. See also anti-ballistic missiles
game of chicken, 111. See also rational action theory
game theory, 102, 107. See also rational action theory
Gardiner, P., 58
Gates, E. M., 31
gene-pool, ix
Geneva Accords, 207, 223
Geneva Conventions, 235, 238, 260
Geneva Protocols, 260
Genghis Khan, 164
Germany, 8, 12, 16, 27, 46, 120, 155, 169, 170, 171–2, 192, 203, 211, 233, 238
German invasion of Poland, 16, 233
German war production, 20, 147
Giap, General Vo Nguyen, 189, 206–7, 223
Gibraltar, 259
Gilbert, M., 31, 117, 152, 154
global containment of communism, 25, 161, 162, 174, 184
global reach, 158, 161, 162
Goering, H., 46
golden bridge, 112
Gomorrah, operation, 146. See also Bombing Offensive
Goodwood, 125. See also Battle of Normandy
Gott, R., 31
Gowing, M., 181
Gray, C., 33, 57, 96, 117, 183, 184, 185, 262
Greece, 20, 159, 186
Great Patriotic War, 98
Grisez, G., 261

Griswold, W., 180
Grotius, H., 232, 260
Guderian, H., 31, 61, 84, 89, 129–32, 139, 152–3
guerrilla war, 92, 195, 199–200, 204–7
Guernica, 19
Guevara, Che, 189, 206–8, 223
Gunder, Frank A., 205, 222

Hague Conventions, 260, 261
Hamburg, 146, 261. See also Bombing Offensive
Harris, A., 145–8
'hearts and minds' campaign, 201. See also Vietnam War.
hegemony, 6, 11
Helsinki Agreement, 262
Hempel, C., 35, 37, 57, 58
hermeneutics, 21. See also explanation
herrenvolk, 6
Hesse, M., 35, 57
Hilferding, R., 192
Hinde, R. A., 58
Hinsley, F. H., 30
Hiroshima, 237, 261
Hitler, A., 6, 9, 12–15, 18, 20, 23, 27, 30, 31, 46, 52, 61, 63, 82, 93, 101, 117, 126, 130, 132, 139, 141, 170, 181, 182, 190, 229, 233, 234, 241, 242, 266
Hong Kong, 259
Hook, S., 58
hot line, 111
Howard, M., 84, 153
Hue, 223
Hungary, 61, 159
Hunan, 197. See also Long March
human rights, 4, 117, 257, 258
Husky operation, 117, 149
Hyde Park Agreement, 181
Hydrogen bomb, 161, 165

ICBM, 161–7, 171, 244, 249, 251, 254. See also ballistic missiles and deterrence.
Iceland, 168
idealism, 50, 227
ideology, 9, 95, 210, 224, 228, 239, 258, 266
immament purpose, 41. See also explanation

imperialism, 2, 4, 7, 39, 121, 192, 233, 237–8. See also Lenin
inaction, see rational action theory
incommensurability, 34. See also Clausewitz and rational action theory
indirect approach, 88, 138–41, 144, 148–51. See also Liddell Hart
India, 103
Indo-China, 110, 181
induction, see explanation
inertia, 67
INF, 167, 171, 175, 185, 257
infinite regress, see explanation
intentions, see explanation
internal security, see national security
International Bank (IBRD), 181, 262
international conventions, 2, 234, 253
International Monetary Fund (IMF), 181, 262
instrumentality, see rational action theory
intervention, 188–9, 212, 234
IRA, 223
Iran, 254
Iranian coup, 257
Iran-Iraqui War, 118
Iron Curtain, 160
irrationality, see rational action theory
Ismay, Lord, 146
isolationism, 159
Israel, 213
Italy, 8, 12, 20, 23, 82, 148, 155, 169, 181, 248
Italian Campaign, 144
Iwo Jima, 261

Japan, 8, 12, 21, 54, 120, 148, 155, 158, 178, 185, 203, 238, 251
Japanese Emperor, 54
Japanese invasion of China, 197, 201–2, 221
Japanese Peace Treaty, 182
Japanese surrender, 237
jet aircraft, 20
Johnson, L. B., 25, 31, 223, 260
Jomini, 91, 116
Junkers, 87 and 88, 132
Jupiter missile, 183, 247–8
justification, see explanation
just war, 6, 227, 230, 231–9

Kahn, H., 106, 112, 118, 152
Kaiser, Wilhelm, 241
Kampuchea, 223
Kant, E., 41
Kaplan, M., 58, 119, 240, 262
Kaufman, W., 118
Kennan, G., 181
Kennedy, J. F., 110–12, 182, 247, 262, 267, 268
Kennedy, R., 119, 262
Kennedy, Sir John, 117, 152
Kiangsi, 198, 200. See also Mao Tse Tung
Kiev, 61
Kissinger, H., 255–6, 262
Kitson, F., 223
Korea, 159, 162, 180, 260
Korean War, 181, 236, 270
Kritik, see Clausewitz
Krushchev, N., 112, 260, 262
Kurile Islands, 180
Kuang Chang, 198

landing craft, 143, 148–51
Laqueur, W., 223
lasers, 155
Latin America, 204, 223
League of Nations, 4, 13, 233, 237, 260
lebensraum, 141–2
Le Duan, 206, 223
Leigh-Mallory Transportation Plan, 124–5, 146
Lenin, V. I., 29, 189, 192–6, 197, 201–2, 204, 206, 208, 210, 217, 219, 221, 260
liberal-democracy, 23, 226, 266
Liddell Hart, B., 19, 31, 88, 116, 135–9, 140, 153
Lithuania, 233, 261
Ljubjana Gap, 149
Locarno Treaties, 13, 130, 233
logic of the situation, 77, 95, 114, 228. See also explanation
Long March, 197, 200–2, 221
long-range bomber, 12, 246
Lorenz, K., 58
Louch, A. R., 58
Low Countries, 15, 118
low-intensity operations, 189, 215
Luftwaffe, 46, 113, 127, 132, 141, 142, 209, 242

MacArthur, D., 182
Machiavelli, N., 2, 29
machine warfare, 139–40
MacMurray, J., 58
Macnamara, R., 118, 182, 255, 267, 270
Macmillan, H., 183
Maginot Line, 140
Mahan, A. T., Admiral, 180
Malayan anti-terrorist campaign, 208–9, 223
Manchu dynasty, 196
Manchuria, 237
Mandates, 180, 213, 261
Mandelbaum, M., 180, 183
Manhattan Project, 31, 158. See also atomic bomb
Manstein, E. von, 82, 89, 139, 153
March, J. G., 58
Marshall Aid, 181
Martin, L., 182
Marx, K., 29, 41, 221
Marxism, 3, 24, 97, 187, 190–4, 198, 204, 205–8, 226
Marxist contradictions, 192
Marxism-Leninism, 198, 266
Maude, F. N., Col., 84
maximisation of profits, 192
maximisation of satisfaction, 192
maxims, see Clausewitz
means, see rational action theory
means-ends, see rational action theory
Mediterranean, 148
megatonnage, 166
Merton, R., 58
Mesquita, B. de, 117
metaphysics, 21, 50
metropolis-satellite relations, see Gunder, Frank
Middlebrook, M., 154
Middle East, 189, 236, 254, 257
Middlemas, K., 152
Midgley, M., 58
military-industrial complex, 158
Mill, J. S., 57
Millennium, 145
mini-max, see rational action theory
Minuteman missile silos, 254, 256
Minuteman 111 missile, 166, 183, 256
MIRV, 166–7, 183, 247, 253–4, 255, 256. See also ballistic missiles

Mises, von, 95, 117
missile gap, 182, 247
mistakes, see rational action theory
Moloch, ix
Molotov-Ribbentrop Pact, 24, 53, 84
Moltke, von, 64
monopoly capital, see Lenin
Montgomery Lord, 21, 85, 125
Moravia, 10, 30. See also Munich Agreement
mores, 21
Morgenstern, D., 118
Morgenthau, H., 30
Mortimore, G. W., 58
Moscow, 61
multi-national corporations, 205
Munich, 141
Munich Agreement, 9, 13, 30, 98, 129, 242, 250, 266
Munich crisis, 113, 117
Mussolini, B., 190, 208
mutual assured destruction (MAD), 183, 255. See also deterrence
mutual defensive deterrence, see deterrence
MX missile, 166–7, 183, 251, 254

Nagasaki, 237, 261
Napoleon, Emperor, 66, 91
Napoleonic Wars, see War
Nardin, T., 260
Nash, Ogden, 269, 270
Nassau Agreement, 183
nationalism, 25
Nationalist government in China, see Kuomintang
national liberation movements, 159, 163, 204, 212
national-socialism, 190
national security, 7, 10, 66, 80, 156, 168, 187, 211, 231, 232, 242, 245, 246, 249, 264–5, 268. See also power-security hypothesis
NATO, 96, 160, 168, 171–5, 181, 184, 226, 244, 246, 251
natural selection, ix, 190
Nazi government, 144, 209, 260
N. E. France, 170, 241
negative capability, see rational action theory
Netherlands, 118

Neumann, John von, 118
neutrality 11, 12
New Economic Policy (NEP), 260. See
    also Lenin
New Order, 159. See also Hitler
Nicholson, M., 100, 117, 119
nihilism, 210
Nitze, P., 118, 262
Nixon, R., 157–8, 247, 252, 255
non-combatants, 234, 235
non-intervention, 188
non-proliferation, 182
normative theories, see explanation
North Africa, 84
North African campaign, 141, 143, 238
Northern Ireland, 223
North Vietnam, 22, 26, 54
nuclear stalemate, 40, 92, 163, 170,
    187, 244, 268. See also deterrence
nuclear strategy, see deterrence and
    scientific strategy
nuclear weapons, see atomic bomb,
    hydrogen bomb, and ballistic
    missiles
nuclear umbrella, 160–1
Nuremberg Principles, 231, 260, 261

Oakeshott, M., 58
Occupation of Japan, 158, 237
Occupation of Prague 1939, 15, 98,
    141
occupation zones in Germany, 160
offensive deterrence, see deterrence
oil, 12, 18
Okinawa, 261
Olympic operation, 261
operational research, 90. See also
    rational action theory
operativ, 129–32. See also Guderian
ostpolitik, 250, 256
Overlord operation, 117, 146, 149

Pacific War, 150, 328
pacta sunt servanda, 9, 30
Pakistan, 103
Palestine, 261
Palestine Liberation Organisation
    (PLO), 212–13
Palma, G., 222
panzer division, 20, 45, 131
Paret, P., 84

Pas de Calais, 124
peace, 4, 7, 9, 27, 232
Peace of Riga, 261
Peaceful Nuclear Explosions Treaty,
    253
Pearl Harbor, 237–8
people's war, 203
perception, xi, 81
Pershing missile, 175, 184
Petain, Marshall P., 142
Pipes, R., 262
piracy, 5
Pointblank, 146. See also Bombing
    Offensive
poison gas, 122, 234
Po ku, 198, 222
Poland, 13, 14, 16, 23, 66, 83, 84, 93,
    126, 140, 159, 233, 243, 261
Polaris missile, 183
Polish corridor, 261
Pol Pot, 205, 223
Pomeroy, W. J., 221
Pope, His Holiness the, 122, 224
Popper, C. R., 38–40, 56, 57, 95, 117
Port Arthur, 180
Poseidon missile, 183
Potsdam Conference, 250
Power, 39, 44–5, 87, 114, 202, 241–2,
    265. See also rational action
    theory
power security hypothesis, 8, 10–17,
    42, 80
power politics, 67
practical reasoning, x. See also
    explanation
Prague, 30
praxeology, 95
praxis, 205
prediction, see explanation
pre-emptive war, 23, 174, 188, 234, 249
prescription, see rational action theory
pressure group terrorism, see terrorism
principle of concentration, 199
prisoners of war, 258
probability, see explanation
'propaganda of the deed', 211, 215. See
    also terrorism
propaganda war, 211, 216. See also
    terrorism and war
proportionality, 235–237. See also just
    war

protracted war, 200–1, 207. See also
    Mao Tse Tung
proxy wars, 40, 189, 214, 238
purpose, see explanation
Pyrrhic victory, 67, 95

racial state, 6, 191
racist theory, 13, 19, 190
Radice, H., 222
radio-active poisoning, 234
Raeder, Admiral, 261
rain dancing, 101
Ranke, von, 61
Rapoport, A., 84
rationalisation, see rational action
    theory
rational action theory, 36, 44, 47, 86–7,
    93–102, 108, 110, 114, 156
rationality, 9, 13, 21, 23, 29, 39, 40, 47,
    52, 62, 77, 89, 94, 112–13, 135,
    137, 155, 162, 176, 187, 201, 210,
    218, 244, 258, 259, 263
  irrationality, 66, 67, 79, 83
  action, 17, 21, 28, 36, 41, 43–53, 55,
    90, 191, 231, 236, 260
  inaction, 18, 25, 43–4
  rationalisation, 18, 23, 39, 51, 54,
    55–6, 72, 78, 218, 263
  prescription, 9, 15, 16, 17, 18, 22, 23,
    42, 62, 63, 73, 87, 89, 98, 113, 134,
    189, 191, 210, 228, 230, 264
  means-ends relationship, 43–8, 57,
    67, 73, 77, 79, 87, 90, 94, 101–2,
    112, 120, 142, 151, 163, 165, 168,
    175, 176, 179, 201, 206, 210, 211,
    216, 218, 224, 258, 263, 269
  commensurability, 52, 63. See also
    Clausewitz
  mistake, 17–18
  instrumentality, 35–6, 43–4, 64, 101,
    112, 191, 230, 231, 235, 264, 266
  capability, 32, 38, 44–5, 53, 57, 141,
    157, 165, 179, 224
  negative capability, 46, 87, 90, 96,
    107, 113, 122
  worst-case analysis, 46, 68, 96, 98,
    179
  decisional theories, 86, 90, 93, 101–8,
    113
Reagan, R., 31, 117, 175–6, 248, 252,
    253, 257, 258, 260

realism, see power-security hypothesis
realpolitik, 10, 105, 232
reason-giving explanation, see
    explanation
reciprocal action, 232
reciprocal compliance, 230, 238, 260.
    See also just war
Red Army, 194, 196. See also Lenin
Regensburg, 146. See also Bombing
    Offensive
regulative rules, see explanation
reparations, 6, 13, 232
resistance, 186, 204, 209, 235. See also
    terrorism
retaliatory capacity, see deterrence
revolution, 2, 25, 40, 187
  Russian, 190–6
  Chinese, 196–204
revolutionary situation, 195, 205, 207
revolutionary war, 2, 6, 189, 201, 203,
    204, 225, 235
Reynaud, P., 152
Reynolds, C., 30, 31
Rhine, 118
Richardson, L. F., 37–8, 57
Romania, 159, 169
Roosevelt, F. D., 118, 148–51
Rostow, E., 262
Rowan, H. R., 182
'roving rebel bands', 200. See also Mao
    Tse Tung
Rubicon, 90
Ruge, F., Rear Admiral, 261
rule of law, 4, 7, 227
rules, see explanation
Ruse, M., 58
Russia, 233, 241

Saar, 262
Salazar, President, 190
SALT, 1, 174, 247, 249, 252, 255, 256,
    257, 262
SALT, 11, 249, 253, 256, 262
Saward, D., 30, 117, 154
Saxe, Marshal, 62
Scandinavia, 15
scenario, 1, 20, 22, 40, 107, 115
Scheldt, 118
Schelling, T. C., 104, 118
Schilling, W. R., 183
schismogenesis, 37–8

Schlieffen Plan, 64, 170, 241
Schweinfurt, 146. See also Bombing
    Offensive
scientific strategy, 1, 62, 93, 116
scientific theory, see explanation
Sea Lion operation, 141, 153
Seaton, A., 152
SEATO, 182
Second Front, 145, 148
Second World War, see World War II
security, see national security
security dilemma, see power-security
    hypothesis
self-determination, 13, 126, 212, 233,
    242, 261
Senate of the United States, 253, 255,
    262
Sentinel-Safeguard ABM system, 156,
    174, 177, 247, 252, 255, 257
Shaw, M., 261
Shingle operation, 150
Sicily, 148
Sino-Soviet split, 184
situational logic, see explanation
Siracusa, J., 181
slavery, 5
Slovakia, 30
Slovenia, 30
Smith, B. L. A., 119
snorkel, 20
socialism, 187
socio-biology, ix, 39
social-Darwinism, 6, 13, 190
Somme, battle of, 139
South Africa, 259
South East Asia, 204
South Sakhalin, 180
South Manchurian Railway, 180
South Vietnam, 25
sovereignty, 7, 232
Soviet navy, 105, 112, 268
soviets, see Lenin
Soviet Union, 13, 20, 23, 54, 61, 96,
    117, 121, 143, 155, 159-60, 168,
    214, 237, 244, 246, 249, 251, 253,
    257, 267
Spain, 181
Spanish Civil War, 19, 130, 188-9
Special Operations Executive (SOE),
    211
Spector, R. H., 261

Speer, A., 182
Spitfire, 129
Sputnik, 183
SS 18 missile, 166
SS 20 missile, 175, 185, 246, 251, 257,
    262, 267
Stafford, D., 219
Stalingrad, battle of, 139, 238
star wars, see Strategic Defence
    Initiative
state terrorism, 187, 189, 208, 213. See
    also terrorism
statistical generalisation, see
    explanation
Stoler, M., 152
Strategic Air Command, 161
Strategic Defence Initiative (SDI), 28,
    167, 175-9, 183, 248-9, 251-4,
    256, 257, 267-8
strategic trusts, 158, 180
strategy, see Classical Strategy, and
    Scientific Strategy
Stealth bomber, 180
structural functionalism, 30, 40
Stuka dive bomber, 128
submarine, 122, 234
subsumption theory, see explanation
subversion, 8, 163
Sudetenland, 30, 242
Suez crisis, 99, 259, 260
Suez Canal, 159
sufficient conditions, see explanation
Sun Tsu, 59-60, 117
surprise, 133, 142. See also blitzkrieg
surplus value, 192
Sweden, 169, 182
Switzerland, 162, 169, 182
symmetrical reciprocity, 37
systems analysis, 40, 101, 107-8

Talbot Strobe, 183
tank, see armour
Tannenberg, battle of, 181
T34 tank, 139
tautology, see explanation
Tedder, Lord, 152
Teheran Conference, 118
teleology, see explanation
Templewood, Lord, 30
ten year rule, 129, 152
terror, 194

terror bombing, see area bombing, and
    Bombing Offensive
terrorism, 40, 187–96, 202, 204–17,
    235
Teschen, 261
'testing the means employed', see
    Clausewitz
Tet Offensive, 207
Thatcher, M., 260
theory, see explanation
theory of action, see explanation
theory of inter-dependent decision, see
    rational action theory
theory of protracted war, see Mao Tse
    Tung
theory of rationality, see rational
    action theory
Thirty Years War, 58, 224
Third Reich, 159, 190
Third World, 189, 204–5, 214
Thor missile, 183, 247
threat, 40, 58, 92, 113, 230, 241, 243.
    See also deterrence and power-
    security hypothesis
Threshold Nuclear Test Ban Treaty,
    253, 262
throw-weight, 166
Tiso, Father, 30
Tokyo, 261
total war, see war
torture, 209
trench warfare, 139
Triad, 166, 183, 247, 254
Trident missile, 183, 254
Tripartite Treaty, 233
Trotsky, L., 195
Truman, H. S., 182, 237, 261
truth, see explanation
Tsarist Empire, 126, 201
Tsarist Russia, 193, 196, 197
Tsunyi Conference, 197–8, 222
Turkey, 109, 248
Turok, B., 221

Ultra, 85, 153
unconditional surrender, 20, 104, 141,
    158, 237
united front tactics, 202, 207
United Kingdom, see Britain
United Nations, 4, 40, 181
United Nations Conventions, 261

United States, 12, 13, 25, 54, 121, 144,
    148, 155, 160–2, 168, 214, 231,
    233, 237, 243–4, 249, 250, 253,
    254, 255, 259, 267
untermenschen, 238–9

Vansittart, Lord, 30
Veale, F. S. P., 154
verification, see explanation
Versailles Treaty, 12, 13, 14, 82, 130,
    142, 159, 233, 241, 243, 261
Vickers medium tank, 129
Vienna, 149, 157
Viet Cong, 297
Vietnam, 179, 206, 250
Vietnam War, 22, 25, 26–7, 54, 99,
    118, 159, 174, 201, 214, 236, 255,
    259, 260, 270
Vilna, 261
Vlassov, General, 261
Vom Kriege, see Clausewitz
V1 and V2, 161

Walsh, W. H., 58
Walters, F. P., 30
Waltz, K., 30
Waltzer, M., 266
Wang Ming, 198, 222
war:
    total, x, 15, 16, 20, 65–7, 80, 97,
        103–4, 120, 138, 141, 145, 164,
        170, 178, 210, 218, 225, 232, 236,
        242, 258
    limited, x, 22, 67–8, 105, 122, 141,
        165, 168, 169, 170, 178, 236, 238,
        259, 270
    cabinet wars, 5, 65, 67, 140
    Napoleonic Wars, 55, 65, 67, 80, 121
    people's war, 187, 218–19
    psychological war, 210, 213, 217
Wardlaw, G., 223
warfinpersal, 38
war guilt, 16
warlordism, 197, 202
Warsaw Pact, 168, 175, 246, 251
war winning strategy, 176–7
weapons procurement, xi, 40, 87, 155,
    165, 242
weapons technology, 7, 20, 80
Webster, C. K., 152
Wedemayer, A. C., 154

Wheeler-Bennett, J., 117, 184
Wilkinson, P., 223
Wilson, D., 222
Wilsin, H., 184
Wohlstetter, A. J., 118
'window of opportunity', 166, 177, 254
Woodward, Llewelyn, 30, 152
World War I, ix, 8, 12, 13, 46, 89, 121,
    128, 134, 137, 138, 192, 212, 230,
    234, 243, 261
World War II, ix, 6, 54, 82, 104, 115,
    120–1, 186, 211, 230, 231, 235,

237, 249, 250, 252
worst case analysis, see rational action
    theory

Yalta, 180, 261
Yenan, 207
Yugoslavia, 20, 186

Zenophon, 21
Zionist terrorism, 213. See also
    terrorism
Zitadelle operation, 140